The Clays of Alabama

The Clays

Published at Lexington by

# of Alabama

A PLANTER-LAWYER-POLITICIAN FAMILY

Ruth Ketring Nuermberger

1958 —

the University of Kentucky Press

COPYRIGHT © 1958 BY THE UNIVERSITY OF KENTUCKY PRESS
COMPOSED AND PRINTED AT THE UNIVERSITY OF KENTUCKY
LIBRARY OF CONGRESS CATALOG CARD NUMBER: 58-6600

*The publication of this book has been possible partly by reason of a grant from
The Ford Foundation*

To G. A. N.

PREFACE

RESIDENCE IN THE SOUTH does not guarantee understanding of that region, but it is likely to help. I have enjoyed two salient advantages in the study of southern history: a long residence in the South and a close association with one of the great collections of southern Americana. The graduate student going to a southern university to study southern history not only immerses himself in the South's past, but is catapulted into the contemporary South with all its changing currents, yet with its viewpoints so distinctive from those of other regions. So it was that I went to Duke University, there to make many southern friends and to try to understand their attitudes, while absorbing facts of the South's past. Later, as curator of manuscripts in Duke University Library, I had the unparalleled opportunity of viewing the whole kaleidoscope of southern history, as I handled and examined the thousands of manuscripts that poured into the George Washington Flowers Collection.

This study of the Clay family, begun under the late Professor William Kenneth Boyd, was first written as a doctoral dissertation. Since then it has been several times rewritten, with the addition of much new material. Acknowledgments of indebtedness can be only partial, for in the accumulation of a body of historical knowledge, the historian gathers from a multitudinous number of sources, of which books, archives, and manuscripts are only the most obvious.

For specific assistance of various kinds I wish to thank the staff of the Alabama Department of Archives and History; the Stack and Reader Division of the Library of Congress for the use of study facilities; Professor Roy F. Nichols; Dr. Reinhard Luthin; Professor Nannie M. Tilley; Dr. Mattie Russell, present curator of manuscripts at Duke University; Allene Ramage FitzGerald; Elizabeth Montgomery Sloan; and the late Mrs. Bettie V. Adams. To my husband, Gustave A. Nuermberger, I am indebted for sympathetic encouragement and for numerous critical readings of the manuscript.

Washington, D. C.   R. K. N.
August, 1957

CONTENTS

1

A Plantation on the Frontier

ON A NOVEMBER DAY in 1811, young Clement Comer Clay rode into the rising frontier town of Huntsville. His visible resources were two horses, one Negro servant, a few lawbooks in his saddlebags, and a small amount of money. He was the typical early nineteenth-century young man "on the make," come to seek fame and fortune in the West.[1] Here he would establish home and family, plantation and slaves; here he would practice law, and serve his section and state in many capacities. From here he would go as a Jackson man to Washington, where, successively as representative and senator, he would work zealously for the Jacksonian program and aid his constituents by obtaining relief legislation for land debtors. There in the next generation his eldest son, as a fiery young senator from Alabama, would lift an eloquent voice in behalf of state rights.

Huntsville lay in the great valley of the Tennessee, at first within the bounds of Mississippi Territory, but soon becoming the northern section of the new state of Alabama. This land into which Clement Comer Clay had come was by report a veritable "Garden of Eden" where mild climate and wondrously rich soil bestowed indubitable riches. To the immigrant from the East the great valley opened out before his eyes a broad and verdant expanse of plain, bounded by rolling hills and a blue haze of low mountains. From the beginning this geographic curiosity, the Tennessee Valley, played its peculiar part in the life and history of Alabama. In the first place it did not really belong to Alabama, for geographically and economically it was tied to Tennessee and the Upper South rather than to the remainder of Alabama and the Lower South. Furthermore, the valley was always in conflict with itself, for the level portions were in soil and climate "elegant cotton country," while the coves, ravines, and hilly terrain were to become the province of the small farmer. The resulting divergence of interests caused strange things to transpire politically, for while the planters soon became the ruling class, their small-farmer constituents often had to be appeased.[2]

The Tennessee Valley, however, was not all of Alabama. To the southward streached a wild, hilly, desolate, infertile country, depressing to observe and difficult to pass through. This area formed a barrier between North and South Alabama, dividing the state into two great sections which felt alien to each other. The hill country itself was gradually settled by farmer folk of unprosperous and suspicious natures. Central Alabama, with its pine and oak uplands merging into the great cotton-producing Black Belt, was not extensively settled until the years 1830-1850, while the less fertile land toward the Gulf was in general the last section to attract population.[3]

But soil was not the sole consideration of the pioneer; to him transportation was of equal importance. The first settlers chose the rich river bottoms bordering navigable waters; thus it was that the Tennessee Valley and the Alabama and Tombigbee river lands drew the first accessions of population.[4]

Only a few islands of settlement yet punctuated the wilderness that had become Mississippi Territory in 1798. Most important were Natchez on the Mississippi and St. Stephens on the Tombigbee. The newest, centered at Huntsville, was in "Old Madison"

---

[1] Thomas McAdory Owen, *History of Alabama and Dictionary of Alabama Biography* (Chicago, 1921, 4 vols.), III, 342 (cited hereinafter as Owen, *Dict. Ala. Biog.*).

[2] Richard Ellis to John Clopton, Aug. 25, 1815, John Clopton MSS; John Gee to Joseph Gee, Sept. 24, 1816, Sterling Gee MSS; John Campbell to David Campbell, Dec. 16, 1817, David Campbell MSS.

[3] Saffold Berney, *Hand-Book of Alabama* (Birmingham, 1892, 2d and rev. ed.), 432; Alabama Geological Survey, *Report on the Valley Regions of Alabama*, by Henry McCalley (Montgomery, 1896-1897, 2 pts.), pt. I, 10; Alabama Geological Survey, *Special Report No. 14, Geology of Alabama*, by George Irving Adams (University, Ala., 1926), 25; Herdman Fitzgerald Cleland, "The Black Belt of Alabama," *Geographical Review*, X (Dec., 1920), 379-81.

[4] Leonard Moore to John Moore, Jan. 8, 1820, Leonard Moore to John Singleton, Jan. 25, July 15, 1820, Richard Singleton MSS; Thomas Perkins Abernethy, *The Formative Period in Alabama, 1815-1828* (Montgomery, 1922), 58.

County, a triangular area between Tennessee's southern boundary and the Great Bend of the Tennessee River, ceded by the Indians in 1806. According to tradition, John Hunt had examined the site of Huntsville in 1805 and had settled there with his family in 1807. He selected his location because of the "Big Spring." In that limestone country, "springs," actually underground rivers coming to the surface, are a common geologic feature. Such a river wells up beneath a semicircular bluff just west of Huntsville's public square. For a century and a half it furnished that town's water supply, and today it flows through a beautiful small park. So perfect a source of water naturally attracted settlers. In consequence, the town as well as the county, and, indeed, the entire Tennessee Valley, grew with astounding rapidity in the boom years from 1809 to 1819.[5]

Madison County, the Indian agent explained in 1809, already had "upwards of 2000 Souls who came from the East, West, North, and South and have brot. with them their passions, and there [sic] virtues— When civilization and refinement shall be well established, this will be a desirable part of the United States."

The elements of "civilization and refinement" soon arrived, as the "Alabama fever" for rich lands brought "many gentlemen from the Eastern States very considerable capitalists . . . some of them having a hundred slaves in family and frequently accomplished ladies." "Town is full of gentlemen from Virginia Kentucky and the Carolinas' who like ourselves," wrote a Virginian, "have been exploring the country." The large number of such men was the most striking feature of Huntsville's early development. Within a few years they transformed "a straggling village of squatters" into "a town of brick buildings." Huntsville, one observer could write in 1818, "has more the appearance of a commercial seaport than any Town I have seen of this side of the Allegany [sic] with the exception of Nashville. Its growth with that of the whole surrounding country in population and in wealth exceeds anything I have ever heard of." "This place does

---

[5] U. S. Department of State, *Territorial Papers of the United States*, ed. by Clarence Edwin Carter (Washington, 1934-   ), V, *Mississippi*, 684-89 (cited hereinafter as *Territorial Papers*); *Niles' Weekly Register*, I (Jan. 25, 1812), 388; Thomas Jones Taylor, "Early History of Madison County," *Alabama Historical Quarterly*, I (Spring, 1930), 110f, (Summer, 1930), 152 (cited hereinafter as *Ala. Hist. Q.*). In the summer of 1957 Huntsville's water supply began to come from outlying reservoirs. Edward Chambers Betts, *Early History of Huntsville, Alabama, 1804 to 1870* (Montgomery, 1916), 21-27.

more business in an hour than yours does in almost a week."[6]
A critical-minded journalist, Anne Royall, thus described Huntsville: "The town stands on elevated ground, and enjoys a beautiful prospect. It contains about 260 houses, principally built of
brick; has a bank, a court house, and market house. There is a
large square in the centre of the town, . . . and facing this are
the stores, twelve in number. These buildings form a solid wall,
though divided into apartments. The workmanship is the best
I have seen in all the states; and several of the houses are three
stories high, and very large. There is no church. The people
assemble in the Court House to worship. Huntsville is settled by
people mostly from Georgia and the Carolinas—though there are
a few from almost every part of the world;—and the town displays
much activity. The citizens are gay, polite, and hospitable, and
live in great splendor. Nothing like it in our country."[7]

One of those who lived in "great splendor" was LeRoy Pope,
Huntsville's real founder, who had come from Petersburg,
Georgia, in 1809. Pope was a capitalist, a banker, a large slave-
holder, a shrewd speculator, but withal a man vitally interested
in developing the new community where he was staking his
fortunes. He quickly purchased the land around the "Big Spring,"
and the town laid out there he called Twickenham, a name soon
abandoned in favor of Huntsville.

Accompanying Pope in the migration from Georgia to the
Tennessee Valley was his son-in-law, John Williams Walker. A
Princeton graduate and a man of outstanding ability, Walker was
soon active politically and was elected the first United States
senator from North Alabama. Pope and Walker, together with
other Georgians, soon managed to gain political ascendancy in
Huntsville, and were sometimes called the "Georgia Party."

This powerful Georgia clique was not universally popular, however, and so Virginians, Carolinians, and others soon found a
common interest in opposing the Georgians. Typical of the
Virginians active in promoting Huntsville's early growth were

6 Return Jonathan Meigs to Timothy Meigs, May 8, 1809, Return Jonathan Meigs
MSS; John Campbell to David Campbell, Dec. 16, 1817, James Campbell to Elizabeth
Campbell, Nov. 18, 1818, Richardson Owen to John Owen, Dec. 22, 1820, David
Campbell MSS.

7 Anne (Newport) Royall, *Letters from Alabama on Various Subjects: to Which
Is Added an Appendix, Containing Remarks on Sundry Members of the 20th & 21st
Congress, and Other High Characters, &c. &c. at the Seat of Government* (Washing-
ton, 1830), 43f.

two physicians, Dr. David Moore, who, in addition to practicing medicine, served in the Alabama legislature for many years, and Dr. Thomas Fearn, who was a bank director, owner and operator of the waterworks, and builder of a canal to provide navigation from the town to the Tennessee River. The concentration of many men of talent and ambition in this frontier community sharpened competition decisively. The young town swarmed with young lawyers who were soon to become politicians, each jockeying for advancement and public office. For fifty years they made Huntsville the most influential political center in North Alabama.[8] These were the men who were to be the associates and competitors of young Clement Clay.

Clement Comer Clay was born on December 17, 1789, in Halifax County, Virginia, the son of William Clay, a Revolutionary soldier, and his wife, Rebecca Comer. About 1795 William Clay joined the westward migration and settled in Grainger County, East Tennessee, where Clement and his seven brothers and sisters grew up. Clement's education began under his great-uncle, Hopkins Muse, and continued at Blount College in Knoxville. This infant institution, which grew into the University of Tennessee, opened in 1804 and housed in a two-story frame building, numbered Clement Comer Clay among its first half-dozen students. He was graduated in 1807.[9]

Clement then read law under Hugh Lawson White, and in December, 1809, at the age of twenty, he was licensed to practice. Equipped with this unusually good education for one reared on the frontier, Clement, with youth's enthusiasm, soon sought wider opportunities than appeared to exist in the old home. No doubt he was influenced in his choice of a location by the fabulous tales that were current about the Alabama country and by the fact that his sister Margaret and her husband, John Bunch, had already settled in Madison County. While visiting them in the spring of

[8] Charles Colcock Jones, Jr., *The Dead Towns of Georgia* (Savannah, 1878), 236ff; Taylor, "Early Hist. of Madison Co.," 89; Ruth Ketring Nuermberger, "The 'Royal Party' in Early Alabama Politics," *Alabama Review*, VI (April, 1953), 81-85; Frank Lawrence Owsley, "John Williams Walker," *Ala. Rev.*, IX (April, 1956), 100-19.
[9] Reginald Fitz Hugh Bigg-Wither, *Materials for a History of the Wither Family* (Winchester, Eng., 1907), 169-72; Zachary F. Smith and Mary Rogers Clay, *The Clay Family*, Filson Club *Publications*, no. 14 (Louisville, 1899), 79; *Dictionary of American Biography* (New York, 1928-1936, 21 vols.), VI, 171f (cited herinafter as *DAB*); Owen, *Dict. Ala. Biog.*, III, 342; Stanley J. Folmsbee, "Blount College and East Tennessee College, 1794-1840: The First Predecessors of the University of Tennessee," *East Tennessee Historical Society Publications*, no. 17 (1945), 22-50.

1810, Clement had purchased a half section of land from John Bunch. Coming as a settler in 1811, Clement Clay set himself two goals: first, to become a landowner and planter; and second, to strive for success as a lawyer. During his first eight years in Huntsville he acquired these land holdings: 800 acres in Township 4, Madison County, for which he paid prices varying from two to six dollars per acre; two town lots in Huntsville for which he paid $1,200 cash; and a plot of less than two acres adjoining the town for $1,465 cash.[10]

The Tennessee Valley experienced two periods of land speculation which ended disastrously in the general economic collapse of 1819. The first comparatively mild boom came in 1809, when the lands of "Old Madison" were opened to sale at the Nashville land office, where "about 24000 acres have been sold in three weeks for a sum exceeding Sixty thousand dollars." Prices did not skyrocket, however, until 1817, when the pressure of incoming settlers made it imperative to survey and put on the market lands on the north side of the Tennessee River. Furthermore, predicted the register of the Huntsville land office, these lands "would sell generally as high, & perhaps higher than any lands of the united States ever sold further, a great number of families (some considerable planters) have settled on those lands, who will of course select the most desirable situations of good water & Soil." Excitement rose to a peak as sales began on February 2, 1818, and during the next two weeks lands in the first six ranges of townships were sold for nearly $2,500,000. "Never did lands sell better in the United States," declared Receiver John Brahan.[11]

In the fever of buying, many settlers paid from twenty to one hundred dollars an acre for cotton lands, "more than *double* the sum they would have given before the sales commenced," while town lots were bid in for as much as five thousand dollars. But along with bona fide settlers had come swarms of speculators, who organized themselves into companies and designated one or two of their members to do all the bidding at the sales. Their scheme was to minimize competitive bidding, obtain the best lands at low

10 Alabama Archives, Alabama State Tract Book, Madison County, p. 162; Alabama Archives, Register's Journal of Sale of Public Lands, 1814-1816, Book C, Huntsville, pp. 162, 606, 623; Madison County Archives, Deed Record B, pp. 3, 177, Deed Record H, p. 44.
11 John Read to Josiah Meigs, April 17, 1817, John Brahan to Josiah Meigs, Feb. 18, 1818, Territorial Papers, XVIII, Alabama, 84f, 260f.

rates, and then resell to boom-dazzled settlers at high prices. But by the time the sales began, local citizens had united to outsmart the speculators. Led by John Brahan, receiver of public moneys at the Huntsville land office, the local men pushed bidding up until speculators and settlers alike were buying at greatly inflated prices. In the furious bidding, Brahan himself ended up with 44,677 acres and an indebtedness of $318,579. The down payment of $78,901 he blandly made from federal funds. Under pressure from the secretary of the treasury for a settlement of his accounts, Brahan assigned all his property to the United States. Valued at just over $46,000, it included 1,260 acres of land, several town lots in Huntsville, and $31,425 in notes due Brahan. Among the trustees charged with administering this property so that the government recovered its money were Clement C. Clay, John W. Walker, LeRoy Pope, and Obadiah Jones, the new receiver.[12]

Those not actually on the spot took a sounder view of the situation, as is evidenced by one of Clement Clay's Virginia friends who wrote, "The high price of Lands in your part of the Country has entirely destroyed all my calculations on a removal it would not be in my power to make any kind of a purchase . . . when I shou'd have to give three or four times the real value in the purchase. I do think the People in your Country are runaway in their Opinions as to the Value of Lands the purchaser must have more ways to pay than I have or never intend to pay the last payments at all—"[13]

Early in 1819 the bubble burst with consequences graphically described by one on the scene: "I cannot but say that I am even gratified to see the sufferings of some individuals at that place in consequence of their voracious insatiable thirst for speculation. . . . They have got involved head over heals [sic] in debt; the price of cotton has fallen to a moderate price; they have no means of extricating themselves; but must stop still and sweat for their avarice & folly. Brahan will be considerably injured if not ruined; and the fur will be jerked off old Pope and some of his ill-gotten

12 U. S. Congress, Senate, 24 Cong., 1 Sess., *Documents* (Ser. 283), Committee on Public Lands, Report upon Bill H. R. 124, May 11, 1836 (Doc. No. 367); Gordon T. Chappell, "Some Patterns of Land Speculation in the Old Southwest," *Journal of Southern History*, XV (Nov., 1949), 471-74 (cited hereinafter as *JSH*).

13 George Mason to Clay, Sr., July 5, 1818, Clay MSS. (In footnotes, Clement Comer Clay will be referred to as Clay, Sr., and his son, Clement Claiborne Clay, will be cited as Clay, Jr.)

gains will go into the pockets of others. These men with several others of the same class have now got large debts running on them at ten per cent a month! ! ! "[14]

All these events occurred under the land system established in 1800, by which a settler could purchase from the government a minimum of 320 acres at two dollars per acre, with a down payment of one-fourth the purchase price, the remainder to be paid in four years. Under this system many purchasers were unable to complete their payments. Reform came in the new land act of 1820, which abolished the credit system, reduced minimum tracts to 160 acres, and set the price at $1.25 per acre, cash.[15] The new law brought anguished cries from thousands of unhappy purchasers who under the spell of the boom had blithely assumed fantastic obligations and now were in imminent danger of losing both their land and investment. These people, who could not possibly raise cash to pay for their lands, sent a stream of frantic petitions to Congress for relief. The story of forfeitures, relinquishments, and relief legislation is closely related to Clement Clay's political career, for he worked constantly to aid such people as "The Hunters [who] speak of forfeiting there [sic] lands and purchasing them in at other sales for Cash, they think it will save them a deal of Money, there [sic] Land Cost them very high and are very good but in my opinion they will be Troubled before they pay for them, Eighty-five Thousand Dollars is no Trifling sum—"[16]

Clement Clay was never deeply involved in land speculation, though he took advantage of the relief laws of the 1830's, thereby acquiring clear title to 640 acres of Madison County land which formed his first plantation, named "Oakley." Later purchases in adjoining Jackson County of some four thousand acres became his "new plantation." His investments in town lots were made with an eye to profits, and that flier in 1819, when he paid $1,465 for less than two acres, was certainly a touch of speculative fever.

Clay's marriage in 1815 to Susanna Claiborne Withers ultimately increased his capital, for when her father, John Withers, died in 1826, Clement Clay became executor of the estate. He

14 James Campbell to David Campbell, April 20, 1819, David Campbell MSS.
15 Payson Jackson Treat, *The National Land System, 1785-1820* (New York, 1910), 151.
16 Leonard Moore to John Singleton, July 15, 1820, Richard Singleton MSS.

acted in that capacity until 1834, when a new agreement among the heirs gave most of the real estate to a son, Augustine J. Withers, while to Clement Clay went nineteen Negroes and all personal property not otherwise disposed of, which included horses, mules, cattle, hogs, furniture, and the crops standing in the fields. Offsetting these gains, Clement Clay and Augustine Withers assumed all remaining debts of the estate.[17]

Clement Clay's early successes as a lawyer in Huntsville are very inadequately recorded, but his fee book containing entries from June 1, 1814, to October 18, 1815, gives a partial idea. During that period he noted the receipt of fees totaling $685.12½, as well as "cash won" (presumably at cards), $73.75, and "cash lent," $117.00. The abundance of litigation gave all the young lawyers a good chance at success. "The bars of Alabama are very much crowded all thro' it," wrote one of them. "The circuit court docket of Huntsville contains at each term no less than 800 causes for trial. . . . The bar at Huntsville is respectable but composed almost entirely of young men who have not been engaged in business longer than myself," remarked another.[18] Among all these lawyers Clement Clay was sufficiently outstanding to be appointed one of the first supreme-court justices of the new state.

However numerous his legal, civic, and political activities became, planting remained basic for Clay as it did for nearly all others of his class. Not only was it the one most respected occupation to which all aspired, but it provided a style of living that gave prestige, and it was the economic base which enabled the planter to seek and hold public office without being dependent on salary or reelection.

The problems of plantation management were always in Clement Clay's thought, and they revolved around the three major elements: cotton, corn and pork, and Negroes. In the lush new land of the Tennessee Valley, cotton flourished amazingly. With prices high, the impulse was to plant more and more cotton, to buy corn and pork from East Tennessee, and with cotton profits to buy more land and Negroes. Clay followed this pattern in some

---

[17] Madison County Archives, Probate Court, File Case No. 660, containing Last Will of John Withers, Sept. 14, 1825, and Agreement of Settlement & Partition, Oct. 14, 1834.

[18] Clay, Sr., Fee Book, 1814-1815, Clay MSS; John Campbell to David Campbell, Dec. 6, 1819, James Campbell to David Campbell, Oct. 23, 1821, David Campbell MSS.

degree over a period of twenty years. Whether in the feverish early days or in later years, Clay was a progressive and careful planter who managed his affairs with as much skill and success as did other members of his class who were also practicing lawyers and politicians.

The cotton crop was every planter's major concern. During the spring and early summer he worried about the amount of rainfall, which was likely to vary from a surplus that would put the crop "in some danger from grass" to a paucity which could make the prospect "rather discouraging because of insects and want of rain." "The season," Clay on one occasion remarked, "has been unusually dry at the Jackson place,—so much so as to threaten the entire exhaustion of the wells." Crops were generally good in 1822, 1823, and 1824, but those of 1827 were, as one planter wrote, "uncommonly sorry owing to a severe drought." "This has been the most disastrous season for the agriculturist, that has ever been experienced since the settlement of Alabama," commented a Huntsville newspaper. The cotton crop throughout North Alabama and Tennessee would not exceed "one half the usual quantity per acre," while there were "neighborhoods, where scarcely a bushel of corn per acre will be made." In the midst of this gloomy situation Clay's crop was pronounced "the finest . . . seen any where in this part of the country."[19]

If Clay kept systematic plantation records, they have long since been lost; consequently, estimates of cotton produced are necessarily incomplete. In 1821 only seventy acres remained standing after a bad season made "it advisable to plough up the greater part of the new field." In 1828 the crop was "much shorter than . . . anticipated." That of 1829 totaled at least 76 bales and probably more. The Withers plantation (under Clay's management) produced 50 bales in 1833. In later years production increased, especially after Clay's "new plantation" in Jackson County came under extensive cultivation. Here the crops yielded from 85 to 120 bales, and in 1845 a high of 200 bales was reached. On the overworked soil at "Oakley" production steadily declined

19 R. W. Withers to Clay, Sr., Sept. 1, 1827, Clay, Sr., to Clay, Jr., June 24, 1833, Clay, Jr., to J. W. Clay, July 10, 1843, Clay MSS; Sterling Gee to Nevill Gee, July 1, 1827, Sterling Gee MSS; Andrew Mitchell to Placebo Houston, July 14, 1827, Placebo Houston MSS; Huntsville *Alabama Republican*, Oct. 24, 1823; Huntsville *Southern Advocate*, June 10, 1825, Sept. 7, 1827.

to as little as 20 bales. Hence, admitted a member of the family, "former neglect must be repaired e'er the crops will yield much."[20]

These vicissitudes only serve to illustrate the constant concern with plantation affairs. During his frequent absences from home, Clay's letters reflected acute anxiety about plantation matters and were often full of specific inquiries and instructions. In one such letter, Clay directed his overseer to "fix up stalls, in my stable, . . . to build one or two more such cabins, as Nanny's and Ben's," and not to neglect "hauling out manure, and ploughing his cotton-land," but before all these things he must "first gather his crop of cotton—and let Frank gin it & bale it, & let it be carried to Triana, and delivered in the warehouse of the Toneys," and then "let the other hands haul in the corn." Throughout the earlier years, management of the plantation during Clay's absence fell to his wife Susanna, whose ability and experience kept everything running smoothly. Seldom were both away for an extended period, but on two occasions Susanna did accompany Clement, now a congressman, to Washington for the session, leaving the plantation to the oversight of her mother and brothers. It is to be feared, however, that the pleasures of congressional society were lost upon Susanna, whose mind dwelt on domestic anxieties. "Please say," she wrote her mother, "if the negroes have their clothes, including the children? I fear you are worried to death, and often blame myself for imposing so great a task on you. Do take care, first of yourself, whatever becomes of pecuniary matters —I am in dread of consequences, with regard to our plantation!"[21] In later years Clay's three sons, Clement C., Jr., John Withers, and Hugh Lawson, assumed part of the burden of management, although they never displaced the overseers.

A long succession of overseers served the Clays on their three plantations. Two of the earlier ones, named Blake and June, were good managers. Not so much could be said for William J. Long, who "could not have done his duty" to produce the "indifferent cotton" of the crop in 1829-1830. He was presumably superseded in 1833 by a man named Gray on the Withers estate. Of another

[20] Susanna Clay to Clay, Sr., June 11, 1821, Dec. 5, 1828, July 6, 1841, William McDowell to Clay, Sr., June 11, 1830, Maria Withers to Clay, Sr., Dec. 24, 1833, H. L. Clay to Clay, Sr., June 15, 1841, Clay, Jr., to Virginia Clay, Feb. 22, 1846, Clay MSS.
[21] Clay, Sr., to Susanna Clay, Nov. 16, 1834, Susanna Clay to Mary Herbert (Jones) Withers, March 26, 1834, Clay MSS.

overseer, Susanna wrote, "Wright is a bad manager and I expect will injure . . . [us] a great deal." In 1841 Clement, Jr., wrote, "I have employed a man by the name of John D. Tanner, to attend to the Oakley place, & have agreed to pay him ($185.00)." Tanner turned out to be "a good manager." On the Jackson plantation, George W. Justice was overseer for many years, and was succeeded by Jonathan W. Camp. Of another overseer, one of the family wrote, "I discharged Weems, at father's request, last Sunday. The plantation is barren of everything to eat—8 or 9,000 *lbs* pork to buy, only corn enough made to support the place two months longer and about ninety three or four bales of cotton, of which 20 are in the field."[22]

With two, and for several years three, plantations to look after, it is easy to understand that Clay had to delegate management to several persons. During the growing season no good planter neglected to inspect his crop at least once in two weeks. Clay's Jackson plantation lay twenty miles east of Huntsville, while "Oakley" was southwest of the town. Some of the family would spend three or four days at Jackson, return to town, and then go to "Oakley" and to the Withers estate, which was six miles west of Huntsville. Susanna Clay often stayed for a week or two at Jackson looking after the meat and meal, the Negroes' clothes, the gardens and the livestock, for it was here that most of the Negroes were stationed and hence the greatest oversight was necessary.

The third vital element in planting economy was the Negro. In the course of twenty years Clay reached the status of a large slave-holder. Before 1820 he held at least seven slaves. One of these he had brought with him from Tennessee, two had been given to Susanna as a wedding gift from her father, and the remaining four Clay had bought for a total of $2,850. The decade 1820-1830 was the period of his most rapid investment in labor. During these years Clay purchased eighteen slaves for $6,494. In 1824-1825 he hired five others who belonged to his sister, Cynthia Barrett, and a slave boy from the Withers estate was given to Clement Clay's small son, John Withers Clay. That these figures are incomplete is attested by the census records of 1830, which list Clement Clay as possessing 52 slaves, thus putting him among the 42 largest

22 William McDowell to Clay, Sr., June 11, 1830, Susanna Clay to Clay, Jr., Feb. 1, 1834, Clay, Jr., to Clay, Sr., Feb. 6, 1841, H. L. Clay to Virginia Clay, Jan. 2, 1855, Clay MSS.

slaveholders of Madison County. The county had in 1830 a total of 2,307 families. Of these, 1,278 families, or over 55 percent, were slaveholders. Holders of one to ten slaves totaled 851, and 427 owned more than ten Negroes. Of this number 42 planters had more than 50 slaves. The two largest slaveholders were LeRoy Pope with 165 and James Manning with 224 Negroes.[23]

By the final settlement of the Withers estate in 1834, Clay received 19 additional Negroes. This brought his total force to 71, enabling him to expand operations on his "new" Jackson County plantation. Here cultivation began about 1833, Negroes being moved there as needed until in 1840 a force of about 40 slaves was at work. Clay did not expand his labor force much during the 1840's; indeed, it may have diminished, for the Panic of 1837 and the subsequent depression had a crippling effect on his financial condition, and it appears that he was forced to sell some of his slaves. Occasional purchases and natural increase gave Clay a labor force of 70 by 1860.[24]

While the Clays always made an effort to raise a goodly portion of their corn and pork, still they often found it necessary to purchase large quantities of one or both commodities in East Tennessee. In 1826 hogs raised on the plantation provided over six thousand pounds of pork "salted and put away" in the smokehouses. Unfortunately, bad weather conditions or imperfect curing sometimes threatened the meat supply. "I have taken the greatest care of our pork," wrote Susanna Clay, "having had it salted twice but am sorry to say that I found [it ne]sessary [sic] to take the bones out of some and to sepperate [sic] the joints of all I do [not] think that it will be entirely lost. . . .I think it will be nessessary [sic] to buy four thousand weight of pork it is now selling at two & a half." At "Oakley" "every hog that would make bacon was killed," twenty-two in one season and fifty in another, but it was almost always necessary to purchase pork for this plantation, sometimes as much as 15,000 pounds.[25]

That the Clays were good masters is beyond doubt. Their forty

23 Clay MSS, *passim* (information from bills of sale and other references to slaves); 5th Census, 1830, Alabama, Madison County, Population Schedules, *passim.*
24 Clay, Sr., to W. F. Withers, Sept. 16, 1843, Clay MSS; 6th Census, 1840, Alabama, Madison County, Population Schedules, pp. 169-70, Jackson County, p. 70; 8th Census, 1860, Alabama, Jackson County, Slave Population, p. 439.
25 Susanna Clay to Clay, Sr., Dec. 31, 1826, Jan. 8, 1828, H. L. Clay to Clay, Sr., Dec. 7, 1843, Dec. 19, 1846, Clay, Jr., to Clay, Sr., Dec. 25, 1847, Clay MSS.

years of planting illustrate the various aspects of slavery as the region grew from the frontier to an established society. On the frontier, cotton culture meant strenuous work for both slave and master. Then the land was new and productive, but required clearing; prices were high, and planters were "on the make." Then the lure of big profits or, on occasion, the absence of the master might have the result detailed by Clement Clay, Jr., who wrote, "I was at the plantation last saturday & the crop is in fine order but the negroes are most brutally scarred & several have ran off."[26] This happened when an overseer was himself completely callous or was driven to strive for a big crop by a demanding employer. The instance related by Clement, Jr., occurred during his father's absence, and was perhaps never repeated, for the Clays were people of sensitivity and reasonableness, and so were not likely to demand the impossible of either overseer or Negro.

Like the majority of masters, the Clays not only felt a vital economic concern for their Negroes, but entertained a real and strong affection for faithful and efficient servants. But in some cases disciplinary measures were unavoidable. The Clays were, however, quite long suffering, and they put up with many a shiftless Negro rather than invoke severe punishment or break up a family by selling the offending individual. Occasionally a member of the family would avow a determination to sell rather than be further troubled.

A sick Negro was capital in jeopardy; hence the Clays, as careful masters, did not omit medical care for their slaves. When he was away in distant Washington or elsewhere, Clement never failed to inquire about the health of his Negroes, and in reply Susanna would detail what she had done to cure their ills or to keep them healthy. Climate, scant sanitation, and the Negro's own carelessness conspired to make him a victim of many diseases and the first sufferer in an epidemic. Every malarial summer took its toll of illness, as did that of 1841, when Susanna Clay wrote, "several of the negroes are sick with chills and fevers . . . none dangerously." Disaster fell, however, in 1852, when two Clay grandchildren, seven Negro children, and several adult Negroes died. Commenting on their misfortunes, Clement Clay, Jr., wrote, "poor little Cornelius died on the 3d. . . . We have lost 5 negroes this

26 Clay, Jr., to Clay, Sr., May 28, 1832, Clay MSS.

year! . . . God knows I would cheerfully have manumitted poor Eliza any day of her illness to have cured her." Six weeks later the situation was even worse when he had to announce "the death of Lydia's youngest child of whooping cough. This made the 7th negro we have lost since 1st March—⅓ of our number! We have lost . . . not less than 2,500 $ . . . in about six months."[27]

The affection often existing between slave and master is something of a tradition, but it would be difficult to find a more striking example than the letter of Hugh Lawson Clay describing the death of his body servant: "Jim died last night at 7½ o'clock. You know how devotedly attached and faithful he was to me, and know what must be my feelings in writing, the melancholy intelligence of his death. He had the care and attention of physicians and friends and all that *could* be done to recover him, or to alleviate his pain, was done. It is a subject of remark, that no other servant in the place would have been attended in sickness with as much care and constancy as he was. The young gentlemen of the place, when I became prostrated by anxiety and fatigue from watching, sat by his bedside, *day and night,* administering to his wants rather with the solicitude of friends, than with a thought of his being a slave and their inferior. . . . I feel desolate—my most devoted friend is gone and *his place* can never be supplied by another placed in his situation—"[28]

During the decade 1850-1860 the Clays made sizable investments in railroad stock and put smaller sums into bank and turnpike stock, but the bulk of their capital was still in land and Negroes. "Oakley" was disposed of, so that all farming operations were concentrated at the Jackson County plantation. By this time the three Clay sons were grown and were themselves slaveholders. But since none of them engaged in planting prior to 1865, they made a practice of hiring out their slaves. Negroes were customarily hired for a year, beginning in January. Hugh Lawson Clay managed this business for the family and followed a policy which experience had proved successful with their Negroes. "I permit them," he explained, "to choose their masters for the year, see that they are well-treated and have their clothes, and then they must behave themselves and give me no trouble." Hiring prices

27 Susanna Clay to Clay, Sr., Aug. 31, 1841, Clay, Jr., to Virginia Clay, Aug. 12, Sept. 30, 1852, Clay MSS.
28 H. L. Clay to Susanna Clay, Feb. 20, 1846, Clay MSS.

varied greatly with time, place, and most of all with the individual Negro. In the 1850's a mediocre slave would bring in $75 a year, but a skilled mechanic commanded as much as $250. In 1858 twelve Clay slaves were hired out for a total of $1,250.[29]

The financial base upon which southern society rested was a vast credit structure universally known as the factorage system. Whether the planter sold his crop to a local factor or shipped directly to a well-known firm in a city, his cotton ultimately had to reach a large market such as Memphis, Mobile, or New Orleans in the west, Savannah or Charleston in the east. Transportation was particularly difficult for Clay and his neighbors in the Tennessee Valley, where the Muscle Shoals impeded river navigation. During high water, however, shallow-draught boats could navigate the shoals and transport cotton to one of the Mississippi River markets. By 1850 Charleston and Savannah were bidding for Tennessee Valley cotton. Boats went eastward, upriver, to Kelly's Ferry; thence the bales were transshipped by wagon the 35 miles to Dalton, Georgia, and from there went on the new railroads to the Atlantic coast. No Tennessee Valley cotton went to Mobile, because Alabama lacked north and south transportation facilities.

The factor performed many services. On the cotton itself these included weighing, sampling, draying, mending, storage, and finally sale to a larger factor or broker. The charge for all this, plus the factor's 2½ percent commission for selling, made a total levy on the planter's crop of 8 to 12 percent.[30]

Clement Clay's position was not altogether typical of planters generally. The Clays always lived in Huntsville, a town of considerable size and a trading center. Thus Clay sold his cotton to a factor in Huntsville and purchased his supplies directly from the merchants of Huntsville, who were often cotton buyers too. The credit system was essentially the same, however, whether the planter lived in rural isolation or near a town.

The cotton crop of 1840, reported one of the family to Clay,

[29] H. L. Clay to Virginia Clay, Jan. 2, 1855, List of Notes and Bonds Due C. C. Clay, Jr., Jan., 1858, Clay MSS; James Benson Sellers, *Slavery in Alabama* (University, Ala., 1950), 195, 211f.

[30] Henry Watson, Jr., to Henry Watson, Sr., Feb. 10, 1834, Feb. 6, 1839, J. A. Wemyss to Henry Watson, Jr., Jan. 4, 1851, Henry Watson MSS; Huntsville *Democrat*, Sept. 1, 1847; Alfred Holt Stone, "Cotton Factorage System of the Southern States," *American Historical Review*, XX (April, 1915), 559-61 (cited hereinafter as *AHR*); Charles Shepard Davis, *The Cotton Kingdom in Alabama* (Montgomery, 1939), 141-68, 180-88.

"has been sold at an average of 9 cts per pound—& I see from the Bill of sale it leaves you in debt to your commission merchants about $1500. The crop bro't you, I believe about $4200." This was a normal condition for most planters. In good years they were likely to put profits into more Negroes and land, and in bad years the factor accepted their overdrafts at an additional charge of 2½ percent. Clay's 200-bale crop of 1845 would, the family hoped, "go far towards paying off his debts."[31] While it may have produced a temporary alleviation, the whole credit system continued in all its complexities to harass the Clays as it did every planter. They, like many another, fell deeper and deeper into debt as investments and expenditures year after year exceeded income. Loans, debts, credits, investments, land and slave transfers accumulated over the years until Clay himself did not know how his affairs stood. Only the debacle of war and Clay's subsequent death revealed the hopeless tangle. It is certain that in the century of its history the Clay estate was never free from debt.

[31] Clay, Jr., to Clay, Sr., Aug. 10, 1841, Clay, Jr., to Virginia Clay, Feb. 22, 1846, Clay MSS.

2

Clement Clay Enters Politics

CLEMENT COMER CLAY was not one to hide his talents. He was no more than settled in Huntsville when he began to take an active part in all local affairs, civic, political, and educational. One of Clay's first services was as a volunteer in the Creek War of 1813-1814, when Andrew Jackson made Huntsville his base of operations. Having returned from this campaign, Clay soon became involved in a personal difficulty with Dr. Waddy Tate. Both men were wounded in the duel that followed. In educational affairs Clement Clay was for many years a trustee of Greene Academy, chartered in 1812 and opened in 1823. Here his own sons and many other Huntsville boys were educated. Clay also served as trustee of Madison Female Academy and sponsored other schools from time to time. He was a member of long standing and a one-time president of the Madison County Bible Society, and as a stockholder in the Huntsville Library Company he was entitled to draw books "every Tuesday and Friday from half past 11 o'clock a.m. to half past twelve."[1]

When President James Monroe unexpectedly rode into Huntsville on June 1, 1819, Clement Clay spoke for the committee which welcomed him to "our remote and humble village," and arranged a dinner in his honor. Next day "at 4 o'clock, the President and suit [sic] together with more than one hundred of the most respectable Citizens of Madison County sat down to a sumptuous entertainment . . . at which Col. LeRoy Pope acted as President assisted by C. C. Clay and Henry Minor Esqrs." Clay's toast was: "Public sentiment—The best shield of merit." On the occasion of Lafayette's arrival in America (1824), Clement Clay, James G. Birney, and three other Huntsville citizens formed the committee to give a public dinner, a ball, and an address of welcome to the famous visitor. In fact, hardly a civic event occurred in Huntsville without Clement Clay's having a hand in it.[2]

Clement Comer Clay's political career began before Alabama attained statehood. Alabama Territory became a political entity on December 10, 1817, and on January 19, 1818, its first territorial legislature met at St. Stephens on the Tombigbee. In that first legislature sat Clement Clay. With him representing Madison County were Hugh McVay, John Williams Walker, and Gabriel Moore, speaker. The seven counties in the territory had a total representation of twelve men. Thus Madison County with four representatives held a dominant place. These twelve young legislators, meeting at the inn of a frontier village, created new counties and altered boundaries of those already established, incorporated an academy, erected two judicial districts, appointed an attorney general for each, and made Clement Clay one of five commissioners to select the best site for the territorial capital. But the most important piece of legislation was that of February 13, 1818, repealing all laws against usury, so that any interest rate adopted by written agreement was recoverable at law. This act, passed in the exuberance of a boom period, was destined to have painful repercussions when the crash of 1819 brought Alabama back to earth and forced repeal (on November 22, 1819), together with relief measures. The incident was for years an unwelcome specter, long haunting the political fortunes of those legislators who had so rashly passed the "Usury Law."[3]

The second session of the territorial legislature convened on November 2, 1818, with twenty members now representing sixteen

1 William and Rebecca Clay to Clay, Sr., Nov. 13, 1814 (letter in private possession); Huntsville *Alabama Republican,* Oct. 23, 1819, Nov. 10, 1820; Madison County Bible Society Minutes, Clay MSS.
2 J. H. Weakley to John Coffee, June 2, 1819, John Coffee MSS; Huntsville *Democrat,* Sept. 7, 1824; Huntsville *Alabama Republican,* June 5, 1819, Sept. 10, 1824. Lafayette did not visit Huntsville. He passed through southern Alabama in April, 1825.
3 James Campbell to David Campbell, March 8, 1819, David Campbell MSS; Alabama (Ter.) Legislature, House *Journal,* 1st Sess., pp. 3-47, Jan. 19—Feb. 14, 1818. (Legislative House and Senate Journals will be cited as *HJ* or *SJ.*)

counties. Acting for the commissioners on the choice of a capital, Clay recommended a site at the confluence of the Cahaba and Alabama rivers. This was adopted and the town of Cahaba was duly laid out. Even though it soon had an "elegant bridge . . . fine houses . . . a fine church & State house," the new capital, unfortunately subject to overflow from two rivers, soon proved to be inaccessible, unhealthful, and generally unsatisfactory. Tuscaloosa became the second capital in 1826. In both sessions of the territorial legislature, Clement Clay was exceedingly active. He served on committees, he introduced bills, he was an active debater, and he kept business moving. Indeed, like most of the members, he was anxious to wind up legislative business and return home to look after his cotton crop and his law practice. Hence he used his "utmost . . . exertions to bring the Session to a most speedy close," which he accomplished on November 21, 1818.[4]

During this session the legislature had petitioned Congress for an enabling act. Congress passed that measure on March 2, 1819, and Alabama was destined to be a state ere the next legislature met. Even before this news reached distant Alabama, eager candidates were seeking election as delegates to the anticipated constitutional convention. When the votes were counted, Clement Comer Clay headed the list of Madison County's eight members.

The convention assembled in Huntsville on July 5, 1819, and chose John Williams Walker as its president. Of its forty-four members, almost half were natives of Virginia; several came from North Carolina, South Carolina, or Georgia; and the remainder were scattered among other states. It was generally considered a very superior body, possessed of much "urbanity & intelligence. It would do no discredit to any country however old and respectable," remarked one observer.[5] On July 7, Clement Clay was named chairman of a committee of fifteen to draft the constitution. Six days later he presented that committee's handiwork, which then became the subject of more than two weeks' debate on the floor of the convention and revision in the committee. Each member "was prejudiced in favour of the forms and mode of

4 Clay, Sr., to Susanna Clay, Nov. 11, 1818, Clay MSS; John Campbell to David Campbell, April 27, 1821, David Campbell MSS; Ala. (Ter.) Leg., *HJ*, 2d Sess., 3-117, Nov. 2-21, 1818; Huntsville *Alabama Republican*, Feb. 20, 1819.

5 John Campbell to John Campbell, Sr., July 10, 1819, David Campbell MSS; Theodore Henley Jack, *Sectionalism and Party Politics in Alabama, 1819-1842* (Menasha, Wisc., 1919), 13.

proceeding he had formerly been accustomed to," so that at first there was not much "harmony." In these debates Clement Clay took an active and leading part. The resulting constitution, with a mixture of liberal and conservative provisions, was modeled partially on the Virginia document of 1776, thereby reflecting the nativity of its makers. The constitution was duly transmitted to Congress, and Alabama became a state on December 14, 1819.[6]

Scarcely had the convention adjourned on August 2, 1819, before the press and public meetings were suggesting candidates for the new state's first officials. One such meeting at Tuscaloosa nominated Clement C. Clay for governor, an honor which he declined, for, "were there no other objection to his offering for that important station, his age would be an insurmountable obstacle to his filling the office." (He would not reach the required age of thirty until after the election.) His neighbors in Madison County proposed Clay for the legislature, but this candidacy he likewise declined, since the legislative session conflicted with the terms of those courts where he practiced and had at that time a large accumulation of legal business.

But Clay was not to languish without honor in the state's first government. On December 16, 1819, he was commissioned judge of the Fifth Judicial Circuit (having been elected by the legislature on December 14), which meant that he automatically became a justice of the supreme court of Alabama. His four colleagues immediately elected him chief justice, and so it was that when he had just turned thirty, Clement Clay occupied the highest judicial post in the new state of Alabama. He served in this office until December, 1823, when he resigned to resume private practice in partnership with James White McClung, a rising young lawyer of Huntsville, to whom Clay had turned over his practice upon becoming chief justice. When Governor William Wyatt Bibb died in 1820, there were those who thought that Clement Clay hankered to be his successor, but if so, he kept that wish to himself.[7]

6 Ala. (Ter.) Convention, 1819, *Journal of the Convention of the Alabama Territory Begun July 5, 1819*, 3-40; John Campbell and James Campbell to David Campbell, July 10, 13, Aug. 11, 1819, David Campbell MSS; Malcolm Cook McMillan, "The Alabama Constitution of 1819: A Study in Constitution-Making on the Frontier," *Ala. Rev.*, III (Oct., 1950), 263-85.

7 John Campbell to David Campbell, Aug. 2, 1820, David Campbell MSS; Huntsville *Alabama Republican*, Aug. 12, 19, 28, 1819, Jan. 29, 1820; John C. Anderson, "The Supreme Court of Alabama, Its Organization and Sketches of Its Chief Justices," *Ala. Hist. Q.*, I (Spring, 1930), 121-23.

As judge of the Fifth Judicial Circuit, Clay found himself very busy. The counties of Jackson, Decatur, Morgan, and Madison comprised the Fifth Circuit, in each of which spring and fall terms of court were held. Clay's first term of court for Madison County brought this comment from the press, "There has probably never been so important a court in the State of Alabama, whether we consider the number and importance of civil cases, or the crowded state of the criminal docket." The following year (1821) Clay held a "most laborious term of three weeks. . . . The number of causes . . . must have considerably exceeded 2,000 many of which . . . must remain untried, although his honor has literally lived upon the bench." . . . "Judge Clay," remarked an astute observer, "is a very young man, of pleasing manners, handsome person, and said to be a man of the first talents in the state. Though this is a new country, I have witnessed very few judges who might rank with Judge Clay in elegance of manners." Even greater pressure of business characterized the courts during the remaining two years of Clay's judgeship. The difficulties of travel, long absences from home, and exhausting hours on the bench, all for a salary of $1,500, were sufficient cause for Clay's return to private practice.[8]

Meanwhile, the young state was beset by money problems, for it had almost no sources of revenue and so had to finance the government by borrowing. Just at this time came the financial crash of 1819. The boom had saddled the people of Alabama with a land debt of eleven million dollars (more than half that of the entire nation), while the crash tumbled thirty-cent cotton down to eighteen cents.

Banking had begun at Huntsville in 1817, when the Planters' and Mechanics' Bank (chartered on December 11, 1816, with a capital of $500,000) opened for business as soon as $50,000 worth of stock had been subscribed. Clement Clay was one of the original trustees as well as a stockholder. The tremendous pressure for money throughout the West led to unsound banking and invalidated all efforts at restraint. On June 23, 1820, the Huntsville bank was forced to suspend specie payment, a circumstance

8 James Campbell to David Campbell, Oct. 23, 1821, David Campbell MSS; Huntsville *Alabama Republican*, March 11, Sept. 15, 1820, Sept. 21, 1821; Anne Royall, *Letters from Alabama*, 130.

which caused Clay to sell his stock at a loss and to withdraw from the board of directors, rather than have any further connection with an institution whose policy he did not approve.[9]

All efforts to force resumption of specie payment failed, so that in February, 1825, Governor Israel Pickens declared the bank's charter forfeited. With their bank closed and its notes no longer legal tender, people in the Tennessee Valley suffered considerable financial distress; but the demise of the Huntsville bank was scarcely regretted by its many enemies, as the following "obituary" attests: "The Huntsville Bank, departed this life on the 5th instant, covered with Glory and dishonor—She died as she had lived, beloved by her friends, and detested by all the rest of the world. . . . She was venerated by the *royal family* as the very essence of all that was good and great, . . . but by all honest men, she was known and felt as the verriest robber that ever disgraced society."[10]

It was a battle between poor and rich, and in it economics and politics became inextricably mingled. The editor of the Huntsville *Democrat,* claiming to be the friend of the poor, was soon labeling capitalists and all who associated with them as belonging to the "Royal Party." The bank, he declared, had "been in the hands of a pack of shavers and extortioners, who have grown fat by grinding the face of the poor, and would have multiplied their oppression ten fold, but for the virtue of a few, who have fought a good fight"; furthermore, "the President of this Bank [LeRoy Pope] did . . . repeatedly declare, that the country people were a parcel of ignorant animals and not able to determine whether this Bank acted correctly or incorrectly." Thus did the label of "Royal Party" begin to operate in Alabama politics.[11]

For "Royal Party" also meant those who had voted for or profited by the Usury Law of 1818. Clay, like nearly every other legislator of the 1818 assembly, had supported the measure, and hence was termed a "Royalist" in some quarters. Though Clay

9 Thomas G. Percy to J. W. Walker, March 15, 1820, John Williams Walker MSS; James Campbell to David Campbell, July 13, 1819, David Campbell MSS; Israel Pickens to William Lenoir, Nov. 19, 1821, Israel Pickens MSS; Huntsville *Alabama Republican,* Jan. 9, 1819, June 23, 1820; William Graham Sumner, *A History of Banking in All the Leading Nations* (New York, 1896, 4 vols.), I, 61; Davis Rich Dewey, *State Banking before the Civil War* (Washington, 1910), 19, 39.

10 John H. Hobbs to Alexander H. Hobbs, March 7, 1824, George Coke Dromgoole MSS; Huntsville *Alabama Republican,* May 28, 1824, Feb. 18, 1825; Huntsville *Democrat,* Feb. 15, 1825.

11 Huntsville *Democrat,* Nov. 25, 1823.

quickly realized the folly of passing the Usury Law and also re-
nounced all connection with the Huntsville bank, he soon found
that it was impossible to convince everyone that he was the
people's friend. Meanwhile, the courts had before them many
cases involving excessive interest charges stipulated during the
single year of the Usury Law's validity. In 1824 the state supreme
court decreed that interest in excess of 8 percent was not recoverable except in specific classes of written contracts, and then for
only limited periods. This good news Clay brought from Cahaba
to Huntsville. "Thus at last," he exulted, "a check is given to
the griping hands of the unfeeling Shylocks of this country."[12]

This was the situation when Clement Clay turned again to
politics. In 1825 his friends had a second time advanced his name
for the governorship and he had again declined to become a
candidate. But he did seek election to Congress in opposition to
Gabriel Moore, whom he cordially disliked. The campaign turned
largely on local affairs—the Royal Party and the Huntsville bank—
though the tariff and relief for land purchasers were issues. Gabe
Moore was wobbly on the tariff, silent on the question of relief
for land debtors, and innocent in the bank scandal. Clem Clay
was consistently hostile to the tariff and a stout advocate of relief
measures, but in the bank matter he was on precarious ground,
for he had been a stockholder and director. He assured voters
that he had urged the resumption and continuance of specie payment "so long as a dollar remained in the vaults," but failing in
this, he had immediately sold his stock at a sacrifice and had *"not
since been, nor am I now a Stockholder,* in that, or any other
Bank." On this the Huntsville *Democrat* gave him hearty support.
But his connection with the bank branded him in the eyes of
many as a member of the Royal Party, whereas Gabe Moore
loudly disclaimed all connection with that notorious faction and
posed as the friend of the poor man.[13]

With these odds Clay's friends urged him to carry on a more
vigorous campaign, but at best the prospects were not very cheer-
ing. In spite of all their efforts they constantly found "a majority
in favour of G. Moor[e]" who "frequented evry [*sic*] grog shop

12 Huntsville *Democrat,* June 29, 1824, June 24, 1825.
13 Huntsville *Democrat,* Feb. 1, July 19, 29, 1825; Huntsville *Southern Advocate,*
May 13, 1825.

in the county and visited every old woman." Mrs. Clay watched the progress of affairs more anxiously than she perhaps realized. She wrote to Clement, "So maney [sic] ungenerous advantages are taken that I should not be astonished if More [sic] should triumph but he can take nothind [sic] in reality from you, you have resources he must ever be a stranger to. But do not think I despair or that your friends think you have no hope, Mr McClung received a letter from Decater [sic] stating you were on rising ground. . . . I had been led allmost [sic] unconsciously to speak of the election with great apparent interest but I assure you I expect to see you (if you should be defeated, releaved, [sic] from a burden for I have allways [sic] thought you consider'd it one, and deriveind [sic] more happiness from your little family than you could ever experience when apart from them." Gabe Moore's vociferous claims together with the misrepresentations common to campaigning brought about Clay's defeat. The vote stood: Clay, 2,070; Moore, 3,973.[14]

Close upon the heels of this came another defeat. When Israel Pickens resigned as United States senator in 1826, five candidates offered to fill the vacancy. After much jockeying in caucus, three of them withdrew, leaving Clement Clay and John McKinley to be voted for by the legislature. In the balloting Clay lost by three votes. The seven Tennessee River counties gave Clay nineteen of their twenty-nine votes and the Northern Congressional District contributed sixteen of its twenty-three, but Madison County gave him only two of its five votes. McKinley's election had the blessing of Andrew Jackson, who hailed him as a better Jacksonian than Clement Clay at this time.[15]

Many complex factors entered into Clay's defeat in 1826. Four years earlier Clement Clay and William Kelly were generally looked upon as the democratic friends of the people in North Alabama, while John McKinley and Henry Chambers headed the Royal faction. In 1822 Kelly was elected United States senator by one vote, "chiefly through the influence of Clay." A little power proved disastrous for Kelly, whose devious course soon antagonized

14 A. W. H. Clifton to Clay, Sr., May 9, 1825, W. F. Withers to Clay, Sr., May 10, 1825, Susanna Clay to Clay, Sr., July 30, 1825, Clay MSS; Huntsville *Democrat*, Aug. 5, 1825; Huntsville *Southern Advocate*, Aug. 5, 12, 1825.

15 Ala. Leg., *HJ*, pp. 29f, Nov. 27, 1826; Huntsville *Southern Advocate*, Nov. 3, Dec. 8, 15, 1826.

most of his friends, including Clement Clay. Now in 1826 when
Clay and McKinley were rivals, Kelly used his influence to throw
the election to McKinley, whom he had beaten in 1822. Further
complication came from the two Huntsville newspapers, which
reversed their customary positions. The *Southern Advocate* supported Clay, while the *Democrat* was fiercely hostile. This anomaly
arose from personal factors. Editor William B. Long of the *Democrat* was the close friend and ally of William Kelly. Their zeal
took a wrong turn, however, when in 1825 they campaigned for
judicial reform which would interpret decisions in the Usury Law
cases so that Kelly's clients would be refunded thousands of dollars
in interest which they had paid while that law was operative.
Kelly's fees in the cases were to be "large and contingent"; he
would receive 50 percent of all amounts recovered for his clients.
While this scheme was encountering strong popular opposition
as being "an open attempt to violate the *constitution*," editor
Long died. Andrew Wills now became chief editor of the Huntsville *Democrat*.

Wills, a Scotsman, had come to Huntsville early in 1824 to be
principal of Greene Academy, of which Clement Clay was a trustee. Difficulties between the trustees and Wills led to the latter's
resignation in December, 1825. Sometime during those two years
Wills, after first associating with some of the Royal Party, decided
that they were the wrong crowd, and so changed his allegiance and
joined Kelly and Long. Thus it was a natural development that
he should become editor of the *Democrat* and that he should
denounce as Royalists, Clement Clay and the other trustees who
had been responsible for ousting him from the academy.

From this stemmed a chain of events growing basically out of
Clement Clay's ambition for office. In the autumn of 1826 editor
Andrew Wills went down to Tuscaloosa, where the legislature
admitted him to its floor for the ostensible purpose of reporting
proceedings. Responsible for this favor was James White McClung,
Clement Clay's law partner and campaign manager in the senatorial election. McClung undoubtedly hoped thus to conciliate
Wills, but the idea backfired and Wills took advantage of his
position to attack Dr. David Moore, one of the most respected
representatives of Madison County. Wills accused Moore of
attaching himself to "that obnoxious party," the Royalists, by

voting for Clement Clay for United States senator. Turning his hostility in another direction, Wills then accused James White McClung of trying to bribe members of the legislature to vote for Clay by promising that Clay, if elected senator, would support the administration of John Quincy Adams. McClung angrily denied this, and the quarrel between the two filled the Huntsville papers week after week. On July 23, 1827, McClung and Wills met on a Huntsville street, and in an exchange of shots Wills was killed. At the subsequent trial Clay was one of the counsel for McClung, who was acquitted by the jury.[16]

Meanwhile, Clement Clay was devoting much of his time and effort to the pressing question of internal improvements for North Alabama. The Muscle Shoals were the chief obstruction to navigation of the Tennessee River, and so it was on this thirty-mile stretch of the river that interest centered. In 1823 Clement Clay became one of three commissioners who were to examine the shoals and report to the legislature. Their lengthy report on November 10, 1826, discussed all the problems and recommended construction of a canal to cost an estimated $487,760. Clement Clay was a charter member of the Muscle Shoals Canal Company incorporated by the legislature on January 13, 1827. A year later (May 23, 1828) Congress appropriated 400,000 acres of relinquished lands to be sold and the proceeds to be used by the state of Alabama in financing construction of this canal. The project was nearer Clay's heart than probably anything else he strove to accomplish. In this initial effort to link the Tennessee Valley by adequate transportation with other parts of the country, Clay gave a prodigious amount of time and hard work with, in the end, disappointingly meager results.[17]

Financing the canal by sale of the relinquished lands would be the chief item of business in the upcoming legislative session. Because of the "unusual importance" of the session, "Many Voters" called upon Clay to be a candidate. He accepted because of his *"earnest desire* to see this *great work* accomplished." In the lively campaign that followed, his opponents argued that Clay would favor giving preference in the sales to those who had previously

16 Nuermberger, "The 'Royal Party' in Early Alabama Politics," 81-98, 198-212.
17 Huntsville *Alabama Republican,* Dec. 17, 1824; Huntsville *Southern Advocate,* Dec. 29, 1826, Jan. 5, March 2, 1827, June 27, 1828; Huntsville *Democrat,* June 13, 27, 1828.

occupied or relinquished the land. This Clay emphatically denied, saying that the proper policy was "to dispose of the land, in the manner best calculated to produce the largest amount of money, *without favour to individuals* who have relinquished or occupy it," and to this end the best method would be sale to the highest bidder.[18]

Clay won the election, and when the legislature convened on November 17, 1828, he was the unanimous choice for speaker of the lower house. A few weeks later Susanna joined Clement in the new capital of Tuscaloosa. Of the town she wrote, "This place is not so large as Huntsville although it has a more imposing aspect . . . the streets are very wide sandy and smooth. . . . There are some handsome buildings finished. The state house and university are progressing." So appeared the raw town to Susanna's unsophisticated eyes, for she had traveled only within the bounds of frontier Alabama.[19]

Meanwhile, Clay was busy with the bill to dispose of the 400,000-acre grant. As drafted, it contained a scheme to classify and price the land on the basis of its desirability. During seventeen days of wrangling over the bill, Clay frequently left the speaker's chair to take part in debate, and on one occasion he "occupied the floor a whole day, and made a most powerful speech in opposition to some features of the bill." He was unalterably opposed to the classification scheme, and strove to convince his colleagues that sale at auction to the highest bidder would bring in more money. Though he failed to change their minds on this, Clay managed to put through several minor improvements before the bill finally passed both houses.[20]

Dissatisfied with some of the Usury Law decisions, this legislature adopted a joint resolution reducing the terms of circuit judges to six years. That change became an amendment to the constitution in 1830. The session also witnessed one of the most curious events in Alabama history, known as the "Trial of the Judges." William Kelly was still trying to win for his clients a refund of interest paid out under the Usury Law. Even though

18 Huntsville *Southern Advocate,* June 20, 27, July 18, 1828; Huntsville *Democrat,* June 13, 27, July 18, 1828.
19 Susanna Clay to Clay, Jr., Jan. 5, 182[9], Clay MSS; Ala. Leg., *HJ,* p. 4, Nov. 17, 1828.
20 Ala. Leg., *HJ,* pp. 17-215 *passim,* Nov. 17, 1828–Jan. 28, 1829; Huntsville *Democrat,* Dec. 24, 1828, Jan. 2, 23, 1829.

the courts had decreed against it, Kelly did not give up easily, and he now came before the Alabama senate, where he presented a lengthy arraignment charging that the conduct of supreme-court justices Reuben Saffold, John White, and Anderson Crenshaw "has been oppressive to my client and injurious to me," and denounced the justices as being unfit for their posts. The entire legal profession came to the defense of the supreme court. During two days of tense hearings Clay and many others testified in behalf of the justices. By a vote of 15-5, the senate declared that evidence against the justices was insufficient for their removal.[21] This brought to a final close the vexations of the Usury Law, and the accusation of Royal Party was no more bandied around the state. William Kelly had failed ignominiously, and soon left Alabama for New Orleans, where he died in obscurity in 1834.

Clay's political position was now greatly strengthened. He was entirely cleared from any accusations connected with the Royal Party, while his success in the legislature and his hearty support of the incoming Jackson administration gave him added prestige. Under these circumstances he became a candidate for Congress in the spring of 1829. His opponent in the campaign was Nicholas Davis of Limestone County. The chief issue was relief for land debtors, and on this Clay had a stronger and more consistent record than Davis. Clay won the election by the small majority of 336 votes in a total of more than 8,000. He had the satisfaction, however, of receiving 2,029 votes in Madison County as against 443 for Davis.[22]

Relief legislation for land debtors had been the chief goal of Alabama's congressional delegation almost from the beginning of the state's existence. The land act of 1820, suddenly cutting off credit, meant financial ruin to many a purchaser. Clamor for aid resulted in the relief act of 1821 which required debtors to relinquish land not yet paid for and apply the sum already paid to the purchase of the tract retained, which must be a minimum of eighty acres with legal boundaries. Interest charges in the future would be remitted for prompt payment, and a further 37½ percent discount was offered to those who would pay up in full before

21 Ala. Leg., *SJ*, pp. 139-89, Jan. 21-22, 1829; Henderson Middleton Somerville, "Trial of the Alabama Supreme Court Judges in 1829," Alabama State Bar Association *Proceedings*, XXII (Montgomery, 1899), 59-96.
22 Huntsville *Democrat*, March 27, April 3, June 26, July 3, 10, 31, Aug. 7, 14, 1829.

September 30, 1822. During the next ten years eleven relief acts were passed, giving assistance to various classes of land debtors. But much still remained to be done, and to this task Representative Clement Clay addressed himself.[23]

[23] Roy Marvin Robbins, *Our Landed Heritage: The Public Domain, 1776-1936* (Princeton, 1942), 38-42.

3

Representative in Congress

ON HIS FIRST JOURNEY to Washington, Clay left Huntsville probably early in November, 1829, stopped in East Tennessee to visit his parents, and there joined his old teacher, Hugh Lawson White, for the remaining distance. They, along with many other members, took "advantage of the late fine weather, to reach the Seat of Government" in the first days of December. Clay and White soon settled themselves at Mrs. Ann Peyton's, one of the more popular boardinghouses for congressmen. Located on Pennsylvania Avenue, between Third and Fourth streets "near Gadesby's," this establishment accommodated one of the largest "messes" in the city. As Clay looked around the dining tables, he found himself one of twelve members, together with assorted wives and relatives.

The twelve men represented ten states, six of them southern. Of the Southerners, Hugh Lawson White, senator from Tennessee since 1825, was most distinguished, while mild-mannered James Knox Polk's major achievements were still to come. Among the others were tall, elegant, handsome Henry G. Lamar of Georgia, and the irascible, frustrated John M. Goodenow, who soon resigned in a huff and returned to Ohio.

As Clay made his way down windswept Pennsylvania Avenue, he could gaze upon the gray-white mass of the Capitol crowned by its squat iron dome. Entering the grounds through an iron gate, he ascended the long flight of steps to the "Grand Terrace."

If he circled the building to the east front, he could contemplate a "lot of probably two acres . . . very beautifully indeed laid off into walks and flower beds." As he entered the Capitol, Clay needed to pause only briefly to examine the then sparse ornamentation of the rotunda. He could proceed at once to the center of Democratic activity, the "Hall of Representatives . . . considered by enthusiastic Americans the 'most elegant legislative hall in the world.' " This "splendid semicircular hall . . . [was] surrounded by twenty-six columns." The walls were draped with "crimson curtains," and between every pair of columns stood "a sofa, on which the members . . . may lounge at their ease." At his "fixed place" each representative had "a comfortable stuffed armchair, and before him a writing-desk with a drawer underneath, of which he keeps the key."[1]

As Clement Clay took his seat in the House of Representatives on December 7, 1829, he was one of 108 new members, all a trifle ill at ease in their new and somber surroundings. Congress was overwhelmingly Democratic. In the House, 142 Jacksonians found only 71 National Republicans to oppose them, and in the Senate, Democrats held an even larger majority. The Twenty-first Congress was reasonably distinguished, though most of its big names were in the Senate. As Clay looked around him in the House, he could see two future Presidents—his own good friend James K. Polk and James Buchanan. There were besides a sprinkling of future presidential candidates, cabinet members, and a larger number who would be governors. The presence of Edward Everett, the orator, George McDuffie, the state-rights protagonist, James Moore Wayne, the great jurist, and Richard Henry Wilde, the poet, gave variety to the assemblage. The states of Virginia, Tennessee, and Kentucky had, on the whole, the most able and distinguished delegations.

The House quickly organized by electing as its speaker Andrew Stevenson of Virginia. Three days later Clement Clay became one of the seven-man Committee on Public Lands. Representing the southeast was eccentric Robert Potter of North Carolina, whose

1 Washington *Daily National Intelligencer*, Nov. 26, 27, 30, Dec. 5, 1829; Anne Royall, *Letters from Alabama*, 225; Glenn Brown, *History of the United States Capitol* (Washington, 1900, 2 vols.), I, 65-67; George M. Whicher (ed.), "Washington in 1834: Letter of Robert C. Caldwell," *AHR*, XXVII (Jan., 1922), 276; "Chamber of Representatives at Washington," *Knight's Penny Magazine* (London, 1832-1845), IV (Oct. 10, 1835), 398.

varied career would be ended by violent death in Texas. Western members of the committee included Jonathan Jennings, who had grown up with Indiana Territory and had been the state's first governor, and broad-faced, black-eyed Joseph Duncan, whose career in Illinois paralleled that of Clement Comer Clay in Alabama.[2]

Clay set to work immediately to prepare relief legislation. On December 17 he put through a resolution requiring the Committee on Public Lands to investigate the expediency of further relief and the advisability of a change in the mode of sale so as to give "a preference in the purchase . . . to actual settlers or occupants, at prices to be *fixed* and *graduated* according to quality of soil and situation." The committee reported a bill on December 30. Clay succeeded in having postponed until September 30, 1830, the sale of relinquished lands in his home counties which had previously been scheduled for February 15. This welcome respite would enable "occupants of those lands . . . to come into the market better prepared to purchase, than they could do at present," since another crop would add to their resources. Meanwhile, John McKinley in the Senate had introduced a relief bill which came before the House for debate on March 11, 1830.

As Clement Clay rose to begin his first major speech, his colleagues saw a man with a strong, determined face and piercing eyes. "He is," noted a contemporary, "a man of talents and learning and of very imposing appearance. His features are handsome and striking and his manners alluring. He is tall and slender, and his hair black, profuse, and glossy. His election to Congress reflects much honor upon those who selected him." Even grumpy John Quincy Adams grudgingly admitted that "Clay is a man of some talent and of much activity and perseverance, a fluent speaker, of very little power, but making up the deficiency of substance by the ardor of his zeal. So it is with almost all the Jackson leaders in the House."

In his first speech on land relief, Clay's arguments revolved around two points: the low price of cotton in contrast with the continuing high costs of labor and equipment; and the fact that

[2] U. S. Congress, House *Journal*, 21 Cong., 1 Sess., p. 29 (hereinafter such citations will use the form: USC, *HJ*, 21:1); Robert Watson Winston, "Robert Potter: Tar Heel and Texan," *South Atlantic Quarterly*, XXIX (April, 1930), 140-59 (cited hereinafter as *SAQ*); Elizabeth Duncan Putnam, "The Life and Services of Joseph Duncan, Governor of Illinois, 1834-1838," Illinois State Historical Society *Transactions* (1919), 107-87.

relief was not for speculators but for actual planters and solid, respectable citizens. On March 15 Clay was able to say, "The Struggle in the House is now over." To achieve this victory, he and the entire Alabama delegation had "laboured with great zeal."[3]

The bill as passed offered three alternatives: if as much as $3.50 per acre had already been paid, the occupant was forthwith given title to such reverted lands; or he might make a further payment of $1.25 or such smaller sum as would bring the total amount paid up to $3.50. Finally, if the purchaser had paid more than one installment, or had bought land priced as low as $2.00 an acre, he might pay off his debt in cash and receive thereby the $37\frac{1}{2}$ percent discount, thus actually obtaining his land for $0.93\frac{1}{4}$ per acre. The act set a minimum price of $1.56\frac{1}{4}$ per acre. Clay admitted this was too high for very inferior lands, but explained that it was the best he could do. Despite the new law's imperfections, Clay declared that "Upon the whole . . . it will be found, in fact, as well as in name, a relief law; under which a very large proportion of the citizens of our state may disenthral themselves from the discouraging and paralyzing embarrassments under which they have labored for the last ten years." The inevitable opposition decried it as a "rich man's law" which would not benefit all classes of debtors, but the Alabama press immediately rose to support of the act and Clay published a fuller explanation assuring his constituents that "a very large proportion of the reverted land will be found, under this act, entirely paid for." When this proved to be true, popular gratitude gave Clay the assurance that he would "have nothing to fear from opposition—at any future canvass—as the People now not Only of Madison Cty but Jackson also have gotten more than they had any reasonable hope of obtaining—" At a public dinner in his honor on July 29, 1830, Clay was acclaimed as the "champion of 'preference rights' and friend of the friendless."[4]

Busy with his committee work, Clay seldom spoke except when debate concerned some phase of public-land policy. But he was

3 John McKinley to [John Coffee], Jan. 25, 1830, John Brahan to John Coffee, March 18, 1830, John Coffee MSS; USC, *HJ*, 21:1, pp. 29, 63, 112, 138, 257, 345, 401, 420, 504; USC, *SJ*, 21:1, pp. 32, 34; USC, *Register of Debates*, 21:1, VI, Appen., xiii; Huntsville *Democrat*, Jan. 8, Feb. 5, April 2, 1830; Anne Royall, *Letters from Alabama*, 225.

4 William McDowell to Clay, Sr., June 11, 1830, Duff Green to Clay, Sr., July 21, 1830, Clay MSS; Huntsville *Democrat*, April 16, 30, Aug. 12, 1830.

always in his seat, following the progress of questions vital to his state. The tariff, removal of the Indians, and the Maysville Road bill were the chief subjects of debate. Clay of course voted to remove the Indians west of the Mississippi; he also favored the Maysville Road bill, and after its veto by President Jackson, he voted to pass it over the veto. It was not long, however, until Clay came around to Jackson's viewpoint on internal improvements.

While Clay attended closely to duty, he was not oblivious of the many excitements abounding in Washington during the winter of 1829-1830. The fever of the "Eaton malaria" rose and ebbed, but its purely social aspects did not trouble Clay, since the feminine portion of his family was in distant Alabama. The Webster-Hayne debate, its implications and consequences, however, were to have their reverberations in Alabama. Not least among events of the winter was the Jefferson Day dinner on April 13. This function, ostensibly to honor the founder of the Democratic party, unexpectedly took on a sinister aspect. Thomas Hart Benton and others "soon discovered . . . that it . . . savored of the new doctrine of nullification; . . . that the dinner was got up to inaugurate that doctrine, and to make Mr. Jefferson its father." At the dinner Clement Clay participated in the twenty-four regular toasts, and then like all, was electrified as President Jackson rose and proposed his famous "Our Federal Union: It must be preserved." As the evening wore on, more than eighty volunteer toasts were offered. Clement Clay in his turn gave, "The distribution of the surplus revenue: The best and fairest mode is to leave it in the pockets of the people who made it—the rightful owners." This sentiment not only expressed his own views, but epitomized Clement Clay's hostility to his distant cousin, Henry Clay.[5]

With the end of the session on May 31, Clay quickly turned his steps homeward, though he stopped in East Tennessee for a brief visit with his parents. For him the summer and autumn were filled with a multitude of tasks pertaining to the plantations, civic affairs, legal business, and politics.

December 2, 1830, saw Clay back in Washington, settled again

[5] Thomas Hart Benton, *Thirty Years' View* (New York, 1854, 3 vols.), I, 148; John Quincy Adams, *Diary*, ed. by Allan Nevins (New York, 1929), 403f; Washington *U. S. Telegraph*, April 17, 1830.

at Mrs. Ann Peyton's boardinghouse with his friends James K. Polk and Hugh Lawson White. Seven of last year's mess were reunited around the dining tables, but there were six new faces, among them Littleton Waller Tazewell, considered Virginia's most brilliant legal mind, and tall, immaculate, resolute-looking Bedford Brown of North Carolina.

Congress met on December 6, 1830, and Clay went to work at once on further relief measures for land debtors. On December 23 he introduced a bill and sent the text to the Huntsville press as corroboration of his activity. "Convinced . . . of the justness and reasonableness of its provisions," Clay on February 15, 1831, made a vigorous speech on behalf of the measure, reviewing again the whole subject and the benefits derived from former measures, but emphasizing their inadequacy to give justice to all classes. He now pleaded for those poorer debtors who had not yet obtained relief proportionate to that "extended to their more fortunate and more wealthy brethren and fellow-sufferers." The bill in question (passed on February 23, 1831) provided that relinquished lands purchased at prices from $5.00 to $14.00 an acre could now be reclaimed without additional payment if the minimum of $1.25 had already been paid. All North Alabama praised Clay for his success in putting through this measure. The Huntsville press reflected the general satisfaction: "Congress has now done every thing for the land debtors of this State, that we could have asked; and while we express our gratitude to government, we must bear in mind the efforts of our faithful representatives."

Nor were their efforts forgotten. Public dinners at Triana and Hickman's Spring attested to the popularity of both Clay and John McKinley. One of the toasts lauded Clay as "Indefatigable and untiring in his zeal; able and successful in his efforts to secure the homes of his countrymen—all proclaim him eminently worthy of the highest honors his State can confer."[6]

Of those prospective honors Clay had in the preceding winter written with the equivocation so often used by those in office, "My time here [i.e., Washington] begins to drag very heavily— . . . I have lost almost all my taste for parties—and, hence, declined two invitations during the last week. I am beginning to think that Congress, is, at least, not the place for the advancement of my

6 USC, *HJ*, 21:2, pp. 96, 134, 139, 315, 343, 348, 433; USC, *Register of Debates*, 21:2, VII, 719, Appen., 18; Huntsville *Democrat*, Jan. 13, March 17, May 26, 1831.

interest, or happiness; and am half inclined, if I could get *decently* out of the scrape, to surrender my claims as a politician. But I do not now percieve [*sic*] how this can be accomplished at present. I do not wish to offend, or injure my friends, who took such an interest—some of them so much trouble to sustain me in my last contest,—and, therefore, feel it a sort of duty to submit my name to the people of the District, *once more*. . . . I have two weeks & four days, yet, to remain here. I fear they will be very long—and may add some grey hairs to the liberal stock I have already. . . . I am beginning to persuade myself that they will add greatly to the *dignity*, and *gravity* of my appearance. Do you not think so?" he asked his young sister-in-law, Mary D. M. Withers, with a touch of humor seldom revealed in his letters.

But by August, Clay's distaste for politics had vanished, and he was reelected to Congress without opposition. Meanwhile, Susanna Clay was making ready to accompany Clement to Washington. She turned over the household to the care of her mother. With the Clays went Susanna's young sister, Ann Withers, and the women's personal maid, Milly. We "intend going," Clay explained to Polk, "thro' Georgia, S. Carolina &c and to take residence of some friends . . . [along the] way. It is our wish," he added, "to board with a small mess—of whom Mr. Mardis, my new colleague (and by the way a very charm[ing] fellow) and his lady will probably be two."[7]

The Clays left home early in November, 1831, and reached Washington simultaneously with a "pretty deep snow" and cold wave which sent the temperature down to 20 degrees and partially froze the Potomac. The Clays and Mardises found their "small mess" at Mrs. McDaniel's boardinghouse "nearly opposite Gadsby's." The only other boarders were John Young Mason of Virginia and Jesse Speight of North Carolina. Intent on deriving every benefit from her wider horizons, Susanna lost no opportunity for "seeing all the sights that are to be found," but young Ann often refused "to go out alledging that it is too exciteing [*sic*] to her nerves to see so much company."[8]

With his work in behalf of land debtors now largely completed, Clay could give more attention to national issues and party

[7] Clay, Sr., to Mary D. M. Withers, Feb. 13, 1831, Clay MSS (Ala. Dept. Archives and Hist.); Clay, Sr., to J. K. Polk, Oct. 17, 1831, J. K. Polk MSS.
[8] Susanna Clay to Mary D. M. Withers, June 14, 1832, Clay MSS; Washington *Daily National Intelligencer*, Dec. 1, 1831.

battles. The United States Bank, the tariff, and Nullification were questions on which Clay had strong convictions. George McDuffie introduced the bill to recharter the bank on February 10, 1832. Clay was not active in the debate which continued through the spring and into the heat of June, but he lost no opportunity to vote against the "moneyed monster" as befitted a true Jacksonian. Jackson's veto of the bank bill gave Clay much satisfaction.

The tariff was a different matter, however. Alabama like most of the South was unalterably hostile to high tariffs, but at the same time Alabama wanted no part of Nullification. Clay's speech on July 12, 1832, during the debate on the tariff bill, closely reflected these views. We are taxed, Clay declared, "unequally; . . . we are taxed oppressively . . . we are taxed unconstitutionally . . . under a system which . . . cannot, which will not be submitted to as a permanent one. . . . Sir, this is not the language of menace." In spite of these strong words, Clay voted for the bill, which passed the House on June 29. Though still protective, it was a considerable modification of the hated act of 1828.

The weary session drew to a perspiring close on Saturday, July 14, recessed over Sunday, and met again at six o'clock Monday morning, July 16, by which time the President had signed the flood of last-minute bills. Adjournment came at 8 A.M. "and by 9 o'clock most of the Members were on their way to their respective homes."[9]

At home again, Clay continued his fight against the tariff and Nullification. On the hustings throughout North Alabama he cried, "I do not pretend that the tariff, as fixed by [this] act, is satisfactory. . . . I shall . . . urge . . . still further reductions of duties . . . until complete justice is done." But, "I am not yet prepared to dissolve the Union, and revolutionize the government. . . . We of Alabama are *Anti-Tariffmen* . . . we are no nullifiers. . . . 'Nullification is neither a constitutional nor peaceful remedy,' but a 'dangerous political heresy.' " Clay's words reflected the majority of Alabama opinion, but there was in the state a strong minority of Nullifiers led by such men as James M. Calhoun (nephew of John C. Calhoun) and Dixon Hall Lewis

9 Mary I. Thomas to Susanna Clay, July 3, 1832, Clay MSS; John Campbell to David Campbell, July 9, 1832, David Campbell MSS; USC, *Register of Debates*, 22:1, VIII, pt. 3, 3457, June 12, 1832; Huntsville *Democrat*, July 19, 1832; Washington *Daily National Intelligencer*, July 16, 1832.

in the south, and David Hubbard in North Alabama, who, Clay feared, might attempt "at the ensuing session of the Legislature, to pass nullifying resolutions." To counteract this danger, Clay busily organized anti-Nullification meetings throughout North Alabama, where, he urged, it was "important that we should be as *unanimous* and *decided* . . . as possible."[10]

Alabama was safe, but that was not true everywhere. The elections showed that South Carolina was ready to "revolutionize the government." There the triumphant state-rights party called a convention which on November 24 adopted an ordinance of Nullification. This was the state of affairs when Clement Clay and Samuel Mardis reached Washington on November 30, 1832, where they found the capital in a state of tension and seething with rumors. Congress assembled on December 3, and next day heard the State of the Union message, which devoted one quiet paragraph to the Nullification crisis. While speculation filled the drawing rooms, the President made ready his proclamation on Nullification, and on December 10 the world knew that Jackson would not shrink from drastic action. A month later he requested from Congress specific authority to use force if necessary to execute the revenue laws in South Carolina.[11]

Administration leaders had decided, however, to offer tariff reduction. Late in December, 1832, Verplanck of New York brought in a bill incorporating such drastic reductions that it got nowhere. The Nullifiers watched and waited while debate on the tariff bill dragged on week after week in the House. Meanwhile, the "Force Bill" was under active consideration in the Senate, and passed that body on February 20, 1833. At this point, Henry Clay adroitly slipped in his compromise tariff bill, which the House passed 119-85, when Clement Clay called for the order of the day on February 26, 1833.[12]

10 John McKinley to Clay, Sr., Feb. 20, 1832, Clay MSS; William H. Crawford to Bolling Hall, Jan. 17, 1832, Bolling Hall MSS; Clay, Sr., to John Coffee, Oct. 20, 1832, John Coffee MSS; Huntsville *Democrat*, Sept. 27, 1832; Huntsville *Southern Advocate*, Oct. 27, 1832; Tuscaloosa *State Rights Expositor and Spirit of the Age*, Jan. 12, 1833.

11 J. R. Poinsett to Andrew Jackson, Oct. 16, 1832, Feb. 9, 1833, Andrew Jackson, *Correspondence*, ed. by John Spencer Bassett (Washington, 1926-1933, 6 vols.), IV, 481, V, 16; USC, *HJ*, 22:2, pp. 1, 15, Dec. 3, 4, 1832; Washington *Globe*, Nov. 26, 29, 30, Dec. 1, 3, 4, 5, 11, 1832; Chauncey Samuel Boucher, *The Nullification Controversy in South Carolina* (Chicago, 1916), 164-227.

12 Washington *Globe*, Feb. 27, 1833; Joseph Howard Parks, *John Bell of Tennessee* (Baton Rouge, 1950), 59-64.

The Force Bill was no longer necessary, declared its opponents. But Jackson continued to press for its passage, and under the guidance of John Bell, it was carried in the House, 149-47. Clement Clay, Samuel Mardis, and Dixon H. Lewis of the Alabama delegation, as well as other southern Jacksonians, voted against it. These "zealous friends of the administration," opposed the bill "from very different motives than those which actuated the nullifiers," observed the administration organ. "Some . . . felt themselves restricted by their State authorities and some thought it unnecessary." But North Alabama soon told Clay that "in voting against . . . [this bill] you did not represent either the feelings or sentiments of your constituents." Clay rushed an answer into print, explaining that he thought the measure no longer necessary when it came to a final vote, but his chief reason for a negative vote was the resolution of the Alabama legislature urging that the federal government use only peaceful and usual means in executing the laws. This the Alabama congressional delegation interpreted as an instruction to vote against the Force Bill. Clay disavowed any personal opposition to the measure. Despite this misunderstanding Clay was reelected to his seat without opposition.[13]

Immediately after passing the Force Bill on March 1, 1833, the House took up Henry Clay's bill to distribute the proceeds of the public lands. Clement Clay, in spite of "personal debility" resulting from a recent "severe indisposition," rushed in to denounce this as "emphatically a tariff measure; . . . the very reverse of what was reasonably to have been expected; it is calculated to heighten still more the excitement, already fearful." The "true policy of the government," Clement Clay argued, was to be found in his substitute bill "to reduce and graduate the price of public lands according to the time it may have been in the market." While others continued the debate until 11 P.M., "the House was frequently in a state of extreme confusion and disorder." This was the condition of the House throughout Saturday, March 2, and until adjournment early Sunday morning. "The hands of the clock were pointing at five as we passed under them out of the Hall," J. Q. Adams noted. Outside the thermometer stood at 6 degrees, "the extremest cold of the winter, and the

13 Clay, Sr., to J. K. Polk, Aug. 19, 1833, J. K. Polk MSS; Washington *Globe*, March 4, 1833; Huntsville *Democrat*, April 11, 18, 25, May 23, 1833; Charles Grier Sellers, Jr., *James K. Polk, Jacksonian, 1795-1843* (Princeton, N. J., 1957), 156-61.

ground covered with snow."[14] On Monday, March 4, 1833, Jacksonians gathered in the House chamber, now restored to sober dignity, to see their hero begin his second term. Snow and cold prevented an outdoor inauguration, but scarcely delayed the homeward journeys of departing congressmen. Clay and the Polks traveled together and reached home safely, but not without adventure, for the Polks barely escaped drowning when their stagecoach, before they "knew it . . . had driven into a swift stream," while Clay was "detained at the mouth of the Tennessee, several days."[15]

At home, Clay soon found himself in the midst of a new problem, trouble with the Creek Indians. Under pressure from restless white settlers and the state of Alabama, the Creeks agreed in 1832 to cede their hereditary lands in eastern and northeastern Alabama, and to move west of the Mississippi. But by terms of the Treaty of Cusseta, those Indians who did not choose to move could remain; white settlers should not enter until surveys were completed; and white intruders already on Indian lands must be removed. Disregarding these restrictions, new settlers rushed in and whites already in the area refused to leave.

Efforts of federal officials and United States troops to remove white intruders resulted in the death of one Hardeman Owens, and brought the troubles to a critical pitch. The Alabama legislature had in 1832 asserted its jurisdiction over the Creek cession and had proceeded to create nine counties from the area. Governor John Gayle declared that the state must have control of its own territory and that no treaty by the federal government could destroy that right.[16]

As he traveled around the state campaigning for reelection to Congress, Clement Clay saw how serious the situation had become. Disturbed by rumors of an order *"for the removal of all white settlers,"* Clay hurriedly wrote to Secretary of War Lewis Cass to

[14] USC, *Register of Debates*, 22:2, IX, pt. 2, pp. 1915-33, March 1, 1833; John Quincy Adams, *Memoirs . . . Comprising Portions of His Diary from 1795 to 1848,* ed. by Charles Francis Adams (Philadelphia, 1874-1877, 12 vols.), VIII, 533.

[15] Marquis James, *Andrew Jackson: Portrait of a President* (Indianapolis, 1937), 624; J. K. Polk to Clay, Sr., March 25, 1833, Clay MSS; John Coffee to Andrew Jackson, March 25, 1833, Andrew Jackson MSS, vol. 83.

[16] National Archives, Record Group 75, Interior Department Archives, Indian Affairs Office, John Gayle to Lewis Cass, Aug. 20, Oct. 2, 1833, Lewis Cass to John Gayle, Oct. 22, 1833 (cited hereinafter as NA, RG 75); Thomas Chalmers McCorvey, "The Mission of Francis Scott Key to Alabama in 1833," Alabama Historical Society *Transactions*, IV (1899-1903), 142, 145-48.

learn the truth. If "removals should take place, . . ." Clay asserted, "incalculable distress and injury, to many hundreds of our citizens, will be the consequence." Following this up with a lengthier and more fully reasoned protest, Clay argued that "*the President does not think he has the constitutional right to remove settlers . . . by military force. . . .* My chief object, . . ." however, continued Clay, is "to suggest a remedy . . . [namely] that the operations of the government might be confined to mere civil process" and that additional agents be "employed to locate the Indian reservations in the shortest practicable time—which . . . would supersede all necessity for a removal of settlers who are peaceful." Sounding an alarmist note, Clay added, "I have just been informed that a Nullifier . . . was recently in Talladega, offering the service of a regiment in defence of the Settlers. All this is stuff & deserves the reprobation of every friend of his country. But I mention it to show you, how eagerly any apparent cause of dissatisfaction is seized upon by those malcontents to stir up discord & spread disaffection to the Government."[17]

As excitement increased, Governor Gayle bombarded the War Department with protests, while at the same time he implored the settlers to abstain from violence. Back in Washington, Clement Clay rushed to the War Department to repeat his earlier arguments. The upshot was that the government sent Francis Scott Key to Alabama, empowered to offer a compromise solution on the lines which Clement Clay had proposed: the surveys were to be completed by January 15, 1834; meanwhile, no settlers would be removed except from tracts allotted to those Indians not moving westward. This policy, combined with Key's charm and tact, led Clement Clay to "the confident . . . belief that the causes which lately seemed to indicate probable collision, between the Federal and State authorities, will soon cease to exist." Actually, the federal government had backed down, and Alabama had won in a situation skirting perilously close to Nullification.[18]

The summer of 1833 was exceptionally busy for Clement Clay. He traveled over much of the state, campaigning, renewing the

17 NA, RG 75, Clay, Sr., to Lewis Cass, April 18, Oct. 8, 1833; Huntsville *Democrat*, May 23, Nov. 14, 1833.
18 NA, RG 75, John Gayle to Lewis Cass, Aug. 20, Oct. 2, 1833; Henry Watson, Jr., to Henry Watson, Sr., Jan. 26, 1834, Henry Watson MSS; Huntsville *Democrat*, Dec. 19, 1833; Mobile *Commercial Register and Patriot*, Sept. 10, 12, 21, 24, 28, Oct. 1, 3, 7, 10, 14, 15, 16, 18, 19, 22, 24, 25, 28, 29, Nov. 1, 2, 6, 7, 12, 1833.

personal touch with his constituents, and hearing their views on current questions. As autumn approached, he wrote to his friend Polk, "Mrs. C. will accompany me to Washington. In what mode we shall travel is yet undetermined—probably, however, in a private conveyance. We must communicate hereafter, and endeavour to meet on the way." The two families reached Washington on November 23, where they, and the Mardises as well, took up residence at Mrs. Clement's boardinghouse on Third Street. Except for Joseph W. Chinn of Virginia, the other boarders were Yankees.

The summer and autumn had brought much excitement on the national scene. President Jackson had removed William Duane and appointed Roger B. Taney as secretary of the treasury. On September 26, 1833, Taney announced the removal of government funds from the Bank of the United States, in accordance with Jackson's determination. This controversial action was the basis for one of the stormiest sessions in congressional history. The Twenty-third Congress had unusually able members: among them were (former or future) five presidents, three vice presidents, four presidential and three vice-presidential candidates, sixteen cabinet members, two justices of the United States Supreme Court, twenty-one diplomatic and consular agents, and thirty-four governors of states. Henry Clay, Calhoun, and Webster led the probank majority in the Senate; in the House, however, Jacksonians held the majority, led by the unflagging labors of James K. Polk, who was now chairman of the Ways and Means Committee. In this powerful post he displaced George McDuffie, a probank man in league with Calhoun. Clement Clay now moved up to become chairman of the Committee on Public Lands. In that capacity he brought in the customary bill to reduce and graduate the price of public lands.[19]

To a degree, the conflicts of the session were focalized in the contest between Polk and McDuffie. This began with Taney's report on removal of the deposits. McDuffie gained the initial advantage by getting this report referred to the Committee of the Whole. The following day, Clement Clay brought forward the customary resolutions referring the President's message to appro-

[19] Clay, Sr., to J. K. Polk, Aug. 19, 1833, J. K. Polk MSS; Carl Brent Swisher, *Roger B. Taney* (New York, 1935), 238; Eugene Irving McCormac, *James K. Polk, A Political Biography* (Berkeley, 1922), 37; Sellers, *Polk*, 213-22.

priate committees. McDuffie immediately opposed reference of the financial and bank portion to Polk's Ways and Means Committee. Clay stood fast, however, and at the same time Polk moved to reconsider the order referring Taney's report to Committee of the Whole. After four days of debate, Polk carried his motion to reconsider, 124-102, and so won the first round in the battle.

For two months the fight between Polk and McDuffie continued. Clement Clay and James Polk have left no records of the strategy they must have planned so carefully in the third-floor rooms of Mrs. Clement's boardinghouse. Certainly the two worked hand in hand to outsmart McDuffie and the probank men. They succeeded on February 18, 1834, when Clay called for the main question and the House voted, 131-98, to refer Taney's report to the Ways and Means Committee. When that committee reported some two weeks later, McDuffie attempted to stifle the question; Clement Clay prevented this. Polk's report concluded with four resolutions which declared that the Bank of the United States should not be rechartered; public deposits should not be restored to the bank; selected state banks should continue as depositories of public funds; and a select committee should investigate the books and activities of the Bank of the United States. Administration and probank forces now lined up for a month's debate on these resolutions.[20]

On March 25, 1834, Clement Clay defended Polk's report in a speech "replete with sound argument, and . . . based on sound facts." Clay denounced the bank for its "assumption of power" and declared that by arguing for restoration of the deposits, probank men "really intend . . . ultimate recharter of the bank . . . however it may be disclaimed." On the basis of precedent Clay defended Jackson's dismissal of Duane and found Taney's removal of the deposits entirely legal. But returning to the "monster," he cried, "The bank has been corrupt and unfaithful in its fiscal agency; . . . Enough to sustain these charges was proved . . . in 1832, . . . developments since have made the evidence full and conclusive." Bad as were the bank's influence over the press and Biddle's personal despotism, even worse was the bank's sudden contraction of credit "at a rate that must inevitably produce great

20 USC, HJ, 23:1, pp. 26, 31, 52f, 87f, 345f; USC, Debates, 23:1, X, pt. 2, pp. 2168-70, 2206f, 2731, 2868-70; J. Q. Adams, Memoirs, IX, 98f.

commercial embarrassment to all, and perhaps irretrievable ruin to many. It follows . . . that the pecuniary prosperity of every community would be much more safe in the power of local banks." State banks, Clay concluded, are fully capable of providing "a medium of exchange between remote parts of the country. . . . We are not dependent on a Bank of the United States; and God forbid we ever should find ourselves in a situation so humiliating. . . . May the power that guided and protected our fathers in their revolutionary conflict, guard and preserve us from this worse than colonial bondage."[21]

Debate concluded on April 4, when the House, by adopting Polk's report, approved Jackson's removal of the deposits. The mounting excitement of the session caused Susanna Clay to exclaim, "I fear that our country, is on the eve of revolution. God, protect it from ruin, should be the prayer of all—I feel that I am weak and ill informed in the science of government, but I trust that I can disern [sic] sufficiently to tell *truth from falsehood* —and oppression from freedom." The session came to a hot and humid conclusion at seven o'clock on the evening of June 30, 1834, "after as hard a day's work as has been done during the session. The members are nearly all gone," wrote an observer the next day. Clement and Susanna and their servant pushed homeward as rapidly as possible and arrived safely after a "perilous & fateaguing [sic] Journey of three days & nights," following their brief stopover with the elder Clays in East Tennessee.[22]

Meetings in both Madison and Jackson counties endorsed Clay and the Alabama delegation who "have truly represented the feelings and wishes of this State" in supporting Jackson's removal of the deposits. A large political rally in Tuscaloosa displayed even greater enthusiasm, in spite of a rainstorm which delayed the dinner and somewhat diluted the "substantial and sumptuous viands" placed on "two parallel tables, ONE HUNDRED AND TEN YARDS in length, (on which were placed 648 plates)." Before a crowd of no less than "TWELVE TO FOURTEEN HUNDRED persons . . . Messrs. King, Clay and Mardis, . . . responded to the sentiments

21 USC, *Debates,* 23:1, X, pt. 3, pp. 3141f, 3146-51; Huntsville *Democrat,* April 24, 1834.
22 Susanna Clay to Clay, Jr., April 1, 1834, William Clay to Clay, Sr., Sept. 16, 1834, Clay MSS; Benjamin B. French to his father, July 1, 1834, B. B. French MSS; USC, *HJ,* 23:1, X, pt. 3, p. 3159; J. Q. Adams, *Memoirs,* IX, 120-22; McCormac, *Polk,* 34; Sellers, *Polk,* 221f.

which were given in compliment to them, in a most felicitous and effective manner." Clay then "rose and delivered a most eloquent and effective speech . . . [in which he] exposed . . . the course which has characterised the mammoth Bank and its advocates . . . and held it up as it deserved, to the scorn and indignation of an insulted people. . . . Mr. Clay was very frequently cheered with bursts of deafening applause." At a dinner in Columbia, Tennessee, honoring James K. Polk, one of the toasts complimented "Hon. C. C. Clay, of Alabama—the *firm, independent and unflinching* supporter of the administration. *When the hour of danger came,* he did not court his political enemies, or wait in silence, to see which was the strong side. With such men the republic is safe." This, commented the Huntsville *Democrat,* was evidence that Clay "owes his political elevation, not to his suavity of manners, or the personal predilection of friends, but to his own intrinsic merit. Amidst the general defection . . . at Washington last winter . . . Alabama possessed in the person of Judge Clay a firm and efficient public servant, whose inflexible honesty, not only withstood the seductions, but also the menaces of the bank. . . . None but noble souls can trample [the] attractions [of money] under foot. That Judge Clay has done, and thereby secured to himself a moral elevation, which places him entirely out of the reach of his low, . . . malignant enemies."[23]

Clay was indeed at the peak of his popularity, but across the line in Tennessee there were ominous rumblings as the Jackson party began to split. It all stemmed from the speakership contest in Congress. Aspiring to that post, Polk had waited more than a year for the vacancy which came when Andrew Stevenson resigned on June 2, 1834. But things went awry for Polk, and on the tenth ballot John Bell became the new speaker, supported, as he admitted, "by the opposition and elected by them." Bell had been drawing away from Jackson for some time. Now in active opposition, he joined forces with Hugh Lawson White, while Polk, Felix Grundy, and Cave Johnson remained stanch Jacksonian leaders both in Congress and in Tennessee.[24]

The breakup of the Jackson party in Tennessee was only one

23 Huntsville *Southern Advocate,* May 27, Sept. 30, 1834; Huntsville *Democrat,* Sept. 2, Oct. 1, 15, 1834.
24 Clay, Sr., to J. K. Polk, Sept. 13, 23, 1834, John McKinley to J. K. Polk, Aug. 13, 1834, J. K. Polk MSS; Parks, *John Bell,* 70-72.

part of the rising tide of opposition. Even in such a Jacksonian stronghold as Alabama, party cleavage was spreading over the state, and the opposition counted many new adherents, especially in the Black Belt. But the situation was confused. The Jackson men, aware of their precarious position, labeled the entire opposition Nullifiers. This ruse forced many who distrusted Jackson's policies to remain with the Jacksonians rather than incur the odious accusation of being Nullifiers. The result in the congressional elections was a victory for the Jackson party in Alabama, and in many other states as well. "The triumph of the Administration, and its friends, has been truly glorious," wrote Clement Clay happily.

Consequently he anticipated "a more quiet session than the last." At least it was for Clay personally, since he did not make a major speech during his last session in Congress. His most extended remarks were in opposition to a motion to print a petition for abolition of slavery in the District of Columbia. His restrained words on this occasion scarcely presaged the angry vehemence with which he and his son would in later years debate the slavery issue.[25]

25 Clay, Sr., to Susanna Clay, Dec. 1, 1834, Clay MSS; Henry Watson, Jr., to Henry Watson, Sr., Feb. 10, July 3, Aug. 7, 1834, Henry Watson MSS; Huntsville *Southern Advocate*, May 27, Aug. 26, 1834, Jan. 20, 1835; Jack, *Sectionalism and Party Politics in Alabama, 1819-1842,* 30-36.

4

Governor and Senator

CLEMENT COMER CLAY had reached the peak of his political career. Democrats throughout Alabama agreed that he should be rewarded with the governorship. His years of apprenticeship in politics had had their defeats, but now, by adhering strictly to Jackson, he had come out on top. But living next door to the political ferment in Tennessee had its perils. In the spring of 1835 Clement Clay had to do a tightrope act of campaigning for the governorship while maintaining an equivocal position as to the next presidential candidate. Already the boom for Hugh Lawson White was well under way, and many politicians were in the unhappy position of having to choose between him and Jackson's favorite, Martin Van Buren. A choice was doubly hard for Clement Clay, who had a strong personal affection and admiration for his old legal preceptor, Hugh Lawson White. On the other hand, Clay's unswerving party loyalty demanded that he support the candidate who could preserve party unity. "So far as a personal preference is concerned," wrote Clay on January 1, 1835, White "is decidedly my first choice . . . [but because of the] danger of dividing our party, and thereby . . . losing all that we have been struggling for during the last six years . . . I am adverse to the support of any man, if it should be discovered that he will merely divide our party." As early as May, 1834, Clay's nomination for the governorship was generally conceded, though not until a year later did he formally announce for that office.[1]

In May, 1835, Clay began his campaign for governor by a tour through the western part of the state, where he "saw the village politicians pro and con" and where he expected to find some opposition. None developed, however, until July, when Enoch Parsons was brought out as opposition candidate on an antibank, pro-White platform. Clay countered this unexpected challenge with a lengthy "Address to the People of Alabama," in which he refused to commit himself to any presidential candidate. For Alabama, he offered a platform of internal improvements, particularly construction of a railroad connecting Mobile Bay with the Tennessee River, which would "promote, incalculably, the agricultural and commercial interests of both ends of the State." Both candidates campaigned vigorously during July—Parsons in the north, and Clay in South Alabama. Clay carried the election by a majority of more than 10,000. The exultant Democratic press interpreted Parsons' "Waterloo defeat" as proof of the dissolution besetting anti-Jackson forces in the state.[2]

Clement Comer Clay assumed office as governor of the state of Alabama on November 21, 1835. He devoted most of his inaugural to state and federal relations, the advancement of education, and internal improvements. His first message to the legislature, a week later, discussed all these subjects and was, in addition, much taken up with the dissemination of abolitionist propaganda through the mails. An Alabama grand jury had recently indicted the editor of the New York *Emancipator* as personally responsible for circulating papers of a "seditious and incendiary character . . . tending . . . to incite to insurrection and murder our slave population." Governor Clay now demanded that New York extradite the abolitionist editor and send him to Alabama for arrest and prosecution. New York did not comply.

Clay, in a particularly angry mood, urged a general tightening of slave regulations and persisted in his demand for "prosecution and conviction" of the offending abolitionists. The usually clear-sighted Clay had allowed an emotional fog of hate to blind him to the "delicate and indefinite character" of his claims. Calmer minds opposed the governor's extreme position and warned that

1 Henry Watson, Jr., to Henry Watson, Sr., July 20, 1836, Henry Watson MSS; Huntsville *Southern Advocate*, July 21, 1835.

2 Clay, Sr., to Susanna Clay, May 15, 1835, Clay MSS; Huntsville *Democrat*, July 8, 15, Aug. 19, 1835; Huntsville *Southern Advocate*, July 14, 21, Aug. 25, Sept. 1, 1835.

where "the sovereignty of a State is involved, the exercise of any questionable authority should, if possible be avoided." The press also declared that Clay's demands for extradition would be refused by any state, "and if our Executive were empowered to offer rewards to drag an abolitionist before our civil tribunals, it would lead to a system of individual retaliation, dangerous to the peace and safety of society, and . . . involve the States in fierce and angry collisions about the unsettled rights of sovereignty." Clay was echoing the Jackson line of extreme hostility to abolitionist propaganda.[3]

As executive, Clay faced two major questions: the Creek War of 1836 and the Panic of 1837. The Creek Indians occupied a large territory in the east central portion of the state. They were at this time reduced almost to a state of starvation due to the customary maladministration and to the inroads of white squatters into their territory. Consequently the Indians were gathering in hostile bands, impeding travel, stealing corn and cattle, and burning farm buildings. In February, 1836, General Winfield Scott authorized the muster of a regiment for observation upon the Indians, and Governor Clay was asked to raise five companies of volunteers for service against the Seminoles, who were giving trouble in Florida. Meanwhile, in distant Washington the Creek danger did not seem pressing, so that President Jackson discharged the regiment of observation, a most aggravating procedure to come from an old Indian fighter.

Even without this, Governor Clay was having enough trouble. He had raised the volunteers for service in Florida, and now they were awaiting arms and equipment to be furnished by an officer of the United States army. When that officer failed to appear as scheduled, Clay could do nothing but discharge his volunteers. Two days later, Captain Edward Harding arrived with the arms, but found no troops.

Meanwhile, Clay persevered in his efforts to protect settlers in the threatened area and showered the War Department with proofs of the "impending danger of hostilities." "No force should

[3] Henry Watson to Julius A. Reed, Aug. 23, 1835, Henry Watson MSS; Ala. Leg., *HJ*, pp. 8-10, 28-30, 47-58, Nov. 14-27, 1835; Huntsville *Southern Advocate*, Dec. 8, 1835; William Sherman Savage, *The Controversy over the Distribution of Abolition Literature, 1830-1860* (Washington, 1938), 9-81.

be called out until the exigency provided for in the constitution arises," replied the War Department, but it did give Captain Harding authority to issue arms upon Governor Clay's requisition. Eventually a hostile outbreak did occur, the War Department authorized a call for troops, and efforts got under way to put three thousand mounted infantrymen into the field.

The actual troublemakers among the Indians were bands of young braves who were restless and could not be restrained. Ruling members of the tribe remained friends with state authorities, and many loyal Indians joined forces with the white militia in searching for the offenders. On May 20, 1836, Governor Clay issued two proclamations, one to the loyal Indians, warning them to separate themselves from those who were hostile, and another to the white settlers, assuring them of speedy assistance. After negotiation, the Indian chiefs agreed to emigrate west of the Mississippi immediately, if they were supplied with provisions. This was, of course, the solution that all white residents hoped for, and with presidential sanction, preparations toward that end were soon made. A few skirmishes forced the surrender of over three hundred warriors and the dispersion of the remaining hostile bands. Thus, by the end of June, 1836, the insurrection was practically subdued, although troops remained in the disturbed area for several months.[4]

The opposition lost no time in criticizing Clay for his handling of the Creek difficulty, calling him "an old woman . . . miserably deficient in decision of character." But on the whole, his course met with public approval, and in recognition of his services he was tendered three public dinners. Speaking on these occasions, Clay stoutly denied that he had been remiss or negligent in meeting the Indian danger; the fact was that his efforts to raise troops had been hampered at every turn by red tape and constitutional restraints. When the legislature convened, Clay laid before it a detailed review of his management of the Indian trouble, and then passed on to the question nearest his heart, internal improvements. He urged that Alabama should try to secure from Congress the money accumulated in the "two per cent fund," and reported

4 Ala. Archives, Governors' Letterbooks, 1822-1836, Letters to and from Gov. Clay, Feb.-June, 1836; Ala. Military Archives, Letters to and from Gov. Clay, March-June, 1836; Huntsville *Democrat*, Feb. 24, May 24, 31, July 5, 1836.

that while the 400,000-acre grant of 1828 had not yielded enough money for the complete improvement of Muscle Shoals, a fifteen-mile canal around the worst obstructions would soon be ready for use.[5]

While these local questions were absorbing public attention, economic forces were heading towards a crisis that soon dwarfed all other matters. For several years a boom condition had "given a fictitious value to every description of property," and land speculation had run riot. Jackson abruptly stopped this by his specie circular of July 11, 1836, ordering that payment for lands be made in gold or silver only. This was only one factor in the increasing stringency which the banks were unable to ease. Throughout Alabama the decline set in with falling prices for Negroes and lands; merchants and factors stopped payments, debts accumulated, and distrust spread everywhere. Mobile, the commercial center of the state, was naturally the first place to suffer. Its harassed citizens in April, 1837, appealed for a special session of the legislature and a visit by the governor to see conditions for himself. Montgomery was the next community to hold a public meeting and pass similar resolutions. Clay refused to incur the expense of a special session until more public meetings throughout the state should give him guidance. In remote areas that had not yet felt the effects of the crash, skeptical farmers feared that "the Legislature would be hurried into some measure of supposed Relief which would be highly impolitic and ultimately injurious to the State." But with the situation growing more acute day by day, local meetings everywhere began to demand a special session and legislative relief.[6]

Meanwhile, on May 13 the banks of Mobile suspended specie payment, and that day Clay called the legislature to meet on the second Monday in June, 1837. Plans for relief were numerous, but Alabama was unanimously opposed to any measures which would impair the obligation of contract or injure the state's credit. Some communities suggested the issuance of post notes, but others

5 Henry Watson, Jr., to Henry Watson, Sr., June 22, 1836, Henry Watson MSS; Huntsville *Southern Advocate*, July 12, Sept. 6, 1836; Huntsville *Democrat*, Nov. 15, 1836.

6 Ala. Archives, Governors' Letters, Letters from Citizens to Gov. Clay, April-May, 1837; Henry Watson, Jr., to Henry Watson, Sr., Feb. 6, 1837, Henry Watson MSS; Robert H. Dalton to John Dalton, July 2, 1835, Placebo Houston MSS; R. C. Cummings to David Campbell, Dec. 10, 1835, David Campbell MSS.

thought such a scheme dangerous. The financial class favored a bond issue to be secured on unencumbered real estate. In his message to the legislature Clay reviewed all the proposed measures, but hesitated to recommend a bond issue which would materially increase the public debt. After a month's debate the legislature passed a bill permitting a three-year suspension of specie payments, extending three years' time to bank debtors while at the same time closely restricting future loans, and authorizing the five-million-dollar bond issue. Of this, one million was to be deposited in each of the branch banks.

One other matter before this session was the choice of a United States senator, and on June 19, 1837, Governor Clement Clay was elected to that office without opposition. In consequence, he resigned the governorship on July 17, 1837.[7]

The breathless heat of late summer hung over Washington as Congress met in special session on September 4, 1837. Clement Clay's credentials were presented by Alabama's senior senator, William Rufus King, and Clay became one of the select company of fifty-two United States senators. He occupied desk no. 27, in the second row, the fourth place left of the center aisle. To his right and left were Bedford Brown, the North Carolina Democrat, and Ambrose Sevier of Arkansas. Immediately in front sat Clay's old friend Hugh Lawson White and the young and charming Franklin Pierce. Behind were veteran Felix Grundy and that restless promoter and speculator, Robert J. Walker of Mississippi, soon to be Clement Clay's good friend. "Old Bullion" Benton, Whiggish John J. Crittenden, opposition leader Nathaniel P. Tallmadge, and financial wizard Silas Wright would all wield their influence in the congressional struggle over a solution to the economic crisis.

For President Martin Van Buren had a plan. Prodded by Jackson, and encouraged by his financial advisers, Van Buren proposed to set up an independent treasury which would completely "divorce" the government from all banks. Calhoun liked the idea so well that he deserted the opposition and returned to the Democratic fold. Thus Clement Clay found himself voting

7 Ala. Archives, Governors' Letters, Letters of Citizens to Gov. Clay, May, 1837; Henry Watson, Jr., to Henry Watson, Sr., [Aug. 7, 1837], Henry Watson MSS; Ala. Leg., *Acts Passed at the Called Session . . . June 30, 1837* (Tuscaloosa, 1837), 1-42; Huntsville *Democrat*, May 23, June 27, 1837.

with Calhoun, whom he had once so bitterly reviled as a Nullifier.[8]

The "Divorce Bill," as the Independent Treasury bill was generally known at the time, required "all receivers of public money . . . to keep safely, without loaning or using, all the public money collected by them." Under existing laws this would include the notes of specie-paying banks. To make the divorce complete, Calhoun introduced an amendment requiring payments due the government for taxes, public lands, etc., to be made progressively in specie, so that by January, 1841, the government would no longer accept banknotes, but would be entirely upon a hard-money basis.

But Van Buren could not hold the party in line. Conservative bank Democrats united with Whigs in bitter opposition to the independent treasury, while administration Democrats worked mightily for its adoption. On October 4, 1837, Clement Clay made the final speech in favor of the bill. The "real issue is, bank or no bank." The West and Southwest, he declared, could never forget the sudden and disastrous curtailment of bank accommodations, and "the intelligent and hardy yeomanry of that great region could neither be cajoled, nor terrified" into agreeing to a recharter. The bill passed the Senate 26-21, but was tabled in the House. Not until July 4, 1840, did the Independent Treasury Bill become law. The "Panic Session" adjourned on October 16, 1837, with little to show for its efforts except a measure empowering the Treasury to issue $10,000,000 in interest-bearing notes.[9]

During this session Clay and five other southern members had messed at H. V. Hill's boardinghouse at Third and C streets. On his return in December, Clay joined the Polks in a large, all-southern mess at Elliot's on Pennsylvania Avenue.

Clay found himself busier than ever with committee work, for each senator served on several committees. Clay's assignments were Militia, Engrossed Bills, and Public Lands. This last was by far the most important, for in Alabama and the West generally, public-lands administration was still a very live issue. The panic

8 USC, *Cong. Globe*, 25:1, pp. 17, 22, 27, Sept. 11, 13, 14, 1837; Ransom H. Gillet, *The Life and Times of Silas Wright* (Albany, 1874, 2 vols.), I, 566-626; Hugh Russell Fraser, *Democracy in the Making: The Jackson-Tyler Era* (Indianapolis, 1938), 81-89; Denis Tilden Lynch, *An Epoch and a Man: Martin Van Buren and His Times* (New York, 1929), 409-15.

9 USC, *SJ*, 25:1, p. 55, Oct. 4, 1837; USC, *HJ*, 25:1, pp. 195-97, Oct. 4, 1837; USC, *Cong. Globe*, 25:1, Appen., pp. 108-11, Oct. 4, 1837; Washington *Daily Globe*, Oct. 4, 5, 13, 1837; Huntsville *Democrat*, Oct. 31, 1837.

had only strengthened demands for changes in the land system which would aid hard-pressed settlers. Heading the Public Lands Committee was fiery and energetic Robert J. Walker of Mississippi, who in this and succeeding sessions led the fight in the Senate on land issues.

The Public Lands Committee divided its program into three bills: a graduation bill reducing the price of lands remaining unsold, a preemption bill, and a taxation bill giving states the right to tax lands as soon as they were sold. The law then in force gave a five-year exemption from taxation. On March 29, 1838, Clement Clay spoke at length on the graduation bill. He explained that the "entire quantity of public lands which has been offered for sale, *from the earliest period to 30th September last,* is 172,374,470 acres; and the whole quantity disposed of . . . but 75,025,055 acres, leaving" over 97,000,000 acres of the public domain still vacant and unsold because it was not worth $1.25 per acre. In the southwestern states of Alabama, Mississippi, Louisiana, Arkansas, and Missouri, some 88,500,000 acres had come into the market, of which only 28,500,000 had been sold over periods of ten to twenty years, while in some of the eastern states, lands in the market for thirty and even forty years remained unsold. "Do not these facts demonstrate the inequality of the soil, and the absurdity of one arbitrary price for all the lands in those five states?" A 50-percent reduction in price (i.e. to 62½ cents per acre) would, Clay predicted, result in the sale of 50,000,000 acres, putting into the federal Treasury $31,250,000, a most welcome addition under existing depression conditions. Clay's efforts, together with those of R. J. Walker, Benton, Calhoun, and others with public-land interests, put this bill through the Senate, but it was, as usual, tabled in the House.[10]

The bill to permit states to tax lands as soon as they were sold met the same fate in the House. It passed the Senate on December 28, 1837, after lively debate carried on "to a late hour" by Clement Clay, Henry Clay, Robert J. Walker, James Buchanan, and others. Public-land interests were more successful with the preemption bill, which became law on June 22, 1838. This extended for two years preemption rights as they had been established by the law of 1830. Henry Clay, the bitterest opponent of preemption,

10 Clement Comer Clay, *Speech of Hon. C. C. Clay, of Alabama, on the Graduation Bill, In Senate, March 29, 1838* (n.p., n.d.), 1-8.

fought the bill almost singlehanded, saying that "in no shape in which the bill could be placed, could he be brought to vote for it. The whole pre-emption system was a violation of all law, . . . a system which had for its object to take from the Government the possession of these lands to throw them into the hands of specu- lators." To which Clement Clay replied that he "would take leave to tell that Senator, with perfect deference, that he was wholly mis- taken, and his charge utterly unfounded. . . . The pre-emption laws had been the most effective instruments to prevent fraud, to save the honest settler and cultivator, and put down the most nefarious and heartless system of speculation ever devised."[11]

This small clash between the two Clays was only a spark beside the fireworks of the session provided by the sparring between Calhoun and Henry Clay and by the new and alarming turn in antislavery agitation. Vermont had sent down resolutions hostile to the annexation of Texas or admission of more slave states, and urged abolition of slavery in the District of Columbia. Calhoun replied with six resolutions setting forth his state-rights theory that "the States retained . . . the exclusive and sole right over their own domestic institutions." Calhoun's resolutions were debated in January, 1838. Without entering the debate, Clement Clay voted for the first four, which were all adopted by large majorities. The fifth declared that the attempt of any state or states "to abolish slavery in this District, or any of the territories, on the ground . . . that it is immoral or sinful . . . would be a direct and dangerous attack on the institutions of all the slaveholding states." The long and bitter fight over modification and amend- ment of this resolution brought Clement Clay to his feet to say that he "preferred the original resolution." It was "couched, to be sure, in strong language, but not stronger than the occasion warranted. . . . He . . . wished to see gentlemen march up to the question presented by the Vermont resolutions, and give their votes, yea or nay, whether the institutions of any of these States were open to attack, on the ground that they were immoral and sinful." Clay nevertheless cast his vote for the modified fifth resolution. The sixth was tabled, Clay voting nay to this.[12]

11 USC, *Cong. Globe*, 25:2, pp. 55, 142, Dec. 27, 1837, Jan. 26, 1838.
12 USC, *SJ*, 25:2, p. 144; USC, *Cong. Globe*, 25:2, pp. 55, 144, Appen., pp. 63, 74, 109; J. C. Calhoun to Anna Maria Calhoun, Feb. 7, 1838, *Correspondence of John C. Calhoun*, ed. by J. Franklin Jameson, American Historical Association *Annual Report* (1899), II, 392; Benton, *Thirty Years' View*, II, 98-101.

In Clay's final speech of the session he had another fling at the bank. Van Buren's message had revealed how "the late National Bank," while supposedly engaged solely in "closing its affairs," had in fact not "cancelled the outstanding notes," but had "reissued, and is actually reissuing . . . notes which have been received by it to a vast amount." The Judiciary Committee's bill, introduced on February 12, 1838, empowered the government to prevent by injunction "the issuing, reissuing, or transfer of any such bills, notes," and other paper. Opponents of this bill argued that Congress had no power to pass such a measure, since the bank was unconstitutional in the first place. Clement Clay replied, "All must admit that if we pass a constitutional law . . . we may repeal such act. . . . Can it be possible that there is so much more virtue in an unconstitutional law, that . . . we can never revoke . . . it?" That "would involve the absurdity of making an unconstitutional law better . . . than a constitutional one." Clay and the administration forces had the satisfaction of seeing this measure become law.[13]

The exhausting session finally reached adjournment on July 9, 1838. The long journey to Alabama and back again left Clement Clay a scant four months at home. In that brief time he had to set things aright on his plantations, renew the personal touch with constituents, and do what he could to stave off the effects of the panic on his personal finances. He took his seat again in the Senate on December 3, 1838, one day after Congress assembled. He joined a small mess of senators at Dowson's No. 1 on Capitol Hill, where his messmates were Thomas Hart Benton, William Allen of Ohio, and Thomas H. Williams of Mississippi. This short session accomplished little in the way of important legislation. The perennial bill to reduce the price of public lands once more passed the Senate, but was not acted on in the House. Clay made his one speech of the session on this bill.[14]

The first session of the Twenty-sixth Congress (1839-1840) was Clay's busiest, at least in point of speaking. He made four major speeches in addition to extended remarks on other topics. Having established himself at Mrs. Bannerman's boardinghouse on Pennsylvania Avenue, where two members from Arkansas, one from

---

[13] USC, *Cong. Globe*, 25:2, p. 4, Appen., pp. 82, 287; Washington *Daily Globe*, May 1, 1838; Huntsville *Democrat*, May 26, 1838.
[14] USC, *Cong. Globe*, 25:3, p. 2, Appen., pp. 58-60.

North Carolina, and one from Maine completed the mess, Clay was ready for the opening of Congress on December 2, 1839. The Senate marked time while the House wrangled over a contested election in New Jersey, and then over election of a speaker. The President's message was read on December 24, which meant that no serious work got under way until the beginning of the new year.

Clay's first speech supported Benton on the question of armed occupation of Florida. Benton drew a picture of Florida to be developed by hardy settlers cultivating a rich soil and protected from marauding Indians by blockhouse settlements and small detachments of the regular army. The Whigs, notably John J. Crittenden of Kentucky and William Campbell Preston of South Carolina, opposed the measure. Clement Clay replied to Preston, defending the conduct of officers and troops in the recent Indian wars in Florida. As to settlement with the inducement of free land for those who would fight for it if necessary, Clay said, "There were a great many hardy and industrious men" in the Southwest who would be glad to acquire a freehold of 320 acres in return for "defend[ing] themselves by the strength of their own arms. . . . The plan was practicable [for] it was in this manner that a large portion of the Western country had been settled. . . . [Furthermore], if economy be the object, this plan is better than any other proposed." The bill passed the Senate, 24-15, on January 20, 1840, but was not acted on in the House.[15]

Once more Clement Clay found himself opposing his old enemy, Henry Clay, this time on the assumption of state debts. The immediate occasion was the London Bankers' Circular of Baring Brothers, suggesting a federal guarantee of state debts for the safeguarding of foreign investors. Thomas Hart Benton proposed "a positive declaration in Congress against the constitutionality, the justice, the policy of any such measure" in a series of four resolutions. During lengthy debates on the subject, "Mr. Clay of Alabama, enchained the Senate . . . in a speech of much logical argument and force. . . . Mr Clay's manner of speaking is exceedingly fine," commented the press; "he is fluent, argumentative, and at times truly eloquent." He denounced "this plan of the London bankers, impeaching the good faith and solvency of the States," and reviewed at length Henry Clay's

15 USC, *Cong. Globe,* 26:1, pp. 1-76 *passim,* Appen., pp. 46-49; USC, *SJ,* 25:1, p. 122.

persistent efforts for assumption under various guises. Clement Clay had the satisfaction of receiving wide commendation in the Democratic press and of voting for Benton's resolutions, which the Senate adopted by large majorities.[16]

Alabama and Georgia senators united in pushing a bill to settle claims for loss of property in the recent Indian wars. Clay spoke on March 12, 1840, in behalf of this bill, which passed the Senate a week later but was not taken up in the House. In debates on the Cumberland Road bill, Clay had a chance to drag in his favorite subject, the price of public lands. Federal appropriations for the road were to be repaid from the "two per cent funds" accruing to the states through which the road passed. Clay objected that remaining lands were too poor to sell at existing prices; hence the states could never repay the cost of the road. Besides, he declared, federal appropriations for this road were unconstitutional, since it benefited only four states. To the question, "Did not the Senator from Alabama vote for the Maysville road bill?" Clay responded, "With all candor and frankness, I answer, I did. . . . *I frankly admit my vote was wrong.*"

Clay had another opportunity to dwell on a favorite theme when he spoke on the preemption bill. This provided a two-year extension of the measure he had introduced in 1838, and corrected a few unsatisfactory provisions of that act. With a presidential campaign at hand, preemption was now even more a party issue, and a vote getter in the increasingly powerful West. Consequently, the bill passed both houses by large majorities. In his speech Clay took occasion to review the working of preemption and to show that it had not led to decreased revenues from the sale of public lands.[17]

In an election year, campaigning is not unknown in the halls of Congress. Clement Clay made the most of his opportunity in connection with the report of the Committee on Militia, of which he was chairman. He repudiated entirely Secretary Poinsett's plan for an enlarged and better trained militia. This plan, explained Clay, was not really Poinsett's; it had originated with William

[16] USC, *Cong. Globe*, 26:1, p. 224, Appen., pp. 125-27; Washington *New Era*, Feb. 3, 1840; Huntsville *Democrat*, March 14, 1840; Benton, *Thirty Years' View*, II, 171-76.
[17] USC, *Cong. Globe*, 26:1, pp. 103, 279, Appen., pp. 298-302, 359-60; R. M. Robbins, "Preëmption—A Frontier Triumph," *Mississippi Valley Historical Review*, XVIII (Dec., 1931), 343-49 (cited hereinafter as *MVHR*).

Henry Harrison and other "black cockade Federalists" back to Henry Knox, the first secretary of war. This gave Clement Clay the opening to turn his speech into an attack on Harrison, the Whigs, Federalism, and the tariff. For five more weeks the session dragged on until adjournment came on July 21, preceded by the customary feverish activity and night sessions.[18]

Long before Congress adjourned, Clement Clay was collecting ammunition for the campaign. To a New York Democrat he wrote, "I wish to undeceive the people of Alabama, on one or two matters . . . in the pending contest for the Presidency. I . . . want authentic evidence . . .

"1. That Harrison was nominated through the influence of the Abolitionists . . .

"2. That Harrison is *supported* and Van Buren *opposed* by the great mass of *Abolitionists* . . .

"I wish . . . [to] present the proof in authentic shape to my constituents—and, indeed, the entire South."

Clay attended the Democratic National Convention in Baltimore, where as chairman of the nominating committee he presented the name of Martin Van Buren. The Alabama congressional delegation soon issued an "Address to the People of Alabama." The burden of this document was to denounce northern Whigs as abolitionists, to urge Democratic unity, and to declare that Harrison's election would mean the triumph of "nationalism, bankism, and abolitionism," while the southern states would become mere "provinces, inferiors, and vassals of the Northern States and Northern men."[19]

Clement Clay hastened home to take his part in the campaign that was already well under way throughout the country. During the past three years Clay had spent nearly twenty-four months in Washington. And in that time politics in Alabama had undergone decided changes. Whigs had become so numerous that they were sure to carry the Black Belt and they threatened other sections. With five congressional districts in Alabama, the Democrats must hold three to maintain their ascendancy. The Democrats were very strong in North Alabama, but elsewhere the contest was

18 USC, *Cong. Globe*, 26:1, Appen., pp. 534-43; Huntsville *Democrat*, July 11, 1840.
19 Clay, Sr., to Azariah C. Flagg, April 28, 1840, Azariah C. Flagg MSS; Democratic Party, National Convention, Baltimore, 1840, *Proceedings* (Baltimore, 1840), 18-19; Huntsville *Democrat*, May 23, June 6, 1840; John Witherspoon DuBose, *Life and Times of William Lowndes Yancey* (Birmingham, 1892), 88.

close. Many state-rights Democrats who had joined Whigs on the Nullification issue were now, however, returning to the Democratic fold along with their leader, Dixon Hall Lewis.

At the height of the campaign, Clay addressed the citizens of his home county. In reviewing the twenty-six years of his public life, "he could recollect no time more momentous than the present." He denounced "as base and unholy" the "coalition between the Northern abolitionists and Southern Whig politicians." As "a sentinel placed by the people of Alabama upon the watchtower of their liberties," he solemnly warned them of the "extraordinary exertions . . . [being] made to overthrow those principles of Democracy upon which the very existence of this government depends." Clay "spoke something more than three hours and a half, and was listened to with the profoundest attention by from five to six hundred of our citizens."[20]

In November, Alabama's electoral votes went to Van Buren, but this was little enough consolation as Democrats surveyed the sweeping Whig victory. With two congressional districts in the Whig camp, Alabama Democrats took counsel on precautionary measures and came up with the general-ticket system which Governor Arthur Pendleton Bagby recommended in his message to the legislature. This would abolish congressional districts and elect representatives on a general, statewide ticket. Thus Democrats proposed to use their heavy North Alabama majorities to elect an all-Democratic delegation to Congress. After a bitter contest in the legislature, the general-ticket system was adopted.[21]

Meantime, Clement Clay reached Washington once more, "after a most dangerous passage over sleet, ice & snow," besides "having barely escaped" being "run over by the cars" at Petersburg. He settled down at Mrs. McKnight's boardinghouse on Pennsylvania Avenue with an all-western mess which included three members from Arkansas, Lewis F. Linn of Missouri, and Augustus Caesar Dodge of Iowa Territory. Winners and losers assembled, but not much was accomplished at this "lame duck" session of the Twenty-sixth Congress. Nevertheless, the Democrats made the most of their final opportunity to discomfit the Whigs on the public-

20 Huntsville *Democrat*, Aug. 29, 1840; Jack, *Sectionalism and Party Politics in Alabama*, 66-72.

21 Ala. Leg., *HJ*, pp. 20, 328, Nov. 22, 1840, Jan. 8, 1841; Huntsville *Democrat*, Dec. 12, 1840, quoting Wetumpka *Argus*; DuBose, *Yancey*, 95-116; Jack, *Sectionalism and Party Politics in Alabama*, 75-79.

lands issue. Thomas Hart Benton introduced his "log cabin" bill making preemption a permanent policy. As chairman of the Public Lands Committee, Clement Clay reported the bill on January 4, 1841, and on the fifteenth gave it his powerful support in a long and able speech. Democrats were strong enough to pass the bill in the Senate, 31-19 (on February 2, 1841), but the Whigs' delaying tactics prevented its consideration in the House. Thus were Democrats denied a last-minute victory.[22]

At eleven o'clock on Thursday morning, March 4, 1841, Clement Clay was in his seat in the Senate to witness the swearing in of John Tyler as vice president. At twelve the entire assemblage proceeded to the east portico of the Capitol to witness the inauguration of William Henry Harrison. A cold, northeast wind chilled the multitude that heard his inaugural address. The Senate remained in session until March 14, to confirm appointments of the new administration. Many of these were not pleasing to southern Democrats. The appointment of Francis Granger as postmaster general particularly aroused Clement Clay's ire and led him to seek "authentic evidence" that Granger "has fully committed himself to the views of the *Abolitionists*." Equally obnoxious was the appointment as minister to Great Britain of John Sergeant, whom Clay called "Federal Abolition attorney for the state Abolition Society of Pennsylvania." Speaking for the Democrats, Clay avowed, "Altho' beaten, we are not subdued— and, for one, I shall avail myself of all fair means to enlighten the people of the South upon the various questions upon which they have been duped & deceived." In this state of mind Clay departed from Washington and reached home "by the Southern route" on March 27, 1841, only to be called back for a special session beginning May 31.[23]

This extra session of Congress necessitated a special election in Alabama. Operating for the first time under the new general-ticket system, Alabama sent an all-Democratic delegation to Congress. But dissatisfaction was widespread, and even Democratic

22 Willie P. Mangum to Charity Mangum, Dec. 9, 1840, W. P. Mangum MSS; USC, *Cong. Globe,* 26:2, pp. 138, 230, Appen., pp. 81-88; Robbins, *Our Landed Heritage,* 80-85.
23 David Hubbard to George Smith Houston, Feb. 24, 1841, George Smith Houston MSS; Clay, Sr., to Azariah C. Flagg, Feb. 19, 1841, A. C. Flagg MSS; USC, *Cong. Globe,* 26:2, pp. 231-56; James A. Green, *William Henry Harrison, His Life and Times* (Richmond, Va., 1941), 391-93. Sergeant declined the post.

leaders admitted that the general-ticket law "may not have been a wise measure." In the regular August elections voters repudiated the idea, and Alabama returned at once to the district system.

Hurrying back to Washington, Clay stopped long enough in East Tennessee to find his parents in "distressing circumstances" from illness and old age. He took time for "a bowl of toddy" with a neighbor, who on returning to Huntsville reported to Susanna that he had seen Clement in "good health, and better spirits" than usual. When Congress assembled on May 31, 1841, William R. King was the only member of the Alabama delegation in his seat. Clement Clay arrived on June 2 and joined King and James Buchanan in a very small mess at "Mr. Beale's" on Capitol Hill. Alabama's special election, on May 20, gave only ten days for returns to come in and for representatives to settle their affairs and make the long journey to Washington. This was an impossible schedule; hence Alabama had no representatives in the House until June 7, and the last one straggled in on the twenty-third. For the first time in his congressional service, Clement Clay was in a minority of 22 Democrats against 28 Whigs.[24]

Henry Clay led the Whigs in Congress. The chief measures of his program were repeal of the subtreasury, the incorporation of a national bank, and distribution of the proceeds of the public lands. All of these, as well as other Whig measures, were enacted into law. Clement Clay made no major speech and took little part in debate, but formed one of the phalanx of Democratic senators who by their negative votes obstructed so far as possible the Whig program. When Tyler, by his vetoes of the two bank bills, broke with the Whig party, it became for the Democrats "a triumphant session. . . . They had broken down the whig party . . . crushed it upon its own measures. . . . The Senate had done it." On this note Clement Clay ended his service in the United States Senate.[25]

[24] Ala. Leg., *HJ*, April 19-28, 1841 [microfilm copy of MS journal; no pagination]; David Hubbard to G. S. Houston, Feb. 24, 1841, G. S. Houston MSS; Susanna Clay to Clay, Sr., May 29, 1841, Clay, Jr., to Clay, Sr., July 27, 1841, Clay MSS; Huntsville *Democrat*, April 10, Aug. 21, 1841; DuBose, *Yancey*, 103; Jack, *Sectionalism and Party Politics in Alabama*, 80-82.
[25] Benton, *Thirty Years' View*, II, 219-22, 240-45, 353-57, 372-73; Nathan Sargent, *Public Men and Events* (Philadelphia, 1875, 2 vols.), II, 123-41; Lyon Gardiner Tyler, *The Letters and Times of the Tylers* (Richmond, 1885, 2 vols.), II, 39-103; "Diary of Thomas Ewing, August and September, 1841," *AHR*, XVIII (Oct., 1912), 97-112.

Clay's long absences from home, combined with four years of depression, had brought his personal finances to such a precarious state that he saw no alternative but to resign his seat in the Senate. In a letter of November 12, 1841, to the Alabama legislature, he submitted his resignation and commented at length on the political situation. "Alabama," Clay proclaimed, "has never wavered, nor faltered—she has stood firmly and immoveably by the Republican faith . . . the principles, which it has been my pride and pleasure to sustain throughout my public life, are now in the ascendant. Indeed, were it otherwise, I would not . . . withdraw . . . my humble support. Although not in power, the Democratic party never was stronger than at the present moment."

When Clay's letter was read in the Alabama senate, a motion to print 2,000 copies was defeated. In the house "an agitated discussion took place," led by Charles McLemore (Whig), who said, "My object in rising is to express the profound contempt I feel towards the author of the foul, slanderous and lying letter just read. . . . I am not inclined to sport with so low and infamous billingsgate as Clement C. Clay has thought proper to indulge. . . . Nothing but the brain of a fiend would have invented the calumny, and none but a villain's tongue give it utterance. . . . True, sir, the Whigs are in a minority on this floor; but they have rights." William Lowndes Yancey replied to this tirade in a full and dignified defense of Clay. It was Yancey's first speech before the legislature, and it established at once his reputation as an orator.[26]

The Alabama legislature elected retiring Governor Arthur Pendleton Bagby to succeed Clay in the United States Senate. Whigs circulated a "corrupt bargain" tale to the effect that Bagby would hold the senatorship for two sessions and then resign so that Clement Clay might return. The Democratic press vehemently scorned the charge.[27]

Clay's resignation did not send him into immediate political oblivion. Only a few months later, anxious Democrats urged him to become a candidate for the next state legislature. This offer

26 Ala. Leg., *HJ*, pp. 67-73, Nov. 15, 16, 1841; Clay Scrapbooks, VI, 48f; DuBose, *Yancey*, 194f.
27 Dixon Hall Lewis to J. C. Calhoun, Nov. 2, 1842, *Correspondence Addressed to John C. Calhoun, 1837-1849*, ed. by Chauncey Samuel Boucher and Robert Preston Brooks, AHA *Annual Report* (1929), I, 179; Huntsville *Democrat*, Dec. 18, 1841; Mobile *Register and Journal*, Jan. 9, 1943.

he declined, though not without expounding his ideas on the proper solution of the bank question which was the main issue of the campaign. Early in 1842 Governor Benjamin Fitzpatrick appointed Clay compiler of a new digest of Alabama law to replace that by John Gaston Aikin, then ten years out of date. Clay undertook this task and submitted his work to the next legislature, where it immediately became the object of party feuding when the Whig chairman of the judiciary committee brought in the majority report to reject the digest. James White McClung, however, pushed his minority report, and "the bill to receive the work was passed by a vote of 65 yeas and 18 nays," five Whigs voting with the majority. "Thus has this attempt to rebuke the Hon. C. C. Clay, for his letter of resignation to last winter's legislature, signally failed; and it is an honour to the five Whigs named that party malice could not force them to do an unjust act." The following June, Clay unexpectedly received an interim appointment as a justice of the Alabama supreme court to fill a vacancy caused by the resignation of Henry Barnes Goldthwaite, who was a candidate for Congress. The entire Clay family privately hailed with joy this windfall (with its salary of $2,250), which they hoped would succor their languishing finances. To this end Clay became a candidate for regular election to the post, but when Goldthwaite lost the congressional contest, he set about retrieving his former judgeship, and in the election (by the legislature) he succeeded in defeating Clay.

This was Clement Comer Clay's last bid for public office. As a politician, his greatest virtue throughout his career had been party loyalty; his greatest fault had been his tendency to contentiousness. This trait appeared during his early youth in Tennessee when he had been a party to a long-drawn-out feud over a lost hog. Soon after coming to Alabama he had engaged in a duel with Waddy Tate; and later Clay had been the central figure in the controversy which caused McClung to shoot Andrew Wills. In consequence of the voting on his digest of the laws, Clay in 1843 engaged in a squabble with James Robinson, Madison County member of the legislature who had voted against accepting the digest. This disagreement became so acrimonious that mutual friends intervened to settle it and prevent a duel. In 1845 the whole Clay family was involved in a misunderstanding with

Nathaniel Terry, unsuccessful candidate for governor. But this was the way of politics in North Alabama.[28]

In spite of controversies, Clement Comer Clay had retired to the eminence of Alabama's elder statesman. Now more than fifty years old, he fittingly turned over active politics to his eldest son, Clement Claiborne Clay. But from long years of habit the elder Clay kept a sharp eye on politics, and he resumed once more an active participation in civic and county affairs. For almost twenty years longer, "Governor Clay" (as he was usually called) wielded an enduring influence in Alabama politics.

[28] Clay, Jr., to Virginia Clay, June 15, 1843, Clay, Jr., to J. W. Clay, July 10, 1843, Benjamin Fitzpatrick to Clay, Sr., Oct. 22, 1843, Clay MSS; Ala. Leg. *HJ*, pp. 14, 132-39, Nov., 1842—Jan., 1843; Huntsville *Democrat*, May 28, June 4, 1842, Jan. 21, 1843; Mobile *Register and Journal*, Jan. 12, 1843.

5

The Clay Family Grows Up

CLEMENT COMER CLAY in 1811 had come to Huntsville with slender means, but high ambitions and boundless energy. Four years of effort gave him an established law practice, a plantation, several slaves, and a house on his town lot on Clinton Street. Clement was then ready to marry. His bride, on April 4, 1815, was seventeen-year-old Susanna Claiborne Withers.[1] Susanna was the daughter of John and Mary Herbert (Jones) Withers, who had come to Madison County in 1808. The Withers family was proud of its English origin as well as its Virginia background dating from 1752, when William Withers had settled in Dinwiddie County.[2] There Susanna was born on July 23, 1798, and there she lived the first ten years of her life. Her transfer at so young an age to the unsettled wilderness of Madison County meant that Susanna's education was curtailed and that a frontier environment was the predominant influence in her formative years. Though surrounded by the unavoidable crudities of the frontier, Susanna imbibed from her parents that sure knowledge of gentle birth and family superiority which had become the New World's substitute for titles of nobility. Susanna was a very conscious aristocrat. Her limitations of education and experience she therefore felt most keenly in later years, when she occupied a position of social prominence. She wrote of it thus: "I have felt my usefulness thwarted all my life in consequence of my deficiency . . . and now I find that I must attend, and learn what I might with ease have accomplished years ago—but I had not the opportunity of knowing its importance till late in life—"[3] "Attend" she did, for Susanna learned constantly from her well-educated husband, and in teaching her children, she necessarily relearned the lessons of her childhood. Inordinate ambition drove Susanna Clay to self-improvement; her eagerness for wealth exhibited itself in parsimony and careful management of household and plantation; the scramble for position in frontier society was reflected in her tendency to advise all members of the family on the conduct of their lives, and particularly in her anxieties for her children. This combination of ambition and anxiety made her somewhat neurotic in later years. In the first years of her marriage, however, Susanna exhibited a timorous dependence upon her husband.

Clement and Susanna Clay's three children were Clement Claiborne (December 13, 1816—January 3, 1882), John Withers (January 11, 1820— March 29, 1896), and Hugh Lawson (January 24, 1823—December 28, 1890).[4] The care and solicitude expended upon these three boys would do credit to parents of any time and circumstance. Their training and education received much attention, with the result that they were "one of the best educated families in North Alabama." Little Clement was at once his parents' pride and despair—pride because at the age of five he "appears to take great delight in his book"; despair because he was an extremely delicate child, which probably accounts for an oil portrait of the five-year-old. Young Clement's earliest visit to his paternal grandparents in East Tennessee furnished the occasion for his first letter. He was fluent if not entirely orthodox in form and spelling. "When i arrived they were all verry glad to se me. ant and unkle kendrick Were not here. Gramama said that she Expected them on saturday, if they were not, there then, she did not ExPect them at all. ant Bunches family and ant hitowers family were all well as far as We know. ant sinthy has a nother daughter Which is not yet Named. unkle green has told myster White, that I can go, in his carriage. he intends coming

1 Madison Co. Archives, Marriage Record, vol. I.

2 Robert Edwin Withers, *Withers Family of the County Lancaster, England, and of Stafford County, Virginia, Establishing the Ancestry of Robert Edwin Withers, III* (Richmond, Va., 1947), 27, 189.

3 Susanna Clay to Mary Herbert (Jones) Withers, March 26, 1834, Clay MSS.

4 *DAB,* IV, 170; Owen, *Dict. Ala. Biog.,* III, 343; Tombstones, Maple Hill Cemetery, Huntsville, Ala.

if noting hapens. on the twenty 5 of this mon gran p^{a}pa intends coming t^{h}ey are trying to Persuad^e granmama to cone, But she Wilnot come. you may expect us all, on the twenty fith or sith of september. i read evry day to unkle, Green, as you have told me. my journey Was a little tiresome for the first an last day, the stage being crowded very much. i roed Behind myster Wite from knoxville to gran papas."[5]

Withers and Lawson (as the two younger boys were called) were not equally precocious. After a start under their mother's tutelage, all three boys went to one of the local teachers. "Lawson," his mother noted, "is much more studious than formerly— I have sent him to Mr. Phelan. . . . I was fearful I could not continue to give him the same attention I had done." The frontier did not abound in educational advantages, but the opening of Greene Academy in 1823 provided an institution which, despite its many vicissitudes, gave a "respectable" training to many generations of Madison County boys. Here the three young Clays were prepared for college in Greek, Latin, mathematics, and English grammar. As a trustee and as a parent, Clement Clay attended the semi-annual examinations to observe the progress of his own and his neighbors' sons. In 1828 and 1829, Clement, Jr., Withers Clay, and Jones Mitchell Withers (Susanna Clay's young brother) were all students at Greene Academy. In the latter year Clement, Jr., "was examined in Virgil; Greek Delectus; and . . . gave an Original Oration on Patriotism." In 1833 Withers was reading "Tacitus and Sophocles's Oedipus Tyrannus." The latter, he explained, "I find . . . exceedingly hard, but have not despaired, keeping in mind the old and true adage, 'Perseverance conquers all things.' " Anticipating a proper reward for his perseverance, Withers added in a postscript, "I have taken the liberty without your leave, of having a new spring put to the lock of your gun, that I might shoot ducks, for which I hope and expect your pardon."[6]

Summers were filled with visits to the plantations, a journey to "the springs," and often by the specter of an epidemic or at least the perennial danger of malaria. In 1826 Susanna wrote, "Hunts-

5 Susanna Clay to Clay, Sr., June 11, 1821, Clay, Jr., to Clay, Sr., and Susanna Clay, Sept. 8, 1826, Clay MSS. Clement Comer Clay's sisters and their husbands here mentioned were: Cynthia and Alston Hunter Green, Maacah and William P. Kendrick, Margaret Muse and John Bunch, Nancy and Epaphroditus Hightower. "myster Wite" was James M. M. White, son of Hugh Lawson White.

6 Susanna Clay to Clay, Sr., Dec. 5, 1828, J. W. Clay to Clay, Jr., Nov. 22, 1833, Clay MSS; Huntsville Democrat, Aug. 22, 1828, Aug. 14, 1829.

ville is more unhealthy at this time than I ever knew it," and consequently she had sent Withers and Lawson to the country, while "Clement & Jones [and the Negroes] I make take cream of Tartar or salts every other day." A week later she and Clement, Jr., joined Clement, Sr., at Blount Springs, a popular North Alabama resort in Blount County, some sixty miles south of Huntsville. They found that "the improvement in the accommodations both on the road, and at the springs are very great." Blount Springs now boasted "a large *Boarding House,* with more than 30 comfortable cabins," while the proprietor promised the best of food and liquors, and an abundance of game and fish for "Gentlemen fond of sport."[7]

Sometimes sport of a different kind could be found closer home. Schoolboy fights, especially with the Pope-Percy-Walker clan, brought a long letter from the Clay boys to explain in much detail to their father how Withers had been set upon by Charles Percy. Young Clement had come to his brother's aid, and this led to another fight between Clement, Jr., and Willis Pope, who "jumped on me," Clement related, "& threw me down & bruised my face a little." "As we went on home he was taunting & provoking me . . . when I went up to him & struck him & after bruising his face & being pulled off of him I went on home. . . . The trustees met & suspended him for two weeks & myself for one, & C. Percey was given 6 licks & brother Withers 1. . . . The trustees . . . blamed him from beginning to end but they blamed me for attacking him the second time. But," continued Clement, "I appeald to my own breast to know whether I was to suffer his reproach taunts & *abuse* without a murmur & my conscience approved my actions.

"I have studied my algebra & read during the week of my suspension . . . & I commenced school this morning with the desire to keep out of all scrapes if possible but to fight when struck & to strike when my character is calumniated or my brothers imposed on. I think candidly that I have acted right & my breast is free from remorse of conscience."[8]

At the age of sixteen Clement was in the midst of feverish preparation to enter the recently opened University of Alabama.

[7] Susanna Clay to Clay, Sr., July 14, 1826, Clay MSS; Huntsville *Alabama Republican,* May 17, 1822.
[8] Clay, Jr., to Clay, Sr., May 28, 1832, Clay MSS.

From Washington his father urged him to "assiduity and exertion" so that he might enter the junior class, but warned him not to be discouraged if he did not succeed, and then continued, "Let me remind you, my son, of the importance of now continuing your exertions to improve & establish your hand-writing. Purchase good paper, tho' it may cost a little more, and practice writing for the mere purpose of improvement. I am very willing that you should consume a few quires of paper, now, that you may write an easy, expeditious and neat hand." To paternal admonitions Withers responded with a promise to "endeavor to 'improve my mind, purify my heart, and curb my passions.' " But studies rested lightly on the youngest, which led Susanna to ask "why . . . Lawson is still in the same book? . . . I know he has abilities, if he will only exert them." He "is not improving . . . as he ought to be. . . . He is no doubt indolent . . . and will never do what he thinks is not expected of him."[9]

Clement, Jr., entered the University of Alabama in January, 1833. The school had been in operation less than two years and was subject to all the handicaps of infancy and a frontier environment. The site at Tuscaloosa was chosen in 1828, construction soon began, and on April 18, 1831, the first students enrolled. But nothing went smoothly, for aside from confused finances, the president, Dr. Alva Woods, was so unsuccessful as an administrator that he antagonized the faculty and created conditions which led to a riot among the students. This occurred when young Clement was a senior. He was not the type of boy to engage in such rowdyism, but he sent his father a full account of the affair.

"It gives me much pain to inform you of the sad state of affairs in our colledge [sic].— Matters have been growing worse & worse every day, till, on saturday night, there was an open & audacious rebellion. About ten student[s] at 9 oclock, collected on the blowing of a horn, & commenced dressing themselves in white— Mr Hudson ran into the room in which they were, & succeeded in detecting two or three—left them & returned to his room—a bottle was thrown at him, but did not strike him—the assailant unknown—they, after this dispersion, met again with their horn & a tin-pan in the Campus, with pistols & clubs—commenced

[9] Clay, Sr., to Clay, Jr., Dec. 15, 1832, Susanna Clay to Mary H. J. Withers, March 26, 1834, Susanna Clay to Clay, Jr., April 1, 1834, Clay MSS.

firing—shouting &c—Mr Tutwiler went out to them, & they left him, & came in pursuit of Dr Woods—met him coming to this dormitory & began to throw brickbats at him—he ran & as he turned the corner of the house a pistol was fired in the direction towards him—he availed himself of an open window & jumped in it—they, fortunately, on his turning the corner, ran around the opposite side of the house, & not seeing him went in the cellars, & then to the woods, to find him—he then came to all the rooms & marked all out,—went in his own room with out a light—the insurgents by this time had added ten more to their number & returned—unable to find him they rocked his windows, &, finally started up stairs to take him out if he *should* be in it—he went in some of the other rooms, & some person telling the disguised company that he was not in his room, they came down & paraded over the lot in every direction—Dr Wallace [i.e., Wallis] came out, & they told him if he approached it was at his peril, cocking their pistols at the same time—he, prudently, stopped—told them the impropriety of their conduct & begged them to desist—they ran off & he went home—Dr Woods, in the mean time, escaped over home without their knowledge—they broke in the chapel—rung the bell—stoned Mr Hudsons windows, & about 1 oclock stillness was procured by their own drowsiness. Mr Tutwiler, alone, among the Faculty commanded some respect from them. I would not risk my life in Dr Woods situation for his salairy [*sic*]; for I believe that there are students in colledge [*sic*] who would shoot him if they did not fear the laws of the land. There is a constant firing of pistols from dark till midnight during some nights in the week. It will injure the colledge [*sic*] very materially thro'out the union. This day Dr Guild remarked to me that without a *change in the Faculty* it must fall."

This was only the beginning of difficulties that continued for several years. A more formidable riot in 1837 led to the resignation of Dr. Woods and the entire faculty. The resulting reorganization set the institution on its way to permanence and growth.[10]

Meanwhile, at the commencement of August, 1834, seventeen-year-old Clement and ten others were graduated with the A.B. degree. Clement's oration on "The True Sources of National

10 Clay, Jr., to Clay, Sr., Feb. 24, 1834, Clay MSS; Henry Watson, Jr., to Theodore Watson, March 23, 1834, Henry Watson MSS; James Benson Sellers, *History of the University of Alabama* (University, Ala.; 1953), I, 3-66.

Greatness" presaged his political career. What to do next was now his most pressing problem, and so he asked his father's opinion on "whether it will benefit me more to spend a year or two at Cambridge, or remain here as a resident graduate." Whatever the decision, he was ready to abide by his father's "better judgment." As to his need for further education, Clement, Jr., added, "I am very deficient in my Historical knowledge. . . . My education is not have [sic] way completed, & my knowledge only respectable.— I do not entertain the most distant idea of quitting school or commencing a profession—I am unprepared." This obedient precociousness did not, however, diminish the constant flow of parental admonition. Clement's mother, with an eye to his cultural attainments and an embarrassing consciousness of her own deficiency, wrote from Washington, "*I again beg you will correspond in French*— Every day convinces me of the necessity of understanding that language." While Clement tended to favor Harvard as the place of his future study, his father preferred the University of Virginia, and after weighing the merits of both institutions, they settled upon the latter.[11]

With the purpose of entering this school, Clement set out with his father in November, 1834, on a three-week journey which took them first to East Tennessee for a very brief visit with William and Rebecca Clay. Upon resuming their journey, they found an old enemy, Gabe Moore, in the stage. "Neither Father nor myself spoke to Moore," but "disregarding his pestilential atmosphere for at least 170 miles," added Clement, Sr., "I scrupulously kept up the same unbending non-intercourse . . . which I have observed toward him for the last ten, or twelve years." After an overnight stop in Washington, they went on to West Point, New York, to visit Jones Mitchell Withers, Susanna Clay's young brother, who was a cadet there. On their return they stayed two days in New York, where friends showed them the "most interesting parts" of that "great, great commercial Emporium." They reached Washington at 11 P.M., Sunday, November 30, scarcely more than twelve hours before Congress was due to assemble.[12]

11 Susanna Clay to Clay, Jr., Feb. 1, 1834, Clay, Jr., to Clay, Sr., Feb. 28, April 7, 1834, Clay MSS; Huntsville *Southern Advocate*, Aug. 26, 1834.
12 Clay, Jr., to Susanna Clay, Nov. 16, 1834, Clay, Sr., to Susanna Clay, Dec. 1, 1834, Clay MSS.

On their way northward they had stopped at Charlottesville, Virginia, where young Clement's enthusiasm for further education was somewhat dampened by his unfavorable impression of the University of Virginia. "To speak frankly," he wrote his mother, "I was disappointed. The dormitories I will not room in— . . . Besides, I found the students, mostly, wild, harum scarum, tho'tless & dissipated, without that that [sic] noble emulation, constant application, & high minded bearing, I had wished to see. The Professors, tho' able, seemed uncommunicative & morose. The buildings & the lawns have an air of stiffness, contractedness, & tiresome uniformity, that was unpleasant to look on. In fact, father, I think, was not so well pleased, &, on noticing my unfavourable remarks, said he would send me, yet, 'to Cambridge if he did not fear my constitution would be injured.' I would go most readily. However, I shall try to content myself at Charlottesville, & . . . make myself a scholar. I shall attend the Lectures on the modern Languages, Mathematics & natural Philosophy—three tickets." Clement did not have an opportunity, however, to learn whether he could either content himself or become a scholar at Charlottesville, for an attack of influenza kept him in Washington all winter.

But his time was not totally lost there, for young Clement had his first contact with national politics and Washington society. "I really do not like Washington," he confided to his mother. "I hear nothing but politics hummed from morning till night. One eternal crowing over the vanquished enemy—one constant backbiting of the foe." By the new year, Clement had recovered sufficiently to go out socially, as he reported to his mother. "The 6th I went to the Presidents to dinner, where I saw political enemies smile over the festive board & talk in apparent friendship around the social fireplace. Mr Webster conducted Mrs Jackson (the Gen.ˢ daughter in law) to the table, the President Mrs Webster. After supper Miss Taney was performing on the piano, & the President called out play & sing 'auld Land sine." [sic] Miss Taney declined singing, & Mr W.[ebster] unbending his senitorial [sic] dignity stepped forward & sung it—strange harmony it would seem where all was discord. (Mr Taney & Mr W[ebster], you know, have been abusing one another for the last 12 months . . . I tho't, myself, Mr W.[ebster] felt his wine of which he drank a great deal. After the song ended the President said familiarly, 'Clay, I think you could sing,' as if pitting him. Father replied he had 'not gotten up to the singing point yet.' "[13]

The elder Clay's candidacy and election as governor of Alabama in 1835 considerably influenced the family's activities for the next two years. Young Clement became his father's secretary, along with Jones Mitchell Withers. Alabama did not provide a governor's mansion, and so to serve as executive headquarters, Clay obtained "Dr. Drish's house," installed two servants, and brought his son Withers to Tuscaloosa to enter the university. The next year Lawson came for the same purpose. The two younger boys remained at the university through the academic year of 1837, but did not receive degrees. As to the household arrangments, young Clement explained that "Tom milks & cooks, & Hannibal will clean up the rooms, brush shoes &c." Governor Clay spent most of the summer of 1837 in Huntsville, leaving Clement, Jr., to handle routine correspondence and such other duties as he could properly carry out in his secretarial capacity. It was useful training for a prospective politician, quite as valuable as more formal education. Susanna as usual worried about her son off in Tuscaloosa alone. When the slave Garland died, she feared an epidemic, but Clement, Jr., assured her that Garland died of apoplexy. "He was, perhaps, the most valuable negro father owned, & his place cannot be easily supplied," noted Clement.[14]

Clement Comer Clay's election in June, 1837, to the United States Senate created new opportunities for the boys' education. And fortunately, the opening of the special session of Congress on September 4 coincided with the opening of the University of Virginia on September 1. Thus it came about that Clement, Jr., and Withers both entered that university in 1837. Clement enrolled in law, while Withers signed up for ancient and modern languages and mathematics. The following year Lawson joined his brothers. In spite of several illnesses, Clement managed to complete his work and was graduated in law on July 4, 1839. Two years later (July 3, 1841) Withers Clay was the first out-of-state student to receive the degree of Master of Arts from the

[13] Clay, Jr., to Susanna Clay, Dec. 26, 1834, Jan. 8, 1835, Clay MSS.
[14] Ala. Archives, Governors' Letters, Clay, Jr., to Clay, Sr., Jan. 30, 1836; Clay, Jr., to Susanna Clay, Aug. 7, 1836, Clay MSS.

University of Virginia. Lawson was a student for two sessions, but did not obtain a degree.

During these years the boys' opportunities were extended in other directions. Withers spent considerable time in Washington, where he frequented the Senate gallery and "heard Mr. Calhoun's reply to . . . Mr. [Henry] Clay. . . . Each spoke 4 or 5 times & were so excited at one time that it was feared . . . the affair would end in a duel, but they were both in good humours when they closed." He went "to see Forest [sic] three nights—attended the President's levee on Thursday evening last—will be at a party this evening—and perhaps another tomorrow evening." He went to church "with Mrs. Polk . . . & heard the minister denounce the practice of attending theatres, calling them 'the devil's pro-tracted meetings.'" In 1841, and again in 1843, Withers made extensive journeys to the north and east, seeking collections for northern law firms as a means of increasing the family's legal business and income. Susanna was "pleased, that Withers, is per-mitted to see so large a portion of his country, tho, the many recent . . . steamboat disasters causes me some little anxiety to know that my child is safe." Indeed, with all three sons absent, Susanna's anxieties and "full heart" led her to write, "I am thinking of you all—and wishing that I could see each at this moment—tho I could not tell which would receive my . . . arms about his neck first? The one who looked palest I expect."[15]

The three young Clays were now nearly ready to embark on their careers. Clement Clay had done a great deal for his sons— perhaps too much, for they were never forced to rely on them-selves as their father had been. Susanna Clay's ambition pushed all three boys into the law. For Clement this was a natural talent. But Withers and Lawson read law in a desultory fashion and later practiced it with indifferent success. Withers, with a deeply religious nature even in his student days, was best fitted for the ministry. He was for many years a vestryman of Huntsville's Church of the Nativity (Episcopal). His was a yielding, quiet nature, not inclined to vigorous exertion. His placid temperament

15 Clay, Sr., and J. W. Clay to Clay, Jr., March 12, 1838, Susanna Clay to Clay, Sr., Aug. 31, 1841, Clay, Jr., to J. W. Clay, July 10, 1843, Clay MSS; University of Virginia, *Catalogues*, 1837-1840, pp. 6, 61; *A Sketch of the History of the University of Virginia* (Washington, 1859), 16, 32; Richmond *Enquirer*, July 16, 1839, July 16, 1841.

made him especially compatible with his mother. Lawson, on the other hand, "has made your mother an old woman before she e'er dreamed of it," Susanna once remarked. He was the masculine counterpart of his mother in spirit and temper. Consequently, the two were always clashing. He had her pride, plus a masculine arrogance in his youth that could be very annoying. Lawson had a desire to study medicine, but his mother looked upon the law as the only proper profession, and so pushed him into it. His temperament leaned toward a life of action and adventure, but he lacked the independence and perseverance to carry it out, and so was to a degree frustrated. Clement, Jr., had qualities of character which enabled him to steer a middle course, being neither dependent on his mother nor antagonistic to her. Clement's real talent, as it developed from his early youth, led him toward being a scholar. But in the mid-nineteenth-century South, a scholar usually had to pursue the lowly art of teaching in order to make a living. A Clay could not descend to that. And so Clement, with his brilliant mind, his fondness for philosophy and history, turned to the "honorable" profession of the law and to politics, in which he did much preaching of a particular political philosophy, and helped to make some history.

When Clement, Jr., was admitted to the bar on October 2, 1839, his father took things in hand by forming the firm of Clay, Clemens, and Clay, composed of C. C. Clay, Sr., C. C. Clay, Jr., and Jeremiah Clemens. This continued until 1841, when Clemens withdrew. Jere Clemens (December 28, 1814–May 21, 1865) had been educated at the University of Alabama and at Transylvania University. In later years he served in the Alabama legislature and in the United States Senate, and was the author of several historical novels. His love of adventure, dissipated living, hostility to secession, and ultimate unionism progressively antagonized the highly moral and strictly state-rights Clays. Clement, Jr., and his father continued to do business at their office "in the new brick building, on the Public Square, immediately West of the Court House." This arrangement lasted until January, 1846, when Clement, Jr., was elected judge of the Madison County court. Withers then became his father's partner.[16]

After some years of dillydallying, Hugh Lawson Clay retired to

16 Huntsville *Democrat*, Oct. 19, 1839, May 15, 1841, March 26, 1845, Feb. 25, 1846.

"Oakley" plantation and devoted the summer of 1843 to reading Blackstone. There, removed from the "bright eyes, pretty faces and all the paraphernalia of fashionable life," with his books as his "only company," Lawson finally succeeded in learning enough law to pass the stiff examination his father set him, and not long thereafter he was admitted to practice. Early in 1845, determined to rely on himself, Lawson hung out his shingle down the river in Tuscumbia. There he boarded at the tavern and hired out his servant Jim, who as a waiter afforded "no little amusement" by his "pompous dignity and self-confidence . . . moving around the dining-room." But Lawson's success as a lawyer was not marked, and when the faithful Jim died early in 1846, his master reluctantly packed up and came home. Legal business was so dull in Tuscumbia that Lawson was not making expenses; hence he proposed "removal to some place where my services professional would be required," but strangely enough he could not "gain the consent of any member of the family." They all, he complained, "wish me to return to Huntsville and finish an existence, miserable in dependence and satiety." The result, he predicted, "will be to make me a mere cypher, or what is worse, a parasitical plumb [sic], clinging to the family stock [sic] for sustenance in life." Declining a partnership with his father and Withers, Lawson declared, "I wish . . . to leave for any western or Southern place, where money could be made, and, dependent upon whatever industry and mental energy I possess, strive against that opposition, with which most young men must contend."

But family pressure prevailed, and Lawson remained in Huntsville, where he soon joined his brother Clement in law practice. Of this arrangement Clement, Jr., wrote, "Altho' I think I cd. make as much alone & shall only divide my means . . . yet, he is my brother & I had better make less money & live even poor, if I advance his future thereby & secure his happiness. Hence, rather than see him wandering off to Miss. or to Texas,—alone & friendless & unhappy, I wrote to him to come back and try his proposition with me." The partnership lasted for only a year.[17]

Lawson was destined to uphold the military reputation of the family. In the flood of southern patriotism occasioned by the Mex-

17 H. L. Clay to J. W. Clay, Aug. 7, 1843, H. L. Clay to Clay, Sr., Jan. 10, 1845, Feb. 20, 1846, H. L. Clay to Virginia Clay, March 11, 1846, H. L. Clay to Susanna Clay, March 14, 1846, Clay, Jr., to Virginia Clay, March 20, 1846, Clay, Jr., to Clay, Sr., April 19, 1846, Clay MSS.

ican War, he obtained a captain's commission, recruited a company of eighty-five volunteers, and in May, 1847, went off down
the river with his men. They reached Mexico during the summer,
and in October, 1847, they were stationed at Vera Cruz preparatory to the movement upon Mexico City. During his year of
service in Mexico, Lawson did not see much actual fighting, and
after returning to Huntsville, he resumed the ordinary round of
legal and managerial activities. The Mexican campaign, however,
had its benefits; a member of the family observed that he had
"never in his life, seen such a decided change in any one for the
better—that [Lawson] has lost all of that *overbearing* temper,
which . . . he too often exhibited and that he was popular and
respected among the *best* class of officers." The Mexican venture
compensated somewhat for Lawson's thwarted ambition to seek
his fortune on the frontier.[18]

Lawson continued for some years to be one of the more eligible
young bachelors of Huntsville. He doubtless cut quite a figure
as he courted the girls, with, as he described himself, his "long
beard, moustache and hair, dressed in a checked jean's coat, a
brown fustian vest, striped & cross barred pants, and heavy winter
boots, not to omit a soft felt hat, of the 'Wide-awake' style, and you
have my *tout ensemble* as I pay visits. . . . As it is the only fancy
suit I ever wore, I intend to have the benefit of it." At one time
he and Withers were competing for the same girl, a circumstance
which led Clement, Jr., to remark, "I wish some woman wd dis-
card [Lawson] & cure his vanity."

Several years later, on May 13, 1855, Lawson married his second
cousin, Harriet Celestia Comer (March 28, 1835—March 18, 1902).
Celeste, whom the family called Lestia, was the daughter of Major
Anderson Comer (August 19, 1797—August 28, 1867) and Maria
Louisa (Sanders) Comer of Macon, Georgia. Celeste was a gay,
society-loving girl of the planting class, upon whom matronly
duties rested lightly. For almost two years she and Lawson
boarded at various places in Huntsville. Meanwhile, Lawson
pushed his income up to "seven or eight hundred dollars, besides
other fees due. . . . So that I count upon good $1,500.*00* cash
at the end of December." Early in 1857 they began housekeeping

18 H. L. Clay to Clay, Sr., May 17, 1847, H. L. Clay to Susanna Clay, Oct. 13,
1847, May 3, 1848, Susanna (Withers) Battle to Susanna Clay, June 29, 1848, Clay
MSS; Huntsville *Democrat*, April 7, May 5, 1847.

in a residence belonging to the family. Their well-carpeted "parlor," their "chamber . . . well & comfortably furnished," the "1500 lbs pork and half a beef in the store-house . . . a good cow," and four servants provided "everything absolutely *necessary* to house-keeping." Their only child, Felix Comer, was born in November, 1856, and died in May, 1862.[19]

Meanwhile, John Withers Clay pursued his quiet way. He was content to stay in Huntsville, filling his days with such legal business as came his way and making small forays into local politics and civic affairs. In later years he turned to journalism and became best known as editor of the Huntsville *Democrat*. But early in 1846 his attention was concentrated on Mary Lewis. "I think brother Withers is so badly smitten, as ever luckless wight was— His leisure moments are most frequently spent in her presence and in 'sweet converse' with her, I dare say," commented Lawson. After some "dallying," she accepted him, and they were married on November 11, 1846. Mary Fenwick Lewis (August 21, 1825—March 2, 1898) was the daughter of John Haywood and Mary Margaret (Betts) Lewis. The latter inherited a large estate from her father, Samuel Betts, a merchant of Havana, Cuba, who died about 1822. John Haywood Lewis was a native of Connecticut. Their daughter Mary, a girl of superior intellect, had received an unusually good education, including study in France. Her background was considerably different from that of the Clay family, who never accepted her in quite the same manner as that accorded the other daughters-in-law. In a different environment, Mary might have turned to women's rights or some other reform movement. In Huntsville she kept busy with her music and French, and soon the cares of a rapidly increasing family demanded her attention.

The children of John Withers and Mary (Lewis) Clay ultimately totaled eleven. Of these four died in infancy or early childhood, and another at the age of twenty-one. Mary (Lewis) Clay's scant attention to housekeeping, her preoccupation with intellectual interests, and her outspoken views on many subjects did not leave a very favorable impression on the Clay family.

[19] Clay, Jr., to Virginia Clay, April 28, 1846, H. L. Clay to Virginia Clay, May 10, 1856, Jan. 14, 185[7], Clay MSS; Clay Scrapbooks, III, 44; Huntsville *Democrat*, June 7, 1855; Anne Kendrick Walker, *Braxton Bragg Comer: His Family Tree from Virginia's Colonial Days* (Richmond, 1947), 6.

This was particularly true of Susanna, who was inclined to be critical of all her daughters-in-law. If Withers and Mary were perhaps not entirely congenial, it was in later years fortunate that Withers had a wife with the energy and ability to steer the family through countless difficulties. Nevertheless, Mary Clay's large family kept her closely at home, and it is scarcely surprising that she was a little bitter with her lot as she saw her two sisters-in-law gallivanting over the country with never a care.[20]

High infant mortality was only one manifestation of the physical ills and hazards that beset frontier society. None of the Clay men was robust. Though Clement, Sr., lived an active life, he often complained of poor health, and on several occasions he was seriously ill. Of the sons, Lawson enjoyed the best health, though illness was in part responsible for his failure to return to the University of Virginia and finish his work there. Clement, Jr., and Withers both suffered frequent illnesses. Indeed, throughout his life, Clement, Jr., was handicapped by ill health which incapacitated him at some of the most critical moments of his career. His delicacy as a child caused his grandfather to write, "we were truly gratified to find that . . . our two youngest grandsons are healthy growing & thriving, while we regret very much you have it not in your power to say as much of the eldest." Young Clement's attack of influenza at Washington in 1834 was only one of many illnesses. During the following spring he had extensive dental work done, a luxury not available in Huntsville. Clement's teeth were apparently badly decayed and abcessed—so much so that the dentist filed them off and attached other teeth to the stubs.

During the spring of 1838 and again in 1839, Clement, Jr., was the victim of prolonged illnesses. On both occasions he sought medical advice in Philadelphia and found it necessary to undergo treatment for a kidney ailment. The doctors of Philadelphia now considered him so delicate that the "majority advise me to go to Europe." But, Clement objected, "That is what I have no desire to do. . . . It would defeat or, at least, postpone all my plans for life. I have no passion for foreign travel. I only wish . . . to

20 Madison Co. Archives, Marriage Record A-4, p. 147; Register of Chancery, Record Book, 1849-1851, pp. 349-79; H. L. Clay to Susanna Clay, April 27, 1846, Susanna (Withers) Battle to Susanna Clay, May 8, 1849, Mary (Lewis) Clay to Virginia Clay, March 1, 1863, Clay MSS; James Edmonds Saunders, *Early Settlers of Alabama* (New Orleans, 1899), 517.

prosecute my profession. But when shall I commence? where shall I settle? & how can I secure my health?" Clement compromised by spending several weeks at the Virginia springs, where his health did improve. For the next decade he was able to lead a fairly active life without the interruption of any major illness.[21]

Young Clement's legal career was well under way and he was a rising young legislator before romance overtook him. During the legislative session Tuscaloosa was a favorite resort for designing mammas with marriageable daughters. A bachelor legislator was considered a prize catch, and young Clem Clay was no exception, for as he playfully explained, "I have been to numerous parties & am a sort of lion, because of *my honors, single-blessedness* & good looks and manners." Clement soon succumbed, though not because of maternal scheming, and confessed that "there is a most lovely & beautiful young lady here who has quite *mesmerized* me." The girl in question was Virginia Caroline Tunstall.[22]

Virginia Caroline Tunstall was born on January 16, 1825, in Nash County, North Carolina, the daughter of Dr. Peyton Randolph Tunstall and Ann (Arrington) Tunstall. With the death of her twenty-year-old mother, three-year-old Virginia was given over to the care of relatives, who three years later moved to Tuscaloosa. Here she spent her childhood living first in the home of Henry Watkins Collier, whose wife Mary Ann (Battle) was Ann Arrington's half-sister, and later with Mrs. Collier's brother, Alfred Battle, and his wife Millicent (Beale). Virginia lived a carefree childhood among a host of cousins and absorbed as much education as her high spirits allowed. Sometimes her father paid a visit and took her to Mobile, where her first taste of dancing and the theater gave her ecstatic pleasure. When the educational facilities of frontier Tuscaloosa were exhausted, she was sent in 1839 to the Nashville Female Academy, where she was one of eight graduates the following year. She was now a young lady in Tuscaloosa society, where, two years later, she met C. C. Clay, Jr.

Their mutual attraction had a rapid growth, and "fascinated"

21 Clay, Sr., to Susanna Clay, Nov. 11, 1818, William Clay to Clay, Sr., Feb. 6, 1825, Clay, Jr., to Susanna Clay, Jan. 8, 1835, Clay, Jr., to Clay, Sr., March 15, 1839, Susanna Clay to Clay, Jr., Aug. 13, 1839, H. L. Clay to Clay, Sr., June 15, 1841, Susanna Clay to Clay, Sr., Aug. 31, 1841, Clay MSS; Ala. Military Archives, Clay, Jr., to Col. Philpott, Feb. 18, 1836; Huntsville Democrat, July 12, 1848.

22 Clay, Jr., to J. W. Clay, Dec. 20, 1842, Clay MSS; Virginia Clay-Clopton, *A Belle of the Fifties: Memoirs of Mrs. Clay, of Alabama, Covering Social and Political Life in Washington and the South, 1853-66* (New York, 1905), 5-19.

though he was, Clement had qualms about marrying during a period of depression. He sought his mother's advice, and after describing Virginia as "a great beauty—of elegant figure—of the sweetest grace of manner—of lively & vivacious humor—of superior and well-cultivated mind—of a most amiable & tender heart—& of an excellent constitution," he confessed that he was "almost resolved to address her." While admitting that she had "but little property, yet enough to support her," he argued that she had "no mercenary motive in forming a matrimonial connection," as was shown by the fact that she had repeatedly refused "the hands of wealthy, but undeserving suitors." From his own side Clement argued that he "ought to get married," that he needed "some anchor to give [him] greater stability of character," the "only obstacle" being the fact that he was "poor & in debt," and could not depend on help from his financially harassed father. Clement promised to wait if his parents opposed the idea, and concluded by saying, "After all, it is well to remember that the lady may decline my offer. She has many suitors around her, now, & has a good field for selection." Clement's apprehensions were not realized, however, and after a month's ardent courtship, he and Virginia Tunstall were married on February 1, 1843.

The wedding, which took place in the home of Henry W. Collier, chief justice of the Alabama supreme court, was the most dazzling social event provincial Tuscaloosa had yet witnessed. The bridegroom described it, "According to contract, Virginia & I were married . . . at 7 o clock, in presence of a numerous assembly. Virginia was very much agitated, but I was far more composed than I had any idea I could be. Dr. Robt. W. Withers, Maria & Eliza Jane were present, together with near half of the Legislature. The house had passed a resolution only two days before to hold night sessions . . . but, on motion of Col. Erwin of Mobile, together with a very happy & kind speech in allusion to the proposed departure of a fellow member from a state of single blessedness, the house adjourned."[23]

The bride, though "an unformed girl" of eighteen, was well endowed with innate ability and had already received a good education by standards of that day. With maturity and experience,

[23] Mary Ann Fort to Martha W. Fort, March 18, 1832, Female Academy diploma to Virginia C. Tunstall, Dec. 9, 1840, Clay, Jr., to Susanna Clay, Dec. 23, 1842, Clay, Jr., to Clay, Sr., Feb. 3, 1843, Clay MSS; Saunders, *Early Settlers of Alabama*, 283ff.

her intellectual quickness and native wit ripened into versatility and brilliant social accomplishments. Even in advanced age she never lost her zest for living or her interest in current affairs. Physically she was tall and strong. Her oval face, blond complexion, light chestnut hair, and close-set eyes gave her an appearance typical of many North Carolinians. She was no beauty—Clement's declaration to the contrary notwithstanding—but her conversational powers and charm were ample substitutes for beauty. Her social talents, capacity for making friends, and vivaciousness, as well as her influential family connections, became great assets to Clement in his public career and complemented his more quiet and studious nature.

Wedding festivities continued until the close of the legislative session on February 15, when Clement and his bride set off for home by stagecoach. On the evening of the second day they dashed across Huntsville's public square and down Clinton Street to the Clay residence, which was aglow with candles and bursting with relatives. After a new round of festivities, Clement and Virginia settled down under the parental roof. Here Virginia began her new life, and soon she was completely identified with the Clays.

The Clay house (sometimes referred to in later years as Clay Castle), though not one of Huntsville's mansions, was a spacious, wide, rambling structure, like many southern houses. It was cool in summer, draughty in winter, and comfortable according to the standards of the day. On their plantations the Clays had only rough log houses which provided shelter and work space during their frequent sojourns, but were not intended for permanent family living. About 1829 Clement, Sr., built a summer home on "the mountain"—Monte Sano, a ridge of 1,000 feet elevation, three miles east of Huntsville. Twenty years later Clement, Jr., put up his own residence near by. Both houses (as well as those of the entire summer colony) were burned by Union troops in 1863. In 1859 Lawson Clay built a house in Huntsville. Withers and Mary Clay lived in a residence originally belonging to the Lewis family; this in later years was called "The Old Home" and is the only house yet standing in Huntsville which belonged to any member of the Clay family. The original Clay homestead on Clinton Street became the site of Huntsville's first public high school.

In the early days Huntsville was notorious as a place of high prices. This was due chiefly to the difficulties of transportation, which made bulky goods, such as furniture, expensive. On other goods the selection was somewhat limited in a town the size of Huntsville. Consequently, everyone who journeyed to the east was laden with a multitude of orders from family and neighbors for all kinds of purchases. Susanna's comments to her husband are typical, "You wish me to mention the kind of dress and bonnet I should like to have? One consideration alone, would induce me to choose any—The *wish expressed by you* that I should I am willing to trust your judgement, all I care for is that the dress should last well, and that you should not give too much for it— . . . We are in want of table cloths; sheets, &c. . . . If you can get four (no, two will do), cloth table covers at four or five dollars apiece it would be as well— . . . Think of what in your judgment we want, that your means would justify you in the purchase of I will try and be content under any circumstances."[24] Despite the panic conditions of 1837, Clement, Sr., expended $350.00 on new furniture. The items included a "Spring & cushion seat sofa, Spring seat lounge," a dozen mahogany chairs and a dozen cane-seat chairs, a "Marble top center table," and two dining tables.

Two dining tables were needed because, like most southern households of the nineteenth century, Clement Clay's roof sheltered a large assortment of relatives in addition to his own family. The death of John Withers, in 1826, brought at least four of Susanna's young brothers and sisters under her care and into her household. These four, Ann Eliza Ward, Mary Dorothy, Jones Mitchell, and Maria Herbert Withers were scarcely grown and married before Susanna had the care of two nieces, Susanna Claiborne Clay Withers and Catherine Hawkins Withers, daughters of her brother, William F. Withers.

Clement Clay gave little thought to the cost of his large household until he was beset by hard times. Then Clement, Sr., was with "sincere reluctance" forced to ask his brother-in-law for aid, when he wrote, "Adverse circumstances have been pressing . . . with more severity. . . . My debts & liabilities have accumulated, until I have no alternative, but to submit to legal coercion, or sell

24 Susanna Clay to Clay, Sr., Jan. 24, 1833, James Green to Clay, Sr., Dec. 16, 1837, Clay MSS.

property at a sacrifice. I prefer the latter; and have been . . . advertising my old place for sale . . . without any prospect of success. I would even sell my new place, but have no idea that I could sell it for half its value in cash. The consequence will be that I must sell a large number of negroes, to extricate myself from my embarrassment. Under such circumstances, I must endeavour to curtail my expenses . . . & practice a most rigid economy. Amongst other measures to reduce my expenditures, I owe it to myself and family to call upon you to relieve me from the expenses of your two daughters; at least, so far as regards *education & clothing*. I do not regard their subsistence as of any consequence, but to be compelled to pay out money, when it must be raised by a sacrifice of property, you must yourself agree, would be unreasonable. . . . I shall expect you to advance the amount of Susanna's tuition and clothing for the ensuing year—say one hundred dollars—by the 5th of next month." William F. Withers replied that he had just lost all his property by forced sale, but he promised to send money as soon as he could collect from those who owed him.

Indeed, the Clays had been feeling the pressure of hard times for several years. "Business here is dull," wrote Clement, Jr., to his father in 1841. "There is but little suing done." "Your note for $3000 . . . falls due on the 16th inst. . . . needless to say . . . Uncle A.[ugustine] & I have not the means of paying it." The only way to meet it, Clement, Jr., continued, was to "draw a bill on Fearne, Donegan & Co., of New Orleans . . . payable 6 months from date with interest . . . to save you from a protest."[25]

In bad times or good the Clay household had its share of cultural agencies. Clement, Sr., received a Washington newspaper as well as the local and state journals. As lawyers the four Clay men accumulated a large and valuable legal library, which was partially dispersed and destroyed when Union forces occupied their law office from 1863 to 1866. The Clay women subscribed to the fashion magazines and bought the best sellers and the popular songs, and for the men, a sporting journal was indispensable in that horseracing town.

This was how the Clays lived, surrounded by relatives, served

25 Clay, Jr., to Clay, Sr., July 27, Aug. 10, 1841, Clay, Sr., to William F. Withers, Sept. 16, 1843, Clay MSS.

by numerous Negroes, content with the luxurious discomfort so typical of the South. Here in Huntsville, Susanna Clay filled her days with scolding idle Negroes, making the rounds of kitchen, smokehouse, and garden, supervising all that went on, and worrying over finances or some other current anxiety. Here the daughters-in-law dabbled at housekeeping, did their fine sewing, played the piano, followed the fashions, attended the local parties, and exchanged the town's gossip with neighbors and relatives.

6

Young Clement Tries Politics

POLITICAL EVENTS of 1840 had given Alabama Democrats a severe fright. The general-ticket system they hastened to adopt to guarantee their supremacy in the state in turn so aroused the Whigs that politics remained at fever pitch for some time. In this heated atmosphere, Clement Claiborne Clay launched his political career. He began as junior editor of the Huntsville *Democrat,* a temporary appointment for the duration of the campaign of 1841.[1] This post shortly presented developments not altogether anticipated, the details of which Clement, Jr., related to his father.

"I had a small fight, on an empty stomach, this morning about 5½ Oclock. . . . I walked up to my office before breakfast—met a boy with some plums—bo't some. . . . I had the last one in my mouth when I saw the redoubtable champion, of ink-stand memory, Wm. H. Smith, meeting me, with a stick in his hand. . . . I dropped the plum stone & peell [*sic*] in my hand, to throw on the ground. Smith, approaching me . . . tho't (he says) I had spit a quid of tobacco in my hand, to throw into his face. He drew back his stick, in a menacing attitude. I rushed at him, unarmed, & struck him with my fist, about the same time that he struck me with his stick on my left arm. I ran my left hand in his hair, & had drawn the blood from his nose & face & blued one of his eyes, when his father ran up behind me, . . . seized me by the neck & pulled me back. A man named Bryant, ran between us. . . . Between them they pulled me to the ground; but I bro't Billy down too & gave him several kicks, before they succeeded in disengaging my hand from his hair. . . . Immediately after our separation, I went over to Uncle Augustine's store— He & I armed ourselves & started across the square. When I got within some fifty steps of Smith . . . he retreated to the Advocate Office, & went up stairs. I went to the door & dared him to come out. He came to the head of the stairs, presented a loaded musket & kocked [sic] it. I stood before the door & denounced him as a coward, scoundrel & assassin; but he neither shot nor came out. . . . He has not shown his face since . . . &, I presume the affair will end at this."[2]

Shortly thereafter, a few of his friends urged young Clement to be a candidate for the legislature. But Clement felt "constrained by many reasons . . . to decline running," chief of which was almost certain defeat. The August elections were satisfying to the Clays and to Democrats generally. Benjamin Fitzpatrick, Democrat, won the governorship by a large majority over his opponent, James White McClung. Clement, Jr., reported to his father that "McClung is the worst beaten man ever seen in this state, save Gen. Parsons." McClung complained of *"persecutions,"* continued Clement, Jr., "especially of the Huntsville Democrat, & of its *'Junior Editors'*—who had harassed him. . . . If he had called me by name . . . as the Editor, it would have made me, at least, a hundred friends." The Democrats, summarized Clement, "have gained two members in Mobile & two in Sumter—& the Legislature will be Democratic by a greater majority than at its last session.— The General Ticket, however, will be defeated. . . . It has not gotten the support of the entire party anywhere."

In the spring of 1842 popular opinion was "unanimously disposed to elect Gov. Clay a member of the next Legislature" in order to cope with the "crisis . . . in regard to the monetary institutions of our State." This vote of confidence aroused in the elder Clay "no ordinary emotions" and demanded his "most profound acknowledgements," wherein he declined to be a candidate,

1 At this time the Alabama legislature met annually and its members were elected annually in August. Members of Congress were elected in the August just preceding their assumption of seats in that body in December.
2 Clay, Jr., to Clay, Sr., June 29, 1841, Clay MSS.

but set forth his views on the bank situation. Democratic eyes then fell upon young Clement, who now felt "bound to yield to the wishes of my friends and to tender my services to the people of Madison," and accordingly stated his "principles," concerned chiefly with the bank question.[3]

In August, C. C. Clay, Jr., won his first election, and he took his seat in the lower house of Alabama's legislature on December 5, 1842. Young Clement was "surprized to find a far better tone of moral feeling prevailing on this floor . . . [than he] had antici-pated. I feel some pride," he continued, "in being a member of this body—containing, as it does, a great amount of natural talent, & statesman-like ability. And I feel some constraint in trespassing on the attention of so grave and learned a body. Yet, I have made two or three little speeches, which have been received with con-siderable eclat."[4]

Before attacking the bank question, Democrats of the legislature took the precaution of concocting another scheme to insure party supremacy. Clement, Jr., explained it to his mother: "We have a subject before this House, which opens a fine field for debate, and on which I propose making a speech, on the 2nd Jany next. . . . The question is, shall our State be divided into Districts for our seven representatives on the basis of a mixed population (as heretofore . . .) or on the White Basis? I am firmly convinced," he continued, "that the latter is the true basis, & shall endeavor to make some showing in its behalf." The question was entirely sectional. North Alabama and the hill counties, with large white populations, favored the white basis; South Alabama and the Black Belt cried out against this scheme to diminish their repre-sentation and influence. The Democrats pushed through their white-basis bill by 64-38 in the house and 15-13 in the senate. The defeated Whigs, loud in their anger, entered on the legis-lative journal a forthright protest, declaring the white basis a "direct violation" of the Constitution and an "alarming and dangerous innovation" that "tends to encourage [the abolitionists] in their wicked schemes," while it gives "to the northern part of

---

3 Clay, Jr., to Clay, Sr., Aug. 4, 10, 1841, Clay MSS; Huntsville *Democrat*, May 14, 28, June 4, 11, 18, 1842.
    4 Clay, Jr., to Susanna Clay, Dec. 23, 1842, Clay MSS; Huntsville *Democrat*, Aug. 13, 1842.

the State an undue advantage over the south in electing members to congress,—and to the dominant political party . . . an equally unjust advantage over those who differ with them."[5]

Alabama's banking experience had been uniformly unhappy. Disillusioned with private banking after the crash of 1819, the people of Alabama turned to state banking to solve their problems. On December 20, 1823, the legislature had chartered a state bank (at Tuscaloosa) to be operated entirely with state funds. Between 1832 and 1835 branch banks were opened at Mobile, Montgomery, Decatur, and Huntsville. The charters ran until 1845, and the president and directors were elected annually by the legislature. During its early years, the bank was well managed, but the inflation and speculation of the early 1830's encouraged reckless operation, while the method of choosing the bank's officers led to a fatal injection of politics and resulted in wholesale bribery and liberal bank accommodations to legislators. Then in 1836 the legislature abolished taxation and essayed to operate the state government from bank profits. Just when this utopian scheme seemed about to succeed, the collapse of 1837 destroyed the flimsy structure.

Investigation revealed that legislators owed staggering sums to the bank. One reckless Whig borrower was involved to the extent of $120,436, and an equally notorious Democrat owed $46,049. Whig indebtedness totaled $572,596, and Democrats trailed with a mere $149,312. Many men of both parties, however, were responsible for large additional sums as sureties for their constituents. In the light of these revelations, John A. Campbell and his bank committee recommended the liquidation of those banks unable to resume specie payment, while those that "held out the prospect of resumption, should for a time, be tolerated but disabled from doing further harm by an increase of their debts in the community." To this latter category belonged the Huntsville and Montgomery branches, but those at Mobile and Decatur were to be liquidated. As debate continued, however, opposition snowballed until the legislature was ready to abolish the entire banking system. "We are," wrote Clement, Jr., "in a high fever

5 Clay, Jr., to Susanna Clay, Dec. 23, 1842, Clay MSS; Ala. Leg., *HJ*, pp. 396ff, Feb. 8, 1843; Mobile *Register and Journal*, Dec. 27, 1842.

about the banks still, &, I seriously apprehend, we will wind up one & all. A bitter spirit of hostility vs. them prevails."[6]

In Huntsville, "a public meeting, without distinction of party, at which Gov. C. C. Clay presided" urged the legislature to spare the Huntsville branch. But it was all in vain, as Clement, Jr., informed his father. "The fate of the banks is sealed irrevocably . . . the House has passed the bill to wind up the Huntsville bank. . . . The . . . resolutions of your meeting were read to the house, without effect. Some remarks were made by McClung and myself, against the passage of the bill, but the house, impatient for the sacrifice, did not listen to or heed us." Speaker John Erwin, too, shook his head over the legislature, which "ought to have . . . pursued a more moderate and prudent course . . . but temperate counsel was wholly disregarded—destruction and prostration were the paramount and ruling objects." "We shall have miserably hard times this coming year," predicted Erwin.[7]

This session saw a reconciliation of the Clays and Charles McLemore, who had in 1841 so bitterly denounced C. C. Clay's comments when he resigned as United States senator. Detailing to his father the whole affair, Clement, Jr., explained how "Yancey came to me & said that McLemore . . . wished to have the difference between us amicably settled—that he had wronged you he acknowledged &c. Yancey insisted that we should be bro't together but I told him, that if McL. would come to me, before some of my friends, I would make up with him on his retracting the offensive remarks." Meantime, Clement, Jr., had, McLemore complained, referred to him as the *"Member from Chambers"* and to another as "the gentleman from Autauga," and "asked if it was done to wound his feelings?—" At this point, said Clement, Jr., "I rose & replied, that 'notwithstanding the relations between the gentleman & myself, . . . I was unconscious of making such a distinction [and if done] . . . it was not done to assail the feelings of the gentleman. . . . That I was above such baseness.—'

6 Clay, Jr., to Clay, Sr., Jan. 18, 1843, Clay MSS; Ala. Leg., *HJ*, pp. 93-99, Dec. 19, 1842; Huntsville *Democrat*, Dec. 17, 1842; William Orlando Scroggs, "Pioneer Banking in Alabama," in *Facts and Factors in Economic History: Articles by Former Students of Edwin Francis Gay* (Cambridge, Mass., 1932), 405-15.
7 Clay, Jr., to Clay, Sr., Jan. 30, Feb. 3, 1843, Clay MSS; John Erwin to Henry Watson, Jr., Feb. 10, 1843, Henry Watson, Jr., to Henry Watson, Sr., Feb. 24, 1843, Henry Watson MSS; Mobile *Register and Journal*, Feb. 2, 1843; Huntsville *Democrat*, Jan. 28, Feb. 4, 1843.

So soon as I sat down, McL. rose & said, 'that he was satisfied.
. . . That, it was generally known . . . he had used some abusive
remarks in relation to the gentleman's father, & that the gentleman
had never spoken to him, (McL) for which he did not blame him.—
That those remarks of last winter, were the ebullition of sudden
& violent party feeling, which he had long regretted, & did still
regret. . . . I replied to him, 'that his magnanimity was equal
to his gallantry of spirit. That I should cherish the recollection of
his noble conduct, & that, henceforth, altho' politically enemies,
we should be personally friends.'— He met me half-way, & we
shook hands.— The house applauded us very long & loudly. In a
private interview he told me he would have withdrawn his abusive
remarks during last session, if he had not been threatened with
personal violence from *me,* by indiscreet friends of mine. I believe
he is a magnanimous man, & that he was sincere in all he said."[8]

Clement, Sr.'s, temporary appointment in the summer of 1843
as a justice of the Alabama supreme court was a great financial
blessing, for the salary of "$2250 per annum," noted young
Clement, "is more *money* than our practice will yield him; . . .
he will have to labor less, will be more at liesure [*sic*], can tend to
his plantation better, & relieve himself more readily of his debts.
For these reasons, I am happy to submit to the pecuniary sacrifice
I must expect from a decline of my professional business." Clement, Jr., now deprived of his father's active partnership in their
law practice, was determined to "stand alone, unaided, & dependent on my sole effort." In view of his precarious financial
outlook, he was "declining a call . . . to run for the Legislature,
being fully resolved to labor at my oars faithfully & constantly,
till I can get off the shoals of debt on which I am stranded."
Early in 1844 he extended his field of legal activity by obtaining
a license to "practise as a Counsellor and Attorney at Law and
Solicitor in Chancery in any of the Courts of Law and Equity
of this State."[9]

So 1843 merged into 1844, a presidential election year, when
an aspiring young politician must certainly devote himself to
politics. Activities got under way on March 15, 1844, when young

8 Clay, Jr., to Clay, Sr., Jan. 18, 1843, Clay, Jr., to Virginia Tunstall, Jan. 12,
1843, Clay MSS.
9 Clay, Jr., to J. W. Clay, July 10, 1843, license to C. C. Clay, Jr., Jan. 13, 1844,
Clay MSS; Huntsville *Democrat,* July 13, 1843.

Clement, at a dinner honoring Andrew Jackson's birthday, lauded "the Old Hero . . . with a zeal and feeling rarely equalled by speakers of maturer age." A month later Clement became "assistant editor of the *Democrat,* for the next eight months." In May, both Clement and his father were active in forming the Madison County Democratic Association. After their defeat in 1840, Democrats were now doubly resolved to be everywhere alert and busy. Other local and county meetings kept the Clays active throughout the summer. Late in July, C. C. Clay, Jr., again became a candidate for the legislature.[10]

The big event of the summer, however, was the "Great National Mass Convention" at Nashville on August 15 and 16, 1844. Leading Democrats from all parts of the country were present, but naturally Tennessee, Alabama, and Kentucky had the largest representations. The Clays both attended. Nashville was filled to overflowing with visitors, who "repaired to the Encampment of the People, and there pitched their tents . . . [at] Camp Hickory, . . . in a large umbrageous grove." Cave Johnson presided over the assemblage, and Lewis Cass of Michigan and Gansevoort Melville (younger brother of Herman Melville) of New York were the leading speakers. "There were," the local press explained, "three several stands erected, at suitable distances from each other, and there was continued speaking from each during the day . . . [by] Governor Clay of Alabama, Judge Bowlin of Missouri . . . Col. N. Terry, the Speaker of the Alabama Senate; the Hon E Hise of Kentucky; Judge J. C. Thompson, of Alabama," and many others. "There were," continued the account, "two miles of table on which the GREAT DINNER was served . . . the utmost good order prevailed. It is, true that shout after shout, huzza after huzza . . . continually rent the air, but there was no disorder or confusion, even at the tables. . . . No spiritous liquors of any kind were permitted to be publicly brought on the ground. . . . Not the slightest sign of intoxication was seen. . . . Such was the regulation of the People's Encampment at Camp Hickory."[11]

As the campaign intensified in its final weeks, Polk called his

10 Huntsville *Democrat,* March 20, 29, April 10, 17, May 8, June 5, 12, 26, July 31, 1844.
11 Nashville *Union,* Aug. 6, 17, 1844; McCormac, *Polk,* 274-76.

old friend into service in Tennessee. Responding to this call, Clement, Sr., on October 14 set off for Winchester, Tennessee, where, as he reported to Polk, "The day was bad . . . yet I had a pretty good audience . . . and made an address of more than two hours." At the next town "there was a glorious 'turnout' . . . from two to three thousand voters & 500 ladies. The day was fine and I made an address of 2½ to 3 hours before dinner —after dinner we had two other speakers—and, at night, a splendid exhibition of transparencies, & several other speeches. . . . I never saw more enthusiasm." On October 22, Nathaniel Terry and George Smith Houston joined Clay, and together they held several joint meetings with Whig campaigners E. H. Foster and R. L. Caruthers. At Pulaski and Lawrenceburg the two Whigs would not give "equal or half equal terms," but finally agreed to let Clay speak first, to be followed by Foster. "Pursuant to this agreement," continued Clay, "I commenced at 12 & spoke till 2 o'clock, on the Bank, the Tariff, & Texas—and was followed by Foster in a speech of 2 hours & 25 minutes. . . . the audience was almost entirely *Whig*—they were respectful to me, but applauded F. very much."

Clay and Houston were both on hand for "the great mass-meeting" at Lawrenceburg on October 25. From there Clay was willing to go wherever "most good can be done." So Polk sent him at the last minute to Chapel Hill and Cedar Springs, where "Whig orators . . . misrepresented my votes on the *Pension Bill*. . . . I must ask you to correct the misrepresentation." Even Clement, Jr., was drafted into service for "meetings in Lincoln & some adjoining counties." Young Clement, urged his father, must "attend both. Our Tennessee friends desire it—and, as he has made no speeches in this state, it would be well for him to do it. A great struggle is going on all over the country—in Tennessee it is tremendous— [and] every man who helps, ought, & I think will be remembered." In the view of one Alabama Democrat, Clay's reward should be the cabinet post of postmaster general. Though he received no appointment of any sort in Polk's administration, Clement Clay, Sr., was unfeignedly happy at his friend's success. "Altho'," Clay wrote to Polk, "I never entertained a serious doubt of your election . . . yet, when we take into view the reckless character of the party we had to contend with, and the unscrupulous means resorted to by them, . . . we may regard it as a most glorious victory—second . . . only . . . to the triumph of Jefferson." In a more personal vein, he invited the Polks "to pay us a visit of a few days, before your departure for Washington. It would be a sort of retirement from the bustle and turmoils, by which you have been surrounded for the last six months." A harassed President-elect, however, could find no time to accept this offer from an old friend.[12]

Election excitement had scarcely subsided when Clement and Virginia Clay and Maria Withers set off for Tuscaloosa by stage. Virginia reported a successful journey "with the exception of Maria's feet, which were awfully swollen . . . caused by sitting still so long—she did not get out of the stage to walk one step from Huntsville here— . . . Dan'l B. Turner I trust I have travelled with for my last time," Virginia continued. "He ate up all our fruit cake, & sat on either my lap or Maria's full one third of the way. Colo. McClung reposed his fat sides in like manner." After one night at a hotel, the Clays went to stay with Virginia's relatives, the Colliers. *"The winter* promises to be very gay," chattered Virginia, "the town is overflowing with strangers, and a great deal of visiting. To be in the parlour you might imagine me Miss T. again ! !" They attended many social functions and met Dixon H. Lewis, the successful candidate for United States senator, whose huge size and lack of grooming led Virginia to remark that "he offended more senses than one!"[13]

The legislative session opened on December 2, 1844, when "The members were . . . sworn collectively, all standing, with their right hands raised, as customary." Clay was appointed to the committees on internal improvements and on public printing, and to a select joint senate and house committee to examine the state bank and its branches. This committee reported the net liabilities of the state at more than fourteen million dollars, of which about half was thought recoverable from the banks, while over six millions were written off as bad. The committee accord-

12 J. K. Polk to Clay, Sr., Oct. 15, 29, Dec. 16, 1844, Clay, Sr., to Susanna Clay, Oct. 23, 1844, Clay MSS; Clay, Sr., to D. G. Eastman, Oct. 12, 1844, N. Y. Hist. Soc. MSS; Clay, Sr., to Polk, Oct. 23, Nov. 22, 1844, Clay, Jr., to Polk, Oct. 22, 1844, Thomas Martin to Polk, Oct. 23, 1844, David Hubbard to J. H. Thomas, Nov. 18, 1844, J. K. Polk MSS, vols. 61, 64, 65.
13 Virginia Clay to Susanna Clay, Dec., 1844, Clay MSS.

ingly recommended collection of one-half the debts due the banks
before October 1, 1846, and the remainder within another year.
Collections to date had yielded $600,000 less than the amount
anticipated; hence this recommendation for more time. Another
proposed economy would concentrate bank business in the hands
of a cashier and attorney at each branch, thus dispensing with
presidents and directors.[14]

Both these recommendations went unheeded. A determined
legislature passed the bill requiring payment of one-third of the
debt on June 1, 1845, in spite of vehement protest by Clay and
his North Alabama colleagues that "it is impossible to raise, so
hastily, the large amount of money required." Clay was equally
unsuccessful with the bill to vest selection of bank officials in the
governor, thus removing from "the Legislature the responsibility
of elections . . . [a] power . . . shamefully abused . . . greatly
to the detriment of the State and the discredit of our banks." He
pointed up this indictment by revealing how the president of the
Huntsville bank had favored large debtors by permitting them to
pay their bank debts in depreciated state bonds, and giving one
of them an 8 percent premium besides, thus permitting "a speculation in this case" of about $28,000. "Was this not," asked Clay,
"a breach of the trust . . . and a violation of the public faith?
. . . I know that in exposing his course to censure I must incur
his enmity, and that of his friends, and, perhaps, a relentless spirit
of revenge: but as the representative of a people, whose interests
are committed to his guardianship, I have felt it my duty, when
a proper occasion occurred, to bring before the house, the evidences of his abuse of official power."

In behalf of internal improvements Clement exerted his best
efforts to assign the "two per cent fund" to railroad construction.
He argued eloquently that forty miles of rail between the Tennessee and Coosa rivers would link North Alabama with navigable
waters leading to Mobile Bay. Thus Mobile need not fear that
North Alabama trade would be diverted to Charleston. Clement
rejoiced when the bill passed the house, dividing the fund between
the Montgomery and West Point and the Tennessee and Coosa

14 J. E. Saunders to G. S. Houston, Dec. 2, 1844, G. S. Houston MSS; Huntsville
Democrat, Dec. 11, 1844; Ala. Leg., HJ, pp. 26, 30, 190, 218-20, Dec. 4, 1844, Jan.
5, 13, 1845.

Railroad companies.[15] But many years were yet to pass before the Clays were able to travel over the railroads whose construction they so long and earnestly promoted.

Abolition, too, thrust its unwelcome presence into the deliberations of the legislature. Replying to a northern proposal to abolish the three-fifths clause by constitutional amendment, Alabama resolved "neither to relinquish this right on the request of one State, nor at the bidding of any greater number." Even worse was Massachusetts' sending of Charles Hoar to Charleston to defend Negro seamen. On this subject, Clement's father urged him to "introduce resolutions expressive of unqualified condemnation" and offering to cooperate with South Carolina "in any measure that may be deemed necessary to prevent such unholy interference with her internal police." The Alabama legislature adopted resolutions declaring that in this "insolent attempt to disturb her domestic tranquility . . . each State has a right to guard its citizens against . . . dangers. The right to exercise this power by a State is *higher and deeper than the Constitution*."[16]

Meanwhile, political activity was lively in North Alabama. The campaign for governor got under way early, and the Clays soon found themselves in the thick of the squabble. Among the several aspirants for that office were Nathaniel Terry, Reuben Chapman, and James White McClung, all of North Alabama and all friends of the Clays. While Terry's friends tried to maneuver the Madison County vote for their man, Philip Woodson, editor of the Huntsville *Democrat,* injected a new element by coming out editorially for Daniel Coleman, a judge and merchant of Athens. We "were astounded," wrote Withers Clay, at what "was written by Mr. Woodson, without consulting with father or myself and without our knowledge or connivance or approbation." C. C. Clay, Sr., tried to remain neutral, take no part *"for, or against Terry, McClung, or Chapman,"* and not "engage in a scuffle . . . as to what friend should get the nomination."

Local political meetings throughout the spring of 1845 developed considerable opposition to Terry, who "was handled,

15 Clay, Jr., to J. W. Clay, Jan. 8, 1845, Clay MSS; Clay Scrapbooks, VI, 11, 113, Dec. 31, 1844, Jan. 19, 1845; Ala. Leg., *HJ,* p. 173, Jan. 2, 1845; Huntsville *Democrat,* Jan. 8, 22, Feb. 5, April 16, 1845; Tuscaloosa *Independent Monitor,* Jan. 15, 1845; Mobile *Register and Journal,* Jan. 6, 7, 1845.
16 J. W. Clay to Clay, Jr., Dec. 10, 1844, Clay MSS; Ala. Leg., *HJ,* pp. 202-204, Jan. 7, 1845.

emphatically, without gloves." Because of his "large bank indebtedness" and "his want of dignity & mental & moral culture," he was "very obnoxious to a large portion of the democracy." At the state convention in Tuscaloosa, Terry's friends nominated him and adjourned before the arrival of southern delegates whose boat from Mobile was delayed. This summary action led Joshua Lanier Martin to become the opposing candidate. The contest split both parties; Whigs and Democrats partial to the bank voted for Terry, while most of those anxious for real bank reform voted for and elected Martin by a majority of five thousand. Terry's defeat only made him more angry with the Clays, who, he claimed, appeared *"more distant* than heretofore." A wordy and acrimonious correspondence ensued, in which Terry declared that "the Clay influence in Madison . . . had caused him to lose 300 votes," that Clay had "openly voted for him but secretly opposed him." To these and other charges, Clement, Sr., replied that "I wrote no letter, during the canvass, . . . unfavorable to . . . Col. Terry, or with a view to injure him. . . . I made no untrue or unfriendly statement of Col. T.'s. Bank indebtedness. I did not 'endeavor to keep my Jackson overseer from voting for him.' . . . But, I do not . . . pretend to be the warm or active friend of Col. T's. election." The elaborate charges and countercharges were finally resolved without any physical violence, and the incident ended in chilly neutrality, as Clement, Jr., indicated: "I have met Terry once or twice, &, as he seemed disinclined to speak, I did not approach him, & we have not interchanged any salutations."[17]

"I do not, and never did, owe any Bank, as principal; and do not now owe any Bank as security, endorser, or otherwise," declared Clement Clay, Jr., and continued, "I am . . . opposed to the policy of receiving State bonds at par for good debts due the Banks. . . . I am opposed to the practice . . . of making small debtors pay the full amount of their curtailments, and permitting the large debtors to extend by paying much less." On this platform he was returned to the legislature in the August elections of 1845.

A month later, Clement, Jr., delivered Huntsville's eulogy to

17 J. W. Clay to Clay, Jr., Dec. 16, 1844, Jan. 1, 1844 [i.e., 1845], April 11, 1845, Clay, Sr., to Clay, Jr., Dec. 28, 1844, Clay, Jr., to Clay, Sr., Aug. 10, 1845, Jan. 21, 1846, Clay MSS; Henry Goldthwaite to William Phineas Browne, June 15, 1845, William Phineas Browne MSS; Huntsville *Democrat*, Jan. 1, Oct. 22, 1845.

Andrew Jackson. He filled it with that "romantic elaboration" which characterized his youthful oratory. No less florid was the *Democrat's* editorial comment. "Mr. Clay, besides the many appropriate classical allusions and references and sublime metaphors, embodied within the historical facts of his address, beautiful and fragrant thoughts, equally as honorable to his own mind, as they were merited by the deceased of whom he spoke."[18]

The Clays were no more than settled in Tuscaloosa for the legislative session, when Virginia came down with a very severe attack of pneumonia. Lawson, who happened to be in Tuscaloosa, reported to the family that after a week she was still so ill that "the Doctors . . . found it necessary to cup and blister her." Four days later he wrote that "Brother Clement and myself alternate during the night in watching her," and that morning they had sent to Greene County for Dr. Thomas Withers. On December 22, two weeks after the beginning of her illness, Clement was able to write, "I am happy to inform you, that Va. is convalescing & regarded by her physicians out of danger. Her situation, from the beginning of her attack till saturday morning last was very critical, indeed, at one time tho't to be desperate. . . . I have been obliged, by advice of the physicians & my own feelings, to remain constantly with Va. since tuesday evening last; & have not attended any sessions of the house." After Lawson returned home, he reported to Virginia the effect of her illness in Huntsville: "A great revolution has been effected in our family: we have prayers morning and night and father always asks a blessing at meals! ! ! Your illness was regarded with great solicitude and anxiety by everyone in the family. . . . Prayers were offered in each of the churches for your recovery . . . indeed, your illness produced quite a sensation."[19]

"It has been said to yr. credit," Clement, Jr., later wrote to Virginia, "that you came nr. losing yr. life in electioneering with members for me." Clement was, at this session, one of four candidates for judge of the Madison County court. Reporting to his father on the situation, Lawson wrote, "Bradford, with Hubbard's assistance . . . will run well on the *first ballot*. . . . We think

---

18 Clay Scrapbooks, VI, 117-19; Huntsville *Democrat*, July 23, Sept. 10, 1845.
19 H. L. Clay to Susanna Clay, Dec. 15, 1845, H. L. Clay to Clay, Sr., Dec. 19, 1845, Clay, Jr., to Clay, Sr., Dec. 22, 1845, H. L. Clay to Virginia Clay, Jan. 2, 1846, Clay MSS.

upon having made more than one calculation, with the names of the members before us, that bro. C. will get on the first ballot 58 or 60 votes, Acklen and Bradford will divide the remaining number. Thompson will not make any *run*. . . . Upon the second ballot, it is expected . . . that bro. C. will get 75-85 votes wh . . . will decide the matter." Lawson and Clement's calculations were not quite correct, for it required four ballots to elect Clement Clay to the Madison County judgeship. This result was arrived at after considerable vote trading, and in part through the influence of Clay, Sr.'s former rival, Judge Henry B. Goldthwaite, who, Lawson reported, "spoke of brother C. as a man of fine talent and legal acquirements and as the choice of the people of Madison. Thus, assistance comes from a quarter we had least of all anticipated!"[20]

Clay found himself busy throughout the session. As chairman of the committee on the state bank and branches, he made a detailed report and introduced a bill "to close the affairs of the Banks, and to apply their assets to the payment of the public debt." This bill would economize bank operations by reducing the number of officials at each branch, by placing the whole system in the hands of three commissioners, and by concentrating operations as far as possible in Tuscaloosa. After extensive debate in both houses, the bill finally passed on February 3, 1846. The three commissioners appointed to wind up the banks were Benjamin Fitzpatrick, Francis Strother Lyon, and William Cooper. When Fitzpatrick declined, C. C. Clay, Sr., was appointed "at a salary of $2500." This arrangement continued for a year, when Francis S. Lyon became sole commissioner and for the next seven years gave outstanding service to the state. At the end of that time "the banks were wound up, their bills were at par and the credit of the State was fully reestablished."[21]

Clement's favorite bill to appropriate the "two per cent fund" to railroad construction, passed the house twice at this session and was as often rejected by the senate. "So you see," wrote the exasperated Clement, "this important measure is finally lost by the strange, unreasonable and impracticable opposition of a

[20] H. L. Clay to Clay, Sr., Dec. 19, 1845, Clay Jr., to Virginia Clay, Feb. 15, 1846, Clay MSS; Ala. Leg., *HJ*, pp. 85-87, Dec. 15, 1845.
[21] Clay, Jr., to Virginia Clay, March 8, 1846, Clay MSS; Ala. Leg., *HJ*, pp. 190-94, 442f, Jan. 5, Feb. 3, 1846; Huntsville *Democrat*, Jan. 21, Feb. 11, March 4, 1846.

majority of the Senate." Lawson's account of his journey home
by stagecoach pointedly illustrates North Alabama's anxiety for
improved communications: "I was stalled until 4 o'clock within
8 miles of Tuskaloosa [sic], the next day was turned over by
the carelessness of the driver, . . . and the third day the bolt pin
broke at the Tennessee river and the forewheel of the coach
ran into the river. No one was in the stage and no damage
done. We reached Huntsville at 3¼ o'clock the next morning!"[22]

Communication was the main factor in the big question of the
session, namely "removal." Popular vote in the previous election
had authorized amendment of the constitution to make legislative
sessions biennial and to remove the capital to a more convenient
location. "So long as Tuscaloosa is the Capital, we cannot indulge
a well founded hope of any easy communication between North
& South Ala." Representatives from the western side of the state
"always will oppose every measure calculated to open a market
for our produce & bring us closer to Mobile. . . . The citizens
of East & South seem to sympathize with us & to extend us the
hand of fellowship," commented Clement.

The more easily to carry both "removal" and biennial sessions,
a few wily legislators contrived to join both questions in a kind of
siamese-twin resolution which, the speaker ruled, could not be
divided. This, remarked an observer, "created a good deal of
fluttering" and some bitter opposition; nevertheless, the questions
remained in this form and caused Clement and the Madison
County delegation no little vexation, for, said Clement, "vote as
I may, either for or against the resolutions, I shall not express the
will of my constituents. A large majority voted against removal,
a still larger majority voted for biennial sessions." When the
amendments were adopted, Clement and his colleagues "voted
against the resolutions; believing that in forcing both resolutions
conjointly through the Legislature, the majority for removal were
doing violence to the right of the minority, [and] establishing a
bad precedent." With "removal" carried, excitement rose to fever
pitch over which town should be chosen for the new capital. "The
Removal question," wrote Clement, "is playing havoc with men's
virtue— High bids are offered for removal votes, as I know by

22 H. L. Clay to Virginia Clay, Jan. 2, 1846, Clay MSS; Ala. Leg., *HJ*, pp. 257f,
Jan. 16, 1846; Huntsville *Democrat*, Jan. 21, 28, Feb. 4, 1846.

intimations as broad as dared be made to me, &, it is tho't *Winston* (!!) & possibly other senators are in market. He will vote for removal for a seat in *U. S. Senate,* &, if his vote is needed, his price may be paid!" With eight towns in nomination, it required fifteen ballots to make Montgomery the new capital.[23]

The session closed on February 5, 1846, and Clement shortly returned to Huntsville, leaving Virginia in South Alabama, where she was convalescing from her illness. But he plied her with constant admonitions: "Be prudent, my dearest. . . . You are so pretty & fascinating, that I fear some fine looking fellow will forget you are a married woman & make love to you. . . . Don't expose yourself to night air, in thin slippers, silk stockings, bare arms & neck. . . . I am truly rejoiced to learn that you are taking some exercise, daily. . . . And I do most fervently beseech you to loosen your dresses. . . . I am not fond of wasp waists. . . . And I fondly trust that when you return, you will weigh 140 lbs. . . . It is now my weight, but I am aspiring to 160 lbs. . . . I have ceased using tobacco in every shape, for some time past, & am proving the good effects of it—"

"I am getting on tolerably well, I trust, with the *ermine,*" Clement wrote as he settled down to his new duties as judge of the Madison County court. The remuneration of this office depended on fees which, he estimated, would amount to "$1500 per annum." "With my practice," he explained to Virginia, "& the hire of your negroes & the rent of my office it will yield at least $2500 a year,—a very handsome income for people of moderate desires. I find, too, that the Office will not prove so laborious or irksome as has been commonly supposed; by method, system & order, it will only occupy about one day in the week of my time."

This left him sufficient time to pursue his own practice, such as he detailed in an account of a journey to the Marshall County court, where, "Being on 'my *own hook,*' . . . unpropped by father . . . I was . . . in search of . . . business. I am happy to say that I took notes . . . to the amount of one hundred dollars. I know this is little in comparison with the business of many old lawyers, but it augurs that I may increase by dint of industry & energy in making a support by my profession." That

[23] Clay, Jr., to Clay, Sr., Dec. 22, 1845, Jan. 9, 1846, Clay MSS; W. P. Browne to Thaddeus Sanford, Dec. 11, 1845, W. P. Browne MSS; Ala. Leg., *HJ,* pp. 368-79, Jan. 28, 1846; Huntsville *Democrat,* Jan. 7, 14, Feb. 4, 1846.

summer Clement and his father had the satisfaction of winning
two cases in the Alabama supreme court, which would yield fees
of $150 or $200. Competition in the legal profession was sharp,
however, as Clement noted a few years later when he wrote, "Jim
Robinson . . . has formed a partnership (!) with Egbert Jones.
. . . He is a good lawyer & will, with Brickell, keep us on the
strain constantly to keep up."[24]

Despite a propitious beginning, Clement's judicial career was
not entirely smooth, for in the summer of 1847, M. A. King, a
candidate for the legislature, campaigned against the high fees in
orphans' court. Clement declared that he had never charged fees
in excess of what the law allowed and that he often remitted
fees in the case of small estates, where, he admitted, the law
should be revised. His income of $1600 from fees was not too
high, he argued, "especially when compared with the labors"
involving "the interests of several hundred persons," the auditing
of involved accounts, and the writing of decrees and judgments.
"Altogether," concluded Clement, "it is a very laborious and
highly responsible office." The next legislature revised the county-
court system in an act which reduced fees and required judges to
be in their offices daily from nine to three, thereby restricting
their legal practice to a single county. Consequently, Clay resigned in the spring of 1848. The local press agreed that "a man
of Judge Clay's character and talents could not be expected to
submit to such a sacrifice of interest or liberty."[25]

The rewards of his professional career thus far were not entirely
soul satisfying, as Clement indicated in a letter to his father,
"Since you left home two most important family events have
transpired,—you have attained your 57th yr & I my 30th! It is
a source of unmingled pain to me, to reflect, that having passed
half of my life,—probably, two thirds of it—I have achieved so
little to the credit of myself or family or to the substantial welfare
of my spiritual or temporal interests!— It is scarcely less painful to
think that you who have done so much to promote the temporal
honors & prosperity of your-self & family, & who now are approach-

24 Clay, Jr., to Virginia Clay, March 8, 20, April 9, 28, 1846, Clay, Sr., to Susanna
Clay and Clay, Jr., June 25, 1846, Clay, Jr., to H. L. Clay, May 28, 1852, Clay MSS.
25 Clay, Jr., to Clay, Sr., Oct. 31, Dec. 25, 1847, Clay MSS; Felix Grundy Norman
to G. S. Houston, Jan. 7, Feb. 10, 1848, Richard Wilde Walker to G. S. Houston,
Jan. 10, 1848, G. S. Houston MSS; Huntsville Democrat, Oct. 27, 1847, Feb. 16,
March 29, 1848.

ing the end of your earthly pilgrimage, are still laboring . . . &
denied . . . repose & quiet . . . peace, plenty & contentment
around your own fireside."

Nor was young Clement's vanity flattered when, in the summer
of 1847, some of his friends urged him to try for the seat in Congress which Reuben Chapman had just vacated upon becoming
candidate for governor. Clay declined, saying he was "not so vain
as to expect" election; furthermore, congressional aspirations in
one of his financial status would label him a "political adven-
turer, dependent on the precarious tenure of public office for his
living." "I will not voluntarily illustrate that character in my
own person," declared Clement.[26]

The approach of another presidential campaign brought Clay
again into political activity. He resumed his post as political
editor of the Huntsville *Democrat,* led the local meeting endorsing
Cass' nomination, and spoke at numerous mass meetings and
barbecues. The Democratic defeat in November, 1848, was
reflected in Alabama state politics, where almost unprecedented
turmoil existed. By tradition, one of Alabama's senators was
always chosen from the northern part of the state, while the other
always came from the southern section. When Senator Arthur
P. Bagby resigned in June, 1848, Governor Chapman broke the
precedent by appointing William R. King, a South Alabama man,
to fill the vacancy. And when Dixon Hall Lewis died on October
25, 1848, Chapman added insult to injury by selecting Benjamin
Fitzpatrick, another South Alabamian, to fill that vacancy. These
appointments "by our delectable Governor . . . have excited
very general disapprobation . . . indeed, . . . great *indignation*
is felt & expressed," C. C. Clay, Sr., declared.[27]

While this indignation smoldered, North Alabama's interest
turned once more to internal improvements. A convention of
fifteen states assembled in Memphis on October 23, 1849, for the
purpose of promoting a railroad to the Pacific. Clement Clay, Sr.,
and J. Withers Clay were among the large Alabama delegation at
the Commercial Hotel, where social activity vied with business.
Matthew Fontaine Maury was chosen president of the convention,

26 Clay, Jr., to Clay, Sr., Dec. 18, 1846, Burwell T. Pope to Clay, Jr., June 23,
1847, Clay MSS; Huntsville *Democrat,* June 23, 1847.
27 Clay, Sr., to G. S. Houston, July 19, 1848, Joseph A. S. Acklen to G. S. Houston,
Nov. 28, 1848, G. S. Houston MSS.

but most of the actual presiding fell to Clement Clay, first vice president, since he "had more parliamentary experience than any other Vice Pres^t." Following the convention proper, interested Tennessee and Alabama delegates continued their deliberations on the projected railroad through the Tennessee Valley. Through the efforts of Clement Clay and Thomas Fearn, these delegates voted to reassemble at Huntsville on November 26 to promote a railroad which would ultimately connect Memphis, Tuscumbia, and Huntsville with Rome, Georgia. This set off a real wave of railroad enthusiasm throughout North Alabama, and numerous local meetings to promote the cause took place early in November.

The Huntsville railroad convention opened on Monday, November 26, 1849, at the Methodist church, with Clement Clay, Sr., presiding over an assemblage of some 265 delegates from interested Tennessee and Alabama counties. They adopted a railroad charter to be presented to the Alabama legislature, a memorial asking an appropriation from the "three per cent fund" to aid in building the road, and opened subscriptions for stock in the Memphis and Charleston Railroad. Enthusiasm reached such a pitch that the corporation of Huntsville subscribed $50,000, while private subscriptions totalled $245,000. George P. Beirne and Robert Fearn led individual investors with $100,000 each. Clement Clay, Sr., signed for $5,000; Clement Clay, Jr., for $1,000; and Withers Clay, for $500. In May, 1850, a report-of-progress convention assembled at Tuscumbia, where C. C. Clay, Sr., presided in a "firm, able and impartial manner . . . [and] rebuked with warmth and indignation, the accusation that his county and town were partial to either side of the river." The secretaries reported that subscriptions in Alabama totaled $563,973, of which Madison County had contributed $298,550. Tennessee subscriptions amounted to $764,100, of which $500,000 was in Memphis thirty-year bonds.[28]

Thus after thirty years of effort, Clement Clay had the satisfaction of seeing a tangible beginning made toward improvement of communications for the Tennessee Valley. C. C. Clay, Jr., was one of a committee of thirteen appointed to present the charter to

28 J. W. Clay to Susanna Clay, Oct. 24, 1849, Clay MSS; *Minutes and Proceedings of the Memphis Convention, Assembled October 23, 1849* (Memphis, 1850), 1-24; Huntsville *Democrat*, Nov. 14, 28, Dec. 5, 1849, March 14, May 16, 1850; Huntsville *Southern Advocate*, Nov. 30, 1849.

the state legislature. The several members of this committee lost little time in setting out on the roundabout journey to Montgomery. Clement, Jr.'s account of delays en route explains the cause of "railroad fever" in North Alabama. "Donegan, Lane, Davis & Ragland, were 10 days on the way. . . . We did not reach here until last evening,—owing to the tedious navigation of the river at its high tide, & our delay at Chattanooga & Atlanta. . . . Failing to reach Chattanooga on friday evening in order to take the saturday mornings cars, we were forced either to lie by there till tuesday morning or go on in a hack. Wishing to make all the speed possible, we hired a hack & baggage wagon, & after a very unpleasant & fatiguing trip of 11 hours reached Dalton on sunday night at 9 o'clock. On monday morning we took the cars & ran down to Atlanta—101 miles distant—in about 5 hours. At that place we found the Macon train did not leave till next day. . . . We left the rail road at Griffin & came in fine coaches to the present terminous of the Montgomery & West Point road, where we again took the cars & ran down to the city—71 miles—in four or five hours."

While Virginia concocted stews and plasters in an effort to cure Clement's severe cold, he prepared "to address the people in behalf of the R. R.," and by early January was able to report that both houses of the legislature had passed the charter for the Memphis and Charleston Railroad. He and the committee were disappointed, however, in their efforts to obtain financial aid. Surveys for the road began in the summer of 1850, and by the summer of 1852 work was actually under way, with contracts for five-mile units let out to various persons. Clement Clay, Sr., had one of these contracts, but was for a time handicapped by lack of labor. Both Irish laborers and Negro slaves were used on the construction, at wages varying from six to fifteen dollars per month. It was a great day when the first passenger train rolled into Huntsville from Tuscumbia, on October 22, 1855. Less than a year later the road was completed to Stevenson in northeast Alabama, and at last the Tennessee Valley had reliable communication with the East.[29]

29 Clay, Jr., to Clay, Sr., Dec. 27, 1849, Virginia Clay to Susanna Clay, Jan. 1, 1850, Susanna Clay to Clay, Jr., July 15, 1850, H. L. Clay to Clay, Jr., Aug. 28, 1850, Clay, Jr., to H. L. Clay, June 4, 1852, Clay, Jr., to Virginia Clay, June 28, 1852, Clay MSS; Thomas Butler Cooper to Nancy P. Cooper, Feb. 2, 1850, Thomas Butler Cooper MSS; Huntsville *Democrat*, Jan. 17, 1850, Oct. 25, 1855, March 20, 1856.

While the Clays were busy building a railroad to bring their portion of the South into closer communication with other parts of the Union, mounting sectional strife was driving a political and intellectual wedge between them and the North. David Wilmot's proviso to exclude slavery from the territory acquired by the Mexican War brought many fiery resolutions from the South. And among the most fiery were those engineered by William Lowndes Yancey at the Alabama Democratic Convention in February, 1848. Yancey's "Alabama Platform" demanded protection of slavery in the territories, repudiated popular sovereignty, and refused to support any presidential candidate not subscribing to these ideas. Yancey's highhanded management of the state convention, designed to "force the Baltimore Convention to nominate" Woodbury, "who is supposed to sympathise with Calhoun more thoroughly than any northern man," angered most Alabama Democrats. They were emphatically not "thirsting after *Calhoun Vagaries*— The Convention was strongly scented with that peculiar stench," one observer remarked. When the Baltimore convention repudiated the Alabama Platform, Yancey's stock sank to a new low. "A few more conventions for him to figure in," prophesied an Alabama Democrat, "will make him so ridiculous as to render him perfectly harmless. He to profess [*sic*] a knowledge of what Alabama will do!" But Yancey's refusal to support Cass threw many votes to Taylor, and Cass carried Alabama by the narrowest squeak.[30]

Calhoun and Yancey's first effort to form a southern party had thus backfired, but Calhoun lost no time in making a new attempt. Joshua Giddings' proposal for gradual abolition of slavery in the District of Columbia gave Calhoun his opportunity to call enraged Southerners into a caucus, where he offered them his "Address to the People of the South." But a united southern Whig representation "foiled Calhoun in his miserable attempt to form a Southern party," and his address was "whittled . . . down to a weak milk and water" affair. Even so, most southern Whigs

---

[30] F. G. Norman to G. S. Houston, April 13, 1848, A. C. Matthews to G. S. Houston, June 6, 1848, G. S. Houston MSS; Joseph G. Rayback, "The Presidential Ambitions of John C. Calhoun, 1844-1848," *JSH*, XIV (Aug., 1948), 350f; DuBose, *Yancey*, 212ff; Lewy Dorman, *Party Politics in Alabama from 1850 through 1860* (Wetumpka, Ala., 1935), 27-31; James Garfield Randall, "Senator Bagby of Alabama," *SAQ*, X (April, 1911), 169; Allan Nevins, *Ordeal of the Union* (New York, 1947, 2 vols.), I, 9-12.

and some Democrats refused to sign. Before the inner workings of this incident percolated to Alabama, the previously anti-Calhounite Clays led a Huntsville assemblage which promptly endorsed the address. Withers Clay offered resolutions declaring it "just in its sentiments and patriotic in its objects; and we, therefore, cordially approve it." Other resolutions urged the Alabama legislature "to prepare the State to sustain" Virginia "to the last extremity" in that state's expressed determination to act, if Congress interfered with slavery in the territories. Objection to such precipitate action brought to their feet "Gov. Clay, C. C. Clay, Jr.," and others "in favor of . . . immediate adoption of the preamble and resolutions," which were then read "and were adopted unanimously."[31]

The chief result of Calhoun's address was the call for the Nashville convention to assemble in June, 1850. The Clays and other southern-rights leaders plugged vigorously for a strong stand, and some even advocated secession, while alarmed Alabama Whigs began to oppose the whole idea of a southern convention. When the Alabama legislature appointed delegates to the convention, that assumption of authority so angered North Alabama that "the people were called upon to take the matter into their own hands." C. C. Clay, Jr., presided at the Huntsville meetings for this purpose, where local dissension became painfully evident. Leading the southern-rights element, Clay urged the necessity of resisting every invasion of southern rights and of holding the convention, which, he declared, would not favor secession. The Whig and unionist elements, led by George P. Beirne, opposed the convention altogether, and in the voting, Beirne's hostile resolutions were adopted, two to one. But this only brought a more impassioned plea from C. C. Clay, Jr., who then "addressed the meeting in a very feeling strain," denouncing opposition to the convention "as suicidal to the South" and imploring his fellow townsmen not "to make a party question of the great issue," on which there should "be but one side in the slave States." Meantime, most of the unionists who had voted for Beirne's report went home,

[31] Robert Toombs to John J. Crittenden, Jan. 22, 1849, *Correspondence of Robert Toombs, Alexander H. Stephens, and Howell Cobb,* ed. by Ulrich Bonnell Phillips, AHA *Annual Report* (1911), (Washington, 1913), II, 141f (cited hereinafter as Toombs-Stephens-Cobb, *Correspondence*); Huntsville *Democrat,* March 14, 1849; Nevins, *Ordeal of the Union,* I, 222-25.

thinking the business of the evening done, whereupon Clay's resolutions were "put to the meeting and carried without a dissenting voice." So spoke the southern-rights faction, who then proceeded to adopt unanimously Withers Clay's resolution asserting that "we, citizens . . . of Madison County, feel authorized to declare that the resolutions which have just been passed . . . expressed very nearly the universal sentiments of the people of this county, and that there are very few who dissent from the propriety of holding the Nashville Convention." Reuben Chapman was Madison County's delegate to the Nashville convention, and Withers Clay attended as correspondent for the Huntsville *Democrat*.[32]

The convention's hasty retreat to a position of moderation resulted in its general endorsement by all factions throughout the South. Clement Clay, Sr., led the Huntsville meeting of endorsement, while the strongholds of southern-rights sentiment experienced a revulsion of feeling and went unionist. The more perceptive began to regret "the effort which has been made to identify the Democratic party with immediate secession," fearing that it would give the state over to the Whigs; hence the only course lay in waiting and working for greater southern unity.

By this time those measures which became the Compromise of 1850 were coloring southern opinion. Clement Clay, Sr., was at first very hostile, loudly proclaiming "*the right of any State in the Union to secede . . .* when the Union ceases to be beneficial," though he admitted that he was "not in favor of secession and disunion at the present time." He urged "resisting the aggressions of the North . . . by the most rigid system of commercial and social non-intercourse." The Clays were soon active in organizing a Southern Rights Association in Madison County, of which Clement, Sr., became president.[33]

Meanwhile, the Clays were not exactly practicing commercial and social nonintercourse with the Yankees, for in the summer of 1850 Clement, Jr., and Virginia were traveling in the North. The furniture purchased back in 1837 had grown a little shabby,

---

[32] Huntsville *Democrat*, April 4, May 9, 1850; Dorman, *Party Politics in Alabama*, 43; Nevins, *Ordeal of the Union*, I, 248.

[33] W. R. King to Bolling Hall, Nov. 19, 1850, Bolling Hall MSS; Southern Convention, Nashville, 1850, *Condensed Proceedings* (Jackson, Miss., 1850), 3; Huntsville *Democrat*, Aug. 15, Nov. 14, 1850, Feb. 13, 27, 1851; Montgomery *Alabama Journal*, July 17, 24, Aug. 2, 5, 12, 16, Nov. 12, 1850.

and so Susanna commissioned them "to select for her a dining sett of china; two rocking chairs for the parlor & a pair of candelabras; . . . two dozen chairs—one dozen for the sitting room & the other dozen for the chambers; a passage lamp, and, in the event you are offered the dining sett upon fair terms, a tea sett, to correspond in style. . . . To pay for these articles, father authorises me to say you can draw on Bradford's house, for the necessary amount."

Having spent on their travels and purchases nearly a thousand dollars in the course of the summer, Clement, Jr., expressed himself emphatically from Philadelphia: "We have found nothing cheaper here, however, than in Charleston; & I am so opposed to helping these Northern folks with my money, that I am reluctant to spend a cent with them. I have found this city & N. York swarming with southern tourists or invalids, seeking pleasure & health in the midst of our enemies, & disbursing among them 2,000,000 annually, according to the common estimation,—instead of expending it in the south to aid & advance our own institutions & our own people! No wonder that their cities & watering places grow & flourish while ours languish or decline. Every step I take here & every word I hear makes me more southern in feeling & principle. . . . I shall at least go home more attached to the south & more resolved than ever to stand by her first & the Union next."[34]

Clay was no mere "tourist" in enemy territory, but an "invalid" seeking relief from a chronic cough and other respiratory ailments. The Philadelphia doctors pondered his case for two weeks, scouted "the idea of [his] being threatened with consumption . . . but apprehend[ed his] cough's terminating in asthma," and solemnly advised sea bathing. An excursion to Rockaway Beach convinced Clement that this was not the cure for him, and so he deserted the Philadelphia medicos. After a short sojourn in New York City, where he tried to drum up some legal business to aid the family finances, Clement and Virginia moved on to the "Hydropathic Water Cure" at Brattleboro, Vermont. This treatment, then very popular, consisted principally in wrapping the patient in icy sheets wrung from spring water, putting him to bed under many blankets, and leaving him helpless for several hours. Frequent cold baths, copious drinking of spring water, a simple diet, and regular hours were other features of the cure. Clement continued

34 H. L. Clay to Clay, Jr., June 25, 1850, Clay, Jr., to H. L. Clay, July 22, Aug. 25, 1850, Clay MSS.

this regimen until late October, 1850, when he considered himself much improved, although he would not "venture to speak in public this winter." But on the road home his cough returned with such severity as to detain him in Petersburg, Virginia, where he was under the care of a relative, Dr. Thomas Withers.[35] Only a few weeks of his customary activities at home were enough to prove that Clement was still not cured. So he and Dr. John Young Bassett set out early in February, 1851, to seek in Florida the health which eluded them both.

They traveled to Chattanooga by boat, thence to Savannah by train, and from there to Lake Monroe, one hundred miles south of Jacksonville, Florida. From this point Clement journeyed by horseback for some ten weeks over the interior of Florida. "My rides," he reported, "were somewhat fatiguing, but they secured me two of the greatest comforts of life, a keen appetite & sound sleep. . . . I am satisfied," he continued, "that there is wonderful virtue in this climate. . . . I shall be in the saddle almost daily . . . till I reach home,—which will require from 20 to 30 days travelling. I shall thus prove the virtue of horseback exercise . . . my cough has quite ceased & I think my throat must be almost well." The result of almost a year's rest and curative effort gave Clay sufficient strength for his senatorial career.[36]

Clement Clay, Jr., was thus absent from the state during the period of greatest disruption in political parties incident to the secession movement of 1850. In the August elections of 1851, the southern-rights party suffered a defeat that "seems to be disastrous," commented a Clay-inspired editorial. Old-line Democrats soon began a reorganization of their party in order to participate in the national election of 1852 and to regain control of the state. Early January, 1852, found Clement, Jr., in Montgomery, where he was counsel for several cases coming before the Alabama supreme court. He was also on hand, though not a delegate, for the "Convention to Reorganize the Democratic Party," which appointed delegates to the Baltimore convention

35 Clay, Jr., to Clay, Sr., Aug. 12, Nov. 4, 1850, Clay, Jr., to H. L. Clay, Nov. 1, 1850, Clay MSS.
36 Clay, Jr., to Virginia Clay, Feb. 5, March 19, 1851, Clay, Jr., to Clay, Sr., Feb. 15, 1851, Clay, Jr., to J. Y. Bassett, March 16, 1851, Clay MSS; John Young Bassett MSS, 1851, passim. Clay's letters are published in Norwood Olin (ed.), "Letters from Florida in 1851," Florida Historical Society Quarterly, XXIX (April, 1951), 261-83. Bassett died of tuberculosis on Nov. 2, 1851.

and chose presidential electors. When one withdrew, the other electors appointed C. C. Clay, Jr., to fill the vacancy. The ticket, headed by Franklin Pierce, with William Rufus King of Alabama for vice president, was strong throughout the state, and the Democratic party went into the campaign with great confidence. As Clement, Jr., prepared to carry on an active campaign, Virginia Clay took a different approach to politics.[37]

Virginia Clay, having persuaded both herself and the family that she needed expert medical attention, set out in May, 1852, under the escort of "brother Lawson" for various points in the East. Stopping first at Charleston, South Carolina, they improved the time in sightseeing and in making useful political and social contacts, particularly with the Rhett family. They proceeded northward, stopping at various water cures, and finally ending up at Brattleboro, Vermont. While they were bumping along over New Hampshire railroads, Virginia learned that presidential candidate Franklin Pierce was at his home in nearby Concord, and nothing would do but they must hasten there and make his acquaintance. Pierce had known Clement, Sr., in Congress and Lawson in the Mexican War, so that there was some excuse for the impromptu visit. Frank Pierce rose so gallantly to the occasion that Virginia found him as "fascinating & warm hearted as as [sic] a genuine Southerner. He left me," she continued, "quite enamored—saying his wife & himself wd. call in the morning. At 10 he came & desired me to drive with him. I thanked him & prepared myself, so as not to detain him an instant, (for he is pushed to death) & he was promptly at my side. We rode in a covered Chaise, with a splendid Morgan horse. . . . I told him among other things that I wd reach home in time to welcome you from yr. political campaign &c.—& a great many delicate & complimentary passes occurred wh I will tell you when we meet. . . . Mrs. P. called, a pleasant, delicate, intellectual looking lady. She staid half an hour, & left, after passing all the courtesies possible for the occasion. . . . Gen'l was in our parlour 4 or five times & thinking we had recd. our full share of his precious

[37] Clay, Jr., to Virginia Clay, Jan. 12, 1852, Clay, Jr., to H. L. Clay, May 28, 1852, Clay MSS; Henry W. Hilliard to Millard Fillmore, Jan. 26, 1852, Millard Fillmore MSS, vol. 30, p. 176; Huntsville *Democrat*, Aug. 7, 1851; Huntsville *Southern Advocate*, Aug. 13, 1851; Montgomery *Advertiser and Gazette*, Jan. 24, 1852; Dorman, *Party Politics in Alabama*, 65-74.

time & attention, we concluded to leave & did so that P. M.,"
but not before they had received an autographed copy of Haw-
thorne's campaign biography from Pierce himself, and his friend,
Thomas J. Whipple, had "complimented" them with "a bottle
of Champaign."[38]

Clay's plans for a vigorous campaign throughout the Huntsville
congressional district went awry when sickness fell heavily upon
the family. Clement spent most of the summer helping to nurse
Withers' sick children, and when little John Withers and Cara
Lisa both died, he had little heart for politics. Withers and Mary
Clay now had only one living child, little Clement, who posed
another family problem, for Clement and Virginia had almost
adopted him and were deeply attached to him. Now, Clement
wrote, "his parents . . . will demand more of his company than
heretofore . . . [and] it will be best for the child's happiness
. . . that he be weaned of his love for us; . . . I am, therefore,
resolved to see less of . . . the little fellow & . . . to break him
of calling Va. 'ma' & me 'pa,' & to teach him to call us aunt &
uncle." Added to these family troubles was the loss of seven
Negroes by death, which impelled Clement to admonish, "Be as
economical as possible, as we have lost a great deal in our negroes
—not less than $2000." During August, Clement spent many
nights at his Uncle Augustine Withers' plantation helping to
nurse that family, most of whom were ill with typhoid fever.[39]

To the middle of August, Clement had made but one campaign
speech, and even then he was "not prepared to canvass," but
during October he worked to make up for lost time. His state-
rights leanings in 1850 were made the most of by his Whig
opponent, Thomas Bibb Bradley, who tried to bury Clay "in
the dark cavern of Secession." Clay, however, kept to the straight
party line in speeches "replete with facts" proving the abolitionist
tendencies of the Whig party and showing how all factions of
Southerners were now "pledged, by the adoption of the Georgia
Platform, to secede and dissolve the Union, if Congress committed any further aggressions on Southern rights." The election
was a sweeping victory for Pierce and the Democratic ticket in
Alabama. Late in November, Presidential Elector Clay pro-

38 Virginia Clay to Clay, Jr., May 22, Oct. 4, 1852, Clay MSS.
39 Clay, Jr., to H. L. Clay, July 30, 1852, Clay, Jr., to Virginia Clay, Aug. 2, 15,
Oct. 4, 1852, Susanna Clay to Virginia Clay, Aug. 22, 1852, Clay MSS.

ceeded by horseback to Montgomery. Of his journey he wrote to Virginia, "After numerous adventures by day light & by night, I reached Ashville . . . rode 44 miles, via Montevallo . . . & stayed that night at a miserable house . . . where I got nothing to eat for supper, & was forced by my good democracy to breakfast at daylight on potatoes, cornbread & coffee without sugar—all cold as charity. . . . rode . . . 18 miles . . . and dined sumptuously, on ham, boiled rock fish, chicken, various vegetables, coffee, potato custard, & rich cream &c.

"Reached Govr. Fitzpatrick's last night. . . . [He] was very kind & attentive. . . . Left there at 8 this morning, arrived here [i.e., Montgomery] at 12, got shaved, had my hair & beard trimmed & done up *comme il faut,* & took a good dinner." As for his official duties, he wrote, "Tomorrow we will meet in the Capitol at 12 noon, cast the vote & elect a messenger.— The next day I will start for home."[40]

Before Clay entered the Senate, he suffered a bitter defeat in the campaign of 1853. Responding to numerous "calls" upon him to become a candidate for Congress, he said, "I feel that I should disappoint my friends and, perhaps, do myself an injustice, by refusing to comply with their wishes." Clay's opponent was Williamson R. W. Cobb of Jackson County, who had represented the Huntsville district since 1847 and continued to do so until 1861. He was "a tall, long-armed man, of some intelligence and more shrewdness," with little education and crude manners, but with a wonderful ability to draw votes from the poorer classes, although he himself was a man of some property and owned seventeen slaves. He was a typical southern demagogue, but he never had the political machine or the power to carry out his program. Nevertheless, one after another the aristocrats of North Alabama fell before him; in 1847 the victim was William Acklin; in 1849 and 1851 Jere Clemens tried and failed; and now in 1853 Clem Clay was to try his lance. Clay too went down in defeat, for Cobb carried every county except one. Before the public, Clay accepted defeat gracefully, denying that he felt any "malevolence or chagrin," since he had not sought the candidacy but had made the canvass only at the insistence of friends who had over-

40 Clay, Jr., to Virginia Clay, July 11, Aug. 15, Sept. 20, 30, Nov. 30, 1852, Clay MSS; Huntsville *Democrat,* Nov. 4, 1852; Dorman, *Party Politics in Alabama,* 81.

estimated his strength. Clay's defeat was the greater because of the strong unionist sentiment throughout North Alabama, which threw nearly all Union Democrat as well as many Whig votes to Cobb. On this situation Clement declared his "abiding confidence, that the time is not far distant, when this sentiment will, again, prevail in this District, and the advocate of State Rights, instead of being reviled as a Disunionist, will be respected as thereby maintaining the Union."[41]

"It is certain that Chapman, Hubbard, Clay, Acklin, Houston & Walker all are intriguing for a seat in the Senate." Thus in one sentence did Albert J. Pickett summarize the chief topic of speculation among Alabama politicians in the fall of 1853. Bolling Hall, southern-rights Democrat and a candidate (though unsuccessful) for the speakership of the legislature, was the clearinghouse for political news during that autumn. "This senatorial question is truly a ticklish one"; hence it "will be the duty . . . of each democratic member of the Legislature, to guard against any guerrilla attempts of the whigs to elect some fishy, unreliable democrat . . . to prevent a repetition of the game played off four years ago, by which the well ascertained will of the Democratic party . . . was outrageously defeated." Two United States senators were to be elected, and while Benjamin Fitzpatrick was generally agreed upon as the choice of South Alabama, the multiplicity of Democratic candidates in North Alabama made selection there highly uncertain. Many Democrats felt that "the only safe plan at this time will be to take one from north and one from south Ala one from the union men and from the state wrights [sic] men any attempt to Elect bouth [sic] from either wing of the party would give the whigs control of the Legislature and at the next Election the controul [sic] of the state."[42]

Democrats throughout the state were willing to vote for any suitable candidate on whom North Alabama could agree. One of the most interested analysts of the situation at this time was C. C. Clay, Jr., himself. Reviewing the candidates, he wrote, "Clemens

41 Huntsville *Democrat*, April 21, 28, May 5, 19, Aug. 4, 25, 1853; William Garrett, *Reminiscences of Public Men in Alabama for Thirty Years* (Atlanta, 1872), 396.
42 R. F. Houston to G. S. Houston, Aug. 22, 1853, G. S. Houston MSS; Nathaniel Davis to Bolling Hall, Sept. 2, 1853, George L. Walder to Bolling Hall, Sept. 6, 1853, Gappa T. Yelverton to Bolling Hall, Sept. 9, 1853, John Hardy to Bolling Hall, Oct. 13, 1853, Albert J. Pickett to Bolling Hall, Oct. 1, 1853, Bolling Hall MSS; Montgomery *Advertiser and State Gazette*, Sept. 14, Nov. 18, 1853.

. . . swears he will be elected as he was before . . . if he cant
be elected by the Democratic party, he will be by the whigs, if he
can.— I do not think he can be elected by either party. L. P.
Walker will be urged forward by some friends; but, as his Democracy only dates back as far as '44, the old men of the party think
his probation not long enough. . . . Maj. Hubbard, Col. Acklin
& Col. Humphreys are all true men & have some friends. Genl.
Houston claims are urged by the *Union* Democrats . . . and
favored by the Whigs. . . . And, last & perhaps least of the list
of patriots who are willing to serve their country, is your humble
servant. . . . however . . . I am not willing to be elected by
the defeat of my own party, or by any sacrifice of its principles
or usages.—I confess to you that I desire an election, because I
feel that I have been beaten by an ass for the H. of Rep.,
because of my state right principles & thro' a combination of
Whigs & pseudo-Democrats, who falsely represented me as a
Disunionist. . . . I do not claim a Senator from N. Ala. as
a right,—I never did. . . . But, as a matter of policy, I think it
would be best to elect one Senator from this region. It would
tend to harmonize the party, to remove sectional strife, &, if chosen
from the State rights wing, to revive the sinking fortunes of the
party in this section. You see that the Whigs here are determined
to unite with the Union Demos. . . . & thus crush the State
rights men who aspire to any office. Without some help—we
will be crushed—"[43]

Democrats caucused on November 23, and "at about the hour
of midnight, nominated for the U. S. Senate, the Hon. Benj.
Fitzpatrick and C. C. Clay, jr., esq." after fifteen ballots. "We
learn," continued the press account, "that on the 1st ballot, Clay
received 21 votes, Walker 13, Houston 10, Chapman 9, Hubbard
5, Clemens 3, & Lyon & Mason, each, perhaps several. . . . Clay
then rose gradually to 45 votes wanting only 2 votes to make two
thirds of the members present—when a Southern member moved
to nominate him by acclamation, which was done. No other
candidate received more than 17 votes on any of the ballotings,
which shows that Judge Clay was the decided choice of his party."
Election by the legislature was only a formality following nomination by the caucus, for the Whigs were too weak to offer any

[43] Clay, Jr., to Bolling Hall, Sept. 30, 1853, Bolling Hall MSS.

real opposition. Consequently, Clay and Fitzpatrick were elected on November 28, 1853, by large majorities. Thus was Clay's defeat avenged.[44]

The election was a victory for the southern-rights wing of the Democratic party, for Alabama now had two senators committed to state-rights principles, though they were at the same time faithful Democrats. It left the strong unionist faction unrepresented and caused the Whig press to complain that Clay was "not the choice of North Alabama" and that he had been "forced upon the Legislature by the operation of the caucus system." The Democratic press, however, rejoiced in Clay's election, and his Huntsville friends invited him to a supper in celebration of the event. This honor Clement was forced to decline, because, as he explained, "I shall leave in a day or two for Washington City, and must employ the brief period of my stay here in arranging my private business, preparatory to a long absence from home."

[44] Ala. Leg., *SJ*, pp. 82f, Nov. 28, 1853; Clay Scrapbooks, VI, 299; Huntsville *Democrat*, Dec. 1, 1853; Montgomery *Advertiser and State Gazette*, Nov. 26, 1853; Montgomery *Alabama Journal*, Nov. 27, 1853.

7

Senator from Alabama

ON DECEMBER 8, 1853, Clement and Virginia Clay set out for Washington, traveling by boat up the Tennessee River to Chattanooga. Here they "took the cars," and at Dalton several other members of the Alabama delegation joined them. There was Benjamin Fitzpatrick, whose broad shoulders, erect carriage, and strong, handsome face made him a distinguished-looking senator. His limited education and mediocre talents were offset by a strict honesty, a devotion to public economy, close attention to duty, and a bent for politics. Political advancement had come to him in part through his marriage into the prominent Elmore family of South Carolina and Alabama. Going to Washington with him now, however, was his second wife, Aurelia Rachel Blassingame, a plump, southern-looking young woman several years his junior. The picturesque member of the party was James Ferguson Dowdell, a large, loosely built man, whose Georgia drawl, naivete, conscious rusticity, and open disregard for the affectations of Capital society delighted everyone, even those of his women friends who were constantly trying to "improve" him.

Not the least of the delegation was Clay's erstwhile opponent, the shaggy-headed, ungrammatical, nasal-voiced Williamson R. W. Cobb, to whom Virginia gave a frosty greeting. Clement Clay, now thirty-seven, was about to become the youngest senator of the Thirty-third Congress. His recently grown, full black beard and mustache lent him a proper senatorial dignity and filled out a rather gaunt face. His tall, thin figure, classic features, black hair and eyes gave him a scholarly and aristocratic appearance which prevented his looking much like a politician. Virginia Clay, at twenty-nine, had attained an agreeable and handsome maturity, and had become a brilliant conversationalist. She now needed only the exhilaration of Washington society to give her a sparkle which mere youth had never conferred.[1]

After many delays and frequent changes, their "Congressional Special" clattered into Washington about two o'clock in the morning, and the weary travelers hastened to the National Hotel, where they had reservations. Dowdell, well muffled in a large shawl and slouch hat, went in to claim their rooms, but returned crestfallen to the hack, saying no rooms were to be had. The scornful and more traveled Clement, also shawl-wrapped and slouch-hatted, strode in to see what he could do, but he was equally unsuccessful. Then Virginia took the situation in hand, and amid her torrent of protests fortunately mentioned the names of the party, whereupon the startled night clerk assured her that he had rooms for them. Within a few days the Clays and Fitzpatricks were established in the boardinghouse of Charles Gardiner on G Street, near Thirteenth. Though distant from the Capitol, this location was convenient to the various government departments and to the White House.

One reason for the Clays' choice of a small mess was that now, after ten years of marriage, Virginia was expecting a child. Her pregnancy terminated unfortunately, however, in a stillbirth. These circumstances, together with a long convalescence, kept Virginia out of the stream of Capital society during her first winter in Washington.[2]

On Wednesday, December 14, 1853, the day after his thirty-seventh birthday, Clement was sworn in as senator, his credentials being presented by R. M. T. Hunter of Virginia. As Clement went to his seat on the front row, left of the center aisle, he could cast an attentive if somewhat confused eye over the select club of which he was now a member. That front row seat, apparently

1 Clay-Clopton, *Belle of the Fifties*, 19-23; Garrett, *Reminiscences of Public Men in Alabama*, 395, 586, 715; Dorman, *Party Politics in Alabama*, 120f; *DAB*, VI, 439.
2 Susanna (Withers) Battle to Susanna Clay, Oct. 22, 1852, Clay, Sr., to Clay, Jr., Jan. 9, 1854, Virginia Clay to Susanna Clay, April 1, 1854, Clay MSS; Washington *Union*, Dec. 17, 1853.

so advantageous, was not favorably viewed by the senators, for it was most distant from the warmth provided by four fireplaces and two franklin stoves at the back of the chamber. Clay's immediate neighbors in chilliness were William Wright, wealthy industrialist of New Jersey, and Stephen Adams of Mississippi. Across the aisle sat Fitzpatrick, Judah P. Benjamin of Louisiana, and soon, handsome and forceful Albert Gallatin Brown of Mississippi. Directly behind Clay were Andrew Pickens Butler of South Carolina, and R. M. T. Hunter. In the third row an imposing quartet sat side by side, namely, aging but still formidable Lewis Cass of Michigan, opportunist Jesse D. Bright of Indiana, egoist Salmon P. Chase of Ohio, and self-righteous Charles Sumner of Massachusetts. To the right of the aisle and in the warmer areas of the third and fourth rows could be seen William H. Seward, Stephen A. Douglas, and Ben Wade of the smoldering black eyes and fierce dark face. On that first day Clement Clay had an opportunity to hear nearly half the sixty-two members as they presented petitions and introduced bills in line of routine business.

Clement Clay and his fellow senators at this moment stood on the brink of momentous events all too unforeseen. A new chief executive, as yet untried, was facing his first Congress. Franklin Pierce had been elected upon a platform endorsing the Compromise of 1850 and promising no disturbance of the sleeping sectional and slavery issues—issues which, it was hoped, had been laid to rest forever, but as it turned out, were even then being disinterred. Pierce's election had been a glowing triumph for the Democracy. Party ranks in the South, so distorted and broken by the secession issue of 1850-1851, were once more normal, and the election of a "northern man with southern principles" was for many a pledge that the Democracy was still national and the South still in control. But beneath this surface accord, dissension soon began to bubble, for Pierce was not a skillful party manager; indeed he had few loyal friends in Congress, but among those few who stood by him, one of the most faithful was young Senator Clay of Alabama.[3]

[3] USC, 33:1, *Official Directory* (2d ed.), front.; Christian Frederick Eckloff, *Memoirs of a Senate Page (1855-1859)* ed. by Percival G. Melbourne (New York, 1909), 5; Roy Franklin Nichols, *Franklin Pierce, Young Hickory of the Granite Hills* (Philadelphia, 1931), 201f, 210, 216, 276, 305, 308, 319.

With committee assignments already made before he took his seat, Senator Clay found himself a member of Commerce, Claims, and Pensions, and later in the session he was also appointed to the Committee on Enrolled Bills. His colleagues on committee were not particularly congenial to Clay. The only other Southerner was the suave, urbane, handsome, and artful Judah P. Benjamin, whose background and interests were very different from Clay's. Among the eighteen members on the three committees, seven were Easterners, five came from the Northwest, five were Whigs, and five showed various degrees of antislavery leaning. Indeed, the big four of abolitionism were distributed among the three committees. Of these, the slightly built William Henry Seward, gray-eyed, cold, unexcitable, and unimaginative, sat on the Commerce Committee. Though a mental giant, as a speaker he was indistinct of voice and strained of manner. He never retaliated to the many attacks upon him, but there were those who thought him "in a quiet way, an exceedingly good hater." Very different was the handsome, erudite Charles Sumner, whom Clay later denounced as "a sneaking, sinuous, snakelike poltroon." Clay, like many others, cordially despised Sumner. Scarcely less obnoxious for their antislavery views were Salmon P. Chase and Ben Wade, both of whom sat on the Claims Committee. Chase's pomposity and ambition, joined with Wade's toughness and profanity, made the two Ohio senators a very remarkable pair. Vigorous, genial, charming Hannibal Hamlin of Maine belied his New England origin. As chairman of the Commerce Committee, his ability and his moderate antislavery views were respected by Southerners and Northerners alike. Clay's other colleagues on Commerce were the aging but erect, strong, and benevolent-looking Henry Dodge, Wisconsin pioneer, and Michigan's Charles Stuart, pro-South Democrat. But Clay's most congenial friend was George Wallace Jones of Iowa, chairman of Pensions. Eighteen years earlier, Clement Clay, Sr., and Jones (then delegate from Wisconsin Territory) had become close friends; now the latter welcomed young Clement. Though always associated with the Northwest, Jones was southern by education, temperament, and viewpoint. His alert, wiry figure, his luxuriant black curls, fastidious dress, winning smile, and polished manners made him a favorite among the ladies, especially since he was a constant attender at social functions and a tireless dancer.[4]

On December 22, 1853, Clay made his first report from the Committee on Claims. The freshman senator did not, however, venture into the realms of oratory, but rather was the careful observer learning the rules, doing his committee work, finding his way to the departments, and trying to become a useful member as rapidly as possible. So it was that he sat silent through the excited and unquenchable flow of oratory expended on the Kansas-Nebraska bill.

That well-known and notorious measure, so closely associated with Stephen A. Douglas, needs only the briefest review here. On the day Clay took his seat, Augustus Caesar Dodge, the tall, mournful-faced Iowa senator, introduced a bill to organize Nebraska Territory. Douglas reported the bill from the Committee on Territories on January 4, 1854; on January 16, Archibald Dixon of Kentucky offered an amendment specifically repealing the Missouri Compromise. Dixon's intransigence forced Douglas to accept the amendment and line up the Democratic party and the executive branch in behalf of repeal. Thus Kansas-Nebraska became a party and an administration measure.

Because of Virginia's illness, Clay just missed the opening gun when on January 30, Douglas blasted the abolition forces. During the next five weeks twenty-two senators made set speeches on the bill. Through the climactic day and night of March 3, 1854, Clement Clay watched the dramatic scene, the packed galleries, the surge of debate between Douglas and the antislavery forces, and helped to vote down Chase's obstructing amendments. Finally "at ten minutes to five o'clock, a. m.," Clay and thirty-six other weary senators cast their votes for the bill. The Senate, considering itself "entitled to a rest of three days," recessed "at five minutes to five o'clock on Saturday morning, after a continuous

4 USC, *SJ*, 33:1, pp. 31f, 413; USC, *Cong. Globe*, 33:1, p. 1554, June 28, 1854; Eckloff, *Memoirs of a Senate Page*, 56; Henry Stuart Foote, *Casket of Reminiscences* (Washington, 1874), 123-25; Robert Douthat Meade, *Judah P. Benjamin, Confederate Statesman* (New York, 1943), 88f, 170-72; George Fort Milton, *The Eve of Conflict: Stephen A. Douglas and the Needless War* (Boston, 1934), 117f; Albert Gallatin Riddle, *The Life of Benjamin F. Wade* (Cleveland, 1887), 179, 215; Charles Eugene Hamlin, *The Life and Times of Hannibal Hamlin* (Cambridge, Mass., 1899), 231, 276f; Maunsell B. Field, *Memories of Many Men and Some Women* (New York, 1874), 290; John Carl Parish, *George Wallace Jones* (Iowa City, 1912), 3, 67.

session of seventeen hours." Other than by his vote for it, Clay's views on the Kansas-Nebraska bill are unrecorded. Simply as an administration measure he would have voted for it, and probably at this time he considered it an important southern victory, though later developments caused him to change his mind. Meantime, Clay had promised the Georgia delegation to support their candidate for governor of one of the new territories.[5]

Kansas-Nebraska also touched Clay in one other curious incident. Jeremiah Clemens, former Alabama senator, was loitering in Washington under cover of land-claims business, where, as Clement reported, he was "boarded at the National Hotel & provided with wines, liquors & other appliances for corrupting Congress,—all at the expense of his clients. He gives dinners, suppers, treats, gambles &c. &c. He looks very rubicund & bloated." It was widely rumored that Clemens would soon go into Pierce's cabinet, a contingency which caused Clement, Sr., to warn his son that "you & Gov. Fitzpatrick" must place the President "in possession of the facts, the damning facts" of Clemens' "political treachery, . . . reckless and unprincipled . . . conduct . . . [and] bad moral habits." Clemens soon lost executive favor when, in reporting a conversation with the President on the Nebraska bill, he claimed that it was Pierce's "*decided opinion* that Douglas's bill was a proposition in 'favor of freedom' and . . . if it should pass, although we might absorb the whole of Mexico, *not another slave State would ever come into the Union.*" With Kansas-Nebraska now an administration measure, Pierce could not tolerate the report that he had expressed "*great surprise at the opposition it met with from the North, and equal surprise that the South should be willing to take it.*" Under executive pressure, Clemens retracted, saying he had "*misunderstood* the purport" of the President's remarks, but added that he himself had never been "in favor of the principle of the bill. . . . I thought the South must be the loser. I think so now." Clemens' analysis was only too accurate.

Pierce's stand on the Nebraska issue was not entirely satisfactory to his ardent friend, Clement Clay, who said, "of course

5 USC, *SJ*, 33:1, pp. 55, 62, 77; USC, *Cong. Globe*, 33:1, pp. 175, 532, 1254; Washington *Union*, Feb. 2, March 7, 1854; Baltimore *Weekly Sun*, Feb. 4, 1854; New York *Herald*, March 5, 1854; Milton, *Eve of Conflict*, 112-17, 122-27, 133-43; Nichols, *Pierce*, 320-24, 339.

we do not agree with him in his view of territorial sovereignty."
Clay never had any enthusiasm for popular sovereignty, although
he did not for several years go over to the other extreme of
demanding federal protection for slavery in the territories.[6]

Like Pierce himself, Clement Clay did not have a great deal to
show for his efforts when the first session of the Thirty-third
Congress finally adjourned on August 7, 1854. He had worked
industriously to obtain grants of land to aid in the construction
of three Alabama railroads. With the railroad boom in full swing
in Alabama, Clay himself and many of his constituents were
personally interested in such aid. But the day of congressional
land grants to railroads had not yet dawned. At this session
thirty-one bills were introduced to grant lands in aid of railroad
construction in all parts of the country. The Senate passed fifteen
of these bills, but the House refused to act on any of them. Many
legislators were afraid of the subject, and could find all kinds of
constitutional objections. Two or three years later, however, the
pressure from railroad interests became so strong that the situation
was completely changed. But for the present, Clay's efforts failed,
and he had to be content with the bill to make Tuscumbia a port
of entry, and a very minor school-section bill, as the sum total of
his legislation for the session. But he had other things to his credit.[7]

No southern senator was worth his salt who could not castigate
the abolitionist bloc. Clay's opportunity came late in June, and
his target was that "Proper Bostonian," Charles Sumner. Debate
was on the question of referring a petition of citizens of Boston
praying repeal of the Fugitive Slave Law. "If we repeal the
fugitive slave law, will . . . Massachusetts . . . execute the provision of the Constitution without any law of Congress? . . .
Will Mr. Sumner . . . do it?" asked Butler of South Carolina.
To which Sumner replied, " 'Is thy servant a dog, that he should
do this thing?' . . . Mr. BUTLER. Then you would not obey the
Constitution. . . . Mr. SUMNER. I recognize no such obligation."
This gave the infuriated Southerners just the weapon they needed,

<hr>

[6] Clay, Jr., to Clay, Sr., March 14, April 5, 1854, Clay MSS; Baltimore *Weekly Sun*, Dec. 17, 1853; New York *Herald*, Dec. 14, 1853, Jan. 11, 1854; Washington *Union*, March 28, 30, 1854; Washington *National Intelligencer*, March 28, 1854.

[7] James Freeman Grant to Clay, Jr., July 17, 1854, Thomas Walker to Clay, Jr., July 19, 1854, Clay MSS; USC, *SJ*, 33:1, pp. 468, 489, 614, 628, 635f, 712-88; Lewis D. Haney, *A Congressional History of Railways in the United States* (Madison, Wisc., 1910, 2 vols.), II, 17.

and they lost no opportunity to throw Sumner's words back at him. After two days of angry fidgeting, Clay lashed out at Sumner on June 28, accusing him of falsifying the Senate records, of "want of personal courage," of "readiness to commit moral perjury," and of a "disposition to instigate other men to crime." This "Uriah Heap," this "filthy reptile," should be placed beyond the "pale of society," in that "social degradation which he merits." "I am surprised," Clay continued, "that honorable men, but especially southern men, should so far forget their rights, and those of their constituents . . . as to lend any countenance to such a character as I have portrayed." Clay, the abolitionist baiter, was acclaimed throughout Alabama, where the press reported that "Sumner squirmed and writhed desperately under Mr. Clay's keen, lashing invective." "All rejoice in the high stand, you have taken," Clay's friends assured him.[8]

Among other measures of the session demanding Clay's attention was the homestead bill. This perennial bill usually passed the House, and its defeat, session after session, in the Senate required the intermittent attention of sundry southern members. The current bill, proposing to open lands to alien immigrants as well as to citizens, was more than usually obnoxious. Clay's comments to the governor of Florida summarized southern views on the subject: "Apart from my constitutional objection to it, I regard it as most inexpedient for the South in many aspects. Our lands are generally poor—those in the north & west generally rich. . . . Sagacious self-interest wd prompt poor men . . . to go north to the best lands. . . . Thus the South wd lose by the free farm policy in land, money & population.— Besides, it will prove a most efficient ally for Abolition, by encouraging & stimulating the settlement of free farms with Yankees & foreigners precommitted to resist the participancy of slaveholders in the public domain."

With the homestead bill before the Senate and with reason to believe that Pierce might sign it if passed, R. M. T. Hunter took the precaution of substituting a graduation bill for the "free farms" measure. Following his father's admonition "to be active & speak on the graduation bill," Clay declared, "I am opposed

8 J. L. M. Curry to Clay, Jr., July 18, 1854, Clay MSS; USC, *Cong. Globe*, 33:1, pp. 1517, 1554, June 26, 28, 1854; Walter B. Shotwell, *Life of Charles Sumner* (New York, 1910), 286-91; Grace Greenwood [Mary Jane (Clarke) Lippincott], "An American Salon," *Cosmopolitan*, VIII (Feb., 1890), 444.

to the free farm policy, and I cannot vote for it. . . . I am a friend of the graduation policy, and I wish to see it adopted by this Congress." Since the homesteaders could not muster enough votes to pass their original bill, they followed Clay's urgings to "unite upon the graduation feature" and next day passed the graduation bill, but it was not acted upon in the House.[9]

Of a piece with his views on homesteading was Clay's hostility to the "Indigent Insane" bill. This remarkable measure, instigated by Dorothea Lynde Dix, tireless reformer in the care of the insane, would give ten million acres of public land to the states which would use the proceeds to carry out her charitable aims. Politicians soon discovered formidable objections to this apparently innocent and worthy measure, especially the profits which would accrue to land speculators. Pondering the matter, Pierce soon became convinced of the bill's unconstitutionality, and on May 3, 1854, he boldly vetoed it. Presidential vetoes had been rare up to that time, and the rejection of a humanitarian measure had the added liability of antagonizing all philanthropists. Pierce based his objections to the bill solely on constitutional grounds, explaining that if the grant had been in money, its unconstitutionality might be more obvious but no more fundamental. The public domain, he added, was already pledged for public indebtedness and so was not available for uses ordinarily reserved to the states. Furthermore, such use of public funds would set a bad precedent which might lead to all kinds of state aid. The veto was loudly applauded by southern Democrats, whose opposition to federal distribution in any guise had become traditional.

So impressed was C. C. Clay, Sr., that he asked why his son did not "make a speech in favor of the President's unsurpassed Veto message. If I could not go into a minute constitutional argument, I would, at least, say some thing more than by my vote, in favor of that able, manly & clear document." Senator Clay soon acted upon this parental advice and made his first important speech on June 20, 1854. Clay's argument echoed the veto message on constitutional grounds, with specific application to Alabama. The

9 Clay, Jr., to James E. Broome, July 8, 1854, Clay MSS; USC, *SJ*, 33:1, p. 543, July 21, 1854; USC, *Cong. Globe*, 33:1, Appen., pp. 1703f, July 21, 1854; John B. Sanborn, "Some Political Aspects of Homestead Legislation," *AHR*, VI (Oct., 1900), 30; Robert Watson Winston, *Andrew Johnson: Plebian and Patriot* (New York, 1928), 128-31.

"Indigent Insane" measure, Clay declared, scarcely differed from Henry Clay's distribution bill of 1842. He explained how he could properly vote for grants of land to railroads because "the effect" was "to hasten . . . settlement of the country," but he invoked the words of the framers to prove that "they did not empower Congress to provide eleemosynary institutions in the states." Clay thus reached the conclusion that this act would "usurp the powers of the local authorities, and transgress the sacred boundary of separation between the State and Federal jurisdictions." Finally, he thanked the President for "vindicating the true principles of the Constitution and upholding and maintaining the rights of the States, which are the surest bulwarks against centralism, and the safest guarantees of popular liberty." Clay's speech was "very highly complimented in private by Senators & others," and brought him much repute at home and throughout the country. Many constituents wrote letters of flattering approval from all parts of Alabama.[10]

Thus in his first session Clay had established some of the policies he was to follow through his senatorial career. Already he had shown himself unalterably opposed to free land under any guise. He lost no opportunity to declare his convictions on strict construction and state rights. To advance the interests of Alabama, Clay concentrated on pushing aid for railroad construction and did his share in promoting local bills. As a member of the Committee on Pensions his policy was conservative and hostile. The "whole pension or bounty system," he declared, "is . . . corrupt & corrupting . . . a tax on the many for the benefit of the few; anti-republican & opposed to the true spirit of the constitution." In the Commerce Committee, Clay decried eastern domination, favored anything beneficial to the South, and obstructed his colleagues as much as possible. Indeed, Clay for the most part followed the line his father had laid down twenty-five years earlier. Along with most of his southern colleagues, Clay was struggling

10 Clay, Sr., to Virginia Clay, May 23, 1854, Clay, Jr., to Clay, Sr., June 22, 1854, R. N. Chapman, Jr., to Clay, Jr., July 2, 1854, J. L. M. Curry to Clay, Jr., July 18, 1854, T. A. Walker to Clay, Jr., July 19, 1854, H. S. Shelton to Clay, Jr., July 24, 1854, G. T. Yelverton to Clay, Jr., July 27, 1854, James E. Broome to Clay, Jr., July 3, 1854, Clay MSS; Clay Scrapbooks, VI, 294-96; USC, SJ, 33:1, pp. 361-69; USC, Cong. Globe, 33:1, Appen., pp. 969-72; Huntsville Democrat, July 6, 1854; Helen Edith Marshall, Dorothea Lynde Dix, Forgotten Samaritan (Chapel Hill, 1937), 148-54; Nichols, Pierce, 349.

against the current that was sweeping the nation into a new era where laissez-faire, state rights, and a minimum of government could no longer be dominant principles. In that strained and emotional decade, not the least of Clay's duties was denunciation of the antislavery bloc, and in this Clay soon proved himself so adept that abolitionists began to call him "Copperhead Clay, after the snake by that name, on account of his venomous attacks on those whom he disliked."[11]

When Congress finally adjourned on August 7, 1854, Clement and Virginia hastened to the cooler air of the Virginia mountains. They did not return to Alabama, but spent several weeks at various Virginia springs, and with relatives in Virginia and North Carolina. From the Red Sweet Springs, Clement wrote, "after the . . . many . . . labors . . . of Washington . . . it is a great relief to do nothing but what promotes physical health & enjoyment.— I rise by 6 oclock a. m., take a swimming bath in a large pool . . . dress & walk two or more miles, eat breakfast & ride on horseback 8 to 12 miles before dinner, take a short walk before supper, &, after that meal, dance a few times & retire to bed by 10½ p. m.— Thus I am engaged in cultivating the mere physical powers quite all of my time. I have improved them most sensibly & visibly since coming here; having increased 17 lbs in weight &, as I am assured, most strikingly in appearance. I weighed only 120 lbs on reaching the mountains, . . . & felt scarcely able to walk a mile.— I now look quite as fleshy & rosy as I ever did. . . . Virginia's improvement has been quite as great as my own.— I am treated with marked attention here, & V. with still more—mine, I suppose, to the senator, & hers to the woman."

Clay cut short his vacation in midautumn, because, as he explained, "I wish to reach Washington City by the 20th Octo., at furthest, & go to studying for the winter." While Clement was thus engaged, Virginia was preparing for her real debut in Washington society, and made a trip to New York for a new wardrobe, as well as to enjoy the sights and theater of that metropolis. With Virginia in New York was her young cousin, Evelyn Collier, the first of a series of relatives who were to spend their debutante seasons with the Clays, enjoying the whirl of

11 USC, *Cong. Globe*, 34:3, pp. 324f, Jan. 14, 1857; C. E. Hamlin, *Hannibal Hamlin*, 223; Nevins, *Ordeal of the Union*, I, 152-59.

Capital society. "Ev. & I," wrote Virginia, "will bring home twelve *new* dresses." The piece de resistance of Virginia's wardrobe was a behooped ivory lace evening gown, rumored to have cost three hundred dollars. The expense of maintaining the senatorial standard of living worried even Virginia, for she wrote, "Another thing I know too,—& that is, that at our present rates, —we are bankrupt! . . . Four thousand $ have we spent, & yet the gay winter to go thro' with!"[12]

Living arrangements for the coming winter were a matter of much concern too, and after canvassing various possibilities, the Clays returned to Gardiner's, where they had spent the previous winter. "Ev.," as Virginia explained, "is perfectly willing to stay in a small room, if it is *entirely comfortable*. . . . Hence, the room must be carpeted & kept at a reasonable temperature." In the same house with them were Fitzpatrick and Dowdell of Alabama, while James L. Orr of South Carolina and Alfred H. Colquitt of Georgia roomed nearby and had their meals with the Clays. "We seven constitute the mess—," Clement explained to his mother, "Va., generally, sitting at one end & I at the other of the table. We are on the best terms of friendship & enjoy our quiet, family-like table or parlor meetings very much. . . . We now have a parlor on the first floor," while as for heating, he added, "We burn wood in our chambers & coal in the parlor. Va. has a parlor quite handsomely furnished, & . . . containing a pretty good piano—."[13]

December 4, 1854, saw Clement Clay again in his seat. This short session achieved only modest results in the way of legislation, and Clay himself did not make even one important speech. He pursued his land policy by introducing a supplementary bill to graduate and reduce the price of public lands, but it died in committee, and his bill to improve Mobile harbor passed the Senate but failed of action in the House. His one successful measure provided for a report on the money due Alabama from the 2 and 3 percent funds. To the bounty land bill granting quarter sections of land to all veterans, their widows, and minor children, Clay gave his stout opposition and negative vote, only

12 Clay, Jr., to Clay, Sr., Sept. 17, 1854, Virginia Clay to Clay, Jr., [Nov.] 19, 1854, Clay MSS.
13 Clay, Jr., to Susanna Clay, Dec. 15, 1854, Virginia Clay to Clay, Jr., [Nov.] 19, 1854, Clay MSS.

to see it become a law. On the matter of aid to railroads, Clay at this time made a different approach by supporting James C. Jones of Tennessee in his bill to allow three years' credit for paying the duty on imported railroad iron. The bill passed the Senate but got no further that session. Clay subsequently took over the idea and pressed similar bills of his own in later sessions. In this he reflected the interests of the South and West, where railroads were rapidly expanding, but tariff and iron-manufacturing interests of the East blocked all his efforts.

Though the short session was not usually so brilliant socially, "Ev. and I," wrote Virginia Clay, "have been constantly engaged visiting and filling evening invitations for some weeks past. Mr. Corcoran, the banker, has his levees just as the heads of departments, only on a more magnificent scale far. To-night is his fete and all uppertendom will be there. . . . Judge Campbell's family are very kind and attentive to us, also Mrs. John Bell's lavishes her kindness on me . . . she," gossiped Virginia, "is dying of consumption her enemies say, is only kept alive by her hope of the Presidency." General Winfield Scott "has spoken to me often of Father, and . . . said . . . very many pleasant things of mine and Mr. Clay's youthful looks, 'Certainly not married ten years,' &c. He is a cunning old coon!" Thus Virginia spent the days until March 4, 1855. Upon returning to Alabama, Virginia accompanied Evelyn Collier to Tuscaloosa, while Clement went to Huntsville but later joined Virginia for a vacation at the Gulf resorts and visits with relatives in southern Alabama.[14]

While he was in that part of the state, Clement took occasion to consolidate his position by an address before the Chunnenuggee Horticultural Society. He deplored the geographic sectionalism of the state and the lack of transportation facilities. He pleaded for development of Alabama's resources, particularly coal and iron, and for soil conservation to "prevent the shameful decadence of agriculture so palpable in Virginia and the Carolinas." Alabama planters, he declared, must abandon the one-crop system of cotton culture, and "adopt . . . such restoratives of their worn out lands, as science may suggest and skill may devise."

14 Virginia Clay to Susanna Clay, Feb. 14, 1855, W. A. Battle to Susanna Clay, June 12, 1855, Virginia Clay to Clay, Sr., July 10, 1855, Clay MSS; USC, *SJ*, 33:2, pp. 64, 120, 198, 214, 220, 305, 316; USC, *Cong. Globe*, 33:2, pp. 1, 68, 105, 152, 251, 613, 622f, 748f, 785, 880; Haney, *Congressional Hist. of Railways*, II, 39-44.

Clay strengthened himself in the western half of the state when, as a distinguished alumnus, he delivered the commencement address before the two literary societies of the University of Alabama. His subject, "The Love of Truth for Its Own Sake," was peculiarly adapted to moral abstractions, in which it abounded, and as a product of the Romantic Age, it apparently suited the "very large & cosmopolitan audience." Virginia Clay described the occasion: "This morning dawned clear & tropically bright, the thermometer standing for many hours at 93-4 . . . but it was the Hon: Senators day, & no help for it. So off we put, at a few minutes before ten. . . . Mr. Clay blanched as usual, to a death like pallor, but regaining instantly his self-control, spoke with an ease & elegance, well befitting the dignity of his subject. He spoke nearly an hour & a quarter—but seemed to feel no unhappy effect from the excessive heat . . . compliments from all came more rapidly than we cd. receive them—" This engagement prevented Clay's attendance at a mass meeting of Morgan County Democrats, whom he conciliated with a public letter in which he rejoiced over the disintegration of Whiggery, deplored the rise of the equally obnoxious Know-Nothings, and advised southern-rights men to "prepare for the worst, but . . . not precipitate it by any indiscretion."[15]

During Clement's fifteen months' absence from home, several events of interest had occurred within the Clay family. In the spring of 1854 Clement, Sr., Withers, and Lawson all journeyed to Charleston, South Carolina, as delegates to the great railroad and commercial convention. Lawson went on to Washington for a brief visit with Clement and Virginia. Later in the year Lawson once more determined to seek his fortune in the West, and to that end he and Augustine J. Withers set out for Arkansas and Texas to look for suitable land. Lawson's "first impressions of Texas were unfavorable," however, for he could not accustom himself to the "unbroken waste of naked prairie," nor could he see how planting there could be profitable in view of the scarcity of wood,

15 Virginia Clay to Clay, Sr., July 10, 1855, Clay MSS; *Address of Hon. C. C. Clay, Jr., Delivered before the Chunnenuggee Horticultural Society* [May 4, 1855]; *The Love of Truth for Its Own Sake: An Address before the Erosophic and Philomathic Societies of the University of Alabama, at Its Commencement, in July 1855: By Hon. C. C. Clay, Jr.* These two addresses published in pamphlet form were originally with the Clay MSS, together with most of both the Clays' speeches in Congress. The latter have not been cited in their pamphlet form, since the texts are usually to be found in the *Congressional Globe*.

water, and means of transportation. He was more favorably impressed with parts of Arkansas, but did not purchase, and in the end nothing came of the scheme which Clement had been very anxious to carry out. Meanwhile, Susanna, on a visit to Tusca-loosa, was thrown from a carriage and suffered a broken arm and other injuries which incapacitated her for some time.

After the failure to purchase Arkansas lands, Lawson returned to Huntsville, soon married, and settled back into the rut of desultory law practice. Clement, Sr., had retired, but left Withers "the use of his name in the firm." Lawson often proposed abandoning the law, but was never able to suggest "another pursuit . . . better in a pecuniary point of view. I am," continued Withers, "studying my cases assiduously . . . & shall endeavor to recover what I have lost. . . . There is, evidently, a strong combination . . . in favor of Walker, Brickell, & Cabaniss, which . . . gives them a decided advantage over any other firm in town. . . . I wish now that you [Clement, Jr.], brother L. & I had formed a partnership years ago. . . . We might have formed a triple cord, which could have successfully resisted all such combinations."[16]

Withers was not without political ambitions, and in the autumn of 1855 he sought election as solicitor for the Huntsville judicial circuit. So it was that Withers and Mary Clay journeyed to Montgomery, followed in a few days by Virginia and Clement, the latter being one of a committee appointed to seek legislative aid for the Memphis and Charleston Railroad. Mary Clay was "enjoying herself greatly" on a rare excursion from home while Withers electioneered among the legislators, and they all attended Alabama's first state fair. Clement of course took this opportunity to mend fences among the county politicians, whom Virginia proceeded to dazzle with her charm and sophistication. As for the solicitorship, Clement feared that Withers would "get no vote from Madison." And so it turned out; Withers did not get the caucus nomination, and the solicitorship went to John Spinks Kennedy. While he was in Montgomery, Withers participated in a movement by leading Democrats to organize "all persons

16 Virginia Clay to H. L. Clay, April 11, 1854, H. L. Clay to Clay, Jr., Dec. 15, 1854, Clay, Jr., to Clay, Sr., Sept. 17, 1854, Virginia Clay to Susanna Clay, Nov. 24, 1854, J. W. Clay to Clay, Jr., Feb. 8, 1855, Clay MSS; "The Great Southern Convention in Charleston," *De Bow's Review*, XVI (June, 1854), 632-41, XVII (July-Sept., 1854), 91-99, 200-13, 325-26.

of whatever former party" into the "Democratic and Anti-Know Nothing party."[17]

Clement and Virginia waited in Montgomery for the Fitz-patricks, and together they set off for Washington on November 28. They were all finally established in Mrs. Smith's boarding-house near Fourteenth and F streets. In describing their situation, Virginia wrote, "we had far more trouble than usual in finding suitable apartments. . . . Our mess, so far from being willing to separate, insisted upon being enlarged . . . we have in two blocks, some twelve Senators, among whom are, Bell, Slidell, Weller, Brodhead, Thomson of N. J. who are married & house-keeping, to say naught of Butler, Benjamin, Mason & Goode, in a mess near us. . . . Our mess is a very pleasant one,—Orr, Shorter, Dowdell[,] Sandidge & Taylor of Louisiana, . . . with the young senator Pugh of Ohio & his bride wife, the Gov. & madam [Fitzpatrick] & ourselves compose the party. Taylor . . . is a true democrat, & Pugh is as strongly anti-free soil as we. Indeed, we keep free-soilers, black Republicans & Bloomers, the other side of the street. They are afraid to even enquire for board at this house."

Virginia's words reflected the increasing sectional tension. Nor was it diminished any by the failure of the House to elect a speaker. For two months the Senate marked time. "I think," predicted Clement Clay, "the ultimate election of Banks quite certain," and indeed, that event took place on February 2, 1856. Meanwhile, both domestic and international affairs pointed to the need for getting the President's message before the public. And so early in January, Pierce sent in that document, which, Clay reported, "has fallen like a bomb shell among [Republicans]. Its bold proslaveryism has startled all—even his friends. Never has any predecessor talked as plainly or as harshly to the section-alists & fanatics. He deserves the highest honors & deepest grati-tude of the South; but I doubt his getting either."[18]

When work finally got under way in the Senate, Clay introduced

17 J. W. Clay to Susanna Clay, Nov. 11, 1855, Clay, Jr., to Clay, Sr., Nov. 23, 1855, Clay, Jr., to H. L. Clay, Nov. 26, 1855, L. P. Walker to Clay, Jr., Nov. 22, 1858, Clay MSS; Ala. Leg., *HJ*, pp. 96, 101, Nov. 30, Dec. 1, 1855; Huntsville *Demo-crat*, Nov. 22, 29, Dec. 13, 1855; Elizabeth McTyeire Essler, "The Agricultural Reform Movement in Alabama," *Ala. Rev.*, I (Oct. 1948), 250-53.
18 Virginia Clay to Clay, Sr., Dec. 25 [1855], Clay, Jr., to Clay, Sr., Jan. 3, 1856, Clay MSS; Howell Cobb to Mrs. Cobb, Feb. 2, 1856, Toombs-Stephens-Cobb, *Correspondence*, II, 358; Nichols, *Pierce*, 436f.

bills to improve the defenses of Mobile and New Orleans, and to provide greater security of life on steamboats, but both died in committee. His two successful bills extended the pension laws to those Cherokees who had fought with the white militia in 1836, and granted alternate sections of public land to the Coosa and Tennessee Railroad Company. By dint of great effort on the part of Clay, Fitzpatrick, and Toombs, a bill to pay the citizens of Alabama and Georgia for losses by Creek depredations in 1836 was gotten through the Senate by a vote of 21-20, but the House ignored it.[19]

This meager accomplishment represents all that could be done in a session not destined for the ordinary course of legislation, for once more Kansas was the center of attention. Pierce's ambition to execute the Kansas-Nebraska Act fairly was frustrated by the actions of designing and unscrupulous men. What was intended to be a free and equal opportunity for all in the territorial domain had rapidly degenerated into a sordid scramble for gain, plunder, and adventure. The imminence of fighting on the frontier was reflected by equally heated dissension in the halls of Congress, while the recent mushrooming threat of the Know-Nothings and the ominous growth of the new Republican party only added to the general political uncertainty and confusion. "Every thing," wrote the impressionable Virginia Clay, "is in excitement & confusion. . . . 'Fusion' reigns in truth; & Southern blood is at boiling temperature. . . . There is a Black Repub. or worse at every corner of our political fence, & if ever the gap is down, we are gone! I wish," Virginia continued to her father-in-law, "you cd. be here, to witness the scenes daily enacted in the Halls of Congress,—to hear the hot taunts of defiance hurled into the very teeth of the Northerners by our goaded but spirited patriots. I expect every day to hear of blood shed & death, & wd. not be surprised at any time to *witness* the civil war of Kansas."[20]

Along with these blows to the administration, the South saw its presumed victory transformed into defeat as its efforts to people Kansas failed. It was not much consolation that New England emigrant-aid companies were not a startling success, when in the

19 USC, *SJ*, 34:1, pp. 132, 145, 165, 181, 229, 348, 367, 473, 513, 569, Feb. 25, 28, March 3, 13, April 3, May 22, 29, July 23, Aug. 1, 7, 12, 1856; USC, *HJ*, 34:1, pp. 1017-19, May 21, 1856; USC, *Cong. Globe*, 34:1, pp. 349, 489, 645, 809, 2052f.
20 Virginia Clay to Clay, Sr., Dec. 25 [1855], Clay MSS; Huntsville *Democrat*, Dec. 6, 1855; Nichols, *Pierce*, 407-15; Milton, *Eve of Conflict*, 186-200.

whole South, Alabama alone could muster only one small and unsuccessful expedition. Major Jefferson Buford of Eufaula, Alabama, led about four hundred men to Kansas, but the anti-slavery faction was so hostile that they were unable to settle, and within a year most of the members had drifted back to Alabama. The expedition had cost nearly $25,000, of which Buford himself contributed over $10,000. Clay gave Buford his warmest support and sent fifty dollars, a sum amounting to three dollars per capita for his slaves, which, he assured Buford, was "far less" than he wished to give.

Looking at actualities, any southern man could well ask, "What better will it be for us, if under the Specious cry of *'popular sovereignty'* the free soil rabble of New England devotes Kansas ... to free-soil—than if Congress should directly apply the *'Wilmot proviso'*? While we are for the Kansas Act—because of its righteous repeal of the *Missouri restriction*—our North. friends . . . sustain it because it deprives us of the territories under Squatter Sovereignty. . . . I want . . . *our rights* in the territories defined." Fearful of "civil war in Kansas," Clay predicted that "If the South do not rush to its rescue this spring & summer the Emigrant Aid societies will abolitionize it before the end of the year. . . . If we do not deter them with numbers, they will become aggressive & insurrectionary in the fall."[21]

In line with the President's recommendation, Douglas, on March 12, 1856, brought in a bill authorizing formation of a state government in Kansas. Debate on the bill brought Clay to the oratorical heights of his career in a two-hour speech which was distinguished less by its reference to the "Contest in Kansas" and more by its "intensity of Southern spirit." Clay began with a sweeping defense of that "true patriot" and "enlightened statesman," Franklin Pierce. Proceeding to the "Policy of Black Republicanism," Clay described it as deliberate misrepresentation, making the South appear to be the aggressor. Furthermore, the Republicans dared not risk a presidential campaign on straight abolition issues, since they had no assurance that "the Northern

21 Clay, Jr., to Clay, Sr., March 10, 1856, Clay MSS; William F. Samford to Bolling Hall, Nov. 9, 1855, Bolling Hall MSS; Eufaula *Spirit of the South,* Jan. 22, 1856; Walter Lynwood Fleming, "The Buford Expedition to Kansas," *AHR,* VI (Oct., 1900), 38-48; William Orlando Lynch, "Population Movements in Relation to the Struggle for Kansas," Indiana University, *Studies in American History Inscribed to James Albert Woodburn* (Bloomington, Ind., 1926), 381-405.

people are yet prepared to sustain them in an open assault upon the constitutional rights of the South"; hence they complained of the "wrongs and injuries of the north" at the hands of an aggressive South in "possession of the high places of the government." To refute this Republican line, Clay developed an elaborate argument claiming that since the Revolution the South had gained only 50 percent in area while the North had increased by nearly 1,100 percent. From this he concluded that "No impartial mind can contemplate the history of these territorial contests without being impressed with the arrogant demands" of the North "and the generous but unwise concessions" of the South. "Instead of aggressing," declared Clay, "the South has been retrogressing; instead of encroaching on non-slaveholding territory, she has been surrendering slaveholding territory . . . she has been conceding . . . until she seems almost regarded by northern Free-Soilers as a mere tenant by sufferance." The "tenant by sufferance" was, however, indispensable to the economic system, continued Clay. Southern wealth went to pay revenue, and southern goods (chiefly cotton, of course) formed the basis of northern profits. Southern nonslaveholders were well off when compared with New England labor, which he described as "that system of servitude called voluntary." As for New England, Clay continued, "with all her pious horror of slavery, she gives it daily aid and encouragement, . . . in rewarding slave labor, in using the products of slave labor, in buying from and selling to the slave owner. . . . How magnanimous and unselfish to refuse the slave owner the privilege of enjoying, like herself, the profits of slave labor in peace and quietness!"

The return of fugitive slaves Clay placed on constitutional grounds as obligatory with or without congressional legislation. This led him to the personal-liberty laws of Massachusetts, that state once so righteously incensed at South Carolina's nullification, but now rejoicing in the disgraceful success of her own nullifying activities. Even those abolitionists who conceded the constitutionality of slavery within the states were really working for its destruction by indirect means, and all their activities "are conceived in the wish, and exerted with the expectation, that they will overthrow slavery in the States." Even worse were the Yankee insults which boasted that the South would never leave the Union because it feared slave insurrection. This led Clay to close on an alarmist note by predicting that "whenever Black Republicanism shall take possession of this Government . . . the South . . . will not pause to expostulate, but will boldly throw her sword into the scale and assert her natural privilege of self-defense." Still convalescent from a recent illness, Clay "was obliged, by hoarseness of voice and physical exhaustion . . . to suspend his remarks."

Nevertheless, his effort was "pronounced on all hands *the speech of the session.*" Lewis Cass called it "the greatest speech he ever heard delivered in the Senate Chamber," and other senators were equally lavish in their praise. The Democratic press was generally favorable and claimed that Clay's speech was "spoken of in terms of admiration even by his opponents," though many northern papers were bitterly hostile. Clay's "outburst of indignant eloquence," wrote a Washington correspondent, "was unexpected from one so young and modest, and fell . . . as a clap of thunder in a clear sky."

The elder Clay's comments to his son were less perfervid and reflected more the customary paternal restraint. "I take pleasure in saying (to you) I consider it able, conclusive, and eloquent. You maintain every proposition, I think, most unanswerably. I somewhat feared the correspondents of the various papers, north & south, who spoke of it, had extolled it too much—to be followed by public disappointment. But I am free to acknowledge, that I do not think they did it more than justice. . . . I see your labor must have been great, but I earnestly hope you will meet your reward, in the approval of your own conscience, increased reputation, and the public good it will have accomplished."[22]

One speedy result was Clay's encounter with abolitionist John P. Hale of New Hampshire, that tough-skinned, clever-tongued enemy of Franklin Pierce. Hale loftily declined to answer Clay's "grossly personal" references, adding that it would "require something else besides malignity to redeem imbecility from contempt." Thereupon Clay leaped up to say, "I defy his malice as much as I

___

22 Clay, Jr., to Clay, Sr., April 28, 1856, Clay, Sr., to Clay, Jr., May 10, 1856, Clay MSS; USC, *SJ*, 34:1, pp. 176, 185; USC, *Cong Globe*, 34:1, Appen., pp. 483-90; Huntsville *Democrat*, May 1, 1856; Montgomery *Weekly Alabama Journal*, May 2, 1856; Milton, *Eve of Conflict*, 219-21. In its pamphlet form Clay's speech was entitled, *Speech of Mr. Clement C. Clay, Jr., of Alabama, on the Contest in Kansas and the Plan and Purpose of Black Republicanism: Delivered in the Senate of the United States on Monday, 21st April, 1856.*

contemn his baseness," and assailed him for indulging in insolence under the protection of the senatorial office. "I see," continued Clay, "that he is pleased by this attention. . . . I beg pardon of the Senate for having consumed so much time on one who soils the carpet upon which he treads." To the more moderate antislavery leaders, Clay was in turn more moderate, as appears in his reply to Henry Wilson of Massachusetts. "I have never," declared Clay, assailed "any Senator for condemning the institution of slavery. . . . I do claim, however, as a southron and a slaveholder, that I am no less a gentleman . . . than those who do not own slaves, and were born north of Mason and Dixon's line. Those Senators whom I did assail, . . . and who were distinctly designated by name, have denied to me, and to every Senator sitting upon this floor who owns a slave, all the characteristics of gentlemen. They have imputed to us a crime in exercising that right which belongs to us. . . . Still, these Senators . . . seek and court our society. They come to us with friendship on their brows, but with rancor in their hearts. I do maintain that this is duplicity unworthy of gentlemen."

The southern press gleefully reported "the blasting, withering, crushing and consuming invective which Mr. Clay discharged upon the notorious Hale." But, southern accounts continued, mere words could not convey the "stinging emphasis of tone, the scornful shake of the finger, the intense fury of the eye, the contemptuous and indignant manner," the like of which had not been heard and seen in the Senate "since the days of John Randolph." On "Hale's brazen brow . . . a blush was even seen," while the "rhinocerous hide of the beastly abolitionist quivered under the lash."[23]

Clay was by this time so worn down from work and from his recent illness that he found a short rest necessary. He spent the time in Virginia, at Madison's estate Montpelier, where the beauty of the scenery and the magnificence of the house and grounds greatly impressed him. "I do not wonder," he exclaimed, "that James Madison was a man of great tho'ts. I only wonder that people born & raised among such scenes should ever have little tho'ts."[24]

23 USC, *Cong. Globe,* 34:1, pp. 1099, 1405, May 2, June 13, 1856; Clay Scrapbooks, VI, 285.
24 Clay, Jr., to Virginia Clay, May 16, 1856, Clay MSS.

Sectional excitement reached a climax on May 22, 1856, when Preston Brooks made his notorious attack on Charles Sumner. The abolitionists provided themselves with revolvers and darkly predicted that "some one will be shot down before the session closes." Southern reaction was mixed, but in October, Brooks' South Carolina constituents honored him with a dinner "in testimony of the complete endorsement of his congressional course." Clay received an invitation to this event, but did not attend. Reflecting widespread southern opinion, one of Clay's correspondents wrote that "The manner of administering the Brooks assault is unfortunate—instead of its being the insult intended it makes a martyr of him and sends him back to the Senate for 6 years longer—" which was exactly what happened.

The session dragged on into the summer, hopefully through June, hotly through July, when the thermometer at ninety-two and the interminable Kansas debate vied in creating heat, and wearily into August, when House and Senate deadlocked over Kansas and the army bill. "Staying here now," wrote one member, "is the severest trial I have ever been subjected to. . . . The weather has been . . . such as I never felt for so long a time before. One can scarcely exist much less dress to go into the parlor." Accommodations and food deteriorated with the weather, for "Every body,—boarders, servants and proprietors,—seem fagged out. The only activity is amongst the flies. The table is literally black with them, and no one pretends to brush them off. Even Mrs. Clay has lost her vigor, and says nothing in our behalf."[25]

While Virginia vacillated about leaving for "the springs," Clay spent most of the summer obstructing the rivers and harbors bills, which he fought on a state-rights basis. This attitude did not always give an air of lofty adherence to principle, especially to members of the opposition. "One of Clay's notions," said one of them, "was that the government had no right to appropriate money to improve rivers and harbors. Once he got appointed to the Committee on Commerce, where he made no end of trouble." When an appropriation for a southern harbor came up, "Clay

25 Isaac Bell to Virginia Clay, May 26, 1856, Arthur Simkins and others to Clay, Jr., Sept. 13, 1856, Clay MSS; L. O'B. Branch to Nancy Branch, Aug. 27, 1856, Albert R. Newsome (ed.), "Letters of Lawrence O'Bryan Branch, 1856-1860," *North Carolina Historical Review*, X (Jan., 1933), 47, 52; Moorfield Storey, *Charles Sumner* (Boston, 1900), 151; C. E. Hamlin, *Hannibal Hamlin*, 284; Avery Odell Craven, *The Growth of Southern Nationalism* (Baton Rouge, 1953), 223-46.

insisted that the State . . . should make the improvement, and all the precedents in the history of the government could not drive the idea out of his head. All the other members of the committee favored the appropriation, and after a stormy session Mr. Clay departed from the meeting in a state of high dudgeon, threatening to invoke the aid of his quixotic Southern brethren to defeat the bill."[26]

In the midst of all these excitements, the national party conventions assembled to nominate presidential candidates. Since January, Clay, as a member of the Democratic Congressional Committee, had been busy with arrangements for the convention which opened on June 2, 1856, in Cincinnati. While the Democracy was still national, rifts within the party were painfully apparent. The outlook was not very encouraging for southern-rights men or for their candidate, Franklin Pierce. Douglas was in a strong position, and most Southerners of whatever stripe were willing to accept him as the party's candidate, along with his doctrine of popular sovereignty. But here and there a few bold spirits began openly to question the trustworthiness of the man and the validity of the principle. Extreme southern-rights men could not agree to that kind of popular sovereignty, which meant recognizing antislavery legislation by a territorial assembly. They maintained that slavery could be dealt with only when a constitution was formed, and on this basis southern extremists demanded federal legislation to protect southern interests in the territories against the Douglas brand of popular sovereignty. Conservative southern leaders, however, refused to make the question of secession turn on the securing of such a "useless abstraction."[27]

Not so William Lowndes Yancey, who was working to have leadership of Alabama's Democracy firmly in his grasp. To this end, he addressed an informal convention in Montgomery on January 8, 1856. When the state convention assembled in May, Yancey took control and pushed through readoption of the "Ala-

26 L. O'B. Branch to Nancy Branch, June 30, 1856, "Letters," 47; William McKendree Gwin, MS Memoirs, pp. 123f; C. E. Hamlin, *Hannibal Hamlin*, 223.
27 W. F. Samford to Bolling Hall, Nov. 9, 1855, Bolling Hall MSS; Washington *Sentinel*, Jan. 10, 1856; Huntsville *Democrat*, Jan. 24, 1856; Nichols, *Pierce*, 450-52; Milton, *Eve of Conflict*, 214-17; Roy Franklin Nichols, *The Disruption of American Democracy* (New York, 1948), 10-13; Joseph Hodgson, *Cradle of the Confederacy; or The Times of Troup, Quitman, and Yancey* (Mobile, 1876), 363f; James Eyers Davis Yonge, "Conservative Party in Alabama, 1848-1860," Ala. Hist. Soc. *Transactions*, IV (1899-1903), 507.

bama Platform of 1848." He had also induced the Alabama legislature to pass resolutions endorsing these principles. Not only did
Yancey control the convention, but he was chosen one of the
electors at large, the other being LeRoy Pope Walker. This selection was not entirely satisfactory, as one of Clay's friends explained.
"Both . . . are as distasteful to me, as they are to a large majority
of the Democracy of Alabama, but . . . expediency . . . was the
controlling power." The convention was "obliged to cast about
for those men whose *speaking powers alone* would be most effec-
tual. . . . Neither of the gentlemen referred to are popular men—
never have been and never will be." While these events were
transpiring in Alabama, Clay from his central location was
reporting to his friends throughout the state "how the under
current moves."

And with that "under current" he was not entirely happy.
"Douglass," [*sic*] lamented Clay, "has disturbed Pierce's prospects
for the Pres. by appearing as a candidate, taking off from him the
votes of seven of the western states. I prefer the latter, but would
gladly see either elected.— I think one of them, or Hunter or
Wise should be nominated." Clay nevertheless recognized "the
necessity of reconciling the high protective feeling of Pennsylvania," and so was more or less resigned to Pierce's defeat. He
covered the national convention when he said succinctly, "The
Buchanan men prevailed throughout." Clay's attitude was accurately reflected in the remarks of one of his friends on Buchanan's
nomination: "We regret that Pierce has been thrown overboard
for we know that the cause of it has been his devotion to the
rights of the States, the South included. . . . We will support
Buchanan of course, cheerfully, but he cannot command that
enthusiasm which the name of Frank Pierce would have done."[28]

In Buchanan the conservatives triumphed. His endorsement
of the Kansas-Nebraska bill reassured the South. He was more
acceptable to many conservative Southerners than Pierce, whose
Kansas policy was suspected of harboring free-soil tendencies.

[28] Clay, Jr., to Clay, Sr., March 10, [June 7], 1856, J. L. M. Curry to Clay, Jr.,
May 10, 1856, James E. Peebles to Clay, Jr., [March 11, 1856], Zacharias Lee Nabers
to Clay, Jr., June 11, 1856, Clay MSS; John Letcher to [?], May 28, 1856, John
Letcher MSS; Ala. Leg., *HJ*, pp. 69-72, Nov. 24, 1855; Huntsville *Democrat*, Dec. 6,
1855, quoting Montgomery *Advertiser and Gazette;* Nichols, *Disruption of American
Democracy*, 18; DuBose, *Yancey*, 318f; George Petrie, "What Will Be the Final
Estimate of Yancey?" Ala. Hist. Soc. *Transactions*, IV (1899-1903), 311f.

The nomination of John Cabell Breckinridge for vice president conciliated both the Douglas men and the tariff interests. While Clay admitted the strength of the ticket, he accepted it with regret. As he explained to his father, "The nominations of Buchanan & Breckinridge will, I think, prove very strong—as strong, probably, as any that could be made. In the North, it will command a much larger vote than Pierce or Douglass could have done. Indeed, it will sweep the entire Democracy & National Whigs & take a large number of Anti-Nebraska men. Coming as they do from two tariff states & representing strong protective interests, it will conciliate the support of thousands who would scarcely have voted for Pierce or Douglass, because of their known anti-protective principles. Being liberal about internal improvements, as they are understood to be, it will secure the North West, wh. P. could scarcely have done—perhaps, even Douglass would have lost, in part. Besides, Buchanan has not offended the anti-slavery prejudices of the North as either P. or D. have done, & many will support him there who would not have voted for either of them.

"All this will make it a very strong ticket for the North. As to the South, it will be a safe ticket on the Slavery issues & our foreign policy—so much better than the Know-Nothing ticket, that it will carry quite every Southern state. With the bold & uncompromising platform adopted, the South will feel secure.

"Yet, *entre nous,* & in profound confidence, it does not suit me, or any Southern rights man I have seen who spoke to me confidentially. It is a ticket for the *Union* wing of the Southern Democracy—such as Houston, Cobb of Ga., *et id omne genus.* Pierce was my choice above all men in the South, North, East or West. If we could keep him in office four years longer, the tariff would be bro't down to a purely revenue standard, the Demo. party put upon the true constitutional anti-internal improvement platform, the back bone of Abolition broken or badly strained, & the Govt. fixed in the old republican tack.

"With our present nominees, the issues will not be fairly fought with Abolition & our triumph will be incomplete. . . . The Atlantic states of the South, & the gulf states, except La., will be the only faithful representatives of the strict construction faith & will curse Buchanan as bitterly as the North now abuses Pierce. . . . Of course, I'll not say this except to those who feel & think with me & then, in confidence. I shall do my best for the ticket —if it need my help."[29]

As soon as Congress adjourned (on August 30, 1856), Clay hastened to Alabama to campaign. With Jeremiah Clemens and Henry W. Hilliard touring North Alabama for the American party ticket, Democrats concentrated their big guns in that area. Yancey was already busy there, and as soon as the congressional delegation reached home, W. R. W. Cobb and George S. Houston joined Clay in the campaign. Clay spoke at Auburn and Ashville, among other places. In October, Andrew Johnson came down from Tennessee to help out the cause. The campaign then moved to the Alabama River counties of Marengo, Perry, Greene, Wilcox, and Dallas, where a local committee was organizing a "Grand Mass Meeting" to be held at Union Town on October 24. There Clay, A. B. Moore, F. S. Lyon, and numerous other Democrats poured out an uninterrupted flow of oratory, climaxed on the last day by Yancey's three-hour peroration, "pronounced with accustomed fluency and solemnity." From Union Town, Clay moved on to Montgomery, where he wound up his campaign with a speech at Estelle Hall on October 27, calling on the South to unite with northern Democrats to strike "one stalwart blow for the Union and the Constitution."

When the Maine elections in September forecast a Republican victory, Democrats everywhere took fright and redoubled their efforts. They were rewarded by October victories in Pennsylvania and Indiana, and in November, Buchanan won the Presidency by a small margin. Alabama Democrats rolled up their customary large majority, with 18,000 votes over their opponents. This election saw the end of the American party in Alabama. That state was now ready to go over to a one-party system.[30]

29 Clay, Jr., to Clay, Sr., June 7, 1856, Clay MSS; Thomas Ruffin to Henry Toole Clark, June 25, 1856, Henry Toole Clark MSS; A. H. Stephens to Thomas W. Thomas, June 16, 1856, Toombs-Stephens-Cobb, *Correspondence*, II, 367; Philip G. Auchampaugh, "James Buchanan, the Conservatives' Choice, 1856: A Political Portrait," *Historian*, VII (Spring, 1945), 77-90.

30 Virginia Clay to Clay, Jr., Aug. 30, Sept. 18, 22, 1856, Clay MSS; W. F. Samford to M. P. Blue, Sept. 22, 1856, W. F. Samford MSS; J. Branham to Howell Cobb, Sept. 15, 1856, Toombs-Stephens-Cobb, *Correspondence*, II, 381f; W. Grandin to R. M. T. Hunter, Oct. 18, 1856, *Correspondence of Robert M. T. Hunter, 1826-1876*, ed. by Charles Henry Ambler, AHA *Annual Report* (1916), II, 199; L. G. Tyler, *Letters and Times of the Tylers*, II, 533f; Huntsville *Democrat*, Sept. 18, 1856; Huntsville *Southern Advocate*, Oct. 9, 1856; Jacksonville (Ala.) *Republican*, Oct. 14, 1856; Cahaba *Dallas Gazette*, Oct. 17, 1856; Montgomery *Advertiser and State Gazette*, Oct. 15, Nov. 5, 1856; Montgomery *Weekly Alabama Journal*, Sept. 20, 1856; DuBose, *Yancey*, 329-31; Nichols, *Disruption of American Democracy*, 44-47.

While Clement was helping to elect Buchanan, Virginia Clay spent the autumn visiting relatives in Virginia and North Carolina, particularly the Hilliards of "Millbrook," Halifax County, North Carolina. Virginia also spent a few days at nearby Shocco Springs, which, she said, "deserves its far-famed reputation, for it is a great place. . . . Gov. Biggs," she continued, "came over . . . to 'Shocco' to see me. . . . I found a great many pleasant friends at the Springs, & was such a belle I was almost ashamed of it. I *fear* I shall be in the papers, in such brilliant colors, as will make me blush." Among the cousins was eighteen-year-old Jennie Hilliard, whom Virginia took back to Washington for the winter. But prior to that, the two women went to New York and Philadelphia on a shopping tour. Here they encountered the subjects of current society news, namely Stephen A. Douglas and his bride, Adele Cutts, who were on their wedding trip. Virginia described the circumstance: "Judge Douglass [*sic*] & wife arrived here [Burlington, N. J.] Mond'y night, & I happened to be in the parlor to greet them. Addie looks magnificent & very happy." She asked "the approval of *my taste* . . . in regard to a superb Eugenia robe at 150$ wh. the Judge had sent her. . . . It is regal, & will well become the wearer. . . . Her whole wardrobe is queenly, & her husband says 'my dear' quite matrimonially."[31]

Early in December the Clays were settled once more in Washington, where, Virginia explained, "Nearly all our mess are re-united," with the addition of two babies, young Benny Fitzpatrick and "little Pugh, a pug nosed little buckeye shoot." His mother, the beautiful Theresa Pugh, who looked more like a twentieth-century New Yorker than a nineteenth-century Ohioan, was accompanied by her less dazzling sister. Under Virginia's guidance, Jennie Hilliard was enjoying "the full blaze of fashionable life, . . . enchanted with the novelty of every body & everything." That winter Washington had its share of scandalous rumors circulating through society, which led Virginia to comment, "I constantly feel that I am . . . struggling to pass 'twixt Scylla & Charybdis, for Rumor, with her thousand tongues is ever ready for a victim. Thank Heaven, no breath of scandal has touched our mess, but we do not belong to the fast fancy-dancing

---

[31] Virginia Clay to Clay, Jr., Aug. 30, Sept. 16, [ca. Nov. 22], 1856, Virginia Clay to Tom Tait Tunstall, Oct. 10, 1856, Clay MSS. "Gov. Biggs" refers to Asa Biggs, who was U. S. senator from North Carolina but never governor of that state.

clique as yet." Indeed, their mess was probably more quiet than formerly, for in the rooms of one of its members, Virginia explained, "there is now no little drinking convenience . . . for he lived so fast last year that he well nigh finished himself, & is now trying to regain his lost . . . Health."[32]

Back in the Senate, Clay took a more active part in debate than he had in previous sessions. He introduced several minor bills, most of which did not pass. He pursued his penchant for economy in various ways, one of which was his opposition to establishing permanent clerkships for Senate committees. He especially objected to paying them six dollars a day, and when informed that the salary was to be $1,800 annually, Clay still maintained that this "pay would far exceed the amount of service rendered." In a debate on committee appointments, Lyman Trumbull of Illinois complained that the Republican party was not adequately represented. To this various senators replied that when committee appointments were made at the opening of the Thirty-fourth Congress (December, 1855), the Republican party "had scarcely a formal organization." Clay took this opportunity to call Trumbull's complaint "not only very inappropriate, but very unfortunate. . . . It implies that it is a sectional party." As for the House of Representatives, Clay charged that "the South has been proscribed upon all those committees which involve the consideration of any of her material interests." In this session Clay began his campaign for repeal of the bounties on codfishing. The bounty, dating from 1789, had originally been granted because of a tax on imported salt, as well as to encourage the training of seamen. Now, Clay argued, it had degenerated into a gratuitous payment to a few shipowners, and not to the fishermen themselves.

Clay was able to pursue both his economy line and his hostility to the pension system by opposing a particularly obnoxious Revolutionary claims bill which was largely the work of lobbyists and claim agents. Clay objected to the provisions for payment, not to Revolutionary officers themselves, but to their widows, children, and more remote descendants. The bill, Clay argued, gave to those whose service had been smallest, and neglected those who had risked most. Such legislation, he argued, would extend

---

32 Virginia Clay to T. T. Tunstall, Jan. 25, 1857, Clay MSS. The person referred to was James L. Orr.

government benefits beyond all bounds of reason or of capacity to pay, and would add one more blunder to a pension system already "an amorphous, distorted mass of legislation, framed rather by caprice than by reason." Clay condemned it as "the most monstrous, unjust, iniquitous measure, in the shape of a pension bill, which has ever been proposed in Congress." By one vote the bill was postponed, and so died.

In the last days of the session, the Jefferson Davis and Winfield Scott feud reached the Senate floor. The army appropriation bill would pay to Winfield Scott, now a lieutenant general, salary arrears for that rank dating from 1847. Secretary of War Davis had bitterly opposed Scott's claims, but the attorney general had ruled in favor of Scott. In the Senate debate, Clay championed his friend Davis and made a strong speech opposing that portion of the bill which would pay Scott's claims. "It is not the rank without pay, but the pay without rank that he seeks. It is not the laurel, but the loaves and fishes that he covets," declared Clay. Scott's alacrity in pressing his claims gave substance to this accusation, and his Whig affiliations did not endear him to Clay. Scott ultimately received more than $10,000, which was rather less than half the sum he sought.[33]

"All Washington," wrote Virginia Clay in January, 1857, "is Cabinet-making,—every coterie has its particular pet— & old Buch will have a sad time trying to please *the people.*" Not the least of the pressures on Buchanan was that exerted by Clay and other state-rights men. Alabamians were using that state's large Democratic majority as the basis for advancing several favorite sons, including Clay, Fitzpatrick, Yancey, and Houston. A rumor that Clay would be made secretary of the navy brought congratulations from a distant friend. Fitzpatrick's failure to receive the vice-presidential nomination now gave him an extra claim to consideration for a cabinet post, while Houston, the leading Union Democrat of Alabama, would provide an even stronger conservative force. State-rights elements and the Alabama electors, however, were unanimously behind Yancey, who "fills the idea of a Southern Representative man." Yancey himself was not so

---

33 F. E. H. Stegen to Clay, Jr., Feb. 26, 1857, Clay MSS; USC, *SJ*, 34:3, p. 897, Jan. 16, 1857; USC, *Cong. Globe*, 34:3, pp. 24, 50f, 70, 183, 328-31, 378, 576, 613, 1001-1005, Dec. 4, 8, 10, 23, 30, 1856, Jan. 14, 20, Feb. 5, 28, March 2, 1857; Nichols, *Pierce*, 385-87.

enthusiastic, as his reply to Clay's efforts in his behalf shows. "I am sincerely obliged to you," he wrote, "for the kind words spoken to Mr B—but . . . I desired . . . to let Mr B—be disembarrassed of all considerations respecting me. I have long felt, that I should have prevented my friends urging my name in connection with a cabinet appointment. I feel even now, crippled for future usefulness, if ever we shall be forced to act against Mr B—which God forefend!"

Nor was Yancey the only one who anticipated trouble. The state-rights men had yielded gracefully to Buchanan's nomination; now they wanted their reward in a good cabinet representation. But Buchanan was not so inclined; he did not intend to repeat Pierce's mistake by taking in all shades of opinion. Buchanan's "safe" conservatism brought threats from the more fiery state-righters. Edmund Ruffin darkly advised "a separation as early as may be," and others feared "That the 'fire' ingredient in the comeing [sic] Cabinet may not be of a due proportion." Another was apprehensive "that Buchanan is disposed to compose his Cabinet of men of the Howel[l] Cobb & Orr *stripe*. Is this true—? Can he not make a Cabinet of the JEFF. DAVIS order, of State rights men? Is the South about to be fouled? Is Jas Buchanan a d—n fool? Must the South prepare at once for a dissolution? If so, *good,* I am for it, & the *sooner the better.* . . . You wrote me . . . that Buchanan had some dark spots in his life on the Slavery question. . . . I fear you spoke the truth."[34]

As March 4 approached, these dark forebodings yielded to immediate interest in the inauguration. "The Inauguration Ball," exulted Virginia Clay, "is to be very grand. A house is being erected for the purpose,—some 300 ft. each way, to be gas-lighted, warmed &c. and the refreshments superb." Nor was she disappointed in the only inauguration which she was destined to witness. The procession, with its soldiers, its two hundred marshals conspicuous in their yellow scarves, its Goddess of Liberty drawn by six horses, and the presidential barouche drawn

34 Virginia Clay to T. T. Tunstall, Jan. 25, 1857, W. L. Yancey to Clay, Jr., Feb. 15 [1857], R. H. Leese to Clay, Jr., Feb. 20, 1857, Edmund Ruffin to Clay, Jr., Feb. 2, 1857, Z. L. Nabers to Clay, Jr., Jan. 23, 1857, James Benson Martin to Clay, Jr., March 3, 1857, Clay MSS; Clay, Jr., to James Buchanan, Feb. 11, 1857, W. F. Samford to James Buchanan, Dec. 22, 1856, James Buchanan MSS; Ross Houston to G. S. Houston, Jan. 4, 1857, G. S. Houston MSS; Greensboro *Alabama Beacon,* Dec. 12, 1856; Nichols, *Disruption of American Democracy,* 56.

by four horses, was indeed grand, but the real climax was the inaugural ball, "the greatest . . . ever given in Washington," where a crowd of fifteen thousand jostled each other and consumed untold quantities of oysters, mutton, venison, beef, ham, ice cream, cake, and other delicacies.

Whatever Buchanan might or might not do, it afforded all Democrats considerable satisfaction to see their leader installed in the White House, for to many it signified the prospect of four more years of grace in which to seek a solution of the many perplexities by which they were surrounded. With inaugural festivities over, Clement and Virginia Clay returned to Alabama to watch the boiling of the political pot, which would in all probability determine their future.[35]

35 Virginia Clay to T. T. Tunstall, Jan. 25, 1857, Clay MSS; Huntsville *Southern Advocate*, March 26, 1857; *Harper's Weekly*, I (March 14, 1857), 166.

8

The Road to Secession

CLAY'S POLITICAL FUTURE rested on his being returned to the Senate. His term did not expire until March 4, 1859, a comparatively distant date which would have been of no significance in the spring of 1857 had it not been for the fact that the Alabama legislature met biennially in November. Election would have to be in 1857 or 1859. If the senatorial election were not held until 1859, a vacancy would exist in Alabama's representation from March 4 until December of that year. Hence the question of holding the senatorial election in 1857 required much attention during that summer and autumn.

Clay was of course anxious to receive endorsement in the form of reelection to so desirable a post in which he had worked so hard. In the three and a half years of his service, he had made tremendous gains in popularity. Clay's election in 1853 had admittedly been a compromise among factions, and his enemies vowed that he had intrigued to avenge his defeat for the House of Representatives. This criticism had died away, and now in 1857 the situation bore out Curry's prediction that "The unhappy distraction, which exists in the ranks of the democracy in the Northern part of the State: the personal feuds and local factions, there unfortunately prevailing will . . . all have ceased, and your acknowledged capabilities be conceded and yielded to without controversy." Clay had succeeded so well in taking the "right" stand and giving the "right" vote, that his popularity had grown by leaps and bounds until his friends could say that "never since Alabama's admission into the Union, has she had a Senator of whom she had such just reason to be proud, or who enjoyed such popularity as you do." Not the least element in his success was the rapid growth of state-rights feeling all over Alabama, which made a strong state-rights senator acceptable all over the state.[1]

Clay got his campaign under way as rapidly as possible. During the preliminary part (April-June, 1857) he worked cautiously and under cover, gathering opinion through private correspondence with his political and personal friends, who included most of the editors of county newspapers. Clay first wanted to know how they felt about "bringing on" the senatorial election in the next legislative session, and though he received a divided response, the majority at this time favored postponing election until 1859, when, they predicted, potential opposition would be dead.

The potential opposition was embodied in the person of Governor John Anthony Winston, who strove to complicate the issues by dragging strictly state questions into the field of federal politics. Winston had been elected governor on a platform hostile to any form of state aid for internal improvements, particularly railroads. He carried out this platform by vetoing more than thirty railroad-aid bills. This vigorous policy of economy gained him considerable popularity, especially in the rural sections. Hence some of Clay's friends feared that Winston's opposition would be formidable at this time when he could take advantage of that popularity "to lift him[self] into the Senate."[2]

Rumors were afloat of other combinations and intrigues directed against Clay, one of them involving Yancey, but Clay gave little credence to these stories. After all, he had just tried to get Yancey into Buchanan's cabinet. Clay sounded out a few friends on a

[1] John Gorman Barr to Clay, Jr., May 2, 1857, J. L. M. Curry to Clay, Jr., July 11, 1854, Clay MSS. The time of a senatorial election was not fixed by law, but depended on circumstances, political maneuvering, and such factors as unexpected vacancies caused by death or resignation. The phrase "bring on" was generally used in connection with the legislature's decision to hold a senatorial election during a given session.
[2] J. M. Hudgins to Clay, Jr., May 11, 1857, R. M. Patton to Clay, Jr., June 5, 1857, W. H. R. David to Clay, Jr., May 19, 1857, Noah Alfred Agee to Clay, Jr., June 3, 1857, William Garrett to Clay, Jr., June 5, 1857, Robert Miller Patton to Clay, Jr., June 5, 1857, George S. Walden to Clay, Jr., June 6, 1857, James W. Davis to Clay, Jr., June 15, 1857, D. H. Bingham to Clay, Jr., June 1, 1857, J. T. Heflin to Clay, Jr., June 6, 1857, Clay MSS; Garrett, *Reminiscences of Public Men in Alabama*, 726; Dorman, *Party Politics in Alabama*, 82f.

scheme to change the procedure in nominating caucus from secret balloting to open voting. Though some endorsed the idea, the majority advised Clay to "Make no effort to change what has been the party usage and which it may be said gave you your seat in the Senate." His best policy, they agreed, was to work for the nomination of legislators who were his friends and thereafter trust to his "talents character and public services" to see him "safely thru a nominating caucus."[3]

The second phase of the campaign began in June, when Winston announced his candidacy in an "Address to the People of Alabama," wherein he reviewed the contest up to that point. Various newspapers friendly to Clay had proposed that candidates for the legislature "speak out, and let the people know whether or not they are in favor of bringing on the election of Senator at the next session, and if they are, who are they in favor of?" Winston denounced this as being equivalent to electing senators by popular vote.

After the opening volley from Montgomery (the center of Winston's influence), the Huntsville *Democrat* felt obliged to enter the contest. John Withers Clay, now the editor, laid himself decidedly open to attack, if not censure, by his position of obvious partiality, which he tried to conceal behind words which would have been no more than friendly had they come from anyone but Clement Clay's brother.

"Mr. J Withers Clay is an ass. . . . The inordinate jealousy of the family wont allow them to see . . . a compliment paid to anybody else," stormed Winston to a friend, and continued, "I wish the field kept open. . . . I can help somebody else . . . even if I am not of the number." Publicly Winston denied complicity in any "conspiracy" to "smuggle" himself into Clay's seat. But since these "slanderous assaults" had been made "by Senator Clay's friends," Winston was now forced into "the position of a candidate," and therefore felt it his duty to "accept," and declared that he would be "content to abide the result that shall be obtained" by the votes "of the ensuing Legislature." The issue

3 J. D. Phelan to Clay, Jr., April 22, 1857, J. G. Barr to Clay, Jr., May 2, 1857, John Cochran to Clay, Jr., May 9, 1857, Gabriel B. DuVal to Clay, Jr., May 14, 1857, Z. L. Nabers to Clay, Jr., March 5, Sept. 19, 1857, O. H. Bynum to Clay, Jr., March 5, 1857, T. L. Trubinin to Clay, Jr., May 30, 1857, Clay, Jr., to John Cochran, May 13, 1857, Clay MSS.

was now unavoidably before the state, and battle was joined by almost every county newspaper.[4]

Both Clay and Winston were criticized for engaging in an unseemly squabble befitting the dignity of neither and tending to breed dissension in Democratic ranks. Winston was the more vulnerable, however, and respecting his "Address" a legislator wrote, "Gov Winstons late *pronounciamento* has met with a decidedly unfavorable reception in this section. It has done him no good." Winston's audacity in openly seeking the senatorship was criticized by a large portion of the press. Many who had endorsed his executive career now agreed that in grasping after the senatorship he was "aspiring to a position which neither his talents, education, or intellect qualifie[d] him to fill, with either advantage to the state and Country or with credit to himself," and some declared that his election "would be a disgrace to the State." The fact that Winston was a resident of the Black Belt worked against him, for two senators from South Alabama would break the precedent of sectional division of the honors.

The state Democratic convention in June was full of intrigue, and the story went that Winston and John Edmund Moore of Florence had combined to push the latter for governor, and thereby reconcile North Alabama to the loss of a senatorship by the gift of the governorship. But this scheme did not work, for the state convention nominated Andrew Barry Moore of Perry County in the Black Belt. In spite of these "manoueverings," Clay's friends who attended the convention reported that he had "nothing to fear from any thing that occurred" there.[5]

Clay undoubtedly held the favored position in the contest. Aside from the fact that he would have to be removed from a position he already held, his statewide popularity had been amply demonstrated during the summer. He had the support of the entire Democratic press, and that of many former Whig papers

4 N. A. Agee to Clay, Jr., June 3, 1857, M. T. P. Brindley to Clay, Jr., June 19, 1857, Clay MSS; J. A. Winston to J. H. Weaver, July 14, 1857, Ala. Archives, Governors' Official Correspondence; "To the People of Alabama" [June 19, 1857], broadside in J. L. M. Curry MSS (Ala. Dept. Archives and Hist.)

5 J. M. Hudgins to Clay, Jr., May 11, 1857, D. H. Bingham to Clay, Jr., June 1, 1857, R. M. Patton to Clay, Jr., June 5, 1857, G. S. Walden to Clay, Jr., June 6, 1857, C. M. Jackson to Clay, Jr., June 12, 1857, T. A. Walker to Clay, Jr., June 28, 1857, H. D. Clayton to Clay, Jr., July 8, 1857, Clay MSS; W. P. Browne to W. F. Samford, Nov. 7, 1857, W. P. Browne MSS; Dorman, *Party Politics in Alabama*, 138.

which under state-rights pressure had now become Democratic. The leading party organ summarized the situation, "Every Democratic paper in the State, we believe, except those in Sumter county, the Southern Advocate in Huntsville, and the Advertiser and State Gazette, have either positively expressed or strongly intimated a preference for his re-election. No one paper in the State has condemned or even questioned the correctness of any vote, or speech, or opinion, or sentiment he has uttered in Congress. Certainly he has reason to feel that he has a just and appreciative constituency, and to hope that if he should ask it, his commission will not be grudgingly renewed."

Whether "he should ask it" continued to be a debatable question right up to the last minute, but as the weeks passed, feeling grew in favor of election in 1857. Clay himself wanted the matter settled in 1857, but he and his friends decided to remain quiet and await developments. They believed that the opposition intended to force the election in 1857, with the idea that Winston would be in a stronger position than he could possibly be in 1859.

The opposition made the most of this by saying that if Clay's chances would be weakened by waiting, he deserved to be defeated. Clay's most energetic opponent was his fellow townsman, William Bibb Figures, editor of the *Southern Advocate* and an old-line Whig. This paper, now nominally Democratic, based its opposition to Clay's reelection at this time on grounds of unconstitutionality, lack of precedent, and inexpediency.

The Democratic press declared that it would be almost criminal if circumstances should make necessary the calling of a special legislative session solely to elect a senator; furthermore, in such critical times, Alabama must have a full and uninterrupted representation in the United States Senate. Since the senatorial question had come up, other editors argued, it would be decidedly impolitic to elect anyone else when Clay's term was only half expired, and at the same time the only way to do him justice was through immediate reelection.[6]

Even so, all was not clear sailing, for as one party leader wrote, "There are undercurrents, & cross currents moving hither &

6 Clay Scrapbooks, VI, 135-40, containing clippings from Canebrake *Gazette,* Sept. 4, 1857, Clayton *Banner,* Sept. 3, 1857, Centre *Argus,* Sept. 26, 1857, *West Alabamian,* Sept. 30, 1857, Chambers *Tribune,* n.d., Florence *Gazette,* Sept. 4 1857, and Marion *Commercial,* Sept. 4, 1857; Huntsville *Southern Advocate,* Sept. 24, 1857; Tuscaloosa *Independent Monitor,* Oct. 15, 1857.

thither so that I cannot comprehend what is really going on and it is likely when I get better posted I shall be in a worse quandary still. . . . I would give odds," he continued, "that with Mrs Clay we could elect Mr. C. against the combined influence of every outsider," but, he stipulated, it must "be done only with the concurrence of a majority of the democratic members. . . . I cannot . . . sanction . . . the policy of calling in the aid of our enemies." He was sure, however, that "the democracy want that election disposed of— We shall have enough to distract us hereafter without keeping this open."

Early in the session, the legislature adopted a resolution "to bring on" the senatorial election. Wishing to spare the family "the solicitude to which we have been the prey" prior to and during the crucial party caucus, Virginia Clay did not write until she could tell them "the news of the glorious victory your son has achieved over the whole Opposition." "Winston," she continued, "has behaved well, is and has been . . . very civil; has called on me, decidedly *warm;* has invited Mr. Clay to drink with him both *before & after* the passage of the Resolution!" "Houston," she added, "literally spread himself. . . . He was very polite also. . . . The warmest opposition came of course from North Ala. All of H's. [Houston's] district were of the opposition." After noting the defection of some professed friends, she concluded, "Judas left children surely, though I don't know that the Bible speaks of them." The formality of election occurred on November 21, when Clay, the only candidate in nomination, received all the votes cast.[7]

The Clays soon left for the East, and while Clement got settled at the National Hotel in Washington, Virginia proceeded to New York for her annual shopping tour, where, Clement advised her, "I allow you two weeks before returning to me & another $100 if you need it." In spite of political tensions and financial panic, official Washington was preparing for a gay and lavish social season. "People," wrote Virginia Clay, "are mad with rivalry & vanity, & will eventually wake up wretched. It is said that Gwin is spending money at the rate of 75.000$ pr annum, & Brown & Thompson quite the same! Think of it! . . . Mrs. Toombs . . . says, *they* spend 1800 pr month, or 21.600 pr annum! So we have

7 Virginia Clay to Clay, Sr., Nov. 17, 1857, Clay MSS; W. P. Browne to W. F. Samford, Nov. 17, 1857, W. P. Browne MSS; Ala. Leg., *HJ,* p. 88, Nov. 21, 1857.

concluded that people of modest fortune can remain in 3d stories of Hotels. Our present rooms are very pleasant but the *fare* has been all winter very indifferent, & gets worse & worse." This winter, Virginia's debutante protege was Loula Comer, younger sister of Celeste Clay.[8]

When Clay returned to the Senate on December 7, 1857, he carried the mandate of his state extending his term of service to March 4, 1865. He found the Washington atmosphere tense and riven with two major worries—Kansas and the recent financial panic. While Clay sat in his study on December 3, writing to Virginia, Douglas and Buchanan faced each other at the White House. The President declared that he would recommend adoption of the Lecompton constitution and that he must make support of it a test of party loyalty. Douglas refused, and the interview ended amid threats and insults. The Lecompton constitution, formed by a proslavery convention of doubtful ability and infrequent sobriety, was declared to be adopted on December 21, 1857. In the referendum Kansans voted not on the whole constitution, but on the constitution "with slavery" or "without slavery." The devious means and faked ballots by which the proslavery faction won caused more trouble than even the most unscrupulous Kansan could have anticipated. Through the summer and autumn Buchanan in Washington and Governor Robert J. Walker in Kansas had vacillated and worked at cross-purposes, until the South was ready to revolt against both. Then, under southern pressure, Buchanan decided to leave Walker to his fate and to support the Lecompton constitution as the only way out of an impossible situation.

Buchanan's message was intentionally vague on Kansas, but implied recommendation of Lecompton. Douglas countered with a demand for a new enabling act and a new convention in Kansas. The cabinet split on a compromise plan to admit Kansas under Lecompton and then allow the legislature to submit the constitution to the people. Besides, Douglas would not accept this. Meanwhile, blocs began to form in Congress. If Douglas expected the northern Democracy to follow him, he was disappointed. Only three joined him: Stuart of Michigan, Pugh of Ohio, and Broderick of California; and in the South, only Henry A. Wise

[8] Clay, Jr., to Virginia Clay, Dec. 3, 1857, Virginia Clay to Clay, Sr. [ca. March, 1858], Clay MSS.

of Virginia. But Douglas could count on the Republicans, and most of the Americans. Southern state-rights Democrats were solid for Lecompton, but such was the lineup on both sides that it was a touch-and-go affair throughout. As later returns came in from Kansas, election frauds became even more patent, but Buchanan, despite competent advice to the contrary, determined to push Lecompton through. On February 2, 1858, he submitted it, with the recommendation that under it Kansas be admitted as a state.[9]

While the anti-Lecompton bloc gained adherents, particularly in the House, administration forces began to exert all the pressure they could command. The Senate Committee on Territories had an administration majority, led by James S. Green of Missouri, which left Douglas, the nominal chairman, in the minority. When administration member Fitzpatrick became ill in mid-February, Clay was appointed to this crucial committee and served until March 24, 1858, when Fitzpatrick was able to resume his post. Meanwhile, debate on Kansas became so heated that several fights occurred. On March 15, Senate debate continued throughout that night and until six o'clock the following morning, when the "majority at length yielded, and the Senate adjourned, . . . the night having been consumed by innumerable motions to postpone and to adjourn," though an "occasional speech diversified the scene." Later that morning the anti-Lecomptonites, led by Hale, "had a consultation . . . for the purpose of avoiding such a scene as we had last night," and proposed to end debate the following Monday.[10]

Excitement in Washington was reflected throughout Alabama, and state-rights men were strengthened in their convictions. Clement Clay, Sr., writing to his son, stressed the anxiety he felt "in regard to political matters—especially the admission of Kansas." But even if Kansas were admitted, "I fear it will do us little practical good," he continued, "with a Black Republican Governor and Legislature to initiate the State." On the subject of Democratic perfidy, he declared, "Walker, Douglas and Wise should, each, be hung high as Haman." At the first news "of Douglas's perfidy, I was incredulous—but astonishing and morti-

[9] Nichols, *Disruption of American Democracy*, 127-31, 153-57; Milton, *Eve of Conflict*, 273, 280, 286.
[10] USC, *SJ*, 35:1, p. 1124; USC, *Cong. Globe*, 35:1, p. 1133, March 16, 1858.

fying as it was, it turned out too true. Douglas was once quite a favorite with me—I looked upon him as the proper successor of Mr. Buchanan."[11]

The Alabama legislature, controlled by southern-rights men, unanimously adopted resolutions calling for a state convention "in the event Kansas shall not be admitted . . . with a slavery constitution." Alabama, they further declared, "will and ought to resist, even (as a last resort) to a disruption of every tie which binds her to the Union." State-rights leaders thereupon asserted it was "perfectly clear . . . we should either say nothing at all or provide for the call of a Convention in case Kansas should be refused admission with the Lecompton constitution—" Alabama's "secession in that event is simply a conclusion from premises long since laid down."

Against this background, Clay rose on March 19, 1858, to speak in support of Lecompton and to defend his state and its legislature's resolutions which, he complained, had "been alluded to by Senators in terms of reproach and of ridicule." He saw only two valid objections to the Lecompton constitution: the fact that it had not been submitted to popular ratification, and the report of irregular elections. "In the younger and purer days of our Republic, constitutions were not submitted to the popular vote," declared Clay, quickly disposing of the first point. The question of election frauds Clay sidestepped delicately by arguing that if the Free Soil party in Kansas was as numerous as claimed, they "either dared not, or cared not, to make the laws and mold the domestic institutions of Kansas. . . . They were either submissionists from cowardice, . . . or anarchists from choice. . . . In either case, they are unworthy of our sympathy or countenance." Black Republicans' real objection to Lecompton was "that the right of property in slaves is recognized."

This led Clay directly into a long argument on the constitutional basis of slave property and its imminent peril at the hands of "northern Republicans," many of whom "deny that property in slaves is protected or even recognized by the Federal Constitution." Hence, asked Clay, "What can we expect but neglect and disregard of our claims to protection of our property from those

11 Clay, Sr., to Clay, Jr. [ca. March, 1858], E. C. Bullock to Clay, Jr., March 9, 1858, Clay MSS; Ala. Leg., *HJ*, p. 274, Jan. 11, 1858; Ala. Leg., *SJ*, p. 198, Jan. 13, 1858.

who deny our title? What can we expect but habitual and system-atic insult, injury, and outrage . . . ? I have not," he continued, "been addicted to singing paeans . . . about the Union. . . . Yet . . . the Union of the Constitution, which our fathers made, I love and reverence and would preserve; but this Union without the Constitution, or with it as construed by northern Republicans, I abhor and scorn, and would dissolve, if my power were equal to my will." Thus ended Clay on his customary menacing note.

Nine speeches and four days later, Lecompton passed the Senate, 33-25. It then went to the House, where an amendment providing for resubmission of the constitution to the people of Kansas passed, 120-112. This defeat the administration refused to accept. House and Senate now deadlocked, the House insisting on its amendment and the Senate refusing to accept it. On April 13 the Senate voted for a conference committee and so got under way the English compromise bill.[12]

William Hayden English was a young representative from Indiana who had been in the anti-Lecompton ranks. Now, under the adroit management of Alexander H. Stephens, English was put forward to propose an acceptable compromise. At first many Southerners were recalcitrant, but by careful rewording combined with unrelenting pressure from administration forces, a workable compromise was arrived at. By emphasizing the land grants offered Kansas and soft-pedaling the actual fact of resubmission of the constitution, both sides in Congress were able to save face, and enough votes shifted to pass the English bill in both houses. It became law on May 4, and thus Kansas passed out of politics. The compromise bill had given Douglas a chance to return to party ranks, but when he weighed all the factors and looked at the political situation in Illinois, where he would soon come up for reelection, he stuck to the course he had set, and so the breach in the Democracy widened.[13]

Public opinion throughout the country was much divided on the English bill. Alabama radicals denounced it as a humiliating

---

12 USC, *SJ*, 35:1, p. 280, March 23, 1858; USC, *Cong. Globe*, 35:1, p. 1437, Appen., pp. 144-49, April 1, March 19, 1858.
13 USC, *SJ*, 35:1, p. 403, April 30, 1858; USC, *Cong. Globe*, 35:1, p. 1904, April 20, 1858; Milton, *Eve of Conflict*, 292-96; Nichols, *Disruption of American Democracy*, 164-76; Richard Malcolm Johnston and William Hand Browne, *Life of Alexander H. Stephens* (Philadelphia, 1883), 332f; Frank Haywood Hodder, "Some Aspects of the English Bill for the Admission of Kansas," AHA *Annual Report* (1906), I, 201-10.

concession on the part of southern congressmen, but majority opinion accepted the bill as a distinct recognition of the Lecompton constitution. This attitude snowballed, until editors who had first been grudging in their acceptance of it shifted to a whole-hearted endorsement of the English bill as being actually preferable to the original Senate bill.

In a letter to the citizens of Mobile, Clay defended the English bill and his vote for it with a lengthy argument designed to prove that the South had lost nothing "either in the abstract or . . . in . . . practical results." Following the administration line, he bore down on the land-grant feature, explaining that Congress was right in "refusing to admit Kansas with the immense dowry she asked." Clay touched as lightly as possible on the fact that Kansans "might vote against the terms proposed, not because they were unacceptable . . . but because the Lecompton constitution was unacceptable to them." If Kansas rejected the terms of admission, the South would lose nothing, asserted Clay, for so long as Kansas remained a territory, federal law would protect slavery and slaveholders; whereas if Kansas became a state, she would send two Black Republicans to the Senate and another to the House, and soon exclude "slavery and slaveholders by law from her limits."

Despite this quasi-victory, Clay closed on a gloomy note. The South, he said, "is now powerless in Congress . . . is getting weaker in the Union every year. . . . Disappointed and defeated as the South has been of the legitimate fruits of past federal legislation for her defence, I cannot indulge in those joyous and jubilant anticipations of peace, justice, harmony and fraternity in the future of our Union, uttered by some Southern statesmen, and devoutly hoped for by all." These, he declared, are "the facts as I believe them to exist, . . . notwithstanding they are as disagreeable to me as they can be to you."[14]

While Congress was in the throes of the Kansas struggle, feminine Washington was preparing for the social event of the decade: Senator and Mrs. Gwin's "fancy dress" ball which illustrated California lavishness. Costume was obligatory, except that President Buchanan, members of the cabinet, "and about twenty Senators, were privileged to appear in citizens' dress." The

14 J. W. Clay to Clay, Jr., May 8, 1858, Clay MSS; Huntsville *Southern Advocate*, Sept. 2, 1858; Montgomery *Daily Confederation*, May 1, 3-5, 11, 17, 1858.

thousand or more guests, in "varied costumes . . . made of rich materials" and representing for the most part mythological or historical figures, presented a scene "picturesquely beautiful." Conspicuous by contrast was Virginia Clay, who chose to portray "Mrs. Partington," a currently popular character created by the humorist Benjamin P. Shillaber. Amid the brilliant costumes, the "Widow Partington" appeared in "a plain black alpaca dress and black satin apron" suited to the rustic woman from "Beanville." "It was the one character," wrote Virginia Clay, "assumed during that memorable evening . . . in which age and personal attractions were sacrificed ruthlessly for its more complete delineation." Ten-year-old Jimmy Sandidge served as Mrs. Partington's incorrigible nephew "Ike." The "wit and talent displayed" by Virginia Clay as "Mrs. Partington made a great sensation. . . . The veritable Mrs. Partington never more wittily murdered the King's English" than did Virginia Clay with malapropisms extemporaneous to the occasion. "Shouts of laughter attested to the pure wit of the widow's tale of misfortune, and wherever she stopped there gathered a crowd through which it was impossible to penetrate." There was "a profusion of refreshments . . . with a sumptuous supper at midnight," and a "fine band of music discoursed inspiring strains . . . until daylight . . . before the guests ceased dancing." This was the crowning event of Virginia Clay's career in Washington society, but the excitement of the occasion was so great that it put her to bed for several days afterward.[15]

From time to time during the session, Congress gave attention to questions other than Kansas. One of these was Clay's bill to repeal the fishing bounties, which he reported as chairman of the Commerce Committee on January 18, 1858. Clay spoke on the bill May 4, 1858, arguing that what had begun in 1792 as a legitimate drawback granted to an important industry, had now degenerated into an unwarranted and gratuitous bounty, corruptly administered and used to bolster up a moribund enterprise. The drawback, originally granted because of a heavy duty on imported salt, was now collected for fish preserved by methods other than salt curing. Furthermore, Clay continued, the bounty went to a few

---

15 Clay Scrapbooks, III, 13; Washington *Union*, April 10, 1858; Clay-Clopton, *Belle of the Fifties*, 128; Benjamin Penhallow Shillaber, *Life and Sayings of Mrs. Partington and Others of the Family* (New York, 1854).

shipowners of Massachusetts and Maine, and not to the fishermen
for whom it was originally intended. The old argument that the
fisheries were a training school for seamen was no longer valid,
Clay contended. The two senators from Maine took part in the
debate, and on May 6, Hamlin replied. A respectable body of
New England opinion tacitly favored Clay's bill, however. Indeed,
Clay got most of his arguments and statistics from New England
friends who admitted that cod fishing was no longer profitable
and that repeal of the bounty would actually "result in benefit to
those engaged in the business" by freeing them from various
restrictions, while the fishermen would gain by "specific wages
instead of shares." On May 19, 1858, Clay got his fishing-bounties
bill through the Senate by a vote of 30-25, but it was not acted
upon in the House. He introduced it again in 1859, but by that
time sectional troubles prevented action.[16]

To extreme southern-rights men Buchanan's foreign policy was
no more pleasing than his domestic administration. In their imperialist dreams "Kansas, Cuba, South America all loomed up as
inviting Southern *expansion,* outlet & development. The *dream,*"
mourned one, "has been sadly dissipated." Alabama was particularly interested in Buchanan's Mexican policy because negotiations
at this time were in the hands of John Forsyth of Mobile. His
efforts to adjust boundary difficulties either by purchase of more
territory or by obtaining a protectorate over the desired area
failed, due to a variety of complications, not the least of which
was the undercover activity of Judah P. Benjamin.

Clement Clay saw nothing good about the "proposed protectorate of Mexico." "If we take Sonora," he predicted, "we will
never let it go— . . . While it is being held by U. S. troops
. . . the enterprising & acquisitive Yankees will flock in there,
with their 'notions,' buy lands & silver mines & prepare it for a
non-slaveholding state, before Southern men obtain even a right
of entry with their slaves—now forbidden by Mexican laws." It
would simply be "a good scheme for aggrandizing the North,
already too strong for the South"; furthermore, he continued, "the

16 George B. Loring to Clay, Jr., Jan. 26, 1858, John Kirk Paulding to Clay,
Jr., May 11, 1858, Clay MSS; Clay, Jr., to W. M. Burwell, May 7, 1858, William
M. Burwell MSS; USC, *SJ,* 36:1, pp. 25, 154, Dec. 22, 1859, Feb. 14, 1860; USC,
Cong. Globe, 35:1, pp. 1930-56, 1991-97, May 4, 6, 1858; *ibid.,* 36:1, pp. 214, 759,
Dec. 22, 1859, Feb. 14, 1860; Huntsville *Southern Advocate,* Dec. 21, 1859.

South has no slaves to spare for acquired territories, & unless the foreign slave trade can be reopened, she would best consult her interest by resisting such acquisitions. If she can hold what she has, in the Union, it will be more than Mr. Seward predicts."[17]

Reopening the African slave trade was much discussed at the Southern Commercial Convention held at Montgomery in May, 1858. Even extreme state-rights men were violently divided on the question, while its advocates had to admit there was little real chance of success. The Upper South was almost solidly opposed. The two Alabama senators were on opposite sides. Clay heartily endorsed the idea, though he thought it impracticable at the moment. Fitzpatrick, on the other hand, wrote, "In regard to the reopening of the African Slave trade, without giving you my reasons in detail . . . I am opposed [to] it, and have been as I believe you know, from the time the question was first broached."[18]

During the closing days of the session, Virginia Clay had gone to New York, and while Clement sat in the Senate chamber on a drowsy summer afternoon, business was suddenly enlivened by a flare of tempers and sharp words between Judah P. Benjamin and Jefferson Davis over details of the army appropriation bill. "I knew it must result in a fight," wrote Clay—and indeed Benjamin did send a direct challenge—but "I am happy to say that I was mainly instrumental in bringing about a peaceable settlement highly honorable to both."[19]

When Congress finally adjourned on June 16, Clement and Virginia went to the Virginia springs to recover "from the exhausting effects of the last Session." They then proceeded to Alabama and spent the latter part of the summer at Point Clear, a small resort on Mobile Bay. Late in September they were in Huntsville once more, and a month later they went to Montgomery for several days. From there Virginia reported that "Mr. Clay is the lion of the city, & the people are very anxious he shall show himself at the Fair." In the absence of Edmund Ruffin, who

17 Clay, Jr., to Clay, Sr., Dec. 11, 1858, W. F. Samford to Clay, Jr., Oct. 20, 1858, Clay MSS; F. W. Pickens to George N. Sanders, May 14, 1857, Francis Wilkinson Pickens MSS; James Morton Callahan, "The Mexican Policy of Southern Leaders under Buchanan's Administration," AHA Annual Report (1910), 137-42.
18 Clay, Jr., to Clay, Sr., Dec. 11, 1858, B. Fitzpatrick to Clay, Jr., Aug. 30, 1859, Clay MSS.
19 Clay, Jr., to Virginia Clay, June 9, 1858, Clay MSS; Burton Jesse Hendrick, Statesmen of the Lost Cause: Jefferson Davis and His Cabinet (Boston, 1939), 174.

had been expected to speak, the state-fair committee "called . . . on Mr. Clay to . . . address them, assigning as a reason, that he was *known* to be a capital planter!!!!" This put Clay "quite in a quandary," since he was also scheduled to "address the Epis: Southern University Convention, as the representative of Huntsville." But Virginia had a solution for the problem and urged him "to just quiet his mind, & give them the West Ala. Speech, as hundreds yes thousands will be here who have never heard or read it. Besides," Virginia continued, "he intends giving a grand supper to his friends on Saturday night, & then make them a speech."

Before Clement left Montgomery, he was thrown from a buggy and injured his leg. This resulted in his and Virginia's return to Huntsville, and there, while he was recovering, Clement and LeRoy Pope Walker reconciled their past differences. In an exchange of letters Walker explained how political debts had obligated him to vote against Clement, Sr., in 1843 and against Withers Clay for solicitor in 1855. Clement responded in a tone of conciliation and cordiality, and saw "no cause why you & I, or yr. family & mine, shd not be friends, as yr. father & mine were while they both lived in this town."[20]

Clement's phrase, "while they both lived in this town," was a key to many things in North Alabama politics. The death of John Williams Walker in 1823 at the age of forty had removed one of the most formidable obstacles to Clement Comer Clay's political advancement. Had Walker lived, the rivalry between the two men might have made Clay's political career quite different. Walker's death further deprived his sons of that political tutelage which Clay gave his boys. So the Walkers, though politically ambitious, concentrated on the law and headed Huntsville's most successful legal firm. Thus, while the Clays stayed on top in the political scramble, as lawyers they lost out professionally and financially.

Another great factor in the Clays' political success was their control of the Huntsville *Democrat*. Their influence (tacit but well understood) on the editorial policy of this paper went back at least to the early 1830's, when editor Philip Woodson's daughter Mary married Augustine J. Withers, Susanna Clay's brother. In

20 Virginia Clay to Susanna Clay [ca. Oct., 1858], L. P. Walker to Clay, Jr., Nov. 20, 1858, Clay, Jr., to L. P. Walker, Nov. 19, 1858, John Joseph Byron Hilliard to Virginia Clay, Nov. 2, 1858, Clay MSS; Huntsville *Southern Advocate*, Sept. 23, 1858; Montgomery *Daily Confederation*, Oct. 30—Nov. 8, 1858.

1856 Woodson retired and sold out to John Withers Clay, who then became permanent editor following several periods of temporary editorship.

At the beginning of December, 1858, Clement was sufficiently recovered to set off for Washington, where he and Virginia arrived on December 3, "at 3 p.m.—being 54 hours from home." "My leg," he reported, "is doing very well & gives me but little trouble." They decided to stay at Brown's Hotel, where they had "a small parlor & a much smaller chamber," because it was "the rendezvous of most Southern Congressmen. . . . Hence, it is very agreeable & advantageous." To the nonsouthern residents, Brown's appeared to be "dominated by . . . aristocratic slaveholders" with a "swaggering manner and a retinue of colored slaves."[21]

The national scene presented many vexing aspects, not the least of which was the rise of a tariff wing among northern Democrats, particularly in Pennsylvania. Buchanan, now in a delicate position, found it expedient in his message to recommend tariff modification in the direction of protection. This alienated most southern Democrats, among them Clay, who thought it an "unfortunate . . . departure from the principles of free trade & of the Democratic party & adverse to Southern interests." He admitted that it would "probably command the entire Black Republican support & that of the Southern Know-Nothings, some old Whigs . . . & the Pennsylvania, & perhaps Kentucky & Louisiana Democrats." Though Treasury Secretary Howell Cobb publicly dissented from Buchanan's tariff policy, he did not thereby ingratiate himself with southern-rights men. "If Mr. Cobb had resigned, as he should have done," declared Clay, "he would have done more to reinstate himself with the Southern Rights Democracy than by any act since his defection in '50-51."

When Congress assembled in 1858, the Democratic caucus proceeded to chastise Douglas for defection on Lecompton by giving the chairmanship of the Committee on Territories to James S. Green of Missouri. This caused so much stir in many quarters that Clay predicted an "effort will be made by Douglas & his friends to excite sympathy for him as a wronged man." Clay bristled with hostility and called squatter sovereignty a doctrine

21 Clay, Jr., to Clay, Sr., Dec. 4, 11, 1858, Clay MSS; Mary Simmerson (Cunningham) Logan, *Reminiscences of a Soldier's Wife: An Autobiography* (New York, 1913), 72.

"more dangerous than 'Wilmot Provisoism,' . . . [and a] heresy, which is now adopted by no party but the Black Republican." "The Southern press," continued Clay, "that pities Douglas & defends him as a trusty champion of Southern rights . . . is either ignorant of Southern rights or faithless to Southern institutions. At least, this is the sentiment of Southern Democrats in Congress & of myself."[22]

Sectional and party squabbles were temporarily suspended while senators solemnly discussed the advisability of moving into the new Senate wing of the Capitol, which was almost completed. Clay advised caution. He was persuaded, he said, from his own "observation of the new Hall, that it is not thoroughly dry," and hence the older members "may be subject to rheumatism and other diseases by going into that Hall." Debate disclosed many other reasons against, and an equal number for, moving to the new chamber. The resolution to move was adopted, 26-18, Clay voting against it.

This was Clay's "obstructing" session. He objected to moving into the new Senate chamber; he objected to interpreting the pension laws so as to allow pensions to women who had married Revolutionary soldiers later than 1800; he objected to the chair's ruling which prevented payment of claims for Creek depredations; he objected to the House pension bill on the grounds that it would cost thirty million dollars; and finally, he opposed the bill which would donate public lands for agricultural colleges. As a state-rights Democrat, Clay was unalterably hostile to this "most delusive and seductive measure," this "magnificent bribe tendered to Alabama for the surrender to Federal power of her original and reserved right to manage her own domestic and internal affairs." Arguing on constitutional grounds, he concluded that "the powers asserted in this bill are hostile to the reserved rights and the true interests of the States." Clay's speech had little influence on the vote, however, and the bill passed, 52-22, with nearly all the southern members voting against it. Buchanan came to the rescue and vetoed the measure.[23]

22 Clay, Jr., to Clay, Sr., Dec. 11, 13, 1858, Clay MSS; USC, *SJ*, 35:2, p. 44, Dec. 13, 1858; Milton, *Eve of Conflict*, 263; Nichols, *Disruption of American Democracy*, 225.
23 USC, *Cong. Globe*, 35:2, pp. 187, 190, 192f, 645, 738, 851-54, 1141, 1412f, Dec. 23, 1858, Jan. 28, Feb. 2, 7, 19, 26, 1859; USC, *SJ*, 35:2, p. 278, Feb. 7, 1859.

The session, as Fitzpatrick remarked to a friend, "has been a dull and tame one," yet little was accomplished, and thirteen days before adjournment no appropriation bill had been passed. "We may get through," he predicted, "but it will be after a fashion." Even the social season was a little dull, though one of the enlivening events was the marriage of Virginia Clay's cousin, Virginia Laura Hilliard, to Hamilton Glentworth of New York. Virginia gave the wedding reception at Brown's Hotel, where the guests "found a table with refreshments in one parlor, and the other parlors crowded with persons, some dancing and some not." Apropos thereof, one of the guests confided to his wife that Clingman, Clay, and other senators went "regularly *to dancing school.*" After the close of the session Clement and Virginia returned to Huntsville and spent a quiet summer on Monte Sano at their "mountain home—with ice water—pure air—delightful breezes & freed from that cursed . . . insect musquitoe [*sic*]."[24]

Clay's physical surroundings might conduce to calm, but the political situation certainly was not reassuring. Everywhere the Democratic party was in trouble. From Ohio, George E. Pugh wrote to Clay, "We are pressed, sorely. . . . We can carry the Legislature, in Ohio, if we can carry my own County; but that which once gave four thousand five hundred majority . . . has lately become very doubtful. . . . Buchanan has lost, for us, those famous strongholds which the enemy never was able to storm—to what laurels is he not entitled?"

In Alabama itself the situation was very much confused. Yancey was working doggedly to break up the Democratic party and form a sectional southern-rights party. In this he was aided by William F. Samford, who that summer came out as candidate for governor on a southern-rights ticket. Yancey was also organizing the "League of United Southerners," to which were flocking many former Whigs and Know-Nothings, much to the alarm of all Democrats. Symptomatic of the trend was the establishment in Cahaba of a new newspaper, *The Slaveholder,* which put at its masthead "the names of Robert Barnwell Rhett, sr., of South Carolina, for the Presidency, and Clement C. Clay, jr., of Alabama,

24 Benjamin Fitzpatrick to Asa Biggs, Feb. 16, 1859, Asa Biggs MSS; L. O'B. Branch to Nancy Branch, Jan. 25, 1859, "Letters," 60, 62; J. J. B. Hilliard to Virginia Clay, June 15, 1859, Clay MSS.

for the Vice-Presidency of the United States." Even the Charleston *Mercury* thought that this "nominating a sectional ticket . . . may be somewhat in advance."[25]

Though the summer elections showed a reassuring conservatism in Alabama, the radicals were not ready to give up the fight. To this end they sought to "bring on" the senatorial election in November, when they hoped to elect Yancey over the pro-Douglas Fitzpatrick.[26] Ever since 1855 Yancey had had his eye on the senatorship. He had the solid backing of the extreme southern-rights faction. Fitzpatrick had not carried on an active campaign during the summer, and in some quarters he was criticized for not stating his position more definitely. Still, he felt that he had "nothing to fear" and anticipated success on the third ballot. John A. Winston was still in the running and held the balance of power. According to one observer, "There was unquestionably a clear anti-F[itzpatrick] majority if it could have been concentrated on any one man." Yancey, who had at first been anxious to "bring on" the election, later changed his mind when it was "settled beyond question . . . that he could not be elected." With things in this muddle, men from all factions united in killing the resolution to elect a senator that session.

Clay's quiet summer was interrupted when his fellow townsmen asked for a speech on the "great questions affecting the institution of slavery and the rights of the South," and his "views of Southern policy in this crisis." On September 5, 1859, Clay consumed two hours and a half in expounding his views. Addressing his audience as "Fellow-citizens of Alabama, one of thirty three free, sovereign and independent States, composing a confederation, not a consolidation, a union, not a nation," he progressed from a dissertation on the nature of the government and the purpose of its founders, through the two great slavery compromises, thence to the Kansas-Nebraska act and the proper interpretation of popular sovereignty.

He dwelt long and earnestly on the defection of Douglas, and concluded by saying, "I need not now tell you, that I will not

25 G. E. Pugh to Clay, Jr., June 5, 1859, Clay MSS; Charleston *Mercury*, Oct. 19, 1859; George Petrie, "William F. Samford: Statesman and Man of Letters," Ala. Hist. Soc. *Transactions*, IV (1899-1903), 476f; DuBose, *Yancey*, 376; Dorman, *Party Politics in Alabama*, 142-45.

26 Fitzpatrick's term did not expire until March 4, 1861.

support Mr. Douglas or any one on his platform, although nominated by the unanimous vote of the Charleston Convention, or the Democratic party, or any other party whatever." To Douglas' "Freeport Doctrine" that a territory could by unfriendly legislation exclude slavery, Clay replied, "It is revolutionary doctrine, striking at the foundation of all government. Property is the basis of the social fabric. To protect and preserve it, is the chief end of every government . . . when protection ceases, allegiance ceases. . . . Protection is an inherent right of citizenship, . . . and when you surrender it, you will cease to be freemen. . . . As your . . . servant, I will not do so, at the bidding of squatter sovereignty, National Democracy, or State Rights Democracy,—yea at the bidding of the Legislature or the people of Alabama. If commanded to do so, I will resign my trust, retire to deepest seclusion . . . and . . . become a quiet passenger on the ill-fated bark of the South, as it drifts ingloriously down the stream of Time, into the black and tideless sea of infamy and oblivion." Before his unionist North Alabama constituents, Clay tailored his words to a moderation which neither threatened nor urged secession. Even his old enemy, Figures of the *Advocate,* conceded that "his speech was an able one in support of the position he took, while it was dignified and respectful to those who might differ with him in the policy the South should pursue."[27]

In the two months between Clay's speech in Huntsville and the opening of Congress occurred a terrifying event which had its evil influence on thinking and speaking, North and South, during all that winter. John Brown's raid on Harpers Ferry sent a shock through the South and doubled southern hatred and fear of the black Republicans. While the House struggled in vain to elect a speaker, the Senate filled its time with threats and accusations about the John Brown raid.

To this debate Clay contributed his quota in a speech on the "Invasion of Harper's Ferry—Dangers and Duties of the South." Addressing himself to the Republicans, Clay declared, "The principles you profess . . . the very platform read in our hearing,

27 E. C. Bullock to Clay, Jr., Dec. 30, 1859, Clay MSS; Ala. Leg., *HJ,* p. 108, Dec. 1, 1859; Ala. Leg. *SJ,* pp. 84f, Dec. 2, 1859; *Speech of Hon. C. C. Clay, Jr., on Slavery Issues, Delivered at Huntsville, Alabama, September 5th, 1859,* 1-15, pamphlet with Clay MSS; Huntsville *Southern Advocate,* Sept. 7, 14, 1859; Montgomery *Daily Confederation,* Nov. 20, 1859.

bind you . . . to exert every means within your power to abolish slavery." In declaring that "the negro is entitled to liberty and equality with the white man," Republicans had made "a chasm between the North and the South so deep and wide that it can never be . . . bridged over." "You Republicans," continued Clay, "must entertain a more contemptuous opinion of us than you have even expressed in this platform, if you think . . . we intend to submit to the domination of our enemies." I "indulge in no menace," he declared, as he accused Republicans of "striving to scatter dragon's teeth over the plains of the South, in the hope . . . that there will spring up armed men ready to destroy our domestic institutions, to desolate our fields, and to drench our hearthstones in fraternal blood." The Republicans, he cried in a final oratorical flight, "have themselves created a storm upon which they may ride to power, but which they cannot then control. We hear the low mutterings of its ominous thunder, and sometimes see the fitful gleams of its baleful lightning; and, sir, if no higher purpose could animate us, the mere brute instinct of self-preservation would impel us to prepare for the conflict, and the defense of our rights against that power which threatens their destruction. . . . I speak, sir, as an American Senator, as an embassador [sic] from a sovereign and co-equal State of this Union, with a due sense of my responsibilities to the people of my State, and to the Union—ay, of my responsibilities to myself." The southern-rights press loudly hailed Clay as one of the few who could resist "the seductive atmosphere of Washington" to stand in "the foremost ranks of the small band of true State Rights men who battle devotedly for the South against fearful odds."[28]

State-rights men in the South now declared that "disunion sentiment never was half so deep" before, and waited breathlessly to hear that as a result of the speakership contest, "some sudden collision and bloodshed in the House had precipitated the catastrophe." They began to proclaim that the election of a black Republican President would dissolve the Union. Northern state-rights men urged upon "Union loving people" the duty of "voting against the Republican party." Everywhere the campaign of 1860 was already under way.

In Alabama the first steps took place in several county conven-

28 USC, *Cong. Globe,* 36:1, pp. 121-29, Dec. 13, 1859; Charleston *Mercury,* Jan. 25, 1860.

tions which demanded protection of slavery in the territories and repudiated Douglas as the Democratic candidate. These results were encouraging to Yancey, who now had real hope of controlling the state. When the state Democratic convention met in Montgomery on January 11, 1860, Yancey and the state-rights faction had carefully planned their moves to control that body. Yancey rose at 3:40 to make some preliminary remarks, so that exactly at four o'clock he could move the selection of his temporary chairman. Trying to outmaneuver him, Nicholas Davis of the conservatives also attempted to nominate a temporary chairman, and bedlam broke loose. When the hubbub subsided, LeRoy Pope Walker nominated Francis S. Lyon, and the state-rights men had control of the convention.

The Yancey men were thus able to put through the "Alabama Resolutions" demanding a protection plank in the Democratic platform, without which the Alabama delegates were pledged to bolt the Charleston convention. An emotional legislature endorsed the work of the state convention by passing resolutions requiring the governor "to call a State convention in the event a Black Republican should be elected President of the United States in 1860." The state-rights campaigners around Montgomery had asked Clay to address them on the "questions agitating the country." Because of illness, Clay had not been able to go to Montgomery, but from Washington he covered the subject in a letter. There were, he said, three alternatives: the South could yield to the black Republicans and save the Union; northern and southern Democrats could save the Union if the South gave up all claim to protection of slavery in the territories except the fugitive-slave law; or the South could claim protection for slave property by all departments of the federal government. This, said Clay, would lead either to equality in the Union or to separation, and he urged preparation for the "irrepressible conflict."[29]

29 E. C. Bullock to Clay, Jr., Dec. 30, 1859, W. Byrdsall to Clay, Jr., Dec. 15, 1859, Clay MSS; Ala. Leg., *HJ*, pp. 230, 251, 319, Jan. 18, 23, Feb. 1, 1860; Ala. Leg., *SJ*, pp. 124, 176, 395, Dec. 13, 1859, Jan. 17, Feb. 24, 1860; Montgomery *Daily Confederation*, Feb. 25, 1860; Huntsville *Democrat*, Jan. 18, 25, 1860; William Russell Smith, *The History and Debates of the Convention of the People of Alabama* (Montgomery, 1861), 9 (cited hereinafter as Smith, *Debates of Alabama Convention*); Yonge, "Conservative Party in Alabama," 511; James Leonidas Murphy, "Alabama and the Charleston Convention of 1860," Ala. Hist. Soc. *Transactions*, V (1904), 224f; Sutton Selwyn Scott, "Recollections of the Alabama Democratic State Convention of 1860," Ala. Hist. Soc. *Transactions*, IV (1899-1903), 313-20; Austin L. Venable, "The Conflict between the Douglas and Yancey Forces in the Charleston Convention," *JSH*, VIII (May, 1942), 226-41.

While events were trending this way in Alabama, Clay was striking his blows in the Senate. He and other southern-rights leaders ganged up on Douglas as the one person who had brought the Democratic party to its present unhappy pass. To Clay's charge of inconsistency, Douglas replied, "I am willing to compare records with him as a Democrat. I never make speeches proclaiming to the world that I will bolt a convention if I cannot get my man nominated." In reply, Clay held to the southern-rights line of lofty principle, as he declared "my test of Democracy is fidelity to principle, his test of Democracy seems to be fealty to party." I, proclaimed Clay, "am not the serf of the Democratic party. I think there are occasions when a man who is faithful to his country and to his conscience must repudiate even the acts of a majority of his party." If Clay refused him the "right hand of Democratic fellowship," Douglas countered, "I shall survive the stroke. If I should happen to be . . . the nominee of, the Charleston convention, and he should vote against me, I am not certain that it would diminish my majority in his own State. . . . I am not courting his support." To this, Clay replied that if Douglas "had been as observant of the public demonstrations within my State as I have been, if he had looked more to Alabama and less to Charleston, I think he would have discovered that I am sustained by a very large majority of the party there; and I think the events that are transpiring there this day will satisfy him of this fact."[30]

While the state-rights bloc fought Douglas in Washington and the Democracy seethed in every state, time hastened toward the crisis that was the Charleston convention. There, in the late April heat, the platform committee wrangled for four days and finally brought in a majority report embodying protection of slave property in the territories, while the minority report reaffirmed the Cincinnati platform of 1856 and endorsed the Dred Scott decision. When the convention adopted the minority report, LeRoy Pope Walker, in accordance with instructions, led the Alabama delegation out of the convention. All of the Mississippi, Florida, and Texas members and the majority of those from Louisiana and South Carolina followed, while individual delegates

30 USC, *Cong. Globe*, 36:1, pp. 424, 426, Jan. 12, 1860; Milton, *Eve of Conflict*, 409f.

from Arkansas, Delaware, and North Carolina also withdrew. As the rump convention balloted fruitlessly on a candidate, the bolters assembled at St. Andrew's Hall, but took no action.

Even Yancey, triumphant but weary, and perhaps frightened by the turn affairs had taken, showed the strain in the letter he wrote to Clay: "You have doubtless seen that both conventions have adjourned—making no nominations— The Natl was demoralised —factious & adjourned to save an open disruption— Our's had timid & perhaps wise men in our councils, who were seriously opposed to a nomination here or even a recommendation. . . . But we were unanimous as to the platform and as to the holding another convention at Richmond— Davis was the favorite name with us—tho Lane & Guthrie & Breckinridge had their friends— . . .

"You & our delegation each & all must take an early occasion, in your places, to speak of our action here & must *sustain us*— It is our right & your duty & exigencies call for the aid of every man—

"I send . . . you large numbers of my speeches & our protest. . . . Give them circulation . . . where it will tell on our cause— Do it at once—so as to bear on the election of delegates to our coming state convention— Prompt and efficient action is 'the order of the day. . . . '

"An early occasion & a decided stand by you, Curry, Pugh, Clopton, Moore (& Stallworth if he will) will have vast influence not only in Alabama but over the whole South. . . .

"I write in great haste—amidst much 'noise and confusion' & pray you to excuse any abruptness of manner or phrase— All for the cause, now."[31]

Clay rose to the occasion with a long letter addressed to Edward Asbury O'Neal of Florence, but intended for all state-rights men in Alabama. "The action of our delegates in the Charleston Convention," he began, "meets my cordial approval." From there he went into a bitter denunciation of Douglas and squatter sovereignty, which, said Clay, "differs not so much in kind as in degree from black republicanism." For Republicans "to deny a right and prevent its enjoyment may be only a wrong"; but for Douglas

31 W. L. Yancey to Clay, Jr., May 4, 1860, Clay MSS; Democratic National Convention, Charleston, 1860, *Proceedings*, 18f, 34f; *Statement of So Much of the Proceedings of the National Democratic Convention at Charleston, April, 1860, as Led to the Withdrawal of the Delegates from Certain States* (n.p., n.d.), 1-22; Nichols, *Disruption of American Democracy*, 304f; Murphy, "Alabama and Charleston Convention of 1860," 248; Venable, "Conflict between Yancey and Douglas," 241.

Democrats "to admit the right and prevent its enjoyment is adding insult to injury." "Thus our constitutional rights, as expounded by the United States Supreme Court, *are* to be snatched from us by squatter sovereigns in all the Territories." Warming to his subject, Clay continued, "The black-republicans would countenance the destruction of our property everywhere outside of the State where it is sustained by law—the Douglasites would countenance its destruction in the common territories, if they had control of the Federal Government. And yet we are to be told that if we do not support Douglas we must take Lincoln. The South will hurl contempt upon the miserable alternative."

In everything except slavery, charged Clay, Douglas was already a Republican. "He goes for enlarging the pension system—so do the republicans. He goes for bounties to mail steamers and telegraph companies—so do the republicans. He goes for distribution of the public lands among the States for AGRICULTURAL COLLEGES —so do the republicans. He goes for giving away the public lands to natives and foreigners . . . so as to fill the Territories with squatter sovereigns—so do the republicans. He asserts the right of those squatter sovereigns to exclude slavery from the Territories— so do the republicans. . . . In view of these accordances, and of his co-operation with them in opposing . . . the admission of Kansas under the Lecompton constitution—and the disorganization and division that he has produced in the Northern wing of our party, and now threatens in the Southern wing—is it not natural that . . . black-republicans should sympathise with him and desire his nomination at Baltimore?"[32]

Yancey and the state-righters worked feverishly for a month to control the situation in Alabama, where the Douglasites, under the able leadership of John Forsyth and J. J. Seibels, were straining just as hard for victory. Conventions of both factions met in Montgomery on June 4, where the Douglasites sent a full, uninstructed delegation to Baltimore, while the Yancey faction sent their men to Richmond, but also authorized them to attend the Baltimore convention under the same instructions they had taken to Charleston. While the Democracy was thus occupied, Whigs and Americans throughout the South came to life again, organized

[32] *Letter from Hon. C. C. Clay, Jr., Washington, May 21, 1860* (Washington, D. C., n.d.), 1, 6 (pamphlet in Ala. Dept. Archives and Hist.).

their Constitutional Union party, and nominated John Bell of Tennessee and Edward Everett of Massachusetts.

Watching the Democratic contests going on in most southern states, several leaders in Washington decided it was time to unite in a final effort at party unity. To this end eighteen southern congressmen advised the Charleston bolters "to go to Baltimore and claim their seats." Clay refused any part in this appeal and condemned the Seibels-Forsyth convention as a device "to avoid open discussion and a fair trial before the people whether they will sustain their delegates at Charleston, and . . . summoning . . . a packed jury, predetermined to condemn our late delegates to Charleston, to surrender the principles of the democratic party, and the rights of the States." It would only aid "the delegates from black-republican States of the North in forcing a platform and a candidate upon the democratic States of the South."[33]

The bolters assembled at Richmond on June 11, 1860, but soon adjourned to meet at Baltimore, there to try for readmission. "A great crisis is pending," wrote one of the Yancey phalanx. "If we are denied our seats the breach in the democratic party . . . will become irreparable, I think and what is more it will be the 1st act in the Drama of Disunion." And so it turned out to be, for the convention finally excluded the original members from Alabama and Louisiana, and admitted their new Douglasite delegations. This led to the second bolt, when in addition most or part of the delegates from Virginia, North Carolina, Maryland, Tennessee, and Kentucky withdrew. The story "of the final disruption of the Baltimore Democratic Convention" was told by one of the Alabama-Yancey delegation, who rejoiced in "the reorganization" of all the bolters "into a separate body under the lead of the President of the first convention who . . . proclaimed that self respect constrained him also to resign." "Mr. Cushing was of course proclaimed . . . president of our new organization and then was presented for the first time the spectacle of two democratic National Conventions sitting at the same time. . . . The Douglas convention proceeded to consummate their forces and nominated that political traitor for the presidency. . . . Our convention

33 *Letter from C. C. Clay, Jr., Washington, May 21, 1860,* 7; Huntsville *Southern Advocate,* May 30, 1860; Yonge, "Conservative Party in Alabama," 517; Dorman, *Party Politics in Alabama,* 159; DuBose, *Yancey,* 477-79.

concluded its labors by nomination of J. C. Breckinridge of Kentucky for President and Genl. Joseph Lane of Oregon for Vice President. One of the best soundest and strongest tickets we could have made up."[34]

The Douglas convention had nominated Benjamin Fitzpatrick for vice president because, said one Yanceyite, he was "the person most likely to distract and divide the party in our state." Fitzpatrick was "in great tribulation," for by "accepting it he severs himself from the true democracy of his section and by rejecting it he leaves to perish many of his personal friends who have taken the Douglas shute in Alabama." Fitzpatrick finally declined, saying that the "distracting differences at present existing in the ranks of the Democratic party . . . distinctly admonish me that I should in no way contribute to" them. The party then nominated Herschel V. Johnson of Georgia. This was the final break between Fitzpatrick and Clay; henceforward they had neither social nor political associations. Shortly after leaving Washington, Virginia Clay wrote, "The Gov. [Fitzpatrick] & family left a few days after we did, with sore hearts. . . . The Mad. wished to stop at the M. W. [Montgomery White Sulphur Springs]. . . . Fitz did not know we were there or she wd. never have desired to stop. She was too much cut. The Douglasites one & all were cursing the Gov. up & down when we left."[35]

Amid these excitements, Clay was going into a rapid physical decline and was rumored to have consumption. Illness kept him off the Senate floor from May 11 to May 24; he returned for two days, and then was out for the rest of the session. He turned over his Senate business to Robert Toombs, who urged Clay not to worry "about such matters at least as I can attend to for you." The Clays (including Withers, who had come up to observe the Baltimore conventions) reached the Virginia springs late in June, when Clement's illness became so serious as to keep Virginia "wretchedly uneasy." Here, she wrote, he "bears his sickness

34 W. P. Browne to Margaret Browne, June 20, 25, 1860, W. P. Browne MSS; DuBose, *Yancey*, 480; Milton, *Eve of Conflict*, 469-77; Nichols, *Disruption of American Democracy*, 318f.

35 W. P. Browne to Margaret Browne, June 25, 27, 1860, W. P. Browne MSS; B. Fitzpatrick to W. Ludlow and Others, June 25, 1860, W. L. Yancey MSS; Virginia Clay to Celeste Clay, July 6, 1860, Clay MSS; Herschel Vespasian Johnson, "From the Autobiography of Herschel V. Johnson, 1856-1867," *AHR*, XXX (Jan. 1925), 317; Shepherd H. Roberts, "Benjamin Fitzpatrick and the Vice-Presidency," *Ala. Hist. Soc. Transactions*, IV (1899-1903), 357-64.

with much more fortitude than he did in W., for I think he is sicker, & God knows he was ill enough there. Whether *anything* will ever cure his cough remains to be seen." By mid-July, Clay had improved enough to go on to Huntsville. He and Virginia spent the summer at "Cozy Cot" on Monte Sano, where Clement was somewhat better. His chief difficulty now was asthma, although on Monte Sano he could "breathe easier & sleep more."[36]

Under these circumstances, Clay could only watch the campaign from the seclusion of his mountain home and write a few letters in support of the Breckinridge-Lane ticket. With three candidates in the field, the followers of each had some hope of success in Alabama. Bell men had the smallest support, and late in the campaign authorized their electors to vote for any candidate who could defeat Lincoln. Douglasites were under the leadership of John Forsyth in Mobile and J. J. Seibels in Montgomery, but had their greatest support in North Alabama. A splinter group calling themselves the Southern Rights Opposition, made up of ultra-state-rights men who had formerly been Whigs or Americans, at first refused to cooperate with any of the three organized factions, but ultimately joined the Yanceyites and supported Breckinridge. Throughout the campaign the Yanceyites were the strongest faction. Yancey campaigned vigorously through Alabama, in other parts of the South, and finally assaulted the enemy in the North and East.

During October, in two public letters Clay repeated his unqualified endorsement of Breckinridge and Lane as the only candidates who could preserve the rights of the South. He shuddered to contemplate the future if either Douglas or Bell were elected, and he predicted again that in the end Douglas and his party would be in the ranks of the black Republicans. When Seibels charged that Clay had formerly favored Douglas, but now had reversed himself, Clement replied that he had never wanted Douglas and would never have voted for him except as a choice of evils. Few true Southerners, Clay continued, would have supported Douglas even before his Kansas defection. And now after Douglas' speech at Norfolk, where he had admitted he would aid Lincoln, if necessary, in maintaining the laws against any resistance, Clay was more

[36] Robert Toombs to Clay, Jr., June 14, 1860, Virginia Clay to Celeste Clay [July] 6, 1860, Clay, Jr., to Clay, Sr., Aug. 16, 1860, Clay MSS; L. O'B. Branch to Nancy Branch, June 17, 1860, "Letters," 76; USC, *SJ*, 36:1, pp. 458-502.

bitter than ever. He was surprised and mortified that Douglas still had any support in the South.[37]

Late in October, Clay's asthma became so bad that his life was despaired of, and he set out for Texas with the hope of finding relief in a different climate. This was a harrowing moment for Susanna Clay, who, in a fit of remorse and in the fear "that we meet no more on earth," wrote to Clement, "Never did I know the day that I would not have given my life for yours— My sons were my 'Idols.' I worked for them—perhaps, with more zeal than judgment."

While Clement and Virginia were in New Orleans pondering whether to go on to Texas or return home, Virginia's cousin, Dr. Robert Carter Hilliard, arrived and promised to cure Clement if they would go to his home at New Iberia, Louisiana. And so they were soon installed in the Hilliard parlor, converted into a bedroom for the invalid. Within a few days, reported Clement, Dr. Hilliard had "stopped my asthmatic spasms . . . that made me feel that suffocation or strangulation was imminent, if not inevitable." As he continued to improve, Clay wrote, "I still hope to return to H[unts]ville during the Xmas, & to Washington by 7th Jany."[38]

Ill though he was, Clay had managed to write a public letter after Lincoln's election. "I think the cup of our wrongs and injuries now overflows. Since the election of a man to the Presidency pledged to a war of extermination of slavery, the North can offer us no greater insult, or stronger proof of hatred and vengeance." Therefore, Clay declared, "I am for separating from them immediately and making them a foreign people, with whom we will treat or fight, as they elect. Let South Carolina act alone, and at once—the sooner the better. I think Georgia, Alabama, and Mississippi will soon join her, and ultimately, all the slaveholding states."

On November 30, 1860, Clay sent to Governor Moore his resignation as United States senator, effective March 4, 1861, if Alabama did not earlier dispense with his services by seceding from the Union. Clay saw no hope for peace in the Union and

37 M. J. Williams to A. R. Boteler, Sept. 14, 1860, Alexander Robinson Boteler MSS; Huntsville *Democrat*, Oct. 10, 24, 1860; Montgomery *Weekly Confederation*, July 27, 1860; Dorman, *Party Politics in Alabama*, 161-63; DuBose, *Yancey*, 487-537.
38 Susanna Clay to Clay, Jr., Oct. 30, 1860, Clay, Jr., to Celeste Clay, Dec. 8, 1860, Clay MSS.

urged that no "overt act" was necessary. While he wished to see cooperation among the southern states, he argued that separate state action was just as necessary in dissolution as it was in the formation of the Union. If Alabama should decide to submit to "dishonor," Clay had not the "passive spirit to represent her in Congress in her disgrace," nor could he "consent to be the servile messenger of a conquered province."[39]

Clay's position was representative of the immediate secessionists or, as they were sometimes called, the straight-outs. The other large group, the cooperationists, exhibited many shades of opinion. There were those like Fitzpatrick who strongly favored secession but felt that "the Southern States should all go together," or at least "a sufficient number . . . should go out to insure a new confederacy." Other cooperationists wanted a convention of southern states to make one more effort at settlement within the Union. If that failed, they would then secede. Then there were the unionists, who refused to secede but at this juncture united with the cooperationists in the hope of delaying action long enough to reach a settlement within the Union.

While Clay was recuperating, his friends kept him informed of events in Washington. "All the Southern States are represented. The S. C. members are all in their seats, except Keitt," wrote David Clopton. "The Pres.'s message," he continued, "was not satisfactory to any side; denied the right of secession, and also the power of coercion, but says he will enforce the laws. The old man is very anxious to avoid a collision, and wants secession postponed until the 4th March. . . . The general impression, here, with all parties," Clopton felt, "is, that a dissolution of the Union is inevitable. I cannot see how a collision of arms can be avoided. But be that as it may, far rather die a freeman than live a slave to Black Republicanism. . . . The argument is exhausted—farther remonstrance is dishonorable—hesitation is dangerous—delay is submission." On a more personal note he continued, "We have felt your absence very much, and the need of your advice and cooperation in the momentous issues, which are pressing upon

[39] Huntsville *Democrat*, Dec. 5, 12, 19, 1860; Arthur C. Cole, "Lincoln's Election an Immediate Menace to Slavery in the States?" *AHR*, XXXVI (July, 1931), 765f. Clay's letter on the election, dated Nov. 15, 1860, and his letter of resignation, dated Nov. 30, 1860, were published in the Huntsville *Democrat*, Dec. 12, 19, 1860.

us. . . . Your State,—a Southern Confederacy will need your services in council, and it may be, upon the field."[40]

Clay reached Washington on January 7, 1861, just in time to take part in the caucus of southern senators which passed three resolutions recommending that: each southern state should secede as soon as possible; a convention to organize a southern confederacy should meet not later than February 15 in Montgomery, Alabama; and in view of threatened hostile legislation, delegations of the seceding states should remain in Congress until March 4, to obstruct it. Clay was considerably troubled by the obvious inconsistency of such action and went into a long explanation to Governor Moore of how it was the "manifest purpose of the Blck. Reps. in both Hs. of Cong. to use the power they may have, when the Sens. & Reps. of the cotton States leave here to enact every species of Legislation which hate of the South & lust of power & plunder may suggest." As for himself, Clay added, "I do not wish to remain here & if I consulted only my feelings . . . would not stay a day after the secession of my state. . . . I think all the Sens from the Cotton States wd do likewise, if they consulted only their own wishes."

On the same day the Alabama convention assembled in Montgomery. Campaigns in the counties for election of delegates had been heated and close; furthermore, strength of the two factions could not be closely calculated because some delegates had not declared their positions. The straight-outs, however, organized the convention, and the news coming from other parts of the South played into their hands and worked against the cooperationists, who, nevertheless, put up a stiff fight to gain time. Led by Jere Clemens, the cooperationists tried to delay secession until the ordinance should be ratified by popular vote. When this idea was rejected, most of the cooperationists agreed to vote for secession anyway, and the ordinance passed, 61-39.[41]

Even before secession was voted, Governor Moore took the

---

40 David Clopton to Clay, Jr., Dec. 13, 1860, Clay MSS; Huntsville *Southern Advocate*, Nov. 28, 1860; Clarence Phillips Denman, *The Secession Movement in Alabama* (Montgomery, 1933), 101-103.

41 Clay, Jr., to A. B. Moore, Jan. 7, 1861, Clay MSS; Smith, *Debates of Alabama Convention*, 452; U. S. War Department, *War of the Rebellion: A Compilation of the Official Records of the Union and Confederate Armies* (Washington, 1880-1901, 70 vols. in 128), ser. I, vol. 1, 443f (cited hereinafter as *O.R.*, with series number in uppercase roman numerals and volume number in lowercase).

precaution of seizing the federal forts within the state, an act which was accomplished on January 5, 1861. It was not until January 25, however, that he appointed Thomas James Judge a commissioner to negotiate with the United States government respecting the forts, customhouses, and arsenals within the state. In this Alabama was slower to act than South Carolina, whose commissioners were leaving Washington at about the time Judge arrived. The Sumter question was much more acute than the disposition of Alabama forts, and Clay had united with other cotton-state senators to restrain South Carolina hotheads, while at the same time he was urging Buchanan to withdraw federal forces. When T. J. Judge asked assistance, Clay sought an appointment for him with the President. Buchanan offered to receive Judge "as a distinguished citizen of Alabama," but could not recognize him as a person "duly commissioned to negotiate." Judge was highly incensed, and Clay proceeded to browbeat Buchanan not only for refusing "to entertain a peaceful proposition from a seceding State, but on preventing Congress from receiving it." The free people of Alabama, Clay continued, "will not consent that places of power granted by them to the government, for their defense . . . shall be used in aid of their invasion and subjugation."

Clay's final blast was certainly not suitable to be addressed to the executive of a foreign government with which he expected to negotiate. "Left to yourself I think you would withdraw your garrisons and sell us the forts, for you pray for peace and protest against coercion. Take care that your counselors do not compromise your honor and your character by evincing uses of those strongholds at variance with your prayers and protests. A superannuated soldier, whose vanity and ignorance have never failed to provoke contempt whenever he essays to play the statesman, is not competent to advise you. Neither is a mere jurist and scholar, who has lived a recluse. . . . Trust your own judgment and feelings and I think you will correct the errors they have committed by transferring your troops from Southern States . . . to the Western frontier."[42]

42 T. J. Judge to A. B. Moore, Feb. 18, 1861, Clay, Jr., to James Buchanan, Feb. 1, 1861, James Buchanan to Clay, Jr., Feb. 2, 1861, O.R., I, lii, 17-20; Smith, Debates of Alabama Convention, 452f; Montgomery Weekly Mail, Feb. 22, 1861.

During January most southern congressmen kept their seats, though a few left to take part in the secession conventions of their states. Unionists and moderates, led by Crittenden, strove for a settlement, but their defeat on January 15, 1861, extinguished the last hope of one more compromise. Secession had by now become a reality, and the delegation of each cotton state was anxiously awaiting official information of independence. Southern congressmen who were still in Washington united on January 21, 1861, in announcing the secession of their respective states and in making valedictory addresses in withdrawing from the federal councils. It was a solemn moment, fraught with mixed emotions, as Clay rose in his turn to declare that his constituents had now assumed "their separate station as a sovereign and independent people. . . . It is now nearly forty-two years since Alabama was admitted into the Union. She entered it, as she goes out of it, while the Confederacy was in convulsions, caused by the hostility of the North to the domestic slavery of the South. Not a decade . . . has elapsed . . . that has not been strongly marked by proofs of the growth and power of that anti-slavery spirit of the northern people which seeks the overthrow of that domestic institution of the South, which is not only the chief source of her prosperity, but the very basis of her social order. . . . [The people of Alabama] are resolved not to trust to the hands of their enemies the measure of their rights. They intend to preserve for themselves, and to transmit to their posterity, the freedom they received from their ancestors, or perish in the attempt. Cordially approving this act of my mother State, and acknowledging no other allegiance, I shall return, like a true and loyal son, to her bosom, to defend her honor, maintain her rights, and share her fate."

This was an impressive peroration, but two terse comments show better the real secessionist state of mind. Shortly after the Republican victory, Clay had said, "Of course, we cannot live under the same government with these people, unless we control it." And just before he left Washington, Jefferson Davis wrote to Clay, "We have piped and they would not dance and now the devil may care."[43]

43 Clay, Jr., and B. Fitzpatrick to W. M. Brooks, Jan. 18, 1861, O.R., I, lii, pt. 2, p. 7; Clay, Jr., to [?], Nov. 15, 1860, Huntsville Democrat, Dec. 5, 1860; Jefferson Davis to Clay, Jr., Jan. 19, 1861, Clay MSS; USC, Cong. Globe, 36:2, pt. 1, p. 486, Jan. 21, 1861.

9 ～

Confederate Senator

WASHINGTON WAS all confusion as southern officialdom hastily departed. Impatient though they were to get away, the Clays remained while Clement tried to back up Alabama's commissioner Judge in his efforts to negotiate for the Alabama forts. When this failed early in February, Clement and Virginia at last set out southward. Clement was suffering constantly from asthma, and he now became so ill that they were forced to remain in Petersburg, Virginia, with Clay's cousin, Dr. Thomas Withers. As Clement grew worse daily, Dr. Withers urged him to go to Minnesota.

Clement and Virginia reached Huntsville on February 24, 1861, and a few days later, with Lawson Clay to help nurse his brother, they began the long journey to Minnesota. First reports from the invalid were discouraging. "Every one in church prayed for him as they do at every service," wrote Mary Clay. The northern climate soon proved beneficial to Clement, so that at the end of March, Lawson was able to return home.[1]

The excitement of the times and Clement's impatience to be active in the new Confederacy were not conducive to his recovery. The northern latitude was socially uncongenial. Rumors, alarms, and the call for troops hastened his departure, even though, as Clement wrote, "I was improving continuously & rapidly when Lincoln's Proc. & that of the Govr. of Minn. reached me, & I think I shd have been entirely restored to health . . . had I remained there with an easy conscience & a quiet mind. But, after those infamous & insulting bulletins, the demonstrations against 'the Rebels' were so offensive as to become intolerable." And so on April 22, 1861, Clement and Virginia took their departure "& came down the Miss. to Memphis, much to the regret of the few *real* friends we found or made in Minn." They reached Huntsville on April 29, 1861.[2]

Meanwhile, Lawson had gone to Montgomery and obtained a commission. On the day of Alabama's secession he had written to Clement, "Tell Jeff. Davis that I can't bring volunteers, but only a right loyal heart & true hand to him & the South— If *he wants me I am ready*. I know he will be our leader." And so now in May, Lawson was off to Virginia to fight for the Confederacy, and Celeste had gone to her parents' home in Macon, Georgia. Both Lawson and Clement were much concerned about their financial affairs, especially the prospects of collecting money due them, as well as safe arrangements for their slaves and other property. Clement also felt the necessity "to consult & conclude what will be done, or ought to be, for the welfare of the Confederacy," for he, like all Confederates, had no doubt of his own military genius, and so he and his fellow townsman, Edward Dorr Tracy, were concocting "a plan of campaign that Davis could not understand & yet so brilliant as to dazzle & bewilder him."[3]

A few days later the Clays had a warm invitation from Varina Davis to visit Montgomery. "If you are able to come with your wife, and make us a visit we will have the concordances of Washington & Montgomery— I should sincerely rejoice to see you," she wrote. "Believe me time has not cooled the affectionate gratitude I feel for all your sympathy during Mr Davis' illness, to me the darkest hour of my life. . . . You are not able to bear hotel inconveniences but if you will come to us, need only see people when you please— I think too Mrs Clay would enjoy seeing the many friends and acquaintances she has here. . . .

"As to the children, I think you must like them, at best your god child— . . . We all think of going out to Mrs Fitzpatricks this evening, with Constitution Browne & his wife, and Mr & Mrs

1 John Withers to Virginia Clay, Feb. 15, 1861, H. L. Clay to Clay, Jr., March 30, 1861, Clay MSS; Mary Clay to Virginia Clay, April 3, 1861, Ada Sterling MSS.
2 Clay, Jr., to Edward Dorr Tracy, May 4, 1861, Clay MSS.
3 H. L. Clay to Clay, Jr., Jan. 11, 1861, Celeste Clay to Virginia Clay, May 4, 1861, H. L. Clay to Virginia Clay, June 4, 1861, Clay, Jr., to E. D. Tracy, May 4, 1861, Clay MSS.

Toombs to spend a night & day— We expect much pleasure. The Madam seems to be in fine spirits, as is also the Governor— . . . Mrs Mallory is in town on a short visit, Mrs Pope Walker is here, Mrs Memminger, and Mrs Toombs, the latter is the only person who has a house—"

But Clay was not able to go to Montgomery, and spent another quiet summer at his home on Monte Sano, sometimes better, and sometimes worse. He still sought a climate that would give him relief, and contemplated western North Carolina, but his friends advised against it and again urged him to go to Arkansas or Texas. Indeed, Clement was still anxious to buy land in one of those states. Nothing came of these schemes, however, and by September, Clay had improved so much that his sincere desire to do something for the Confederacy and the lure of public life had brought him to change his plans.[4]

During these months of Clay's inactivity, much had transpired in Alabama. Though the convention had voted secession by a large majority, cooperationists and Union men in North Alabama were so strong that a meeting in Huntsville passed resolutions instructing Madison County delegates to retire from the convention if the ordinance of secession were not submitted to popular vote. But at Montgomery even such unionist leaders as Jere Clemens and Nich. Davis were swept along with the tide, and though they voted against secession, once it was passed, they urged that "we must go with the State, or create civil disturbances of the most dreadful character at home." Lawson Clay also predicted "that there will be a successful attempt made to excite the people of N. Ala. to rebellion *vs.* the State & that we will have civil war in our midst." Although this did not materialize, unionist opposition continued. But in March at a Huntsville mass meeting, the secessionists got the upper hand and put through resolutions refusing to endorse activities of the unionist leaders. By this time events had moved so far and so fast that all cooperationists and most unionists were going along with their state and the Confederacy.[5]

Politically the new Confederacy was in chaos. Party lines were

4 Varina Davis to Clay, Jr., May 10, 1861, J. J. B. Hilliard to Clay, Jr., Sept. 11, 1861, R. C. Hilliard to Virginia Clay, Sept. 19, 1861, Clay MSS. The Clays were godparents to Joseph Evan Davis (April, 1859—April 30, 1864), the child that was killed by falling from a porch at the Confederate White House.

5 H. L. Clay to Clay, Jr., Jan. 11, 1861, E. D. Tracy to Clay, Jr., March 6, 1861, Clay MSS; Huntsville *Southern Advocate*, Jan. 16, 1861.

gone. Leaders and constituents alike had shifted views and positions on the many critical questions of recent months and years.
During its short life the Confederate States of America was not to
have political parties in the ordinary American sense of that term;
nevertheless, every officeholder's political antecedents were an
important factor in his election. In spite of the political chaos,
definable groups were striving for immediate control of the new
government. Foremost among these, at the very outset, were the
secessionists—the men who had taken the South out of the Union.
They had led the way when all was in doubt, and now they were
awaiting their reward. Men like Yancey and Rhett expected to
occupy high posts in the new government. In their own eyes
they were the patriots, emulating their forebears of 1776.

But that reward was not forthcoming. The act of secession
itself immediately brought a revulsion of feeling, and the pendu-
lum swung conservative and brought to the headship of the new
state men of less violent views. Their leadership would conciliate
not only the conservatives in the seven seceded states, but would
reassure other southern states which had not yet left the Union.
But it was all bitter to the patriots, as Robert T. Scott, the leading
secessionist of Jackson County, wrote to Clay, "I am not satisfied
as to the workings of the Confederate Government, there is a
screw loose somewhere, to be a submissionist seems to be the best
passport to office and distinction," he complained, pointing to
Joseph C. Bradley, leading unionist of Huntsville. Bradley had
"moved Heaven and Earth," Scott continued, ". . . to divide and
brake [sic] up the Democratic party . . . then . . . toiled like
a Galley Slave . . . to defeat Secession . . . and . . . turned up
Confederate Tax Collector for Ala the most lucrative office I
expect in the State. . . . This is discouraging," Scott mourned,
"and I sometimes, almost dispair [sic] of accomplishing any good
by the Revolution in which we are now involved. Davis was
opposed to Secession and he too has been rewarded for his services— . . . I have heard it whispered that both Davis and Stephens
are reconstructionist. If I could believe this . . . I would be
willing to die. . . . You have the confidence of President Davis
and I hope you can assure me that the charge . . . is false— I
think you should write to President Davis remonstrating against
his appointments from the submission ranks. If he keeps up this

policy he will distroy [sic] the confidence of the only party that can save the country from ruin." So ran the thinking of the secessionists as the time approached for the first elections to office under the permanent constitution of the Confederacy.[6]

The Confederacy was scarcely formed before officeseekers were canvassing their prospects under the new government. A potential successor hastened to inquire whether Clay intended to "retain" his seat in the senate. If not, LeRoy Pope Walker thought he could be elected. Lawson Clay replied that it was Clement's just due to have his "course endorsed by a re-election," and so Walker agreed to take himself out of the picture and *"advocate"* Clay's election to the Confederate senate. Then Walker learned "he would stand a good chance for a Cabinet Appointment" and so hastened to Montgomery, continued Lawson's report to Clement, carrying "a letter from me to Jeff. Davis in his behalf, stating what I know to be your relations towards Pope W. & your estimate of him as a jurist & sound politician. . . . *Telegraph Jeff. Davis* . . . that you would be pleased to have him appointed." Thus was LeRoy Pope Walker made the first Confederate secretary of war and for the time removed from competition with Clay. It was a normal political maneuver, but the Clays could scarcely have done the Confederacy a greater disservice. Walker, though a gentleman of fine mind and integrity, was so poor an administrator that as war secretary he did almost nothing when the post demanded a man of vigor and foresight to organize the war effort while enthusiasm was high.[7]

The summer elections in Alabama only showed that the conflict between factions continued unabated. The wave of revulsion against secessionists had reached its peak and subsided as a result of Davis' conservative appointments. Once more radical feeling was on the upswing, and in the August elections it made decided gains. Secessionists won the governorship by electing John Gill

[6] John E. Moore to W. P. Browne, March 2, 1861, W. P. Browne MSS; Robert Thomas Scott to Clay, Jr., Oct. 11, 1861, Clay MSS; Montgomery *Daily Post*, July 13, 22, 1861 (typescript copy in Yancey MSS); Hendrick, *Statesmen of the Lost Cause*, 170, 191f.

[7] H. L. Clay to Clay, Jr., Feb. 11, 1861, Clay MSS; Jefferson Davis, *Rise and Fall of the Confederate Government* (New York, 1881, 2 vols.), I, 243; Mary Boykin (Miller) Chesnut, *A Diary from Dixie*, ed. by Ben Ames Williams (Boston, 1949), 473; DuBose, *Yancey*, 588. Virginia Clay said that the secretaryship of war was offered first to Clay, who declined it because of his health and urged the appointment of Walker. Davis also offered the choice of any cabinet post to Yancey, who declined and also suggested Walker.

Shorter over his opponent Thomas Hill Watts. Shorter had long been a state-rights Democrat and was a leader in the secession movement. Watts, on the other hand, had been an old-line Whig, had espoused the American party and, in 1860, the Bell-Everett men, but Lincoln's election turned him into a straight-out secessionist. With the governorship firmly in hand, secessionists also had a good chance to control the legislature. That body had experienced a great turnover of personnel, with two-thirds of the senate, and nine-tenths of the house new men. Looking over the new legislature and the prospects, Joshua Coman wrote, "No Conservative man can possibly live in this Sea of Secession—he cant touch bottom no where, the whole thing is straight & dead out against all who stand in that connection. . . . The Conservatives in the August elections, did not even hold their own, but lost on every field. . . . The conservative element is greatly reduced in this body . . . it has been crushed out."[8]

This trend was reflected in the congressional elections. Under the new apportionment, Alabama now had nine representatives. Of the men elected to the permanent congress, only two, William P. Chilton and J. L. M. Curry, had served in the provisional congress. Chilton was an old-line Whig who had joined the secessionists. Curry was an ambitious young state-rights Democrat, though there were those who thought his party loyalty could not be depended on. David Clopton, Francis Strother Lyon, James Lawrence Pugh, and Edmund Spann Dargan were also secessionists, a total of six. The most conservative member was undoubtedly William Russell Smith, who had been a unionist leader up to the moment of secession, but thereafter he went wholeheartedly with his state. Smith's political antecedents were Whig, Union Democrat, and American party, and in 1860 he had been a Bell-Everett leader. Of Thomas J. Foster and John Perkins Ralls little is known. A complete secessionist victory seemed likely in the

8 Joshua Prout Coman to [G. S. Houston], Nov. 6, 1861, G. S. Houston MSS; W. L. Fleming, "The Peace Movement in Alabama during the Civil War," SAQ, II (April, 1903), 115; Dorman, Party Politics in Alabama, 165; Hendrick, Statesmen of the Lost Cause, 178f.

To avoid confusion, only two terms are used to describe political factions. In 1861, secessionists seems best to describe those who had been state-rights leaders and had worked for immediate secession. In the Confederate Congress they became the state-rights faction or party and grew increasingly hostile to Davis. The conservatives seems the best term to apply to those who saw the necessity for a stronger central government. They supported Davis and his administration, for the most part.

senatorial elections, since, according to one observer, "The Secessionists from North Alabama all give the cold shoulder . . . to
any suggestion favoring a Conservative for the Senate. . . . They
say N Alabama must have one of the Senators, but they never
go out Secessiondom for him."[9]

Senatorial candidates were even more numerous than usual.
One aspirant, John E. Moore, "was early on the field, circulating
energetically, largely & warmly," and "insisting that Clay was in
dreadful health good as dead." Jere Clemens, as always, "would
like exceedingly well to be Senator . . . but just now is hardly
in a condition for any pra[c]ticable purposes." It was rumored
that J. L. M. Curry would oppose Clay "and be aided in it by
Fitzpatrick." LeRoy Pope Walker's intentions were not known,
but "The impression is . . . that he & Clay have juggled & the
initiated know all about it. He is not to oppose Clay." "The
Current . . ." continued one conservative member, "is decidely
& unmistakeably in behalf of Clay & Yancy [sic]. Yancys election
is generally conceded & I think beyond all doubt. Clays also, is
almost as certain in my Judgement." Clay himself was not so
certain, but at the end of October, 1861, he set out for Montgomery to look after his prospects.[10]

Gloomy Josh Coman's predictions about the senatorial elections
came true, but the secessionists had no smashing victory. Yancey
was nominated and elected without opposition. But as usual,
North Alabama could not agree on a candidate, and so after much
wrangling in caucus, the various factions placed in nomination
Clement C. Clay, Jr., Thomas H. Watts, Robert H. Smith, and
Richard W. Walker. The contest was between Clay and Watts.
For the first five ballots Clay had a plurality of four to six votes
over Watts, while Walker and Smith each received from six to
twelve votes. After five ballots the latter two were withdrawn,
and the names of J. L. M. Curry of Talladega and George P.
Beirne, a former Whig of Madison, were substituted. These two
developed no strength, however, and were withdrawn after the

---

[9] H. L. Clay to Clay, Jr., Jan. 31, 1860, Clay MSS; J. P. Coman to [G. S. Houston],
Nov. 6, 1861, G. S. Houston MSS; Walter Lynwood Fleming, *Civil War and Reconstruction in Alabama* (New York, 1905), 29; John Witherspoon DuBose, *Alabama's
Tragic Decade: Ten Years of Alabama, 1865-1874*, ed. by James K. Greer (Birmingham, Ala., 1940), 43; Dorman, *Party Politics in Alabama*, 152.

[10] J. P. Coman to [G. S. Houston], Nov. 6, 1861, G. S. Houston MSS; H. L. Clay
to Virginia Clay, Nov. 1, 1861, Virginia Clay to Clay, Jr., Nov. 1, 1861, Clay MSS.
L. P. Walker had resigned as secretary of war on Sept. 16, 1861.

eighth ballot. On the tenth ballot Clay received 66 votes and was elected over Watts, who had 53. As to geographical distribution of the votes, Clay's support came from the representatives of seven northeastern, eight southwestern, and four southeastern counties. Watts carried ten east-central and three southern counties, while the northwestern counties and several others throughout the state divided their votes. Madison County delegates gave their votes to Beirne and Walker, while Jackson County, on the other hand, voted solidly for Clay.

Clay was considerably chagrined over such a hard-won victory and openly expressed his "intention to resign . . . esteeming the circumstances of . . . election, a censure rather than the result a compliment." His friends vigorously condemned this idea, pointing out that such a peevish quitting would only "give a victory to selfish and unprincipled intriguers over your own tried friends." "Your secret enemies and open opponents," elaborated one correspondent, "by bargain, intrigue and secrecy organize a strong force against you. Their plans and purposes are unknown to your friends . . . until the vote is being taken. Yet, your friends, surprised as they were, defeat this labored secrecy and well devised scheme of 'Sam Rice and Co.' Now it is you step in & because the vote was not so flattering as you were led to believe it would be; you propose to punish your friends by giving your enemies another chance to defeat them. Call you this standing by your friends? . . . Think better of this. It is unwise to permit an enemy to know he has wounded or can wound you. It is worse to prove to your *friends* that the malice of your enemies can influence you more than their friendship." Another correspondent declared, "The triumph of your friends *was a grand one*. The combination of your *Union enemies* and the old line Whigs that desired the election of Watts made the opposition formidable indeed, but by the *untiring efforts* of your friends they were over come and completely routed. It appeared to me that the aristocracy generally tried to defeat you."[11]

Clay soon put aside his peevishness and prepared to go to Richmond. He paid up debts and accounts in Huntsville totaling more than $1,700, leaving some $700 in notes yet unsettled. But he was apprehensive, and the future appeared uncertain and gloomy

11 J. M. Withers to Clay, Jr., Nov. 29, 1861, J. T. Bradford to Clay, Jr., Dec. 1, 1861, Clay MSS; Ala. Leg., *SJ*, pp. 107, 111-16, Nov. 20, 21, 1861.

in mid-February when he and Virginia set off "in the rain" for Chattanooga, where congestion of rail traffic plus refugees fleeing from threatened middle Tennessee made delay inevitable. Clement and Virginia reached Richmond, found lodgings with Mrs. Duval, and on February 19, 1862, Clay took his seat in the Confederate senate under the permanent constitution.

Yellow mud underfoot, gray clouds overhead, and incessant rain were the physical accompaniments of that series of military disasters which surrounded Jefferson Davis' inauguration. The collapse in Tennessee began with the fall of Fort Henry on February 6; two days later, disaster struck in the east, when Union forces captured Roanoke Island on the North Carolina coast. On February 16, 1862, Fort Donelson, the last defense on the Cumberland River, fell, leaving the heart of the Confederacy wide open to Union invasion. This last disaster was not generally known in Richmond until February 23, the day following Davis' inauguration. The natural assumption was that Davis had suppressed the unwelcome news on inauguration day.[12]

Clay was soon getting reports from the West. Huntsville's reaction to "our misfortunes at Fort Donelson" was a mass meeting at which leading unionists, "Ad. White, Joe Bradley, & Bob Brickell made speeches & took the highest ground for resistance," wrote J. W. Clay. "Joe said, he was ready to sink or swim with the Southern Confederacy, & stake all he has on the issue." The Confederate army was "rallying" at Murfreesboro, reported E. D. Tracy, though it "seemed in a sad state of disorganization. Our people are . . . recovering from the terrible shock produced by the fall of Fort Donelson and evacuation of Nashville, but many are hesitating in their hearts between God and Baal, & most are far below the heroic spirit which would lead them to prefer a wilderness & a desert, to homes polluted by invaders. . . . This Valley seems entirely overlooked . . . nobody seems alive to its vast importance & few know even where it is. Meanwhile the river is high and you may hear any morning that the enemy are here, but you shall hear at least one gun being fired at them."[13]

Clay's anxiety over personal perils had to be put aside for the

---

12 Clay, Jr., Receipt Book, 1860-1862, Clay MSS; John Beauchamp Jones, *A Rebel War Clerk's Diary at the Confederate States Capital,* ed. by Howard Swiggett (New York, 1935, 2 vols.), I, 111 (cited hereinafter as Jones, *RWCD*).

13 J. W. Clay to Clay, Jr., Feb. 19, 1862, E. D. Tracy to Clay, Jr., Feb. 22, 1862, Clay MSS.

more pressing work at hand. The new congress had much to do. The senate was a select body of twenty-six members. Exactly half of them had previously served in the United States Congress, for a total of ninety-two years. R. M. T. Hunter led with previous legislative service of twenty-one years, while R. W. Johnson with the aid of his Arkansas machine had thirteen years, A. G. Brown, the east Mississippi politician, had fourteen, James L. Orr, that handsome opportunist of upcountry South Carolina, had ten, and Clay had seven. Several others had state legislative experience, and among the most able for their legal attainments were young Benjamin Harvey Hill of Georgia and Thomas Jenkins Semmes of Louisiana. In spite of this body of experienced men in both senate and house, the Confederate congress was universally reviled by those who deigned to comment on it. Of it Alexander H. Stephens said, "This is a very poor Congress. There are few men of ability in the House. In the Senate not more than two or three. Tom Semmes is the ablest. The next are Barnwell, Hunter, and Clay."

Committee appointments gave to Clay the chairmanship of commerce, and membership on Indian affairs and rules. He with Johnson and Orr of the rules committee immediately got to work and five days later reported a set of forty-eight rules for conducting business, which the senate immediately adopted.[14]

The first congress, in the fifty-three days of its first session, deliberated on 52 senate bills and 68 bills originating in the house. Of the 120 bills before it, the congress passed 90. President Davis vetoed six of these. The remaining bills were either tabled, indefinitely postponed, rejected, or pigeonholed in committee. Among the important subjects which failed to become law were senate bills "to make Treasury Notes a legal tender," "to levy a war tax on cotton produced in the year 1862," "to authorize the President to convene Congress at extraordinary times and places," "to limit the production of cotton in the year 1862," and House bills to authorize "the purchase of iron-plated vessels of war" and to provide a coordinator of railroad transportation.[15]

Of the measures enacted into law the most important were the

---

14 Johnston and Browne, *Stephens*, 414; Confederate States of America, Congress, Senate *Journal*, II, 15, Feb. 24, 1862 (Washington, 1904, 58th Cong., 2d Sess., Doc. No. 234, 7 vols.) (cited hereinafter as CSAC, *SJ*).

15 CSAC, Register of Bills and Resolutions of the Senate, 1862-1864 (vol. XI of War Department Collection of Confederate Records, National Archives, Record Group 109) (cited hereinafter as NA, RG 109).

conscription and exemption acts, the act authorizing suspension of the writ of habeas corpus, and the house measure limiting that act. In an emergency category were the act to "regulate destruction of property under military necessity," the house bill "to increase facilities for importing . . . merchandise into the ports of the Confederate States," and, of course, the appropriation measures.

Amid the gloom of recent defeats in the West and the threat of Union forces on the Virginia coast, Clay's friend, Louis T. Wigfall of Texas, introduced the bill to suspend the writ of habeas corpus. It was rushed through both senate and house in one day, almost without debate, and without a recorded vote in either house.

In the first days of March the bill "to regulate the destruction of property under military necessity" was extensively debated and amended in both houses. Dissension arose over methods of indemnifying owners for cotton and tobacco destroyed. By omitting that feature, the bill passed both houses on March 6, 1862. The senate vote of 12-10 showed little party alignment, but the senators who voted for the bill were chiefly from states where enforcement of the law would not be an immediate military necessity. Curry's bill "to increase facilities for importing . . . merchandise into the ports of the Confederate States," making it lawful to unload cargoes on any part of the Confederate coast, was the congressional answer to pressure of the blockade. It passed both houses with little discussion.[16]

Clay sponsored four bills in this session, two of them administrative in nature. The first provided that if an army officer became secretary of war, he should not lose his rank, but only the pay thereof while he received the salary of a cabinet officer. The second concerned succession to the presidency and provided for assumption of office by the president pro tempore of the senate, and then by the speaker of the house in the event of death or disability of both president and vice president. After earlier vain efforts in both houses, Clay on the last day of the session put through a bill "to authorize the employment of drill-masters."

[16] CSAC, *SJ*, II, 28, 29, 32, 35, 38-40, 144f, 159, 161, 213, 215; CSAC, *HJ*, V, 34, 55, 63, 194f, 286, 289, 293; Southern Historical Society *Papers*, XLIV, 65, 99-104, 109f.

Debates of the Confederate Congress were never published in permanent form; hence there is nothing comparable to the U. S. *Congressional Record*. To fill this gap, the Southern Historical Society compiled a record of the debates taken from accounts appearing in Richmond newspapers. Publication began in vol. XLIV (1923) of the society's *Papers*. Vol. L was issued in 1953, by the Virginia Historical Society, and two volumes remain to be published. This source will be cited as *SHSP*.

On April 5, 1862, Clay introduced his "Bill to punish drunkenness in the army." During the winter the problem of drunken soldiers in Richmond had become so pressing that the cabinet had contemplated seizure of grain in the hands of distillers, but decided against such an arbitrary use of power. Early in the session a joint resolution depriving of his commission any army officer found intoxicated passed the senate but failed in the house. Against this background, Clay offered his bill, which the senate debated and amended at length on April 14, 1862. Clay was unhappy about the modifying amendments, but the measure as passed did provide for cashiering, suspending, or publicly reprimanding commissioned officers convicted of intoxication, whether on or off duty.

Davis' message requesting conscription came before congress on March 29, and on April 1, 1862, Wigfall from the committee on military affairs reported a bill which both houses debated and amended at length. It provided for enrollment of all white men of ages eighteen to thirty-five, and extended for three years the term of service of all men then in the army whose one-year enlistments were about to expire. Conscription passed the senate on April 11 by a vote of 19-5. The five opponents were the Georgia senators, Orr of South Carolina, Mitchel of Arkansas, and Oldham of Texas. Other state-rights leaders, including Wigfall and Yancey, voted for conscription. The house vote of 54-26 showed much division. In general the Alabama, Arkansas, Kentucky, Missouri, and Texas delegations voted for conscription; Georgia and South Carolina members had a majority in the negative; and the Mississippi, Louisiana, North Carolina, Tennessee, and Virginia delegations were almost equally divided, while several of their members abstained from voting. Yancey brought in the accompanying exemption bill, which passed both houses after considerable debate and amendment. The state-rights men took the precaution of adding a clause to include "all persons who now are exempted by the laws of the respective States."[17]

When congress adjourned on April 21, 1862, McClellan and his Union army were already on the peninsula making ready for

17 CSAC, SJ, II, 154, 161-64; CSAC, HJ, V, 228, 250; Confederate States of America, *Public Laws of the Confederate States of America, Passed at the First Session of the First Congress, 1862-* , ed. by James M. Matthews (Richmond, 1862), 47f (cited hereinafter as CSA, *Laws*); Meade, *Benjamin*, 230.

the advance toward Richmond. An undercurrent of apprehension pervaded the city. Many who could do so left Richmond, among them Virginia Clay, who had gone early in April to visit relatives. To her Clement confessed, "we may have cause to go elsewhere very soon." As congressmen departed, a hostile Richmond press shrieked accusations of cowardice. Vitriolic Wigfall added his voice as he wrote to Clay, "I have not seen Davis since you left. He is I suppose at this time engaged in prayer—ditto Randolph, Cooper & Lee. . . . What Davis's plans are I do not know. I do not know if he even has any. I shall stay here & . . . do what I can, . . . to rouse & lead the people to defend their homes. As to the Government I shall interfere no further with their comfort. . . . I could 'divide myself & go to buffets for ever having attempted to move such a dish of skimmed milk to an honorable action,'" fumed Wigfall, paraphrasing Shakespeare.[18]

For the most part, congressmen hastened homeward to defend their votes, advise the governors and legislatures of their states, hearten their constituents, and set in order their personal and family affairs. Virginia and Clement Clay were not able to reach home, however, for Huntsville was in enemy hands. The Clays spent some time in Petersburg, then Virginia went to Warrenton, North Carolina, while Clement proceeded to Macon, Georgia, where he tried to ascertain what would be best to do. "I am," he wrote, "growing daily more anxious to learn the exact state of things at home, & am resolved to approach as near Huntsville as I safely can, & send a courier with an unsigned & undirected letter to mother, to learn the condition of things." Clay felt a great compulsion "to do something to wrest my home from the Vandals & to rescue my relatives & friends from their oppression. . . . I wish only to know what to do & I will attempt it. I will cheerfully spend all of the little the enemy will leave me, & my life too, to rid N. Ala. of the foe." Clay was not able to accomplish much toward this purpose, however, until after the next session of congress.[19]

In mid-August heat, perspiring congressmen extricated themselves and their baggage from the jampacked trains that crept into

18 Clay, Jr., to Virginia Clay, April 12, 1862, L. T. Wigfall to Clay, Jr., May 16, 1862, Clay MSS; Edward A. Pollard, *Life of Jefferson Davis, with a Secret History of the Southern Confederacy* (Philadelphia, 1869), 220.

19 Clay, Jr., to Virginia Clay, May 29, 1862, Clay, Jr., to H. L. Clay, May 29, 1862, Clay MSS.

Richmond, and plunged into the exhausting search for rooms in the overcrowded capital. The congress assembled on August 18, 1862, and Clay was soon busy with his first bill, S. 57, "to punish and repress the importation of notes purporting to be notes of the Treasury of the Confederate States." This act was aimed at counterfeit Confederate notes printed in the North, which became "invasion money" widely circulated in areas occupied by the Union armies. Clay's bill provided the death penalty for any Union officer, private, or camp follower who, upon capture, was found to have in his possession such forged or counterfeit Confederate notes. Clay deplored this "low cunning" of the enemy and urged that "we are constrained to take some measures for protection against these outrages." The bill passed without debate on October 3.

Pursuing his watchdog and efficiency role, Clay set in motion an inquiry to ascertain "whether all of the officers of the Quartermaster's and Commissary Departments are necessary for the public service." His anxiety over western defenses led him to aid Haynes of Tennessee in a resolution looking to the defense of the Cumberland, Tennessee, and Alabama rivers.

As chairman of the committee on commerce, Clay had little to do, but he did bring in a bill "to Encourage the manufacture of clothing and shoes for the army," which provided for the importation, duty free, of machinery for such manufacture. Clay did his most important work in this session as chairman of the joint committee to investigate the management of the naval department. Appointed on August 28, 1862, this committee took testimony throughout the session, and continued the investigation through succeeding sessions of the first congress.[20]

New conscription and exemption bills took up most of the time at this session. The conscription bill passed by the senate raised the age limit to forty-five years and provided that men inducted "shall be first and immediately ordered to fill to the maximum numbers the Companies, Battalions, Squadrons and Regiments in service," while "the surplus, if any," shall be organized into new units. Yancey and other state-rights men tried to substitute their scheme of a call on the governors for quotas of men, but their

20 CSAC, SJ, II, 237, 245, 252, 275, 297f, 407, 416; NA, RG 109, CSAC, Bills and Res., box no. 6; SHSP, XLV, 220, XLVII, 40f, 47.

effort was beaten down. The state-rights faction in the house, however, passed just such a bill. A conference committee finally agreed on what was substantially the senate bill, and so conscription was saved.

So many uncertainties had arisen under the first exemption bill that a more detailed measure was necessary. Debate grew long winded and furious, especially in the house, over exemption of state officials. Conservatives argued that the Confederate government had a constitutional right to conscript every state official (though that would be inexpedient). Vociferous state-rights men howled that it would be unconstitutional to conscript state officials because that would destroy state governments, which the constitution guaranteed. Exemption of justices of the peace was debated for days and ended with a compromise clause exempting "such State officers as the several States may have declared by law to be liable to militia duty, or may hereafter be exempted by the several States."

But these victories did not satisfy the state-rights group. Yancey, in an especially puerile manner, complained that Alabama did not have as many brigadier generals as other states, and brought in a bill requiring that each state have as many brigadier generals as it had brigades in the field. In judiciary committee, Yancey's archenemy, B. H. Hill, redrafted the bill, but still recommended that it should not pass. Clay joined the majority in helping to defeat Yancey's hyperstatism.[21]

Clay's career was considerably affected by H. R. 8, a bill to increase the pay of privates and noncommissioned officers from eleven to fifteen dollars per month. This bill passed the house on September 13, 1862, by a vote of 74-6. In the house, Charles M. Conrad of Louisiana tried in vain to substitute a provision for homesteads for soldiers, and in the senate a substitute appropriating five million dollars to be distributed by the state governors to indigent families of soldiers was likewise unsuccessful. Clay voted for this amendment and against the original bill, which passed, 14-6. Clay's vote on the unpopular side of this question was to be a decisive factor in his defeat for reelection to the senate in 1863. He and other opponents of the bill were absolutely right

21 NA, RG 109, CSAC, Bills and Res., box no. 6; CSAC, SJ, II, 315, Sept. 11, 1862; SHSP, XLVI, 202f, 214f, 244f, Sept. 4, 22, 23, 26, 1862.

in their argument that this small increase would only add to the inflation and would not actually benefit the individual soldier, while it added a large item of expense to the Confederate budget.

Clay's position on other questions of this session was rather middle of the road, sometimes leaning toward the state-rights faction and other times tending toward the conservatives, but always supporting Davis. Clay actively supported S. 95, which required that if a substitute deserted, the man hiring him should be held to military service. Clay voted with the state-rights men in rejecting S. 81, a bill designed to prevent the advancement of incompetent officers. When Yancey tried to amend the bill so as to continue the system of electing officers, Clay voted against that amendment, but in the final role call on this much-needed measure, Clay voted against its passage.

Many senators continued to be much exercised over the vexed question of martial law, and the state-rights faction, led by Oldham, introduced joint resolution S. 16, which protested the extension of martial law beyond the army and went so far as to declare "that martial law is unknown to the Constitution." A large vote killed this clause, and Clay was then instrumental in tabling the whole resolution. When congress adjourned at five o'clock on Monday, October 13, 1862, much badly needed legislation had not been passed, and the members dispersed at a critical juncture in military events.[22]

Clement and Virginia Clay left Richmond immediately and reached Huntsville on Sunday, October 19, 1862. Bragg's offensive operations invading Tennessee and Kentucky had drawn all Union forces northward, so that for some months Huntsville was once more within Confederate lines. During the remainder of the year Clement was busy with his personal affairs. Once more he paid off debts and bills to the amount of $1,800. After noting that he still owed Lawson $1,318.49 and that his note to Frank Mastin for land on Monte Sano now amounted to $1,165, Clement added, "all my debts wont exceed the sum of $3,000."

Before his constituents, one of Clay's first acts was to defend his vote against the bill to increase soldiers' pay. In a letter to William Bibb Figures, editor of the Huntsville *Southern Advo-*

22 CSAC, *SJ*, II, 314, 369f, 394f, 447f, Sept. 22, Oct. 1, 2, 8, 1862; NA, RG 109, CSAC, Bills and Res., box no. 6; *SHSP*, XLVI, 134, 200f, 247, XLVII, 3f, 31f, 48f; Jones, *RWCD*, I, 157f, Sept. 29, 1862.

cate, Clay reviewed his argument on the danger of inflation, and pointed out that the passage of other measures, such as those to provide clothing for the army, made the increase of pay unnecessary and inadvisable. He concluded, "If I had been only intent on pleasing the multitude, I should have voted the many millions to the soldiers. . . . But, knowing the facts . . . had I done so, I should have played the demagogue. . . . I voted according to the dictates of my own judgment, & have the approval of my own conscience, wh. every honest man prefers to the applause of the multitude."

In Huntsville, Clement and Virginia found conditions unsettled, and there was "little to eat." Lawson Clay was "very anxious" to pay off his debts in depreciated Confederate notes, and Clement did pay for him accounts totaling $258. Both men were much concerned about their slaves, and Lawson proposed that his should be sent to Macon. Later Lawson wrote, "What do you think of Saml Tate hiring father's, your & my men on the Blue Mountain R. R.?" Clement ultimately decided, however, to hire all the Negroes at a niter works in Santa Cave, Jackson County. He also did what he could to add to the comfort of his parents, and among other things, he managed to obtain small quantities of coffee, sugar, and salt for them.[23]

"We left Huntsville for Richmond Jany 8th, 1863 @ 5 a.m.," recorded Clement. They had been warned to "take every precaution against small pox, which is everywhere—in the cars & in the country." Of their journey Virginia wrote, "We rode from Stevenson to Chattanooga in the freight train, the baggage cars on the passenger being unable to receive a single trunk! Arriving at C[hattanooga] we wd. have been forced to go to a small-pox hotel or [re]main in the streets but for the galla[ntry] of an old acquaintance . . . of Washington memory who g[ave us] his room, beds, &c. & furnished . . . wagons to have our baggage [brought] from the depot." From Atlanta, Clement went on to Richmond, while Virginia, the two other women, and the servants went to Macon, Georgia, to stay for the time with the Comers, Celeste Clay's parents. "We fumigated the room at Atlanta,"

<hr/>

23 H. L. Clay to Clay, Jr., Dec. 14, 31, 1862, Clay, Jr., to Clay, Sr., Dec. 13, 14, 1862, Clay, Jr., Receipt Book, 1860-1882, entry under Jan., 1863, Clay MSS; Huntsville *Confederate,* Oct. 22, 1862; Clay, Jr., to W. B. Figures, Oct. 30, 1862, printed in Huntsville *Southern Advocate,* in Clay Clippings.

wrote Virginia to Clement, "had a bed bro't in for Emily & retired soon after you left us. Fearing robbery by chloroform I slept with *all* the money in one stocking & mine & Alice's watches, chatelaines & pins in the other. . . . We slept three in a bed; I in the middle & awoke refreshed."

Virginia and Celeste Clay spent the winter in Macon, expecting each week to join their husbands in Richmond. Meanwhile, Clement and Lawson shared a room at Mrs. Duval's, where "Our board is very high, &, when our wives come, will exceed our pay." But it was impossible to find another room, and so Celeste and Virginia did not get to Richmond at all, for which Clement thought they should be thankful, since that city was "dull as ever" and "besides, the weather has been horrid—scarcely two consecutive clear days—but snow, rain or sleet all the time. I am disgusted with this climate & this mode of life & am resolved to quit it at the end of my term—which is only for one year from day after to-morrow," he wrote on February 15.[24] (Clay had drawn a two-year term in the lots assigning senators two, four, or six-year terms.)

Despite the handicaps of miserable weather, disagreeable living arrangements, high prices, and the general feeling of gloom, Clay had a busy and profitable session. He introduced ten bills, of which five passed. Of the total, six bills were of rather minor importance. Three of these (S. 83, 84, 113) failed to pass. They dealt with the rank of army surgeons, printing of the provisional and permanent constitutions, and heavier punishment for trading through the lines. The three which passed (S. 68, 88, 89) abolished ports of delivery in the Confederacy, reduced the number of commissary and quartermaster officers, and authorized the transference from one jail to another of prisoners whenever that was necessary for their safe custody.[25]

Clay's four important bills dealt with two subjects: absence of soldiers and officers without leave, and naturalization and conscription of aliens. On the former subject, S. 78, which became law, required deducting pay for the period any officer or soldier was absent without leave. As Clay drafted the bill, S. 109 author-

24 Clay, Jr., Receipt Book, 1860-1882, H. L. Clay to Clay, Jr., Dec. 31, 1862, Virginia Clay to Clay, Jr., Jan. 13, 1863, Virginia Clay to Susanna Clay, Jan. 14, 1863, Clay, Jr., to Susanna Clay, Feb. 18, 1863, Clay, Jr., to Virginia Clay, Feb. 15, March 12, 1863, Clay MSS; Jones, *RWCD*, I, 238.
25 NA, RG 109, CSAC, Sen. Reg., XI, 270, 276, 280, 285; CSAC, *SJ*, III, 122, 163, 171, 188f, 224, 262, 274, 283, 290, 312; *SHSP*, XLVIII, 239, XLIX, 118.

ized the discharge of any officer absent without leave. The military affairs committee extended it to include dropping of disbursing officers who failed to make prompt returns, and modified the original bill so as to allow an officer "to furnish reasons for his absence." Clay finally got the bill through the senate on April 24, but it was lost during the adjournment rush in the house. A similar bill became law the next session.[26]

The handling of aliens was a question Clay had deeply at heart. His first aim was to keep them from voting, and to this end he introduced, on March 9, 1863, S. 71, which would prevent the naturalization of all foreigners except those who were serving in the military forces of the Confederacy, and would deny these men the vote until they had been duly naturalized. Clay could not rally much support for his bill, and so he moved to lay it on the table. Two weeks later the senate took up a house bill (H.R. 24) of the same title, but somewhat different purpose. This bill "to repeal the laws of naturalization" was entirely the work of the state-rights bloc, which was bitterly hostile to the act of the provisional congress which retained in force United States laws on naturalization, thereby placing that subject under control of the Confederate government. The state-rights men wanted to repeal these laws, so that naturalization would be entirely under the jurisdiction of each "sovereign state." As Oldham put it, "The Confederate Government had no right to force citizens on the separate States against their will." Orr of South Carolina opposed the bill, arguing that the Confederacy needed foreign mechanics who were "everywhere useful citizens."

Those who favored the bill were thinking not of actual European immigrants, but were obsessed with the specter, as Clay predicted, of "an immense immigration from the United States" after the war, which would overrun the border states. Such immigrants, Clay argued, if not prevented from voting, "would in a very short time grow into a great political power . . . hostile to slavery, which it was our duty to protect." One of the more violent state-rights men, Oldham, boomed, "No man should ever have a vote who was not born and raised on our soil," while Clark

26 NA, RG 109, CSAC, Sen. Reg., XI, 278, 284; NA, RG 109, CSAC, Bills and Res., box no. 7; CSAC, SJ, III, 152, 171, 243, 320, 327f, 339; Bessie Martin, *Desertion of Alabama Troops from the Confederate Army: A Study in Sectionalism* (New York, 1932), 200.

of Missouri cried that Orr's views were "perfectly monstrous," for "if we should allow . . . the meanest of all foreigners, the Yankees, to settle among us and vote, how long . . . would it be before . . . our new border States would . . . become Abolitionist?" Clark would "as soon admit to citizenship a devil from hell!" The senate was overwhelmingly in favor of changing the naturalization laws, but the conservatives prevailed in their view that nothing should be done until adequate modifying legislation could be drafted. And so the bill was postponed until the beginning of the next session.[27]

Public opinion was demanding the conscription of aliens. Responding to this and to his own strong feelings on the subject, Clay introduced S. 105 on April 4, 1863. His bill would immediately enroll "all resident or domiciled male foreigners" of conscript age, place them in the service on "the same footing with citizens," and distribute them among existing army units. "The certificates of Consuls or Consular Agents shall not be taken as evidence of exemption." This was the clincher, for it was by such certificates that most aliens had avoided conscription. Debate on the bill showed considerable opposition and a disposition to postpone it. When it came to a final vote, Clay had only five senators with him, while eleven voted against the bill. Explaining the defeat, Clay wrote, "My bill to enroll aliens was postponed in secret session, from fear of offending foreign nations. Orr, Barnwell, Semmes and others opposed it with great vehemence. I was only aided by Clark. I think we prevailed in the argument, but fear carried the votes against it. The same unmanly passion caused postponement of the bill to repeal the naturalization laws." A feeble substitute for Clay's bill came in the last-minute passage of H. R. 64, which would put into military service citizens of the United States sojourning in the Confederacy. This was particularly directed at the many citizens of Maryland who were living in the Confederacy.[28]

27 CSAC, *SJ*, III, 140, 152, 289, 359; *SHSP*, XLIX, 230f; Ella Lonn, *Foreigners in the Confederacy* (Chapel Hill, 1940), 385f, 391.

28 Clay, Jr., to W. L. Yancey, May 2, 1863, DuBose, *Yancey*, 744; Yancey to Clay, Jr., May 13, 1863, Clay MSS; NA, RG 109, CSAC, Bills and Res., box no. 7; CSAC, *SJ*, III, 340, 414; CSAC, *HJ*, VI, 8, 442; *SHSP*, XLIX, 183, 268f; Jones, *RWCD*, I, 275f; Franklin Barlow Sexton, "Diary of a Confederate Congressman, 1862-1863," ed. by Mary S. Estill, *Southwestern Historical Quarterly*, XXXIX (July, 1935), 62.

In the class of needed legislation which failed to pass was B. H. Hill's bill to establish a court of claims. After lengthy debates and numerous amendments, the senate passed a strong bill on March 24, 1863, but the subject was not taken up in the house, and the Confederacy lived its brief life without having this much-needed court. The votes indicate that Clay and some others who fought a strong supreme court were in favor of a strong court of claims.[29]

Exemption was a most hotly debated subject throughout the session. The "twenty negro" clause had caused so much dissatisfaction that some modification was necessary. The senate's elaborate bill (S. 27), passed on February 25, 1863, was firmly rejected by the house, whose own bill (H. R. 3) would modify only the most objectionable portion of the existing law. Both houses rejected the work of a conference committee, and in the end more mail contractors and state officials could legally avoid military service; but exemption of overseers was restricted to those plantations having twenty or more slaves, whose owners were minors, imbeciles, femes soles, and men actually absent in military service. Overseers could remain with the crop of 1863 until it was harvested, and the law also gave the secretary of war wide discretion in detailing men from the army for special work. The gains in this new law were certainly not worth the time consumed in debate.[30]

Even more vexed and controversial was the question of impressment. Inflation and scarcity of supplies had already made impressment a military necessity in many instances. The need for regulating such seizures and giving them a legal basis became urgent during this session of congress and resulted in a rash of bills in both houses for that purpose. One of them, H. R. 9, copiously amended by both houses and by a conference committee, ultimately became law on March 26, 1863.

The impressment act provided that if a farmer refused to sell his produce at market price, the impressing officer and owner each must select a "disinterested citizen" to appraise the property in question. If these two could not agree, they were to select an

29 CSAC, SJ, III, 195f; William Morrison Robinson, Jr., Justice in Grey: A History of the Judicial System of the Confederate States (Cambridge, Mass., 1941), 501-505.
30 CSAC, SJ, III, 44, 66f, 73-80, 98, 100, 295, 299, 304-308; CSAC, HJ, VI, 435-38; SHSP, XLIX, 95f, 104f, 118, 121f, 136f, 146f, 155f, 166f, 178f; Albert Burton Moore, Conscription and Conflict in the Confederacy (New York, 1924), 72-76.

umpire whose decision would be final. In emergencies, property could be taken and appraisal made afterward. Slaves were to be impressed under state laws or under regulations of the secretary of war, who was also empowered to authorize impressment in any locality where it might become necessary. Another feature of the act was an effort at price control. The president must appoint a commissioner in each state and request the governor to appoint another; these two men would form a board to establish prices to be paid by impressing officers. The board must publish its list of prices every two months, or oftener if necessary. R. M. T. Hunter introduced this feature, but it was a similar amendment by Semmes which passed on March 9, 1863, by a vote which cut through party lines. Clay, Wigfall, and Hill favored it; Yancey, Simms, Oldham, and H. V. Johnson opposed it.

The bill as passed attempted to make impressment a summary matter against speculators by enabling an impressing officer to disapprove the decision of appraisers, take the property, and refer the matter to the board of commissioners. If owners who were producers of the stores gave affidavit that the property was held for their own use and not for sale or speculation, the decision of neighborhood appraisers or umpire was final. Some of those who had worked hardest for the bill thought this distinction was ruinous, and so four of them—Clay, Semmes, Simms, and Sparrow —voted against it. The seventeen who voted for it included all shades of state-rights men and conservatives. It was the state-rights bloc, however, which vociferously opposed the working of the act. Led by Toombs and Governor Joseph E. Brown in Georgia, opposition soon spread to other states, and in the end the law was largely inoperative. It bore heavily and unequally on people near the scene of military operations, and was an important cause of the growing discontent.[31]

Early in the session, the senate took up S. 9, a bill to authorize the Erlanger loan of $5,000,000. The bill passed both houses in secret session with, apparently, little debate. Yancey held out strongly against the bill, arguing that it was a bad bargain and

31 NA, RG 109, CSAC, Sen. Reg., XI, 33, 269, 271; NA, RG 109, CSAC, Bills and Res., box no. 7; CSAC, SJ, III, 47, 50, 56, 143, 189-91, 194, 216; CSAC, HJ, VI, 61, 100-102; SHSP, XLVIII, 58f, 82-84, 205f, 240f, 246f, 256f, XLIX, 12f, 17; Johnson, "Autobiography," 331; Frank Lawrence Owsley, State Rights in the Confederacy (Chicago, 1925), 232-60; Louise Biles Hill, Joseph E. Brown and the Confederacy (Chapel Hill, 1939), 147-50.

that the subject was not a matter for legislation but should be handled by the president. Yancey offered a substitute bill which would empower the president to negotiate a loan of $50,000,000. On this he had the support of Clay, Baker, Henry, Maxwell, and Mitchel; but twelve senators voted against him, and the original bill passed without a recorded vote.[32]

The great debate of the session centered on the question of establishing a supreme court, and in this Clay had a vital part. B. H. Hill introduced the supreme-court bill (S. 3) on January 19, 1863. The first debates revolved around the number of justices and their salaries. Hill's amendment providing for five justices finally prevailed over Yancey's desire for only three and other proposals for four. Then Clay, pursuing his economy line, proposed a salary of $5,500 as against $7,000 provided by the bill. After numerous other proposals, the senate adopted Clay's figure. Clay then offered his amendment which would repeal the forty-fifth and forty-sixth sections of the judiciary act of March 16, 1861. This was the crux of the question, since these sections provided for appealing "upon a writ of error" from the state courts to the Confederate supreme court, thus making that body comparable in power and jurisdiction with the United States Supreme Court. The wordy debates which followed revealed a four-way division of the senate: those who would have only a strong supreme court modeled on that of the United States; those who wanted a strong court but would accept a weaker one; those who would establish the court only if appellate jurisdiction were denied; and those who wanted no supreme court of any kind.

Clay did not himself speak on his amendment, but it was extensively debated. Barnwell proclaimed, "We must preserve the principle of State rights. If this were lost the bond that binds us together was instantly dissolved." On the same line, Yancey declared that "The State Rights majority will alone preserve this government. . . . The powers of the Government must not be strained against the sovereign States." Wigfall, always flashy, attributed the destruction of the Union "more to the Supreme

32 W. L. Yancey, MS notes, "In secret Session, Senate C. S. A. 21st Jany. 1863," Yancey MSS; CSAC, *SJ*, III, 28f, 234, 275f, 287, 329, 333, 361, 387; CSAC, *HJ*, VI, 33-35, 53-55, 117, 274, 350, 376f, 440f, 472; CSA, *Laws and Joint Resolutions of the Last Session of the Confederate Congress (November 7, 1864—March 18, 1865) Together with the Secret Acts of Previous Congresses*, ed. by Charles W. Ramsdell (Durham, N. C., 1941), 164.

Court of the United States than to any one other thing. . . . He regarded it as the greatest misfortune that ever befell the country that a man of Judge Marshall's high character and intellect should have remained for so great a length of time upon the Supreme Bench as to have been able to fasten his principles of a strong central government upon the country." If the Confederacy must have a supreme court, Wigfall "did not desire to see the first intellect upon the bench. . . . A man of towering intellect in this court may become a misfortune to the country." Hill and Henry fought doggedly for a strong court, declaring that "If this amendment should be passed the fatal stab would be given to our new Government." But they were overruled, and on March 18, 1863, the senate adopted Clay's amendment, 16-6, and shortly afterward passed the bill establishing a supreme court without appellate jurisdection by a vote of 14-8. The house failed to act either on this or on a later bill, and so the Confederacy never had a supreme court.[33]

Wigfall's fear of a "towering intellect" at the head of the proposed court may have had some influence on the voting. It was generally believed that Davis would appoint John Archibald Campbell to be chief justice. Campbell, formerly a justice of the United States Supreme Court, was a man of "towering intellect," though of austere personality. He had opposed secession and had not resigned his justiceship until April 29, 1861. Consequently, many people in Alabama and elsewhere felt that Campbell was not a fit person to hold high office in the Confederate government. Campbell had been filling the post of assistant secretary of war since October 21, 1862, and on April 16, 1863, the senate confirmed him by a vote of 18-6, Clay voting for, and Yancey against, the appointment.

The supreme-court debate led to a most spectacular scene in the Confederate senate. B. H. Hill and Yancey, speaking on opposite sides of the question, indulged in heated language, and each accused the other of deliberately making false statements. Hunter, who was presiding, called neither to order, and Barnwell's efforts to get Yancey to retract were in vain. Finally, Hill

[33] T. J. Withers to Clay, Jr., April 18, 1863, Clay MSS; CSAC, *SJ*, III, 20, 32, 36, 38, 176; CSAC, *HJ*, VI, 117, 274, 350, 376f, 440f, 472; *SHSP*, XLVII, 197f, 206f, 208-10, XLVIII, 15, 27, 39, 323; Johnson, "Autobiography," 331; Robinson, *Justice in Grey*, 433.

threw an inkstand which struck Yancey's cheekbone and did some damage, but the injury was not responsible for Yancey's death, as some of his admirers later claimed. Resolutions censuring their conduct were adopted in secret session without a tally of votes.[34]

Jefferson Davis' talent for antagonizing people contributed largely to his troubles as chief executive. He and Yancey had never been friendly, and early in the spring of 1862, Davis' asperity touched off an antagonism that was to grow to large proportions. At that time Clay and Yancey united in pointing out that Alabama had forty regiments in the field but only five brigadier generals, and so the two senators recommended four Alabama colonels for promotion to that rank. The letter, obviously drafted by Clay in careful and respectful language, brought this reply from Davis: "It is the province of the Executive to nominate and of the Senate to confirm or reject. Recommendations are willingly received and respectfully considered by me, but I will not argue as to their propriety and do not recognize the fairness of the within statement of my course, and assumption as to what it should be." Davis apparently viewed the letter not as official business but as a personal insult, and so after endorsing it with these comments, he had returned it to Clay and Yancey. This action rankled for over a year and caused Yancey to write to Davis, "The return to us of that paper and the endorsement, I considered then, and do now, an act of grave discourtesy. . . . I think that the circumstances evince a settled hostility on your part to me, and justify a return of such feelings on my part."[35]

In April, 1863, the quarrel broke out anew over appointment of a postmaster for Montgomery. Clay and Yancey united on one Glackmeyer for the office, but Davis intervened, and when Postmaster General Reagan sent in the nomination, the name presented was E. M. Burton. Clay immediately got busy, but he had small success, as he reported to Yancey, who had already left Richmond, "I had two interviews with the President, and . . . vainly endeavored to persuade him to recall the nomination and

34 Clay, Jr., to Virginia Clay, March 25, 1863, Clay MSS; Thomas O. Butler to Yancey, Jan. 28, 1863, Yancey MSS; CSAC, SJ, III, 49, 301; DuBose, Yancey, 690; Robinson, Justice in Grey, 453-55, 470-73.

35 Clay, Jr., and Yancey to Jefferson Davis, April 21, 1862, Yancey MSS (letter in Clay's handwriting) (This letter and others in this controversy are printed in DuBose, Yancey, and in Ala. Hist. Q., II (Summer, Fall, 1940), 258-60, 336-41); Yancey to Davis, July 11, 1863, Yancey MSS.

send in Glackmeyer." This Davis refused to do. "I told him," continued Clay, " I would not vote for B[urton]. He said: 'Very well. If you think it right to reject a good man because you and your colleague preferred another, do so.' I said: 'I think the Senate will reject him.' Whereupon he became excited and vehement—said the Senate could not dragoon him into nominating their choice, etc., etc. I left him in a bad humor with you, Chilton and myself. I had the nomination continued till next session." Yancey protested bitterly to Davis, "I have never been consulted by you as to a single appointment made by you, in Alabama. . . . And I have particularly noticed your selections . . . from among the most inveterate personal foes I had in Alabama. . . . I . . . believe that you were influenced in the rejection of Mr. Glackmeyer . . . by feelings of personal hostility to myself."

Prior to this development, Yancey had requested a commission for his son, Dalton H. Yancey. But after hearing this from Clay, and becoming convinced of Davis' "personal enmity," Yancey hastened to withdraw the application. Davis countered by asking what authority Yancey had for such a belief. The whole thing was beginning to look like an affair of "personal honor." Yancey, in a wordy reply of June 26, 1863, declined to answer the question, but after pondering the matter decided not to send his letter.[36]

At this point, Clay unexpectedly found himself in the middle of the squabble. Clement and Virginia were in Macon when, early in June, Lawson summoned them to Richmond because Celeste Clay was seriously ill. They arrived in the capital on June 10 and remained for two weeks, until Celeste was convalescing. During that time Davis showed Clay the correspondence with Yancey. Clay's first reaction was open surprise that Davis denied "personal enmity" toward Yancey.

"My desire was to promote peace and prevent discord among all men, and especially my friends," Clay declared, in detailing the whole business to Yancey. "Now, in reflecting on the letters and my interview, I am surprised at my conduct, as well as the President's. . . . His conversation since we met in Richmond, . . .

36 William P. Chilton to Clay, Jr., May 1, 1863, Clay MSS; Yancey to Davis, May 6, June 26, July 11, 1863, Yancey MSS; Clay, Jr., to Yancey, May 2, 1863, DuBose, *Yancey*, 743f; Davis to Yancey, May 26, 1863, *Jefferson Davis, Constitutionalist, His Letters, Papers and Speeches*, ed. by Dunbar Rowland (Jackson, Miss., 1923, 10 vols.), V, 498.

his and his wife's kindness to my brother and his wife during her recent illness, his official position, our past relations and the state of the country, all forbade my having any personal difficulty with him. . . . Hence my calmness and moderation in simply maintaining that I did not think him your friend, had probably told you so, etc.

"I confess, however, surprise, not unmingled with indignation, at his positive and harsh denial of enmity to you—as I am sure all who have heard him speak freely of you, during the last twelve months, must feel. . . . I think your entire correspondence puts you on the vantage ground, and evinces a frankness, manliness, patriotism and magnanimity which will do you honor. You did me only justice, as *he knew,* in saying that I would bear you out in your assertion that you had opposed the Administration with reluctance and regret, and had often expressed it to me. He has often been assured by me that he wronged you and misconstrued your opposition in terming it factious; that you were governed by principle in all your public conduct. I think it must have been a consciousness of the wrong he had done you that prompted his showing me the correspondence between you, in the hope that I would say something to justify him to himself. His official course grows daily more inscrutable, and the more I see of him the less I understand him."[37]

On July 1, 1863, Yancey, suffering from his final illness, "utterly exhausted and greatly emaciated," wrote to Clay to learn "whether Davis appeared desirous of holding on to my regard or no?" To this Clay responded, "I answer, yes! I was surprised to find him unwilling to admit that he was unfriendly to you and much more to have you believe him unfriendly, and I can see no motive now, and saw none then, for his letters to you or his conversation with me, but to prevent making you an enemy." On this note the controversy ended, for three days later Yancey was dead.[38] "Poor

---

[37] Clay, Jr., to Yancey, June 30, 1863, Yancey MSS; DuBose, *Yancey,* 749f.

[38] Yancey to Clay, Jr., July 1, 1863, Clay MSS; Clay, Jr., to Yancey, July 25, 1863, Yancey MSS; Clay, Jr., to Wigfall, Aug. 5, 1863, L. T. Wigfall MSS. Some of these letters are available only in printed or typescript form, and other letters between Clay, Yancey, and Davis have not been found. There is some discrepancy between dates of the letters and context. Writing to Yancey's widow on Sept. 12, 1863, Clay commented, "About a week before Mr. Yancey's death I received a letter from him, dated 13th July /63, wh. was, perhaps, the last he ever wrote. Can you tell me whether he recd. my answer, written two days after receipt of his letter? It would give me pleasure to know that he did." Yancey died on July 27, 1863.

Mr. Yancey!" wrote Celeste Clay. "Who would have thought that bro: Clement would have outlived him?"

On December 16, 1863, Clay announced Yancey's death in the Confederate senate and delivered a eulogy of the deceased, whereupon the senate adjourned for the remainder of the day.[39]

39 Celeste Clay to Virginia Clay, Aug. 13, 1863, Clay MSS; *SHSP*, L, 62.

10 ~

Confusion and Hardship

IN ITS FIRST 364 DAYS, the war had not touched Huntsville. But that town felt much apprehension in the early months of 1862, especially after the surrender of Forts Donelson and Henry. Before leaving Huntsville in early February, 1862, Clement, Jr., had taken all the precautions he could for the protection of his and his brothers' property and the safety of their parents. Only a month later, General G. J. Pillow, retreating through Huntsville, predicted Union invasion. On Susanna Clay fell the burden of deciding what to do in such circumstances, although she appealed to Clement, Jr., to "Write & say what is best." Torn between the advisability of staying in town or going to the plantation, Susanna believed "if we stay here, we may save our property here," while, "If we go to M[onte] V[ista] rude soldiers might molest us with impunity as yr. poor father is too deaf & weak to repel."

Rumors of invasion had been so constant that when Union troops actually did arrive early in the morning of April 11, 1862, they took the town by complete surprise. Under the command of Brigadier General O. M. Mitchel, they quickly seized the telegraph office, railroad station, and considerable rolling stock, including fifteen locomotives in the railroad yards and shops. In spite of the surprise attack, many citizens of Huntsville managed to slip out of town and escape into the mountains. One of these was John Withers Clay, who wrote to Clement, Jr., a graphic account of his adventures. After hiding for some days in the mountains, Withers proceeded to Knoxville, where for the time he stayed with Lawson Clay and received a temporary appointment as superintendent of the Seventh Niter District at a salary of $100.00 per month.[1]

With all three Clay men away from Huntsville, coping with the invaders was in the hands of Susanna and Mary Clay. Mitchel's forces were thinly spread over a long line in the Tennessee Valley and were consequently much harassed by small bands of Confederate troops. This circumstance, together with lax discipline, led to numerous outrages, pillaging, and destruction of property of the civilian population. On August 18, 1862, Clement Clay, Sr., was seized at his plantation, imprisoned along with some thirty other citizens at the Huntsville courthouse, and shortly released to remain in his own house. All the Clays lost property by robbery during this period. But rumor and uncertainty made the three sons even more apprehensive than the actual facts warranted. It was impossible for them to learn just what had occurred, while stories came to them of the burning of their houses, destruction of their furniture and books, and of their families' being driven from home. Not until Clement, Jr., reached Huntsville late in October, 1862, could he ascertain exactly what had happened.

When Braxton Bragg withdrew on May 30, 1862, from his base at Corinth, in the northeastern corner of Mississippi, to Tupelo, fifty miles to the south, Halleck and his Union army were in control of a long arc sweeping from Memphis to Chattanooga. Halleck sent his subordinate, Don Carlos Buell, across northern Alabama toward Chattanooga, but Buell's advance was much slowed by the fact that he was ordered to rebuild the Memphis and Charleston railroad as he went. Thus it was that Buell arrived at Huntsville on June 29, 1862, and set up his headquarters there. While the Union army was in slow motion toward Chattanooga, Bragg devised the bold scheme of moving his army in a wide arc through Mobile and Atlanta to East Tennessee, and from there taking the offensive to liberate Middle Tennessee and invade Kentucky. Bragg himself reached Chattanooga on July 29, 1862, and about a week later his entire army had arrived. Confederate

[1] Susanna Clay to Clay, Jr., March 5, 1862, H. L. Clay to Clay, Jr., April 30, 1862, J. W. Clay to Clay, Jr., May 15, 1862, Clay MSS; Frederick Augustus Mitchel, *Ormsby MacKnight Mitchel, Astronomer and General: A Biographical Narrative* (Boston, 1887), 283f.

raids cut Buell's lines of communication, so that on August 31, 1862, Buell and his Union troops left Huntsville for Murfreesboro, Tennessee. It is not here necessary to go into Bragg's and Kirby-Smith's spectacular but indecisive invasion of Tennessee and Kentucky, except to say that for the next ten months Huntsville was once more within the Confederate lines.[2]

Union troops were gone, but the demoralization they left behind could not so quickly be erased. Many North Alabama unionists welcomed the invader, took the oath of allegiance to the United States, and were soon installed in various offices. Clement heard "that Clemens was Provost Marshall, Lane in some office, Nich Davis thick with the Feds. & just returned from a visit to Andy Johnson at Nashville." Obnoxious as was the conduct of such men, for all practical purposes the crop and Negro situation was more dangerous. The presence of the enemy throughout the growing season seriously curtailed the amount of food crops raised, while demoralization among the Negroes further interrupted crop cultivation and harvesting. Susanna Clay wrote, "If we make bread under existing circumstances I will be content. We cannot make any cotton unless a speedy change takes place. . . . Yr. Father's hogs are reduced to fifty, all told. Cattle in the same ratio. . . . Seed of all kinds are difficult to get. The season & Yankees prevented our saving any. Potatoes are not in market."

A month after Clement, Jr., had placed most of the family's Negroes at the niter works, eleven of them had run off. Those who remained at the plantation refused to work and stole or claimed the livestock, but insisted that they were entitled to receive their customary rations. Susanna Clay spent two weeks at the plantation trying to straighten things out and restore a little of the customary discipline, but she was not successful. "I pray for strength," she concluded, "& trust it will be given." "The negro," she wrote a short time later, "is more to be pitied than blamed. They are ignorant & grasping, as we are, for a happier future! I have a hard time with ours, for they just do as they

2 Clay, Jr., to H. L. Clay, May 29, 1862, J. W. Clay to Virginia Clay, June 4, 1862, H. L. Clay to Clay, Jr., July 11, 1862, J. W. Clay to Clay, Jr., Sept. 11, 1862, Clay MSS; Fleming, *Civil War and Reconstruction in Alabama*, 62-65; James B. Fry, *Operations of the Army under Buell from June 10th to October 30th, 1862, and the "Buell Commission"* (New York, 1884), 13-23; Don Carlos Seitz, *Braxton Bragg, General of the Confederacy* (Columbia, S. C., 1924), 124-26, 138, 152.

list. I try by 'moral suasion' to get them to do their duty & it sometimes succeeds."

In mid-May, 1863, Lawson warned that the enemy was likely to occupy Huntsville again, and urged that his parents and the Negroes be removed to a safe place in Georgia. "The Yankee policy & practice," he elaborated, "is to carry *all* away, men, women & children . . . certainly the property of every one of our family will be sacrificed to their hate, egged on as they will be by personal & political foes who are Unionists." Susanna too felt that flight would be the wisest course, but Clement, Sr., refused to leave his home, and so the two old people, with Mary Clay and her family, met the invader once more when he came on July 4, 1863.[3]

On June 26, 1864, Union forces under Rosecrans began an offensive in Middle Tennessee which forced Bragg and his Confederates to withdraw from their base at Tullahoma, Tennessee, and to concentrate more closely around Chattanooga. North Alabama was once more at the mercy of the enemy, and this time it was worse, for rather than enduring a prolonged occupation, the town and area were subject to raids, which occurred on July 13, 24, August 11, and October 12. Union troops enticed or forced most of the Negroes to go with them, seized most of the food and livestock, burned some houses and barns, and so left the countryside in a chaotic condition and many civilians destitute. The July and August raids left the Clay family with "20. pieces of meat 6 bushs. of meal—250 pounds of flour two cows . . . we can hold out for three months if our provisions are not taken & our servants are faithful," Susanna said.

But the Negroes were not inclined to be faithful; they were, as Susanna expressed it, "worse than free." "We cannot exert any authority," she wrote. "I beg ours to do what little is done. . . . I have to work harder than I ever did, but *am patient* silent & prayerful. Yr. Father cannot realize the times. . . . The negroes are so bold, that Alfred told me . . . if yr. father . . . let the overseer attempt to punish for disobedience, that some would kill the overseer! . . . Yr. negroes are free as ours. Where masters

[3] Clay, Jr., to Virginia Clay, May 29, 1862, J. W. Clay to Clay, Jr., Feb. 1, 1863, Susanna Clay to Clay, Jr., Feb. 28, March 6, 24, 1863, H. L. Clay to Clay, Jr., March 24, 1863, Clay MSS. George W. Lane, a resident of Madison County, was a strong unionist.

are they do better—but all . . . expect that all the negroes able
to go, will do so when the cars run or the Y.s get here." And so
it was, for by the beginning of 1864 friends informed Withers
that twenty-seven of his father's Negroes had gone.

The distressing rumor also came through that "the mother of
Senator C. C. Clay . . . was drawing rations from the Federals
at Huntsville." G. W. Jones soon assured Clement that "Your
father has never drawn rations as reported," but, he continued,
"Mrs. Withers Clay has had a hard time of it has several Federal
officers boarding with her, through whom she purchases supplies
for her family." Another friend informed Clement that "Yr office
is head qrs. for Logan's Medical Director— I took out yr scrapbook
& carried it to Mrs J. W. Clay & sent 'young Clem,' to take out
every other article from the garret room. . . . *All* of J. W. Clay's
negroes have left home—& 'Young Clem' is heroically performing
all the duties of maid, boy &c—her house is occupied by Yanks.
Your mother & father keeps at home, very well, house filled with
Yanks— Every vacant room in town is so filled. . . .

"You have doubtless heard that yr negroes on Mt. Sano have
declared their freedom, occupy yr mountain home, sleep in yr
bed & sheets—use yr china &c. &c. & on a visit from yr mother to
them to see how they were getting on—She was saluted as 'Mrs.
Clay' &c. &c. and told she need give no more orders to them."[4]

As the war dragged into its final months, Mary Clay was able to
get a letter through to Withers, detailing conditions in Huntsville.
"I have two contrabands," she wrote, "who cook & fool about the
house, & scorch my children's clothes. . . . I wish I could afford
to send Clemt. to Mr. Banister to prepare him in Greek & Latin.
. . . The pupils I have, this session, will keep me free from debt,
though we 'live exceedingly plainly.' . . . To-morrow, Miss Bowers
commences her school, . . . & Willie will go, if he is not too busy
gathering up wood. Clemmie is a great blessing to me. . . . I fear
I am depending too much on his strong willing arm. . . . Clemt.
& Willie cut my wood & then take the axe to Ma's & cut her's.
. . . 1½ yrs. have elapsed since I last saw you, & I, still, toil

4 Susanna Clay to Clay, Jr., July 24, 29, Aug. 24, Sept. 5, 19, 1863, J. W. Clay
to Clay, Jr., Jan. 7, 1864, E. L. Autrey to Clay, Jr., Feb. 2, 1864, G. W. Jones to
Clay, Jr., March 14, 1864, Clay MSS; *Daily Huntsville Confederate*, Marietta, Ga.,
Sept. 1, 1863; Montgomery *Weekly Advertiser*, Sept. 30, 1863; Seitz, *Braxton Bragg*,
309-12.

wearily on . . . duty & necessity are stern, unflinching drivers, & I hurry over the rocky, flinty road, & stay not to inquire, if I am worn out. I must work while it is yet day—while I can get employment, & thank God gratefully for it."

One of the most distressing events of this period was C. C. Clay, Sr.'s arrest. It happened this way. When the Confederate army under Hood was in North Alabama, they arrested D. C. Humphreys as a traitor to the Confederacy. When Hood was forced to withdraw and the Union forces returned, their general, James B. Steedman, had C. C. Clay, Sr., and James J. Donegan arrested "as hostages for Humphreys" and was about to send them to Nashville, when Humphreys arrived in Huntsville, whereupon Clay and Donegan were released.[5]

Under the spur of war conditions, the usually quiet Withers Clay had almost as many adventures as his more active brothers. During the first Union occupation of Huntsville, Withers had been forced to suspend publication of the Huntsville *Democrat* when he fled to East Tennessee. He had returned to Huntsville early in October, 1862, and resumed publication, issuing the paper as Volume I, number 1, of the Huntsville *Confederate*. The demand for news was so great, however, that in the following spring Withers decided to publish a daily paper, and so on May 18, 1863, the *Daily Confederate* made its initial appearance. But again the coming of the enemy forced Withers to suspend publication on July 1, 1863.

Warning telegrams of the second invasion of Huntsville reached Withers just as he was "leaving the Church with the dead body of our infant, Ellen Jordan, born on the 25th June & dying on the 1st July." Withers immediately sent his presses, type, and paper to Chattanooga, took "painful" leave of his wife and children who "bore it with equanimity," drew most of the family's money from the bank, sent the silver and other valuables to South Alabama, arranged for transference of the remaining Negroes to a safer place, and himself left Huntsville by train on July 2, 1863. He reached Chattanooga on July 4, and there resumed publication (on July 21) of the *Daily Huntsville Confederate*, but not for

[5] H. L. Clay to Virginia Clay, Jan. 14, 1865, J. W. Clay to H. L. Clay, Feb. 4, 1865, Clay MSS (J. W. Clay's letter quotes extensively from two letters written by his wife, Jan. 5, 15, 1865).

long, since military operations forced him to suspend on August 12. He withdrew to Marietta, Georgia, where he published his paper and did job printing from September 1 to December 24, 1863. Sherman's advance forced Withers to retreat to Dalton, Georgia, where he resumed publication on January 23, 1864, but he continued only until February 16, 1864, when military pressure caused suspension for the remainder of the war.[6]

From north Georgia, Withers Clay worked his way southwestward to Macon, where his sixteen-year-old son, Clement, joined him. Later, at Columbus, Withers wrote, "You need not be astonished, if I start, in a few days, for home via Selma, Meridian, Corinth, Tuscumbia & Decatur." It was December 6, 1864, however, before Withers and young Clement began that journey. With the aid of all varieties of transportation they reached Decatur, Alabama, on December 18, two hours after the train had departed for Huntsville. Clement and another boy set out to walk the remaining twenty-four miles to Huntsville, while Withers waited for the train, "which was not expected to return before two days." When it did return, passengers brought "the news that the Yankees had re-occupied Huntsville." Withers remained in Decatur a week, hoping for a chance to see his family, "but it was vain," and he was only eight miles away from Decatur when Union troops marched into that town. Withers reached Selma, Alabama, on January 19, 1865, and a short time later was in Montgomery, where he began work about February 1 as assistant editor of the Montgomery *Advertiser*.[7]

When Lawson and Celeste Clay left Huntsville in early May, 1861, they were destined for a long absence. After several months in Lynchburg, Virginia, Lawson was transferred in the spring of 1862 to Knoxville, where he served on Kirby-Smith's staff. A short leave at the time of this transfer enabled him and Celeste to make their only visit to Huntsville during the war. Shortly after Clement and Virginia left for Richmond in February, 1862, Celeste went once more to Macon, while Lawson proceeded to his new post in Knoxville. In May, Celeste and four-year-old Felix Comer Clay became seriously ill with what was probably a streptococcus throat

---

[6] J. W. Clay to Clay, Jr., July 4 [1863], Clay MSS; Huntsville *Confederate*, Oct. 8, 1862; Huntsville *Daily Confederate*, May 18, 1863.
[7] J. W. Clay to Virginia Clay, Oct. 29, 1864, Feb. 13, 1865, Clay MSS.

infection and scarlet fever which resulted in the child's death at Macon. Thereafter it seemed best that the bereaved parents should be together, and so Celeste went to Knoxville for the summer and autumn. In August, 1862, Lawson suffered a broken leg and encountered much difficulty in finding suitable living quarters where he could be properly cared for. Late in September the bone had knit sufficiently for him to risk the journey to Macon, where he could be comfortably situated in the Comer household. By mid-November he was able to return to duty in Knoxville.

Early in February, 1863, Lawson was transferred to the adjutant general's office in Richmond. There he and Clement shared a room for the winter, while Celeste and Virginia Clay remained in Macon until late April, when both women went to Richmond. Virginia was there only a few weeks, however, for shortly after the adjournment of congress on May 1, 1863, she and Clement traveled once more to Macon. From there Clement wished to go to Huntsville, but his mother advised against it as being too dangerous, and with the constant threat of Union raids, he was not able to visit his parents that year.

In June, 1863, Celeste Clay became so seriously ill that Lawson sent for Clement and Virginia, who reached Richmond on June 10 and remained until the 27th. It was during this time that Clement went to Orange Courthouse to confer with Wigfall. Celeste convalesced in Richmond until late July, when she was able to go to Lynchburg, and later to Blue Ridge Springs, some forty miles beyond.[8]

Upon leaving Richmond, Clement and Virginia returned to Macon, and then proceeded to Chunnennuggee, Macon County, Alabama, "where," Clement reported, "we were delightfully situated & had every comfort that wealth & taste could supply" until their hostess "died suddenly & strangely" on July 26. After that they sojourned with relatives near Columbus, Georgia. As for his own ailments, Clay explained to Wigfall that "the cough I left you with turned out whooping cough, & supervening from my sore throat & asthmatic tendency, it has, I assure you used me very hardly." After Clay's short visit to Montgomery in August, he

8 Robert Brown to Virginia Clay, May 22, 1862, Celeste Clay to Virginia Clay, Aug. 19, 1862, July 29, Aug. 9, Nov. 12, 1863, H. L. Clay to Clay, Jr., Sept. 25, 1862, Clay MSS.

and Virginia spent September and October at Beech Island, the Hammond estate on the Savannah River. During this interval, Clement had a nasal operation in nearby Augusta, Georgia.

On Saturday, November 4, 1863, Clement left for Montgomery to look after the senatorial election, while Virginia proceeded to Macon. Shortly after the election on November 24, Clay returned to Macon, whence, early in December, he, Virginia, and Celeste began their journey northward. Virginia stopped in North Carolina with the Buxton Williamses, where she remained until the beginning of 1864. Clement and Celeste went on to Richmond, arriving December 8, 1863.[9]

Clement described their journey in considerable detail. "We got to Weldon about 8- a.m. found Genl. Cobb, Gov. Harris & Sens. Maxwell & Johnson of Ga there, having failed to make the connection the evening before at that point. We got off from W.[eldon] at 9½—reached Petersburg at 2½ & left there at 4 p.m.— On arriving at Jarratt's . . . [we] walked down to cousin Tom's—found him at dinner . . . had ham, roast beef, turkey, stewed oysters, potatoes, slaw, & pound cup cakes! Of course we took something to eat. . . . We got here [Richmond] at 6½ p.m. . . . being only 2½ hours travelling 22 miles."

Clement went on to explain his living arrangements: "I am at the Misses Murry on Main, nearly opposite Arlington House, & next door to . . . the Wigfall's . . . & have a rear room on 3d floor, with a balcony & southern exposure. . . . I pay $75 a month for room rent & attendance of servants, $40 for coal & gas, & must furnish my own towels!— Lestia will let me have 2 till I can buy. My meals, I am told will cost me $125 pr month.— My board will exceed my pay by 10$ per month." Three days later, Clement reported arrangements to "take my meals, by special favor, . . . in the basement of this house" in the family of a Major Bentley, who had grown up near Huntsville. Mrs. Bentley, a bride of seven months, agreed reluctantly because "she had never kept house," but, Clement continued, "I think I ingratiated myself so much . . . as to secure my stay here as a

9 Clay, Jr., to L. T. Wigfall, Aug. 5, 1863, L. T. Wigfall MSS; Mary Day to Virginia Clay, Sept. 17, 1863, Clay, Jr., to Susanna Clay, Nov. 11, 1863, Loula (Comer) Hammond to Virginia Clay, Oct. 30, 1863, Tempe Williams to Virginia Clay, Nov. 7 [1863], Clay, Jr., to Virginia Clay, Dec. 12, 1863, Celeste Clay to Virginia Clay, [Dec. 9, 1863], Clay MSS.

permanent boarder. I fare very well—tho' plainly. They have an excellent cook; Sally Lund or drop muffins or loaf-bread, or flannel cakes or egg bread with good butter, fair coffee, & spiced round of beef, or stake [sic] or oysters or chipped ham, for breakfast; middling bacon, slaw, potatoes (Irish or Sweet), rice, spiced round & molasses for dinner; good tea & crackers for supper. It is good enough for any body."[10]

Early in January, 1864, Virginia joined Clement in Richmond and remained until the end of his senatorial term on February 17, 1864. During that time, she entertained with at least one supper party and took part in an amateur theatrical performance of Sheridan's "Rivals," which was the big social event of the winter in Richmond.

From this account, it is apparent that the burdens of war fell lightly on Virginia and Celeste Clay. True it is that they were "refugees," forced from their homes by the enemy. Nevertheless, their manner of life was as little changed as possible by war conditions; they were safe from the enemy; they endured no starvation diet; and they were well supplied with clothing and many luxuries that came in through the blockade. Except for two instances, they visited no hospitals, nursed no wounded, and engaged in no war work of any kind, unless helping to keep up morale by their charm and high spirits could be counted as such. "Sister & myself, deserve *no* credit for *any thing*. We have done *as little* for our country as any other two worthless women I know," confessed Celeste Clay.

Late in 1863 one of their friends went through the lines to Memphis, where she procured a pair of spectacles for Clement and "a black & white Poplin dress . . . a pair of corsets—a comb & a pair of gloves" for Virginia. Virginia's favorite cousin, Tom Tait Tunstall, was going regularly through the lines into Maryland for the purpose of bringing various scarce items into the Confederacy. On one of these expeditions he had about $2,000, of which Clement had furnished $700, and Eli S. Shorter $1,000. Tunstall "expected to realise $1000 profit for himself & the same

10 Clay, Jr., to Virginia Clay, Dec. 9, 12, 1863, Clay MSS. The persons referred to are Howell Cobb; Isham Green Harris, governor of Tennessee, 1857-1863; Augustus E. Maxwell, Confederate senator from Florida; and Herschel V. Johnson. "Cousin Tom" was Thomas W. Withers. Jarratt's was a hotel at Petersburg, Va., which also served as the railroad station.

for S.[horter]. If I get my money back, I shall be content," Clement declared. During one of her visits at Beech Island, Virginia Clay obtained a dress of homespun cloth woven by the Hammond Negroes. Early in 1863 Virginia made "a very comfortable & quite an elegant robe de chambre" for Clement. Upon sending it, she explained, "you *will* recognize my old travelling dress, but I hope it *will* be none the less comfortable for that." Then she continued with further admonitions: "Do dress like a gentleman & senator My darling, for *my* sake. Strangers, by scores, who do not *know*, *see* you. Comb yr. hair & beard, & use clean fresh handf's. Won't you?— You look old & dilapidated when you neglect yourself."[11]

But Clement had far more to worry about than his personal appearance. The government of the Confederacy was disorganized by political confusion and dissension centering about Jefferson Davis.

"Has it ever occurred to you that Davis's mind is becoming unsettled? No sane man would act as he is doing. I fear that his bad health & bad temper are undermining his reason & that the foundation is already sapped. God only knows what is to become of us, with such a man at the head of the government. What a sad thing it is that Howell Cobb had not been elected in his place. His patriotic heart & wise head would have taken us safely through. We have now nothing to look to except Congress & what hope can any reasonable man draw from that source?" Thus did Wigfall's words reflect the state of mind of those who were violently hostile to Davis. Even the faithful Clay had been alienated by the incidents of the Davis-Yancey controversy. More in sorrow than in anger Clay wrote of Davis, "He is a strange compound which I cannot analyze, although I thought I knew him well before he was President. He will not ask or receive counsel, and indeed, seems predisposed to go exactly the way his friends advise him not to go. I have tried harder than I ever did with any other man to be his friend, and to prevent his alienating me or other friends. I have kept my temper and good will towards him longer than I could do with any other man than an old and cherished

11 Celeste Clay to Virginia Clay, Dec. 24, 1863, Carrie H. DuBarry to Virginia Clay, Dec. 22 [1863], Clay, Jr., to Virginia Clay, Feb. 15, March 12, 1863, Virginia Clay to Clay, Jr., Feb. 24, 1863, Celeste Clay to Virginia Clay, Feb. 16, 1865, Clay MSS; Ada Sterling, Recollections, April 30, 1903, Ada Sterling MSS.

friend. If he survives this war and does not alter his course, he will find himself in a small minority party."

Wigfall spent the summer trying to confer informally with other Confederate leaders on what future policy should be. "If Barnwell & Hunter could only awaken from their fatal slumber something might yet be done for the country. Do you correspond with either of them?" he asked Clay. "I think Barnwell would listen to you." Wigfall's efforts were not successful, for most of the men approached felt that such an attempt would be useless. If the subject of conference was to be the conduct of the war, "*you know* I am entirely without influence in such matters," R. M. T. Hunter declared. Clay, however, spent several days with Wigfall at Orange, Virginia, where they "talked fully & freely of matters in general."[12]

While Clay and Wigfall were discussing Davis and other problems, matters were coming to a head during the summer of 1863. Overshadowing all else were the great military reverses of Gettysburg and Vicksburg. A feeble counter to these misfortunes was the shimmering and elusive hope of a northwestern confederacy. In the spring of 1863 that subject was ever present in the minds of all serious observers. The Old Northwest seemed almost ready to break away from the Union and join the Confederacy. Clay regarded "events there as the most important, because the North West will not aid the war much longer if the Miss. is not opened to their trade." Opinion in the Confederacy was much divided on the subject, however, for many felt that to bring the nonslaveholding states of the Northwest into the Confederacy would ultimately be fatal to slavery. That remained an unresolved question, for revolt in the Northwest never quite came off.[13]

For politicians and officeholders, 1863 was primarily an election year—a fact largely forgotten since that time. Every seat in the house of representatives would have to be filled, either by returning its incumbent or electing a new man. And the eight

[12] L. T. Wigfall to Clay, Jr., June 12, Aug. 13, 1863, Clay MSS; R. M. T. Hunter to L. T. Wigfall, June 23, 1863, Clay, Jr., to Wigfall, Aug. 5, 1863, L. T. Wigfall MSS; L. T. Wigfall to Joseph Eggleston Johnston, June 15, 1863, J. E. Johnston MSS; Clay, Jr., to W. L. Yancey, May 2, 1863, DuBose, *Yancey*, 743f; Hendrick, *Statesmen of the Lost Cause*, 186.

[13] Clay, Jr., to Virginia Clay, March 22, 1863, E. D. Tracy to Clay, Jr., March 3, 1863, L. P. Walker to Clay, Jr., Feb. 27, 1863, Clay MSS; Eli M. Bruce to W. N. Haldeman, Feb. 17, 1863, Robert McKee MSS; Wood Gray, *The Hidden Civil War: The Story of the Copperheads* (New York, 1942), 115-37.

senators who had drawn two-year terms must either terminate their services or seek reelection. Other factors complicated the election too. The entire delegations from Kentucky and Missouri had been chosen by a minority of the electorate and so held office on dubious constitutional grounds. Large sections of Tennessee and Louisiana were in enemy hands, and Union forces occupied some portion of nearly every other Confederate state. These hard facts forced congress to pass special legislation for conducting the elections in the states affected.[14]

Issues in the summer of 1863 varied somewhat from state to state, but they generally reflected discontent with the government, local or Confederate. In Mississippi, impressment and suspension of the writ of habeas corpus were especially obnoxious. Louisiana voters found the impressment law reprehensible. In Georgia the political pot boiled most vigorously, as Joseph E. Brown, Alexander H. Stephens, and Robert Toombs intrigued constantly against the Davis administration. Toombs made a strong effort for the senatorship, from which vantage point he proposed to strike at Davis. Only through the efforts of Ben Hill was Herschel V. Johnson reelected. Though Johnson was no friend of Davis, he was not the bitter enemy that Toombs had turned out to be.

There was disaffection in every state of the Confederacy, but it varied greatly in extent and intensity. A dangerous situation existed in North Carolina, where a secret peace society was operating and William Woods Holden was openly campaigning for peace. Of the ten congressmen elected there, eight were said to be peace men.

Conditions in Alabama were similar and even more threatening. Disaffection centered in North Alabama and the hill counties, where a peace society had been operating since 1862, though its existence did not become generally known until 1863. When Clay

14 CSAC, *SJ*, III, 383, 414, 421, April 30, May 1, 1863. In February, 1862, the senate had prepared four ballots of two years and four years; five ballots of four years and six years; and four ballots of two years and six years. The thirteen states drew by lot for these; then the two senators of each state drew for the two terms allotted in the first drawing. Senators of La., S. C., Tenn., Tex., and Va. drew four- or six-year terms, and so none of them came up for reelection during the life of the Confederacy. Senators who drew the two-year term and so were up for reelection in the summer and autumn of 1863 were Clay of Ala., R. W. Johnson of Ark., J. M. Baker of Fla., H. V. Johnson of Ga., W. E. Simms of Ky., James Phelan of Miss., J. B. Clark of Mo., and George Davis of N. C. Because of Yancey's death, Alabama was the only state in which both senatorial seats had to be filled in 1863.

visited Huntsville in the autumn of 1862, he had found many evidences of disloyalty, which he detailed in a report to Secretary of War Seddon. By the summer of 1863 that situation had worsened.[15]

Against this background, Clay began to assess the political situation in Alabama. During the preceding year Clay had repeatedly said he would not run for reelection to the senate, but as he got reports of intrigue from Alabama friends, his resolution weakened and he consulted Virginia on the matter. He suggested that by a little judicious visiting in Montgomery, she might accomplish much good, and especially "restore the *entente cordiale*" with the Fitzpatricks, who had been cold ever since the break in 1860. Rumor had it that Clay's chief opponent for the senate would be J. L. M. Curry, who would be aided by Albert Elmore, Fitzpatrick's brother-in-law. "It occurs to me," continued Clement, "that all Fitzpatricks spleen against me might be turned upon Curry if he knew what a Jesuit he is & how he & Yancey are yoked together. . . . Now you may be surprised at this," Clement added, "because I have so often said I did not think I would run again. . . . But Mr. Barnwell, Hunter, Wigfall & Phelan have expressed so much feeling about it & such anxiety that I should, that . . . I have so far changed my purpose as [to] adopt their suggestion. I will not preclude myself from running when the Leg. meets . . . by declaring I will not run in advance."

As matters developed during the summer, it became evident that Governor Shorter would be defeated by Thomas Hill Watts, who had "the inside track." Before election returns were in, Clay warned, "you may look out for the old Whigs & Douglasites taking possession of the Gov's, Cong. & Leg. There is a strong feeling of dissatisfaction with those in office that is very natural & not entirely unfounded, that threatens to throw us all out—especially those regarded as the President's especial friends." Watts won the governorship by an overwhelming majority. Although only three

15 J. W. Clay to Clay, Jr., Feb. 1, 1863, H. L. Clay to Clay, Jr., Aug. 6, 1863, Clay MSS; Joseph E. Brown to A. H. Stephens, May 29, 1863, Robert Toombs to W. W. Burwell, June 10, 1863, Toombs-Stephens-Cobb, *Correspondence*, 618ff; Johnson, "Autobiography," 333; John Knox Bettersworth, *Confederate Mississippi* (Baton Rouge, 1943), 50f; Jefferson Davis Bragg, *Louisiana in the Confederacy* (Baton Rouge, 1941), 267f; Hill, *Joseph E. Brown*, 134f; Fleming, *Civil War and Reconstruction in Alabama*, 133-42; Georgia Lee Tatum, *Disloyalty in the Confederacy* (Chapel Hill, 1934), 107-25; Richard E. Yates, "Zebulon B. Vance as War Governor of North Carolina, 1862-1865," *JSH*, III (Feb., 1937), 69; W. L. Fleming, "The Peace Movement in Alabama during the Civil War," *SAQ*, II (July, 1903), 246-60.

congressmen were replaced, the trend was conservative. Curry was defeated, chiefly because he had supported the Davis administration. Curry's successor, Marcus Henderson Cruikshank, described by one observer as "a little country editor without brains or character," was the law partner of Lewis E. Parsons, later to be known as the scalawag governor of Alabama. In North Alabama the notorious Williamson R. W. Cobb was once more elected, but he never took his seat, and the Confederate congress expelled him as an adherent of the enemy.[16]

This was the situation when Clay went to Montgomery for a few days in August, 1863. The August elections were just over, and Clay was rejoicing in Curry's defeat for congress, but feared "he may be sent to the Senate in Yancey's place," a post for which several Alabama newspapers were already pushing him. The election occurred without incident, however, on August 22, 1863, when Robert Jemison (a former Whig and cooperationist) of Tuscaloosa was chosen by a large majority for Yancey's seat. Clay circulated for several days among the legislators, doing all he could to convince them that he was right in opposing the increase of soldiers' pay. The Montgomery *Advertiser* strongly supported Clay for reelection to the senate.

Clay found the new legislature "composed of a large majority of new men, who had never been in office before & of whom I had never heard. None of my old friends in that body could tell me of the political sentiments or party affiliations of one in ten of those new men. But their acts indicate that they dissent from my views of public affairs & disapprove of my public course. . . . On the whole my opinion is, that the Leg. will elect a Douglas or antisecession Dem. or Curry, to succeed me." Clay's friends, however, thought that Curry could not be elected, and that his friends, if not antagonized, would throw their votes to Clay. Possibly this might have happened, had not the Clay-Curry dispute occurred.

And again the question of increasing soldiers' pay was involved. Curry had voted for the increase, but had later admitted the unwisdom of the bill and said that he hoped the senate would

16 Clay, Jr., to Virginia Clay, March 25, 1863, Clay MSS; Clay, Jr., to L. T. Wigfall, Aug. 5, 1863, L. T. Wigfall MSS; J. L. M. Curry to W. P. Browne, May 13, 1863, W. P. Browne MSS; Burwell Boykin Lewis to Rose (Garland) Lewis, Aug. 11, 1863, B. B. Lewis MSS; CSAC, *HJ*, VII, 12, 125, 275-77, May 3, 31, Nov. 15, 16, 1864; Jessie Pearl Rice, *J. L. M. Curry, Southerner, Statesman and Educator* (New York, 1949), 92.

kill it. After making this assertion to Clay, Curry proceeded at the next session of congress to reintroduce the soldiers' pay bill. Clay was highly incensed at this two-faced action. Curry's purpose was apparently to retain the support of the electorate by favoring a popular bill, while letting Clay assume the odium of standing on the unpopular side. That unpopularity would defeat Clay, and Curry could then be elected to Clay's seat in the senate. At least this was Clay's interpretation of the affair, and there is no doubt that Curry aspired to be a senator.

Consequently, in the capitol at Montgomery on November 14, 1863, Clay, in the presence of witnesses, had a conversation with Curry embodying these views. Clay's verbal castigation did not set off any fireworks, for Curry "bore it all with meekness & only replied that I misunderstood him," Clay reported.[17]

Balloting for the senatorship began in the Alabama legislature on November 20, 1863, and continued through five days and twenty ballots before any one candidate achieved a majority. Balloting began with three men in nomination. Secession, state-rights, and the Davis administration had two candidates in Clay from North Alabama and Curry representing East Alabama. The discontented, conservative, anti-Davis element put forward John Jacob Seibels of Montgomery. Seibels, an outstanding Douglas man in 1860, cooperationist in 1861, and now a leader in the secret peace society, was in favor of ending the war. Clay had a bloc of support which gave him between 26 and 35 votes on the first eleven ballots; Curry had the support of an equal number; Seibels had a bloc of votes varying from 40 to 45.

On the eleventh ballot Clay fell to 26 votes and his friends withdrew his name. On the twelfth ballot Benjamin Fitzpatrick was nominated, and he drew off several of the Seibels votes. Then Seibels was withdrawn, and his friends thereafter cast their votes entirely for Fitzpatrick. Six of the Clay bloc went over to Fitzpatrick, eight gave their votes to Curry, and the remaining thirteen scattered theirs among the minority candidates.

There were several minority candidates, and in the various trial balloons the legislature voted for a total of thirteen persons.

17 Wigfall to Clay, Jr., Aug. 13, 1863, J. W. Clay to Clay, Jr., Aug. 17, 1863, Clay, Jr., to A. Benners and J. T. Taylor, Aug. 21, 1863, Clay MSS; Clay, Jr., to Wigfall, Nov. 15, 1863, L. T. Wigfall MSS; Ala. Leg., HJ, Special Session, Aug. 17-29, 1863, p. 28; Montgomery Weekly Advertiser, Sept. 2, 1863; Rice, Curry, 43f.

William Russell Smith, John Gill Shorter, and John Anthony Winston received one vote each on one or two ballots, and then were dropped. One faithful friend voted consistently for John Cochran on all twenty ballots, and on the thirteenth ballot a small boom netted Cochran eight votes. William M. Brooks was dropped after a trial in two ballots with a high of four votes. Thomas Hill Watts, though governor-elect, received ten or eleven votes on ballots seventeen, eighteen, and nineteen.

After the sixteenth ballot Clay's friends put him in nomination again, and on ballots seventeen, eighteen, and nineteen he received from 17 to 20 votes. But it was apparent Clay could not be elected, or even rise to his former strength of 35 votes. On the seventeenth ballot Richard Wilde Walker was also nominated, but commanded only four votes. After the nineteenth ballot, Clay took the course he had determined upon before the election when he had told his friends "they might withdraw me if they thought proper & I would yield & would do all I could to elect any third man & *gentleman* they might choose," but he could not advise any friend to vote for Curry "who had betrayed me & his country for the sake of office." At the same time, after the nineteenth ballot, the Curry bloc agreed to withdraw their man. Consequently, on the twentieth ballot Richard Wilde Walker was elected senator, receiving 61 votes to Fitzpatrick's 47. Twenty-seven of the Curry bloc and 24 of the Clay bloc united on Walker. Only three of Clay's friends and only two of Curry's voted for Fitzpatrick on the final ballot. And so it was that ten years to the day after his first election to the United States Senate, Clement Clay was defeated for the equivalent Confederate office.

Withers Clay spoke for the family when he expressed pride in Clement's "elevated moral position," delight over Curry's, Seibels', and Fitzpatrick's defeat, and satisfaction with Walker's election. Walker "is a man of talents," Withers continued, "&, I believe, of high-toned integrity & true to the Southern cause—a genuine convert to States' Rights principles long before the war —& a much better, & more reliable man than Pope [LeRoy Pope Walker], &, from what I hear, than any of his brothers."[18] Thus,

18 George S. Walker to Thomas B. Cooper, Nov. 13, 1863, J. L. M. Curry MSS; Clay, Jr., to L. T. Wigfall, Sept. 11, Nov. 15, 1863, L. T. Wigfall MSS; J. W. Clay to Clay, Jr., Nov. 29, 1863, Clay MSS; Ala. Leg., *HJ*, Regular Session, 1863, pp. 136-61, Nov. 20-24, 1863.

after forty-five years of political rivalry, did the Walker clan win a victory over the Clay family.

Clay appeared in his seat on December 9, 1863, two days after the fourth and last session of the first congress assembled. He was now for the first time in his career a "lame duck" senator. Whether or not he now deliberately curtailed his activity, it is true that he introduced few bills in this session. But those in which he did have a hand were exceedingly important.

As chairman of the committee on commerce, Clay brought in four bills, S. 182, 183, 184, and 209, which provided the legal basis for the "New Plan" designed to bring through the blockade military supplies instead of luxuries, and to put cotton sales and shipments entirely under government control. During 1862 and 1863 blockade running had grown into a large and profitable business, but it was in the hands of private individuals, many of them British, who naturally operated solely with a view to obtain the largest profits. Luxury goods afforded larger profits than war materiel. During the summer of 1863 the Confederate government made a beginning at control by demanding that shipowners allot one-third or one-half their space to government cargo. The owners retaliated by charging high freight rates, and the seaboard states countered by purchasing or chartering additional vessels for state-controlled shipping.

Bill S. 182, "To Impose Regulations upon the Foreign Commerce of the Confederate States to Provide for the Public Defense," declared "That the exportation of cotton, tobacco, military and naval stores, sugar, molasses and rice from the Confederate States . . . is prohibited, except under such uniform regulations as shall be made by the President." Introduced by Clay on January 13, 1864, this bill was transferred to the secret calendar, debated, amended slightly, and passed without recorded vote on January 19. The bill became law on February 6, 1864, and on March 5, Secretaries Memminger and Seddon issued regulations pursuant to it, requiring that half the tonnage of each vessel be reserved for the Confederate government.

The companion act, S. 183, introduced, debated, and passed on the same days and also in secret session, was entitled "A bill to Prohibit the Importation of Luxuries, or of Articles Not Necessaries or of Common Use," and included furs, carpets, beverages, laces, firecrackers, furniture, stained glass, marble, wallpaper, gems, jewelry, bananas, coconuts, and oranges. These two acts brought forth loud howls from shipowners, who, for some weeks, were practically on strike. But the government held firm, and gradually the ships went back into operation under the new rules.

The third bill to round out the new system was S. 209, "to Establish a Bureau of Foreign Supplies." Clay introduced this as S. 184 on January 13, 1864. It was debated at length on January 20, 1864, when Oldham offered a substitute bill. A week later the commerce committee abandoned S. 184 and brought in a new and more comprehensive bill, S. 209. It was extensively debated and amended in secret session in both houses, and a conference committee was finally necessary before the bill became law on February 17, 1864. One of the evils besetting Confederate efforts was a multiplicity of purchasing agents in Europe who were competing with each other in the effort to obtain supplies. The bureau of foreign supplies as established by S. 209 coordinated European purchasing operations under one head and also set up a unified agency inside the Confederacy for the purchase of cotton and other produce for export under government control. It also authorized a similar agency for the area west of the Mississippi, which would operate chiefly through Mexico.[19]

Thus did the Confederacy finally achieve the machinery for a workable system of imports and exports, and the means for establishing a sound credit abroad. But it did not become effective soon enough to counteract the deteriorating military and home-front situation within the Confederacy. How large a part Clay had in drafting and putting through this legislation is impossible to say. These were administration bills, which the cabinet and the president agreed upon, and Clay, in spite of his former disagreements with Davis, loyally did his part in supporting them.

Clay's last service was to write and present the "Report of Joint Select Comm appointed to investigate the management of the naval Department under its present head." For nearly two years this committee, under Clay's chairmanship, had taken testimony

19 NA, RG 109, CSAC, Bills and Res., box no. 10; CSAC, SJ, III, 557, 593f; SHSP, L, 31, 35, 41, 76, 226, 258; O.R., IV, iii, 80-82, 186f, 553f; Samuel Bernard Thompson, Confederate Purchasing Operations Abroad (Chapel Hill, 1935), 88-90; Louise Biles Hill, State Socialism in the Confederate States of America (Charlottesville, Va., 1936), 11-13.

from a large number of witnesses and had published much of it in a volume of nearly 500 pages. One paragraph summarized the entire investigation: "The Committee do not deem it necessary to review all the facts . . . or to express their conclusion upon each of them, as the testimony is herewith presented & may be read by all who desire the information it furnished. They think they will discharge their duty by expressing the general result of their investigations. They are gratified that they can state, that, after long, patient & careful investigation, they have found nothing in the administration of the Navy Department that justifies any censure of Mr. Mallory."

The report dwelt on the difficulties of establishing a navy and the paucity of Confederate resources for that purpose. The failures and deficiencies of the navy and the navy department the committee found traceable to unavoidable shortages of material, labor, and money, and not to any negligence or want of energy on Mallory's part. Clay presented this report during the rush of business on the last day of the session.[20]

The first congress ended during the coldest weather of the winter. "There was ice in the wash-basins in our bed chambers," wrote a Richmond resident on February 18, 1864. And on that day Clement Clay found himself without employment. He had for several weeks been canvassing the possibilities for a future occupation, without coming to any decision. Late in December, Clay and Phelan had "agreed to go into the army, . . . even as privates." A week later Clement declared, "One of the Clays must save the honor of the family, by dying or offering to die in defense of his country; & I can best be spared for the sacrifice. . . . I think I can fight or die with the firmness of a soldier—I hope with the grace of a Christian. I am making my arrangements for the field."

As other prospects opened up, Clay's martial ardor cooled somewhat. During the winter he consulted LeRoy Pope Walker on

20 Text of the report, in Clay's handwriting, is in NA, RG 109, CSAC, Bills and Res., box no. 10. It was printed as *Report from the Joint Select Committee, to Investigate the Management of the Navy Department* (Richmond, 1864); the testimony was printed as *Report of Evidence Taken before a Joint Special Committee of Both Houses of the Confederate Congress to Investigate the Affairs of the Navy Department* (Richmond, [1863]). It is also printed in full in U. S. Navy Dept., *Official Records of the Union and Confederate Navies* (Washington, 1892-1922, 30 vols.), II, 1, 431-809 (cited hereinafter as *O.R.N.*); Joseph Thomas Durkin, *Stephen R. Mallory: Confederate Navy Chief* (Chapel Hill, 1954), 224-42, 295-97.

the prospects of law practice in Montgomery. "I feel satisfied," Walker replied, "you would do *well* and I hope you will not think of settling out of this State. As your friend . . . permit me to say that the step would be most injudicious and would, doubtless, subject you to most unjust criticism." Clay also carefully sounded out his prospects for being appointed attorney general, but learned that Davis felt he "must appoint a Whig" to that post. In the early spring another friend proposed to Clay that "if you will get authority for Baylor R. Stewart to exchange tobacco with the Yankees for horses & mules it will be doing our govt a decided service & at the same time make a pile of money of which you shall have half & no one know that you have any interest except *myself*."[21]

Early in April, Davis appointed Clay a colonel of cavalry, in which rank he would report as "Presiding Judge of Military Court for North Alabama." Should he accept this? Clay was in a great quandary and so turned to Wigfall for advice. And he give it copiously.

"I do not think it good policy," counseled Wigfall, "to hold from the Executive a subordinate position after being defeated in your own state. A foreign Mission or a place in the Cabinet would be a matter worth considering. . . . I feel that your position would be better, more independent, higher, your individuality & personal identity better preserved & sustained in holding no office under the Executive Dept. It will be better for you in the future & you must not ignore the future. You have a future & I hope it will be a bright one. Four years is not long. The Presidency itself my dear friend, is not too high for your aspiration. Between you & Davis to day you would get four votes to his one. Do nothing to lose your own individuality. Be your self whether in success or defeat & do not dissolve your connection with Alabama."[22]

While Clay was pondering this advice, Jefferson Davis resolved the whole matter by this directive: "Confiding special trust in your zeal, discretion, and patriotism, I hereby direct you to proceed at once to Canada, there to carry out such instructions as you have received from me verbally in such manner as shall seem most likely to conduce to the furtherance of the interests of the Con-

21 Clay, Jr., to Virginia Clay, Dec. 20, 27, 1863, L. P. Walker to Clay, Jr., March 20, 1864, G. W. Jones to Clay, Jr., March 4, 1864, Clay MSS; Jones, *RWCD*, II, 152.
22 James Alexander Seddon to Clay, Jr., April 13, 1864, L. T. Wigfall to Clay, Jr., April 12, 1864, Clay MSS.

federate States of America which have been intrusted to you."
Davis had been contemplating such a mission for some time and,
as he informed R. M. T. Hunter, had "made attempts to engage
for the service in Canada several gentlemen deemed competent;
but they have declined for various reasons." Among those who
had declined was Alexander H. H. Stuart of Virginia. About
April 27, 1864, Jacob Thompson and Clement Clay accepted the
assignment. Jacob Thompson of Mississippi had been secretary
of the interior under Buchanan, had served with the Confederate
forces until the fall of Vicksburg, and in the summer of 1863 had
been elected to the Mississippi legislature. The third commissioner, James Philemon Holcombe, a distinguished lawyer and formerly a professor at the University of Virginia, had already been
sent to Canada on February 19, 1864. His assignment was essentially legal, though he later cooperated with Clay and Thompson.

Clay hastened to inform Wigfall of what had happened: "I am
on my way to Canada, for the purpose of serving the Country as
I best can. You know how as well as I do. It is a very responsible,
difficult, & delicate duty, for which I am not suited by my talents
tastes or habits. I cannot simulate or dissemble as is tho't necessary
& proper in a diplomatist. I cannot enjoy secret service. . . . I
must incur the perils of the sea & of capture by the enemy. . . .
But somebody must undertake this service in accordance with the
wishes of Congress & I could not shirk it from mere personal
considerations. I would not undertake it alone, but with one who
is regarded as fit to do the bargaining & bartering, I can get along
as a counsellor, perhaps with some credit. Having declined the
Bureau & the military Judgeship, I could not well refuse this
without appearing disinclined to serve anywhere.— I have accepted
it with extreme reluctance, thro' a sense of duty to my country,
& will do my best to serve her faithfully & efficiently."[23]

Here began a reconciliation with Davis, who, Clay wrote, "has
certainly vindicated himself from my suspicion that he was indifferent to my fate. He has tendered me several places without the
least suggestion from me that I wished anything.— He professed

23 Jefferson Davis to Clay, Jr., April 27, 1864, Davis to Jacob Thompson, April
29, 1864, Davis to R. M. T. Hunter, April 14, 1864, *O.R.*, IV, iii, 304, 332; *Jefferson
Davis, Constitutionalist*, VI, 226f, 237; Clay, Jr., to L. T. Wigfall, April 29, 1864,
L. T. Wigfall MSS; Alexander F. Robertson, *Alexander Hugh Holmes Stuart, 1807-
1891: A Biography* (Richmond, 1925), 205-208.

to be my friend & never to have been otherwise, & I am now satisfied that I have misunderstood his feelings toward me." The tragic death of Davis' four-year-old son Joseph, the child to whom Clay stood in the relation of godfather, completed the reconciliation. Concluding his letter of condolence to Davis, Clay wrote, "Be assured, my dear friend, that it has stirred the affections of my heart for you more than all the many favors you have shown me, & that I shall ever cherish a sacred memory of that pledge of yr. affection for me on wh. God has set the solemn seal of death."[24]

After the adjournment of congress, Clement had joined Virginia in Petersburg. Clay was soon busy trying to negotiate a deal by which "Gentlemen of large capital & credit" would purchase 100,000 bales of cotton, for which they would pay "nine (9d.) pence per pound sterling exchange" when the cotton was delivered at Mobile. Memminger and Davis approved the scheme, but it apparently was never carried out.

On April 30, 1864, Clay left Petersburg, where, as he recorded in his diary, "Dear Jeanie & little Matt accompanied me to the Depot." Under the stress of deep emotions they parted after "a long & close embrace & many kisses." An eight-hour delay caused by a minor accident enabled Clay to reach Wilmington, North Carolina, the next day in a calmer frame of mind. From there he sent Virginia a power of attorney and numerous instructions as to his business and financial affairs.[25] On May 6, 1864, Clement Clay, Jacob Thompson, and their secretary, William W. Cleary, sailed for Canada.

[24] Clay, Jr., to Jefferson Davis, n.d., but probably May 1, 1864, Clay MSS. Joseph Evan Davis was killed by falling from a porch on April 30, 1864.
[25] Clay, Jr., to C. G. Memminger, April 25, 1864, Clay, Jr., to William A. Violett, April 28, 1864, Clay, Jr., Diary, April 30, May 1, 1864, Clay MSS.
Jeanie was Clay's pet name for his wife. Matt (born about 1860) was the son of Emily, a Negro slave and personal maid of Virginia Clay. A white father gave the child an almost white skin and features. Matt was raised by the Clays, given some education, became a respectable citizen, and took the name of Clay.

11 ~

Canadian Adventure

ON THE NIGHT of May 6, 1864, the *Thistle,* on which Clay and Thompson sailed, slipped through the blockade and the following day outran a pursuing Union vessel in a five-hour chase. Of this experience Clay wrote, "I did not feel alarmed, but yet not quite as easy as I desired.— Preparation was made for throwing over the cotton & dividing the Govt Gold—$25.000—among us to save it from the Yankees, if captured. And all our papers, tending to show our missions, were put in the bag with the Govt. Dispatches, to be burned."

Clay and Thompson transshipped at Bermuda, where a week's delay enabled them to exchange views with the many Confederates there. They reached Halifax, Nova Scotia, on May 19, 1864. Two days later a "sudden and quite severe indisposition" prevented Clay's accompanying Thompson "in his overland trip thro' New Brunswick to the St. Lawrence, about 200 miles of which had to be performed in an uncovered wagon." During the interval, Clay took stock of public opinion in the Maritime Provinces and made the acquaintance of the Right Reverend Thomas Louis Connolly, Roman Catholic archbishop of Halifax, who "dispenses the most liberal hospitality to every respectable Confederate who visits Halifax." Accompanied by Holcombe, Clay partook of that hospitality and departed with a letter requesting "the attention and kindly services of every Catholic Bishop and Priest and layman with whom he may come in contact."[1]

Clay found an "almost unanimous expression of sympathy and good wishes for our cause" throughout the Canadian provinces, but he had to admit that there was little hope for anything more substantial, for few Canadians disapproved the nonrecognition policy of the British government. Clay also feared that "the tone of the English press is less favorable to us than formerly," and urged expansion of Confederate propaganda in England.

By May 30, 1864, Clay was well enough to travel, but since water transportation had not yet begun, he too had to go overland. "I found the old-fashioned stage the most pleasant conveyance of my entire trip, . . . and was much improved in health and strength by the genial air, exercise, and excitement it afforded," wrote Clay. He stayed two days in Quebec, and went from there by steamboat to Montreal, where he arrived on June 11, 1864.

At Halifax, Clay and Thompson had found James P. Holcombe earnestly carrying out the first portion of his mission. Holcombe had proceeded to Canada under written instructions to investigate the case of the Union steamer *Chesapeake*. If, as the Confederate government was informed, the *Chesapeake* had been captured by a band of escaped Confederates, the cargo would be a legitimate Confederate prize of war. Holcombe's investigation revealed, on the contrary, that the expedition which captured the *Chesapeake* "was devised, planned, and organized in a British colony by Vernon G. Locke, a British subject," who "assumed to issue commissions in the Confederate service to British subjects on British soil, without the slightest pretext of authority for so doing." Consequently, Holcombe concluded, "any claim we might advance to the Chesapeake would be defeated." This decision Benjamin and Davis fully concurred in.[2]

1 Clay, Jr., Diary, May 7, 1864, Clay MSS. Clay's diary as preserved in his MSS covers April 30—May 10, 1864, Sept. 8, 1864, Jan. 31—March 28, 1865. If he kept a diary during the months in Canada, he presumably destroyed it.

The correspondence of Clay and the other commissioners in Canada is to be found in a variety of places. Most of their dispatches are printed in *O.R.*, IV, iii, and *O.R.N.*, *II*, iii. The principal MS record is CSA, State Department Archives (sometimes called Pickett Papers) in the Library of Congress. Material here cited is in Record Letterbook XIV. Clay's own copies of his official correspondence he kept in a letterbook which will be cited as Clay MS Letterbook.

Thomas Louis Connolly to Clay and Holcombe, May 20, 27, 1864, Clay MSS; Jacob Thompson to Judah P. Benjamin, May 10, 1864, Clay, Jr., to Benjamin, June 17, 1864, J. P. Holcombe to Benjamin, April 26, 1864, CSA, State Dept. Archives, Record Letterbook XIV; *O.R.N.*, II, iii, 1101, 1117.

2 Clay to Benjamin, June 17, 1864, Benjamin to Holcombe, Feb. 15, April 20, 1864, Holcombe to Benjamin, April 1, 26, 1864, CSA, State Dept. Archives, Record Letterbook XIV; *O.R.N.*, II, iii, 1072f, 1096, 1101f.

Holcombe was now free to carry out the second portion of his instructions, received just as he was leaving Richmond. "We are informed," explained Benjamin, "that several hundreds of the officers and men enlisted in our service who were captured by the enemy, are now in Canada, having escaped from prison; that they are without means of returning home, although anxious to resume service." These Confederates had escaped chiefly from Johnson's Island, the Union prison camp in Lake Erie near Sandusky, Ohio. On the supposition that there might be as many as four hundred of these men, Benjamin furnished Holcombe with a credit of $25,000 to be used in returning them to the Confederacy. Locating the men and making financial arrangements for their maintenance and transportation involved much work, and ultimately took Holcombe as far west as Windsor. His investigations soon showed that the number of men was much smaller than originally intimated, and did not total much more than one hundred, after weeding out the impostors and those disinclined to return to the Confederate service. By the time Holcombe had completed this business, other events seemed so imminent that he remained for several weeks in order to assist Clay and Thompson.[3]

What were Clay and Thompson instructed to do now that they had reached their destination? Their all-enveloping purpose was to bring about a "disruption between the Eastern and Western States in the approaching election at the North" so that "the three great Northwestern States of Illinois, Indiana, and Ohio could . . . be organized into a Western confederacy, with such advantages as will enable them to dictate terms of peace to the United States Government." Ancillary to the main project were schemes to buy various newspapers, particularly in the Northwest, and to "rig" the gold market. Clay and Thompson would be the masterminds in these schemes, but there must be other and younger men to execute them. To head this service, the Confederate government selected Captain Thomas Henry Hines, who, on March 16, 1864, was instructed to proceed to Canada, but while "passing through the United States . . . [to] confer with the leading persons friendly to . . . the Confederacy . . . [and] induce our

[3] Benjamin to Holcombe, Feb. 24, April 28, May 27, 1864, Holcombe to Benjamin, Aug. 11, Nov. 16, 1864, CSA, State Dept. Archives, Record Letterbook XIV; *O.R.N.*, II, iii, 1035f, 1104f, 1120f, 1187f, 1235.

friends to organize and prepare themselves to render such aid as circumstances may allow. . . . You will likewise have in view the possibility . . . of effecting any fair and appropriate enterprises of war against our enemies, . . . in any hostile operation . . . that may be consistent with the strict observance of neutral obligations incumbent in the British Provinces."[4]

Thomas Henry Hines, a native of Warren County, Kentucky, was a young man of great daring and resourcefulness. He had been a member of John Hunt Morgan's command and was chiefly instrumental in that leader's escape from prison following his famous raid through Indiana and Ohio. Other officers who attempted to carry out various military operations included John Yates Beall and Bennett G. Burley, both commissioned in the Confederate navy, John Breckinridge Castleman, Charles H. Cole, John W. Headley, Robert M. Martin, and Bennett Henderson Young. These eight young men together with Commissioners Clay, Thompson, and Holcombe, and Beverley Tucker, whom Jefferson Davis had sent to Canada to purchase supplies, formed the "hard core" of Confederate operations from Canada.[5]

To them flocked all sorts and conditions of men, and around them swirled endless rumor. Consuls reported their coming; detectives shadowed them; refugees and escaped prisoners besought their aid; politicians, Copperheads, and peace fanatics

4 Benjamin to Slidell, April 30, 1864, *O.R.N.*, II, iii, 1105f; Thompson to Benjamin, Dec. 3, 1864, *O.R.*, I, xliii, pt. 2, p. 933; Thompson to Clay, June 9, 1864, printed in U. S. Cong., 39:1, House Judiciary Committee *Report* no. 104, July, 1866, entitled "Assassination of Lincoln." This report prints letters of Clay, Thompson, and other Confederates in Canada, with the intent of showing their complicity in Lincoln's assassination. The letters were found in captured Confederate archives. (Cited hereinafter as USC, 39:1, HR Jud. Com. *Rep.* no. 104.) Thompson to Mason and Slidell, Aug. 23, 1864, Seddon to Hines, March 16, 1864, printed in Thomas Henry Hines, "The Northwestern Conspiracy," *Southern Bivouac*, V (Dec., 1886–March, 1887), 443, 509. Hines' narrative of activities in Canada is one of the best accounts by a participant. Hines had in his possession (received from Jacob Thompson) the official journal and many letters and dispatches of the Confederate commissioners while they were in Canada. Hines prints in full or in part many of these documents not elsewhere available.

5 Other narratives by or concerning participants are: John Breckinridge Castleman, *Active Service* (Louisville, Ky., 1917), 150f; John W. Headley, *Confederate Operations in Canada and New York* (New York, 1906), 217; Daniel Bedinger Lucas, *Memoir of John Yates Beall: His Life; Trial, Correspondence; Diary; and Private Manuscript Found among His Papers, Including His Own Account of the Raid on Lake Erie* (Montreal, 1865), 86-219; *Famous Adventures and Prison Escapes of the Civil War* (New York, 1893), 158-83 (the section on Morgan's escape was written by T. H. Hines); Jane Ellis Tucker, *Beverley Tucker. A Memoir by His Wife* [Richmond, Va., 1893?], 22. James David Horan, *Confederate Agent, A Discovery in History* (New York, 1954), is a popular account making Thomas H. Hines the central figure. Bennett H. Young published a partial account of his activities in the Louisville *Courier-Journal*, March, 1899.

harangued them; and from the American shore, newspaper correspondents avidly reported all the rumors that floated across the
Niagara River and Lake Ontario.

And what of the qualifications of these men to do the work for
which they had been commissioned? "Inadequate," is the only
answer. True, they had not been President Davis' first choice for
the mission. Clay's appointment served two purposes: it found a
job for a defeated senator and rewarded his loyalty to the Davis
administration. In appointing his old friend Jacob Thompson as
head of the mission, Davis had a man of vigor, administrative skill,
and experience. As a young man on the Mississippi frontier,
Thompson's unrelenting work had brought him wealth as a
planter and lawyer, and success as a politician. He was serious,
humorless, and tended to be domineering. Neither Thompson
nor Clay, however, had talents suited to fomenting a revolution
or directing secret-service operations. They were not experienced
in judging the type of men who would now surround them; they
were both too credulous, too trusting, and too optimistic about
what could be accomplished with the resources at their command.
They were not quite so gullible, however, as some of their
subordinates, especially Hines and Castleman, thought them to be.

Clay and Thompson soon found that their clashing tempera-
ments would make close association disagreeable. For this reason
primarily, Thompson set up his headquarters in Toronto, and
Clay joined his genial friend Beverley Tucker at St. Catherines,
where the springs gave them an excuse for sojourning in search
of health. Holcombe settled down at the Clifton House in nearby
Niagara Falls.[6]

Thompson had already opened a bank account in Montreal,
and the commissioners were adequately supplied with funds.
Holcombe received a total of $33,000, divided as follows: $5,000
for handling the case of the *Chesapeake*; $25,000 for returning
escaped prisoners; and $3,000 for his personal compensation and
expenses. These funds were in the forms of bills of exchange, a
letter of credit on Liverpool, and $500 in gold coin. The amount

6 Jefferson Davis to R. M. T. Hunter, April 14, 1864, Davis to Jacob Thompson,
April 7, 1864, *Jefferson Davis, Constitutionalist*, VI, 220, 226; Castleman, *Active
Service*, 133, 143; P. L. Rainwater (ed.), "Letters to and from Jacob Thompson,"
JSH, VI (Feb., 1940), 95-111; J. F. Bivins, "The Life and Character of Jacob
Thompson," Trinity College Historical Society *Papers*, ser. II (Durham, N. C.,
1898), 83-91.

of money in Thompson's hands totaled at least $900,000, and perhaps more. He and Clay carried with them $25,000 in gold. During the summer, Thompson transferred at least $100,000 to Clay, who disbursed it on his own responsibility.[7]

Immediately upon his arrival in Montreal, Thompson began a series of "conferences with representative men of the North, with a view to forming in the outset some basis which should govern our opinion as to the best course to pursue thereafter." On June 9, 1864, he sent Thomas H. Hines to Windsor, Ontario, for a preliminary interview with Clement L. Vallandigham, and two days later Thompson himself had a long conference with that gentleman.

Vallandigham was the leader of the peace Democrats. His vigorous opposition to the war had caused Lincoln to banish him to the Confederacy in May, 1863. Confederates received their visitor with considerable reserve, however, for Vallandigham never advocated an independent confederacy; he simply opposed the war and envisaged a reconstruction of the "Union as it was" with the Democratic party in political control. A month's leisurely travel, interspersed with conferences, brought Vallandigham to Wilmington, where, on June 17, 1863, he embarked for Canada. There he was received with considerable fanfare, and settled down at Windsor, where he was still living almost a year later when Hines and Thompson conferred with him.[8]

In the Northwest, secret societies favorable to the South and hostile to Lincoln had existed from the beginning of the war. As the conflict dragged on, these disaffected elements became more active, and in February, 1864, reorganized their scattered and autonomous societies into the Sons of Liberty, with Vallandigham as supreme commander. From him, Thompson learned about the organization, and decided that such widespread discontent might be utilized to benefit the Confederacy. That discontent expressed

7 Benjamin to Holcombe, Feb. 24, 1864, CSA, State Dept. Archives, Record Letterbook XIV; *O.R.N.*, II, iii, 1935f; Benjamin to Thompson, April 28, 1864, New York *Herald*, July 28, 1872; Clay, Diary, May 7, 1864, Clay to Thompson, Aug. 3, 1864, Clay MSS; Clay to Benjamin, Sept. 12, 1864, *O.R.*, IV, iii, 636; Thompson to Clay, [ca. Dec. 1, 1864], USC, 39:1, HR Jud. Com. *Rep.* no. 104, p. 14.

8 Thompson to Mason and Slidell, Aug. 23, 1864, Hines, "Northwestern Conspiracy," 502, 508; Jones, *RWCD*, I, 334, 357f, May 27, June 22, 1863; Davis to Bragg, June 8, 1864, *Jefferson Davis, Constitutionalist*, V, 507f; Edward Chase Kirkland, *The Peacemakers of 1864* (New York, 1927), 34-39; Elbert J. Benton, *The Movement for Peace without a Victory during the Civil War*, Western Reserve Historical Society *Collections*, Publication no. 99 (Cleveland, Ohio, 1918), 36-46; George Fort Milton, *Abraham Lincoln and the Fifth Column* (New York, 1942), 176-79.

itself in much talk about breaking off the states of Ohio, Indiana, and Illinois and forming them into a northwestern confederacy. Such a revolt would be most advantageous to the southern Confederacy, and to this end, Thompson bent "every energy that is practicable" and asserted that "every thing justifies the belief that success will ultimately attend the undertaking." His first financial aid went to engineer "peace meetings" in Peoria and Springfield, Illinois.[9]

While Thompson was thus busy formulating his plans, other events were taking shape of which none had dreamed. Clay, settled at St. Catherines, was receiving a steady stream of visitors. Many a prominent northern Democrat journeyed to Niagara Falls, crossed the Suspension Bridge into Canada, and spent a few days discussing war and politics with Clay and Holcombe, and sometimes with Thompson. Among them were John B. Weller of California, Daniel W. Voorhees of Indiana, James W. Singleton of Illinois, Charles R. Buckalew of Pennsylvania, David A. Noble of Michigan, Washington Hunt, Dean Richmond, Benjamin Wood, and Millard Fillmore of New York. Engineering all this activity were two strange characters: George Nicholas Sanders and William Cornell (Colorado) Jewett.

George N. Sanders, promoter, backstairs politician, revolutionary, and at the same time imperialist, had had a strange career during the preceding twenty years. After promoting the European revolutions of 1848 and leading the "Young America" movement of the 1850's, he joined the Confederate cause and busied himself with various schemes for running the blockade and for building vessels abroad. With the failure of these projects, Sanders dropped temporarily out of sight. But Clay had no more than reached Montreal when he learned "that Geo. N. Sanders is at Niagara, representing himself as sent by our Govt. to encourage peace! He actually talked . . . of calling a peace meeting of citizens of the U. S. & C. S. to devise joint action for that end. I hope he will not do so silly a thing, but wish he was in Europe, Asia, or Africa."

9 Thompson to Mason and Slidell, Aug. 23, 1864, Hines, "Northwestern Conspiracy," 509; Hines to Seddon, Dec. 16, 1864, Hines MSS; Thompson to Benjamin, Dec. 3, 1864, O.R., I, xliii, pt. 2, p. 930; Gray, Hidden Civil War, 69-72, 163-68; Ollinger Crenshaw, "The Knights of the Golden Circle: The Career of George Bickley," AHR, XLVII (Oct., 1941), 23-50. Union reports on the Sons of Liberty are printed in O.R., II, vii, 228-366, 626-60, 717-54, 801-803.

William Cornell Jewett was an even more bizarre character. He had had a shadowy, if not shady, career in various parts of the West, and was now obsessed with the idea of obtaining peace by European mediation. To that end he harassed the heads of state at home and abroad with addresses, petitions, and personal appeals. In June, 1864, Jewett too was in Canada. Thus these two irresponsible and irrepressible extroverts had maneuvered themselves into position to be key figures in the "Niagara Falls Peace Conference."[10]

That is the grandiose name for the series of events that occurred July 5-21, 1864. The actual "conference" was confined to a brief meeting between Holcombe and Horace Greeley on July 20. For Greeley, editor of the New York *Tribune,* was another peace fanatic. Opposed to the war at its outset, he had vacillated between anguished cries for peace and feverish support of that war when emancipation became a goal. Union military reverses of the spring and summer of 1864 had produced in Greeley such feelings of despair that the idea of peace was once more an obsession with him.[11]

Peacemaker Jewett, now sure that he was running the show, sent throbbing appeals to his old friend Greeley, who replied, "induce the Confederate chiefs to make an open proposition to the federal Government, setting forth the best terms they are prepared to offer." Two days later, busybody Jewett had everything lined up, and informed Greeley that "I have . . . just left Hon. George N. Sanders. . . . I am authorized to state . . . for our use only . . . that two ambassadors of Davis & Co. are now in Canada, with full and complete powers for peace. . . . Will you come here?" he telegraphed. "Parties have full power."[12]

10 Clay to Benjamin, June 17, 1864, CSA, State Dept. Archives, Record Letterbook XIV; Mallory to Davis, Aug. 16, 1862, Benjamin to Sanders, Oct. 28, 1862, *O.R.N.,* II, ii, 46, iii, 579f; Merle E. Curti, "George N. Sanders—American Patriot of the Fifties," *SAQ,* XXVII (Jan., 1928), 79-97; Merle E. Curti, "Young America," *AHR,* XXXII (Oct., 1926), 34-55; Kirkland, *Peacemakers of 1864,* 68-72.

11 Kirkland, *Peacemakers of 1864,* 51-67; Ralph Ray Fahrney, *Horace Greeley and the Tribune in the Civil War* (Cedar Rapids, Iowa, 1936), 155-60; William Harlan Hale, *Horace Greeley, Voice of the People* (New York, 1950), 275-80.

12 Greeley to Jewett, July 3, 1864, New York *Herald,* July 25, 1864. The correspondence of the whole episode was first published in Buffalo and New York City newspapers July 22-25, 1864, and a few days later in many Confederate papers. Frank H. Severance, "The Peace Conference at Niagara Falls in 1864: An Episode of the Civil War," *Peace Episodes on the Niagara,* Buffalo Historical Society *Publications,* XVIII (Buffalo, N. Y., 1914), 79-94. Citations to this and other secondary works already cited will not be repeated in succeeding notes.

Whether Jewett or Sanders thrust ambassadorial rank on the Confederates, that assumption so impressed Greeley that he forwarded the documents with an impassioned letter of his own to Lincoln. Sobbed the overwrought Greeley, "our bleeding, bankrupt, almost dying country also longs for peace. . . . A frank *offer* by you to the insurgents of terms . . . will . . . prove an immense . . . advantage to the National cause: It *may* save us from a Northern insurrection."

Lincoln pinned down Greeley's hysteria with this instruction: "If you can find any person anywhere professing to have any proposition of Jefferson Davis in writing for peace, embracing the restoration of the Union and abandonment of slavery, whatever else it embraces . . . he may come to me with you . . . he shall . . . have safe conduct. . . . The same if there be two or more persons." Sanders quickly assured Greeley "that Hon. Clement Clay of Alabama, Professor James P. Holcombe of Virginia, and George N. Sanders, of 'Dixie,' are ready and willing to go at once to Washington, upon complete and unqualified protection being given."[13]

Now that he was on the brink of action, Greeley shrank from further involvement, writing to Lincoln that the Confederate commissioners "would decline to exhibit their credentials to me, much more to open their budget and give me their best terms. . . . I have neither purpose nor desire to be made a confidant, far less an agent, in such negotiations." During the next five days, Greeley stalled while his and Lincoln's communications crossed each other in the mails and on the telegraph wires. On July 15 the exasperated Lincoln wrote, "I am disappointed that you have not already reached here with those Commissioners. . . . I not only intend a sincere effort for peace but I intend that you shall be a personal witness that it is made."

This letter Lincoln sent to New York by his secretary, John

13 Jewett to Greeley, July 5, 6, 1864, Greeley to Lincoln, July 7, 1864, Lincoln to Greeley, July 9, 1864, Robert Todd Lincoln Collection of the Papers of Abraham Lincoln, vols. 160, 161 (Library of Congress). With the manuscripts is a page-proof pamphlet of the correspondence with deletions proposed by Lincoln. Greeley would not agree to the deletions, and so the proposed pamphlet was not published in the summer of 1864. The correspondence is printed in *The Collected Works of Abraham Lincoln*, ed. by Roy P. Basler (New Brunswick, N. J., 1953-1955, 9 vols.), VII, 435, 440-43, 451, 459-61, 482f, 485, 489f, 494 (cited hereinafter as Lincoln, *Collected Works*); Sanders to Greeley, July 12, 1864, Buffalo *Commercial Advertiser*, July 22, 1864; New York *Times*, July 22, 1864.

Hay, who delivered it to Greeley "a few minutes after . . . 6 a m" on Saturday, July 16. Greeley still objected, saying that "some one less known would create less excitement and be less embarrassed by public curiosity"; still, "if the President insisted on his going he would go, but he must have an absolute safe-conduct for four persons." Hay (duly authorized by Lincoln) wrote the safe conduct and gave it to Greeley, who said, "I will start to-night; I shall expect to be in Washington Tuesday morning if they will come."[14]

Greeley reached Niagara Falls on Sunday, July 17, and immediately addressed this note to Clay, Holcombe, and Thompson: "I am informed that you are duly accredited from Richmond as the bearers of propositions looking to the establishment of Peace. . . . If my information be substantially correct, I am authorized by the President of the United States to tender you his safe conduct . . . and to accompany you at the earliest time that will be agreeable to you." Jewett and Sanders were the ball passers in this play between Greeley and the Confederates, but Jewett refused to be relegated to a minor role and insisted that he was calling the signals. Greeley's letter was, said Jewett, the "result of my negotiation for initiatory steps to a peace. . . . He and myself will meet . . . the honorable gentlemen . . . at the Suspension Bridge, and proceed . . . to Washington."[15]

But it was not quite that simple. Clay and Holcombe were, to say the least, startled upon being addressed as "duly accredited" emissaries of the Confederate government. They worked over their reply for a day and came up with an equivocal document which disclaimed any powers to negotiate, but added, "We are, however, in the confidential employment of our Government and entirely familiar with its wishes and opinions. . . . We feel authorized to declare, that if the circumstances disclosed in this correspondence were communicated to Richmond we would be at once invested with the authority to which your letter refers, or

14 Greeley to Lincoln, July 10, 1864, Lincoln to Greeley, July 15, 1864, Hay to Lincoln, July 16, 1864, Lincoln, Collected Works, VII, 440-43; John Hay, Letters of John Hay and Extracts from Diary, selected by Henry Adams, ed. by Mrs. Hay (Washington, 1908, 3 vols.), I, 212 (cited hereinafter as Hay, Letters and Diary).

15 Greeley to Clay, Thompson, and Holcombe, July 17, 1864, James Murray Mason MSS (copy enclosed in Clay and Holcombe to Mason, July 18, 1864); Buffalo Morning Express, July 22, 1864; New York Times, July 22, 1864; Jewett to Sanders, July 17, 1864, New York Herald, July 25, 1864.

that other gentlemen clothed with full powers would be immediately sent to Washington. . . . We respectfully solicit, through your intervention, a safe conduct to Washington, and thence . . . through your lines to Richmond."

This reply completely confused Greeley, who hurriedly telegraphed Lincoln "to solicit fresh instructions," explaining that "I have communicated with the Gentlemen in question & do not find them so empowered as I was previously assured." To Clay and Holcombe, Greeley promised to "transmit" his "further answer . . . at the earliest moment."

While they were awaiting Greeley's "fresh instructions," Clay and Holcombe rushed a dispatch to James Murray Mason in London, with copies of the notes interchanged with Greeley through July 18. "It seems to us," exulted the commissioners, "that a great change has come over Mr. Lincoln . . . & that he now contemplates an amicable adjustment between the North & the South, either in reunion or as separate & independent Governments. . . . The South will not, in our opinion, consent to reunion, but . . . would . . . as an independent Government . . . agree to . . . a treaty of amity and commerce, and possibly of alliance." Greeley, they believed, was "sincerely desirous of peace, even at the cost of our separation."[16]

What was the basis for this optimism? So far as Clay and Holcombe knew, they were being offered safe conduct to Washington with no strings attached. Greeley had failed to mention Lincoln's terms, namely, "restoration of the Union and abandonment of slavery," laid down on July 9 and repeated on the 15th. This omission put all the parties in a false position, but in any case, Clay and Holcombe "were so deeply impressed with the grave responsibility which would attach to any action we might take . . . that we telegraphed to Colonel Thompson to meet us at St. Catherines and unite in our deliberations."

Early on Tuesday, July 19, Greeley informed the commissioners that "further instructions . . . must reach me . . . by noon tomorrow." Clay and Holcombe replied, "One or possibly both of us, may be obliged to leave the Falls today, but will return in time

16 Clay and Holcombe to Greeley, July 18, 1864, Greeley to Clay and Holcombe, July 18, 1864, Clay and Holcombe to Mason, July 18, 1864, J. M. Mason MSS; Buffalo *Morning Express*, July 22, 1864; New York *Times*, July 22, 1864; Greeley to Lincoln, July 18, 1864, Lincoln, *Collected Works*, VII, 451.

to receive the communication which you promise to-morrow."
They then hastened to St. Catherines to confer with Thompson.[17]

The "further instructions" were again carried by John Hay,
who had set out from Washington on the evening of July 18,
missed his connection in New York, and arrived at Niagara Falls
just before noon on Wednesday, July 20. The document he
carried is one of Lincoln's most famous.

"Any proposition which embraces the restoration of peace, the
integrity of the whole Union, and the abandonment of slavery,
and which comes by and with an authority that can control the
armies now at war against the United States will be received and
considered by the Executive Government of the United States,
and will be met by liberal terms on other substantial and collateral
points, and the bearer or bearers thereof shall have safe conduct
both ways."

After considerable persuasion Greeley agreed to accompany
Hay across the Suspension Bridge to deliver this message. They
were met at the door of the Clifton House by Sanders, whom Hay
described as "a seedy looking rebel, with grizzled whiskers."
Greeley's arrival brought the curious flocking into lobby and
corridors to see what was going on. Hay and Greeley found
Holcombe (presumably just returned from St. Catherines) having
a late breakfast in his room. He was, Hay noted, "a tall, solemn,
spare, false-looking man, with false teeth, false eyes, and false
hair." Hay handed Holcombe the note and told him that if the
Confederates wished to "send any communications to Richmond
for the purpose indicated, they might be sent through Washington,
subject to the inspection of the government; and the answer from
Richmond should be sent to them under the same conditions."
Hay offered to "be the bearer of anything they chose to send . . .
to Washington." They shook hands around, and Greeley and Hay
departed, escorted to their carriage by the effusive Sanders who
remarked, "I wanted old B[ennett] to come up, but he was
afraid to come."[18]

17 Holcombe to Benjamin, Nov. 16, 1864, CSA, State Dept. Archives, Record
Letterbook XIV; *O.R.N.*, II, iii, 1236; Greeley to Clay and Holcombe, July 10, 1864,
Clay and Holcombe to Greeley, July 19, 1864, Buffalo *Commercial Advertiser*, July
22, 1864; New York *Times*, July 22, 1864.
18 Lincoln, *Collected Works*, VII, 451; Hay, *Letters and Diary*, I, 216-18; William
Roscoe Thayer, *Life and Letters of John Hay* (Boston, 1914, 2 vols.), I, 180; Buffalo
Morning Express, July 25, 1864; New York *Herald*, July 25, 1864.

Dinner restored Greeley's equanimity, and thereafter Hay went off to Buffalo to spend the night. Meantime, Greeley saw Jewett again and authorized him to receive any reply the Confederates might make. Holcombe had telegraphed the latest developments to Clay and Thompson, and Clay replied, "Will be with you at five o'clock. Detain Greeley until I see him." But Greeley, "in view of his mission being ended, through the rejection of the terms of negotiations," had no intention of being detained, and so fled on the first train for New York.[19]

What Clay intended to tell Greeley at five o'clock remains a mystery. If he, Holcombe, or Thompson recorded their first reactions to Greeley's visit and Lincoln's message, those records have long been lost. But it is a safe guess that the President's note induced in the three commissioners a state of considerable excitement, which indeed is apparent even when embalmed in the carefully considered and diplomatic words of their formal reply. Clay wrote that reply, with the aid of Holcombe and the approval of Thompson. In offering a safe conduct "exacting no condition but that we should be duly accredited," wrote Clay, "It seemed to us that the President opened a door which had previously been closed against the Confederate States, for a full interchange of sentiments." Now, Clay continued, "a document has been presented which . . . bears no feature of resemblance to that which was originally offered. . . . It precludes negotiations, and prescribes in advance terms and conditions of peace. It returns to the original policy of no bargaining, no negotiations, no truce with rebels. . . . What may be the explanation of . . . this rude withdrawal of a courteous overture for negotiation at the moment it was likely to be accepted . . . we leave for the speculation of those who have the means . . . to penetrate the mysteries of his Cabinet or fathom the caprice of his imperial will. It is enough for us to say that we have no use whatever for the paper which

19 Clay to Sanders, July 20, 1864, Jewett to Clay, Thompson, Sanders, Beverley Tucker, "and the other Hon. representatives," July 20, 1864, Buffalo *Daily Courier*, July 23, 1864.

The timing of the whole affair seems to be about this: Hay arrived at Niagara Falls at 11:30 A.M., July 20. He and Greeley reached the Clifton House perhaps about 1 P.M., had their short interview with Holcombe, and returned to the International House by perhaps 2 P.M., when they had dinner. Between that and five o'clock Greeley apparently saw Jewett and boarded a train for New York. Just when the telegrams between Holcombe and Clay were sent and received is uncertain, but Clay's answer was apparently received and passed from Holcombe via Sanders and Jewett to Greeley before he departed.

has been placed in our hands. We could not transmit it to the President of the Confederate States without offering him an indignity, [and] dishonoring ourselves."[20]

Greeley was gone, and so Jewett turned this letter over to the New York Associated Press. Meanwhile, Hay was patiently waiting for that same reply, which he expected to be delivered to him. The next morning (July 21) Hay "respectfully inquire[d] . . . when he may expect to be favored with such a message." Holcombe explained that he and Clay had addressed their reply to Greeley, and Hay departed for Washington. Clay spent the next few days having the correspondence of this incident printed, and on July 25 sent it, with a dispatch, to Jefferson Davis. All these documents Clay put into the hands of C. C. Nelson, a Canadian, who took them first to Greeley. Clay wrote to Greeley, "I trust I am not violating the laws and certainly not the proprieties . . . in asking you to facilitate Mr. N.s mission to Richmond for an object which I am persuaded is scarcely less dear to you than it is to me." Whether Nelson ever reached Richmond with the documents is an unsolved mystery.[21]

Meanwhile, the episode was causing a great furor. Bumbling Greeley was attacked on all sides by his journalistic colleagues, who demanded publication of the entire correspondence. This would have put Lincoln in the clear, but the President, feeling that it would be dangerous to publish Greeley's most hysterical effusions, proposed deletion of a few passages. To this Greeley would not consent, and so the matter of publication dropped, with the result the facts have come to light piecemeal over the years.[22]

While Clay and Holcombe were so deeply involved in political activities, Jacob Thompson was developing his own schemes. He

20 Clay and Holcombe to Greeley, July 21, 1864, Buffalo *Commercial Advertiser*, July 22, 1864; New York *Times*, July 22, 1864.

21 Clay to Greeley, July 25, 1864, Clay MS Letterbook; Holcombe to Hay, July 21, 1864, Buffalo *Commercial Advertiser*, July 22, 1864; Clay and Holcombe to Greeley, July 21, 1864, Hay to Clay and Holcombe, July 22, 1864, *The Rebellion Record: A Diary of American Events* (New York, 1861-1868, 11 vols.), XI, 534; Hay to Holcombe, July 21, 1864, Edward McPherson, *The Political History of the United States of America, during the Great Rebellion* (Washington, 1865, 2d ed.), 302. These works, containing most of the correspondence, seem to be the only printed sources for these two letters. Another work covering the whole episode is John G. Nicolay and John Hay, *Abraham Lincoln: A History* (New York, 1890, 10 vols.), IX, 184-200.

22 Greeley to Hay, Aug. 4, 1864, Henry J. Raymond to Lincoln, Aug. 5, 1864, Lincoln to Greeley, Aug. 6, 9, 1864, Greeley to Lincoln, Aug. 11, 1864, Lincoln to Raymond, Aug. 15, 1864, Lincoln, *Collected Works*, VII, 482, 485, 489f, 494.

himself was initiated into the Sons of Liberty during his conference with Vallandigham and James Barrett of St. Louis, adjutant
general of the order. Thompson strove to fan the flames of discontent within the order into a revolt which would seize the
governments of Ohio, Indiana, and Illinois, and "liberate" Kentucky and Missouri. The plan of operation was this: Confederate
officers then in Canada would lead the Sons of Liberty in attacks
on the several prison camps in the Midwest. The Confederate
soldiers thus released would be organized on the spot into a
mighty force which could seize the state governments, strike terror
into the populace, sweep to the Ohio River, and thence to the
Confederacy.

It was a wonderful scheme. The first stumbling block, however,
was the fact that the Sons of Liberty were not pro-Confederate.
They simply wanted cessation of the war and restoration of the
Union. Their hostility to Lincoln stemmed from his policy of
arbitrary arrests and other wartime restrictions on personal rights
and liberties. Still, Thompson thought their discontent was
strong enough to break out into violence, and it could be used
to benefit the Confederacy. Certainly a successful revolt would
divert large Union forces from the lines pressing toward Richmond and Atlanta; it would prove the unpopularity of the war;
and it would force Lincoln to make peace.[23]

July 20 was the date first set for the rising, but as it approached,
the Sons of Liberty found they were not ready, and so a conference
of the supreme council at Chicago on July 19 postponed action
until August 16. From Chicago some of the high officers went on
to St. Catherines to confer with Thompson, Clay, Holcombe,
Hines, and Castleman. At both places Thompson provided tangible encouragement to plans of revolt by distributing financial
aid, which totaled perhaps $200,000. At a second conference in
London, Canada, on August 7, the Sons of Liberty insisted on
another postponement until August 29, the date of the Democratic
national convention in Chicago. The Confederates could do
nothing but agree, though they did their utmost to pin the

23 Thompson to Benjamin, July 9, 1864, New York *Herald*, July 28, 1872 (this
and other dispatches of the Confederate commissioners were published in the New
York *Herald* in July, 1872, as a result of the publicity attending John T. Pickett's
sale of Confederate archives to the U. S. government); Thompson to Mason and
Slidell, Aug. 23, 1864, Hines, "Northwestern Conspiracy," 509.

supreme council down to a firm promise of action on that date. Meantime, all the commissioners were exceedingly busy arranging for the purchase of arms to be distributed among the Sons of Liberty. This was accomplished early in August, with the aid of Ben Wood of New York.[24]

The plot now concentrated on Chicago and the Democratic convention. A small band of Confederates would go to Chicago, assemble the Sons of Liberty into a fighting force, release the Confederate prisoners in Camp Douglas, mount and arm them, and then sweep to the Ohio River. In their most optimistic moments the plotters also envisaged the simultaneous release of Confederate prisoners at Rock Island and Springfield, Illinois, at Indianapolis, Indiana, and at Columbus, Ohio.[25]

Seventy Confederates left Canada on August 27, 1864, and the following night at the Richmond House in Chicago, Hines and Castleman met the officers of the Sons of Liberty. Though thousands of the order were in Chicago for the convention, their leaders had not organized sufficiently for the projected operation, and did not control their members. Hines and Castleman, who had hoped for a force of 5,000, besought the officers to round up their men for an assault on Camp Douglas during the night of August 30. But the Sons of Liberty were men of talk who timidly held back when faced with the prospect of real action and danger. In desperation, Hines then asked for 500 to join him in an attack on Rock Island, but even that number was not forthcoming; and

24 Thompson to Benjamin, Dec. 3, 1864, CSA, State Dept. Archives, Record Letterbook XIV; New York *Herald*, July 25, 1872; Hines to Seddon, Dec. 16, 1864, Hines MSS; Clay to Thompson, Aug. 3, 1864, Clay MSS; [Clay to Thompson], July 11, 20, 1864, USC, 39:1, HR Jud. Com. *Rep.* no. 104, pp. 17f (Clay and Thompson both used pseudonymns while in Canada; Clay signed many of his letters "T. E. Lacy" and addressed them to "W. P. Carson"); Hines, "Northwestern Conspiracy," 507-509, 567; Felix Grundy Stidger, *Treason History of the Order of Sons of Liberty, Formerly Circle of Honor, Succeeded by Knights of the Golden Circle, Afterward Order of American Knights* ([Chicago], 1903), 98f, 117; Castleman, *Active Service*, 145; Milton, *Lincoln and the Fifth Column*, 291.

25 Principal Confederate accounts are in Hines, "Northwestern Conspiracy," 569-74, and Castleman, *Active Service*, 144-59. Union accounts, in addition to works previously cited, are: I. Winslow Ayer, *The Great Northwestern Conspiracy in All Its Startling Details* (Chicago, 1865), 39-59; *The Great Treason Plot in the North During the War* (Chicago, 1895), 163-73; Thomas H. Keefe, "How the Northwest Was Saved: A Chapter from the Secret Service Records of the Civil War," *Everybody's Magazine*, II (Jan., 1900), 82-91; [James Roberts Gilmore], "The Chicago Conspiracy," *Atlantic Monthly*, XVI (July, 1865), 108-20, and *Personal Recollections of Abraham Lincoln and the Civil War* (Boston, 1898), 294-333. Ayer was a detective and Keefe was chief of detectives for the Northwest Department. The military report is in B. J. Sweet to James B. Fry, Nov. 23, 1864, *O.R.*, I, xlv, pt. 1, 1077-80.

so the Confederates were forced to abandon their long-cherished plot. Safety demanded that the Confederates leave Chicago when the convention adjourned, and so they split up, one-third going southward to the Confederacy, one-third returning to Canada, and twenty-two remaining with Hines and Castleman, who now hoped to salvage something by carrying out various smaller exploits in Illinois and Missouri.[26]

The Democratic convention revealed a party sadly divided between peace-at-any-price men, led by Vallandigham, and eastern war Democrats who supported the war either from principle or because of accruing profits. An incongruous result was that the party nominated a war Democrat on a peace platform. George Brinton McClellan was nominated on the first ballot. His running mate, George Hunt Pendleton, represented the peace wing of the party, while Vallandigham and John B. Weller controlled the platform-drafting subcommittee. Their "peace plank" demanded "that immediate efforts be made for a cessation of hostilities, with a view of an ultimate convention of the States . . . to the end that, at the earliest practicable moment, peace may be restored on the basis of the Federal Union of the States."[27]

It was generally believed throughout the North that Clay and Thompson's chief mission was to influence, perhaps control, the Democratic convention. Lincoln himself wrote, "Does any one doubt that what they *are* empowered to do, is to assist in selecting and arranging a candidadate [*sic*] and a platform, for the Chicago Convention?" The New York press asserted that "Hon. Clement C Clay . . . has prepared a Platform and an Address to be adopted by the Democracy at the Chicago Convention." This supposed platform declared for further prosecution of the war "only to restore the *Union as it was*," with "no further detriment to slave property," demotion to menial service for all Negroes in the army and navy, and a permanent status as slaves for all Negroes "not having enjoyed actual freedom during the war." On the same line, Clay's address declared that "The stupid tyrant who now disgraces the chair of Washington and Jackson could, any day, have peace and restoration of the Union, and would have

26 Castleman to Seddon, Sept. 7, 1864, Castleman, *Active Service*, 157-59, 172; Bennett H. Young to Clay, Sept. 2, 1864, USC, 39:1, HR Jud. Com. *Rep.* no. 104, p. 13.
27 Gray, *Hidden Civil War*, 183-85; William Starr Myers, *A Study in Personality: General George Brinton McClellan* (New York, 1934), 450-54.

them, only that he persists in the war merely to free the slaves."
Actually, Clay was "for *peace* and *disunion*," but to his Democratic
friends he said, "You can not elect without a cry of war for the
union; but once elected, we are friends, and can adjust matters
somehow." There is no proof that Clay wrote two such documents, but all the evidence indicated that he did. Lincoln himself
was sufficiently convinced of it to take the time to copy in his own
hand the platform and address as published in the newspapers.[28]

Though the Chicago convention did not adopt his ideas, Clay
was still well satisfied with its work when he wrote, "The platform
means peace, unconditionally. Vallandigham & Weller framed it
—it is recognized as satisfactory by nearly all the delegates . . .
and by the N. Y. News and other peace papers— . . . McCln. will
be under the control of the true peace men— McCln. is privately
pledged to make peace even at the expense of separation if the
south cannot be induced to reconstruct any common govt!"

Clay's satisfaction was short-lived, however, for in McClellan's
letter of acceptance repudiating the "peace plank" of the platform,
he saw "a craven surrender to . . . the selfish partizanship of the
leading war Democrats." A few days later Clay wrote a long and
florid diatribe to his onetime friend, George H. Pendleton, calling
on him to decline the vice-presidential nomination "for the sake
of the . . . cause of state rights & popular liberty which we both
profess to espouse."[29]

Jeremiah S. Black stirred up more peace talk when he visited
Thompson in Toronto. Thompson, Black, and Stanton had all
been friends and colleagues in Buchanan's cabinet. Black strove
to maintain old friendships, but now that Stanton was secretary
of war and a Radical, the rift was wide. Black himself had never
given the war active support. This was the situation in August,
1864, when Black casually told Stanton that he was going to
Canada to see Thompson. Stanton encouraged, even endorsed,
the idea. Black's long, friendly conversation with Thompson
ranged from reminiscence and gossip to a survey of the possibilities

---

28 Lincoln to Abram Wakeman, July 25, 1864, J. L. Talcott to Seward, July 16,
1864, Lincoln, holo. MS [Memorandum on Clement C. Clay, July 25, 1864], R. T.
Lincoln Collection of Lincoln Papers, vols. 161, 162, 163; Lincoln, *Collected Works*,
VII, 459, 461.

29 Clay to Holcombe, Sept. 14, 1864, Clay MSS; Clay to Benjamin, Sept. 12, 1864,
Clay to George Hunt Pendleton, Sept. 16, 1864, Clay MS Letterbook; Charles R.
Wilson, "McClellan's Changing Views on the Peace Plank of 1864," *AHR*, XXXVIII
(April, 1933), 498-505.

for peace and reunion. Black reported to Stanton that the southern people, though anxious for peace, would "not surrender any right to regulate their domestic affairs by State authority," which meant that each state must be free to make its own laws defining "what shall be the legal relations between the black and white races." Concede this, and the southern states would return to the Union, thought Black. Send Clay, Thompson, and Holcombe to Richmond, he urged, as the opening move in arranging an armistice and beginning negotiations. Stanton's reply was icy: "your recent interview with Mr. Thompson . . . clearly proves that the rebel leaders . . . will accept no peace but upon the terms of absolute independence. . . . Believing this to be their purpose, I am not disposed to give the President the advice you recommend." Stanton further violently denied having given his "approbation" of the visit. The break between the two men was complete when Black in reply reminded Stanton that "you . . . very unequivocally expressed your wish that I would . . . go and see Mr. Thompson. . . . You repeated it not less than three times."[30] So ended another effort for peace.

The story would be incomplete without some account of the acts of war attempted by the Confederates. In July, 1864, Thompson sent Captain Charles H. Cole on a circuit of the Great Lakes and lake cities. Cole reported that "Buffalo is poorly protected. . . . I left Cleveland, and . . . met a gentleman who . . . took me around the government works. . . . I went to Chicago where . . . There is an immense amount of shipping. . . . Destroy the different draw-bridges, and then the whole city is accessible by water. Milwaukee is an easy place to take possession of. They have no fort. . . . Lake Erie furnishes a splendid field for operations."

Anchored in Lake Erie off Sandusky lay the U. S. S. *Michigan,* the only armed vessel on the Great Lakes. If the Confederates could capture the *Michigan,* they might release the Confederate prisoners held on Johnson's Island, sweep Union shipping from the lakes, and make attacks at will on the lake cities. Thompson commissioned Charles H. Cole, John Yates Beall, and Bennett Burley to carry out this project. Posing as a young Philadelphia

---

[30] J. S. Black to Stanton, Aug. 24, Sept. 3, 1864, Stanton to Black, Aug. 31, 1864, Jeremiah Sullivan Black MSS; Thompson to Mason and Slidell, Aug. 23, 1864, Hines, "Northwestern Conspiracy," 509; William Norwood Brigance, *Jeremiah Sullivan Black: A Defender of the Constitution and the Ten Commandments* (Philadelphia, 1934), 126-28.

millionaire, Cole took up residence at Sandusky, became intimate with the captain and crew of the *Michigan,* and visited prisoners on Johnson's Island. While perfecting his plans for capturing the *Michigan,* he entertained lavishly. On September 18, 1864, Beall, Burley, and about twenty other Confederates took passage on the *Philo Parsons,* a small steamer running between Detroit and Sandusky. They soon took command of the *Philo Parsons,* and at Middle Bass Island they also captured another steamer, the *Island Queen.* After putting passengers and baggage ashore on the island, they scuttled the *Island Queen* and proceeded toward Sandusky to attack the *Michigan.* But the prearranged signal was not flashed, and so seventeen fainthearted Confederates refused to proceed with the attack. The signal was not given because Cole had already been arrested. He was to have given a champagne dinner aboard the *Michigan* on the night of September 19, after which the ship's capture would be attempted. But his plan was betrayed, presumably by one Maurice Langhorne, to John C. Carter, captain of the *Michigan,* who arrested Cole during the afternoon of September 19. Unable to finish the exploit, Beall made for the Canadian shore, discharged his mutinous crew, and sank the *Philo Parsons.*[31]

Still hoping to accomplish something in the naval line, Thompson furnished $17,000 to one James T. Bates, a Kentucky steamboat captain, for the purchase of a small steamer, the *Georgiana.* The Confederate crew would be under the command of John Yates Beall. Thompson's account of what happened is substantially correct: "She had scarcely been transferred when the story went abroad that she had been purchased and armed for the purpose of sinking the Michigan, releasing the prisoners on Johnson's Island, and destroying the shipping on the lakes and the cities on their margin. The wildest consternation prevailed in all the border cities. At Buffalo two tugs had cannon placed on board; four regiments of soldiers were sent there. . . . The whole lake shore was a scene of wild excitement." Canadian investigation revealed nothing suspicious about the *Georgiana,* principally because the Confederates had not yet had time to get arms aboard. But to avoid difficulty, Thompson soon disposed of the boat. Thus ended

31 Hines, "Northwestern Conspiracy," 568, 699f; Thompson to Benjamin, Dec. 3, 1864, *O.R.,* I, xliii, pt. 2, 932f; Union dispatches *ibid.,* 399, 409, 426-28, II, vii, 850f, 901-906; Lucas, *Memoir of John Yates Beall,* 33-46; Castleman, *Active Service,* 161f; Headley, *Confederate Operations in Canada and New York,* 231-36, 248-52; Frederick Boyd Stevenson, "The Johnson Island Conspiracy: An Episode of the Civil War," *Frank Leslie's Popular Monthly,* XLVI (Sept., 1898), 257-66.

Confederate attempts to control the lakes and release the prisoners on Johnson's Island.[32]

Leaving Chicago on August 31, 1864, Hines, Castleman, and the twenty-two Confederates under them proceeded southward to east-central Illinois, where they remained for the next month in the vicinity of Marshall and Mattoon. They had decided to direct their own activities and found that a strike at the enemy could be made by destroying military stores and shipping at the St. Louis wharves. The entire band went to St. Louis, located the boats, and would have succeeded but for their reliance on "greek fire," a liquid supposed to ignite when exposed to air. Each man went to his assigned boat, broke his bottle of "greek fire," and hastily departed. The concoction flashed into flame but did not ignite boat or cargo. With a supply of matches the Confederates probably would have accomplished their purpose.[33]

Election day, which fell on November 8, 1864, would provide the last opportunity for Confederate action. Thompson labored diligently to coordinate and perfect the plans. About November 1, Hines and his men returned to Chicago, where high officials of the Sons of Liberty had arms, and presumably men, to carry out the assault on Camp Douglas. The trouble this time was that Union detectives already knew enough of the plot to warn Commandant Colonel Benjamin J. Sweet of the impending outbreak. Sweet went into action on Monday, November 7, arresting leaders of the Sons of Liberty, seizing their caches of arms, and capturing some of the Confederates, though Hines himself escaped. This ended the "Northwestern Conspiracy."[34]

[32] Thompson to Benjamin, Dec. 3, 1864, *O.R.*, I, xliii, pt. 2, 934; Union dispatches *ibid.*, 552, 557, 602, 617, and in *O.R.N.*, I, iii, 349, 352, 370-75, 495f; Charles Stanley Monck, Viscount Monck to Edward Cardwell, Viscount Cardwell, Nov. 14, 1864, Canadian Archives, Ottawa, G 12, vol. 69, no. 175, p. 197, Governor General's Office, Letters to Secretary of State, 1864 (Monck was governor general of Canada; Cardwell was secretary of state for colonies in the British cabinet) (cited hereinafter by number: G 12, vol. 69); U. S. State Department, *Foreign Relations*, 1865, pt. 2, pp. 1-90 *passim;* Lester Burrell Shippee, *Canadian-American Relations, 1849-1874* (New Haven, 1939), 156f; Headley, *Confederate Operations in Canada and New York*, 253-55.

[33] Castleman to Clay, Sept. 5, 1864, Castleman to Clay and Thompson, Sept. 24, 1864, USC, 39:1, HR Jud. Com. *Rep.* no. 104, pp. 15f; Castleman, *Active Service*, 157-59, 172-74.

[34] Sweet to Fry, Nov. 23, 1864, *O.R.*, I, xlv, pt. 1, pp. 1076-83; Thompson to Benjamin, Dec. 3, 1864, *O.R.*, I, xliii, pt. 2, p. 934; [Gilmore], "Chicago Conspiracy," *Atlantic Monthly*, XVI (July, 1865), 108-20; Gilmore, *Personal Recollections*, 307-33; Keefe, "How the Northwest Was Saved," *Everybody's Magazine*, II (Jan., 1900), 87-91; Ayer, *Great North-Western Conspiracy*, 61f, 72-85; Headley, *Confederate Operations in Canada and New York*, 284-300.

Jacob Thompson thought he had arrangements made for election-day incendiarism in Cincinnati, Boston, and New York, but the day passed without disturbance in those cities. That was not the end of the story in New York, however, where eight determined Confederates led by Colonel Robert M. Martin persisted in their mission. They had been promised complete cooperation from leading Copperheads, and even absolute neutrality on the part of Governor Horatio Seymour. But Copperhead courage evaporated as 10,000 reinforcements poured into New York, and so nothing happened on election day. The Confederates then set November 25 for action, and on that evening the eight men set fires in ten hotels, three theaters, and in some shipping along the wharves, using again "greek fire." The result was great excitement in the city, but little damage from the fires. All the Confederates managed to return to Canada without capture. A fruitless effort to derail a train near Buffalo ended their activities.[35]

The St. Albans raid on October 19, 1864, was the most spectacular of all Confederate border actions. It is ironical that this expedition against the town of St. Albans, Vermont, planned by B. H. Young and directed by Clement Clay, should have come nearer success than did all the schemes over which Jacob Thompson had labored for months. Lieutenant Bennett Henderson Young, with twenty Confederates under his command, executed the raid. By twos and threes they filtered into St. Albans and spent October 18 reconnoitering and perfecting their plans. Wednesday, October 19, was a chilly, cloudy, threatening day. At 3 P.M. Young and his men went into action on the main street, where they proceeded to rob the three banks of some $200,000, attempted to fire the hotels and other buildings, herded startled and protesting citizens onto the adjoining village green, seized horses on the street and from the livery stables, and shot up the town, wounding two or three people, one of whom later died.

Though not in uniform and without a Confederate flag, they repeatedly asserted that they were Confederate soldiers, carrying out a retaliatory action. After some forty-five minutes of such activity, several Union soldiers at home on leave began to organize the citizens for resistance, whereupon the Confederates mounted

35 O.R., II, viii, 414-16; Headley, Confederate Operations in Canada and New York, 266-300, 323-31.

their horses and made for the Canadian border, fourteen miles distant, under cover of approaching darkness. In hot pursuit rode some fifty irate citizens, led by young Captain George P. Conger.

Great waves of excitement and fear swept over the East. The telegraph operator in St. Albans flashed news of the raid to Montpelier, and then shut up shop and joined in pursuit of the raiders. This left distracted Governor J. Gregory Smith with the impression that Confederates had seized telegraph office, railroad station, and the whole town, and that his family who resided there were in imminent danger. Troops and arms were rushed to St. Albans, and all New England was alerted against future raids, which rumor reported as imminent.[36]

As soon as Young and his men crossed into Canada, they abandoned the horses and most of their weapons (chiefly pistols), and scattered through the countryside on foot. By the morning of October 20, seven of the men had been captured, and Young himself was seized a short time later by some of the Vermonters who had crossed into Canada in pursuit. They threatened immediate shooting or hanging, but he was saved from further rough treatment by the arrival of a Canadian officer who persuaded the Vermonters to yield Young into his custody. Within a few days, fourteen of the Confederates had been captured and taken to Montreal for trial. On October 29, 1864, Seward requested the raiders' extradition under the Ashburton Treaty as criminals guilty of robbery and murder.[37]

On November 7, 1864, the case opened in Montreal police court before Judge Charles Joseph Coursol. Clay retained three distinguished attorneys, J. J. C. Abbott, R. Laflamme, and W. H. Kerr, to defend the prisoners; B. Devlin and —— Ritchie represented the United States; and F. J. Johnson and G. E. Cartier

---

[36] The literature of the St. Albans raid is quite extensive and cannot all be cited here. The most important sources are: [Clay to Benjamin], Nov. 1, 1864, enclosure in Cardwell to Monck, Dec. 31, 1864, Can. Archives, Gov. General's Office, Numbered Files, no. 57, vol. I, Dispatch no. 112; U. S. State Dept., *Foreign Relations*, 1864, pt, 2, pp. 759-814, 1865, pt. 1, pp. 15-17; *O.R.*, I, xliii, pt. 2, pp. 420-56, 914-16. Accounts appeared in most U. S., Confederate, and Canadian newspapers. Fullest reporting is in the Burlington, Vt., *Daily Free Press* (file in Burlington Free Library), Oct. 20, 21, 27, 29, 31, 1864, which carried excerpts from the St. Albans *Messenger* and the Burlington *Times*. Mrs. J. Gregory Smith, "An Incident of the Civil War," *Vermonter*, IV (Jan., 1899), 101-104.

[37] Seward to Lyons, Oct. 29, 1864, U. S. State Dept., *Foreign Relations*, 1864, pt. 2, p. 756; Burlington *Daily Free Press*, Oct. 25, 1864; Headley, *Confederate Operations in Canada and New York*, 260-63.

appeared as crown counsel. The hearing of testimony occupied a week, whereupon Abbott applied for a thirty-day delay in order that the prisoners might send to Richmond for freshly authenticated commissions and other evidence. Judge Coursol granted a delay to December 13, 1864. When the case resumed, Kerr argued that Judge Coursol had no jurisdiction because arrests to be valid under the treaty must be made on warrants issued and signed by the governor general. On this basis Coursol dismissed the case for want of jurisdiction.

Young and his men were thus free on December 13, 1864. On the same day (and with some previous arranging by George N. Sanders, still in his busybody role), Guillaume Lamothe, Montreal chief of police, returned to the raiders the $90,000 found on them at the time of their capture. Devlin immediately protested to the Montreal city council, and after lengthy investigation, the council decided that Lamothe had erred in returning this money entrusted to his custody, and so forced him to resign.[38]

The matter of the money also caused some trouble among the Confederates. In planning the St. Albans raid, Clay had stressed burning the town as the primary objective, with robbery permissible, provided monies thus obtained were turned over to him as agent of the Confederate government. As it turned out, robbery was the raiders' chief accomplishment. Misunderstandings and misrepresentations caused some of the raiders to feel that Clay had deserted them, though Young himself always had complete trust in his superior. Prior to the action, Clay had advanced $2,462 to the raiders, and on October 22, 1864, he put $6,000 in the hands of George N. Sanders for their defense. Before the three trials were over, expenses had reportedly amounted to more than $80,000.[39]

[38] L. N. Benjamin (comp.), *The St. Albans Raid; or, Investigation into the Charges against Lieut. Bennett H. Young and Command, for Their Acts at St. Albans, Vt., on the 19th October, 1864* (Montreal, 1865), 21, 116, 117, 127, and *passim;* Montreal City Council, *The St. Albans Raid: Investigation by the Police Committee, of the City Council of Montreal, into the Charges Preferred by Councillor B. Devlin, against Guillaume Lamothe, Esq., Chief of Police, and the Proceedings of the Council in Reference Thereto* (Montreal, 1865), 3, 78, and *passim.*
[39] Young to Clay, Nov. 21, 1864, Beverley Tucker to Clay, Dec. 9, 1864, Clay MSS; "Lieut. B. H. Young in acct with the Confederate States of America" [ca. Nov. 1, 1864], facs. of MS in Clay's hand, reproduced in Louisville *Courier-Journal,* March 12, 1899, and in *Vermonter,* VII (Jan., 1902), 24; F. L. McChesney to Young, Jan. 5, 1899, Louisville *Courier-Journal,* March 12, 1899; J. D. McInnis to Thompson, Nov. 15, 1864, USC, 39:1, HR Jud. Com. *Rep.* no. 104, p. 14.

Judge Coursol's release of the prisoners was severely criticized by higher law officers of the Canadian government. Under new warrants issued for rearrest of the raiders, Bennett Young and four others were taken into custody near Quebec on December 20, 1864. A new trial began in Montreal on December 27, 1864, this time before the superior court presided over by Justice James Smith. Once more Abbott applied for a thirty-day delay to enable the prisoners to get the needed evidence from Richmond. During the time thus granted (January 11–February 10, 1865), the Confederates sent six messengers (one of them a woman) to Richmond. Two of them, the unidentified woman and Stephen F. Cameron, a Confederate chaplain, managed to make the round trip, reaching Montreal with the necessary documents on February 15, 1865.[40]

After some six weeks of further hearings, Justice Smith gave an opinion entirely favorable to the Confederates. He said, "I . . . hold that the attack on St. Albans was a hostile expedition authorised both expressedly and impliedly by the Confederate States; and carried out by a commissioned officer of their army in command of a party of their soldiers. . . . No act committed in the course of . . . that attack can be made the ground of extradition under the Ashburton treaty. . . . The prisoners cannot be extradited because . . . what they have done does not constitute one of the offenses mentioned in the Ashburton treaty . . . therefore . . . the prisoners are entitled to their discharge." Released on April 5, 1865, the five men were immediately arrested again, this time on charges of violating the neutrality laws. A preliminary hearing some weeks later produced no reliable evidence, and so the men were released on bail. The charges against Young were dismissed on October 27, 1865, whereupon he departed for Europe. High British law officers subsequently upheld both Canadian decisions in the St. Albans case.[41]

Six of the raiders had never been captured. These men presumably made a quick escape from Canada and returned to the

40 Monck to Cardwell, Dec. 15, 24, 1864, Jan. 26, 1865, Cardwell to Monck, Dec. 31, 1864, Can. Archives, Gov. General's Numbered Files, no. 57; Thompson to Benjamin, Jan. 8, 1865, CSA, State Dept. Archives, Record Letterbook XIV; Benjamin, St. Albans Raid, 173-75, 183-93, 213-15.

41 Cartier to Monck, Feb. 21, April 1, 1865, Cardwell to Monck, April 1, 1865, Sir John Michel to Cardwell, Oct. 27, 1865, Can. Archives, Gov. General's Numbered Files, no. 57; Mason to Benjamin, Dec. 16, 1864, March 31, 1865, O.R.N., II, iii, 1250f, 1267; Benjamin, St. Albans Raid, 469, 471.

Confederacy. When the fourteen prisoners were released on December 13, 1864, after the first trial, nine escaped rearrest. Five of these men apparently made their way to New Brunswick and from there by blockade runner to a southern port. The other four remained for a time in Montreal, then moved eastward through heavy snow and severe cold. Guided by a French Canadian, David Têtu, they experienced many adventures and hardships before they reached Halifax, where they took ship for Europe.[42]

So much for the St. Albans raiders; but what had become of the other Confederates under Clay and Thompson's command? Several had returned safely to the Confederacy; others had been captured; and two were soon to be hanged as spies. Of the officers previously referred to, Thomas H. Hines alone escaped capture. After the election-day fiasco in Chicago, he made his way to Cincinnati and thence to Richmond, where he reported to Secretary of War Seddon. Two others, Robert M. Martin and John W. Headley, escaped capture during the war, but were arrested at their Kentucky homes in October, 1865, for their previous activities. Headley eluded his guard and soon received a pardon from President Johnson, but Martin was imprisoned until the summer of 1866. Captured in Indiana on October 1, 1864, John B. Castleman was tried as a spy, but released (through his uncle's intervention with President Lincoln) on condition that he leave the country. Castleman promptly went to Europe via Canada. Charles H. Cole, apprehended on September 19, 1864, for his plot to seize the *Michigan,* was imprisoned for over a year, then handed over to the civil authorities on a writ of habeas corpus, and released without trial in Brooklyn, New York, on February 10, 1866. Bennett G. Burley, who had seized the *Philo Parsons,* was the only one to be extradited to the United States, but he escaped from prison, was never tried, and later returned to his native Scotland. Robert Cobb Kennedy and John Yates Beall were tried by military commission, convicted, and hanged as spies, in spite of all efforts to save their lives. They had both participated in the attempt to burn New York. On the return trip, Beall was captured on December 16, 1864, just before crossing into Canada at Niagara Falls. Kennedy reached Canada, but was captured near Detroit

[42] Henry Têtu, *David Têtu et les Raiders de Saint-Alban: Épisode de la Guerre Américaine, 1864-1865* (Quebec, 1891, 2d ed.), 81-197.

in January, 1865, as he began his return to the Confederacy.[43]

What had been accomplished? In seven months of activity the Confederates had spent over half a million dollars and had employed, directly or indirectly, several hundred persons. But no revolution had occurred in the Northwest; no Confederate prisoners had been released; no peace had been made; and no Democratic victory had come in the election. The Confederates had succeeded only in carrying on a "war of nerves." With hopes vanished for any effective action and with the Confederacy itself near collapse, Benjamin on March 2, 1865, instructed Thompson to close up business and accounts in Canada, to remit all remaining funds to Fraser and Trenholm in Liverpool, and to "Return to the Confederacy as soon as you can."

Though he presumably received this dispatch, Thompson obeyed it only in part. He had remained in Toronto "watching the trial of the famous 'Burley Extradition Case' " until February 14, 1865, when he went to Montreal, where he stayed until April 10. On that date Thompson and his secretary, W. W. Cleary, began their journey to Halifax, and had reached Rivière du Loup, below Quebec, when they heard of Lincoln's assassination. Bad weather and roads detained Thompson there until the end of April, when he went on to Halifax and sailed for Europe, probably in May, 1865. He carried with him some £12,000 of Confederate funds which he finally turned over to Benjamin at Paris in September, 1865. Thompson lived in Europe and Canada until the spring of 1869, when he returned to Mississippi. He was one of the few Confederates who managed to save most of his property and fortune. At Rivière du Loup, Cleary decided to turn back westward, and lived in Canada during the remainder of 1865.[44]

43 Hines to Seddon, Dec. 15, 1864, Hines MSS; Monck to Lyons, Dec. 6, 1864, Monck to Burnley, Jan. 31, 1865, Burnley to Seward, Feb. 4, 1865, U. S. State Dept., *Foreign Relations*, 1865, pt. 2, pp. 7, 64; *O.R.*, II, viii, 279f, 399, 611, 704, 739, 878, 881, IV, iii, 414-16; *Trial of John Y. Beall, as a Spy and Guerrillero, By Military Commission* (New York, 1865), 3-94; Lucas, *Memoir of John Yates Beall*, 86-219; Headley, *Confederate Operations in Canada and New York*, 251, 340-70, 438, 450; Castleman, *Active Service*, 174, 182-88, 196; Jonathan Truman Dorris, *Pardon and Amnesty under Lincoln and Johnson: The Restoration of the Confederates to Their Rights and Privileges, 1861-1898* (Chapel Hill, 1953), 76-78; Stevenson, "Johnson Island Conspiracy," *Frank Leslie's Popular Monthly*, XLVI (Sept., 1898), 265.

44 Benjamin to Thompson, March 2, 1865, New York *Herald*, July 24, 1872; Benjamin to Thompson, Sept. 3, 13, 1865, facs. and text in Castleman, *Active Service*, 201f; *O.R.*, II, viii, 517, 519; Rainwater (ed.), "Letters to and from Jacob Thompson," 104-10; Stuart Robinson, *The Infamous Perjuries of the "Bureau of Military Justice" Exposed: Letter of Rev. Stuart Robinson to Hon. Mr. Emmons* ([Toronto, June 10, 1865], photostatic copy in Rare Books Division, Library of Congress, from original in possession of David Rankin Barbee), pp. 1-3.

Communication between the commissioners and their government was subject to many hazards, and it became increasingly
difficult as collapse of the Confederacy neared. Their greatest
peril arose from the presence among them of spies and traitors, of
whose existence they were only partially aware. Of these, the
most notorious was Richard Montgomery, a doublecrosser who
played both sides. He applied at the War Department in Washington for service as a spy on the Confederates. He then went to
Richmond, where he gained the confidence of Confederate officials,
who sent him to Canada with dispatches. There Ben Wood
recognized Montgomery at once as a spy, and so warned Jacob
Thompson. Montgomery immediately disappeared from Toronto,
but apparently turned up at St. Catherines where Clay and Holcombe, though doubtful of his trustworthiness, used him as a
courier on one or more occasions. Montgomery claimed that he
delivered Confederate dispatches to the War Department in
Washington, where they were copied, and then proceeded to
Richmond with the originals. This went on until November,
1864, when he was carrying Clay and Tucker's dispatches of
November 1. These Stanton considered so important that a fake
arrest was arranged in Alexandria, Virginia; Montgomery was
clapped into Old Capitol Prison, but from there he was soon
allowed to escape, whereupon he returned to Canada with a con-
vincing tale of adventures for the Confederates. To them he was
known as James Thompson.[45]

Delays and dangers in communications caused the highest Confederate officials as well as ordinary folk to resort to the use of
"Personals," published mainly in the New York *News,* a pro-South
paper. Clay's own "Personals" reflected his anxiety: "I am well,"
he wrote. "Have written every week, but received no answer
later than 30th June. . . . Can I leave here before Spring? Answer
by personal in Enquirer." In reply, Secretary Benjamin instructed,
"Your friends think the sooner you return the better. At the
point where you change vessels you can ascertain if it is better
to proceed direct to Mexico."

Clay could accomplish nothing more in Canada, and with the

45 Charles Anderson Dana, *Recollections of the Civil War* (New York, 1898),
238-47; Benn Pitman (comp.), *The Assassination of President Lincoln and the Trial
of the Conspirators* (Cincinnati, 1865), 26-28; William W. Cleary, *The Protest of
W. W. Cleary, against the Proclamation of President Johnson, of May 2nd* (Toronto,
1865), 52-58; *O.R.,* II, viii, 132f, 181, 191, 837; Hines, "Northwestern Conspiracy," 703.

approach of winter, he feared for his health. Besides, he was in imminent danger of arrest for violating the neutrality laws, since testimony in the trial of the St. Albans raiders had proved him responsible for that expedition.[46] And so about December 1, 1864, Clay left St. Catherines, spent a few days in Montreal, and reached Halifax about December 19, after an overland journey. He sailed from that port on January 13, 1865, and reached Bermuda five days later. Transshipping to the blockade runner *Rattlesnake,* he touched at the Bahamas on January 31, and on the night of February 2 the ship ran aground in Charleston harbor. As if that were not enough, the lifeboat also ran aground. "I waded to shore," Clay recorded in his diary, "carrying what baggage I could in my hands. . . . Waded in repeatedly . . . & got wet to my waist. Lost a box . . . a trunk, & much of my own baggage wh. was in the hold of the ship—all being burned in it." A friend took Clay from Sullivan's Island to Charleston, where he spent a day drying out his baggage and then set out in search of his wife. He went first to Columbia, South Carolina, where he "Left a large black trunk, corded . . . in care of Mrs. Genl. Chesnut." He joined two friends in hiring a carriage to take them on to Augusta, Georgia, where Clay destroyed a number of papers concerning activities in Canada. On February 10, 1865, he and Virginia Clay were reunited in Macon, Georgia.[47]

During Clay's absence in Canada, Virginia Clay had passed the time at various places and with mounting impatience. Hearing that the enemy was only six miles away, Virginia left Petersburg on May 7, 1864. Traveling via Danville, Greensboro, and Charlotte, Virginia did not reach Macon until May 13. At Danville, lunch and supper had cost her $25, while her hotel bill was $80. "Will soon be broke at this rate," she noted. "Had to open my bag & get out another hundred dolls. Leave G[reensboro] with $137 in my purse." Celeste joined Virginia in Macon, whence the two women later journeyed to Columbus, Georgia, to visit Celeste's sister, Victoria Winter. As the weeks and months passed

---

46 Clay, Jr., to H. L. Clay, Oct. 29, 31, 1864, H. L. Clay and J. P. Benjamin to Clay, Jr., Nov. 10, 11, 1864, printed in New York *Daily News,* Oct. 31—Nov. 23, 1864 (Each "Personal" appeared in several issues of the paper; Clay used his pseudonym, "T. E. Lacy"); [Beverley Tucker to Clay, Jr.], Dec. 9, 1864, Clay MSS; Cardwell to Monck, April 1, 1865, Can. Archives, Gov. General's Numbered Files, no. 57; Benjamin, *St. Albans Raid,* 387-92.

47 Clay, Jr., Diary, Jan. 31—Feb. 18, 1865, H. L. Clay to Virginia Clay, Jan. 7, 1865, Clay, Jr., holo. memoranda [Feb. 8, May 12, 1865, Jan. 1, 1866], Clay MSS.

with only occasional letters from Clement, Virginia insisted on going to Canada to join him, but was dissuaded by Lawson Clay and Secretaries Mallory and Benjamin, who assured her that Clay would probably return soon. In October, 1864, Virginia went to "Redcliffe," the Hammond plantation on Beech Island in the Savannah River. Sherman's approach sent her, late in January, 1865, to nearby Augusta, Georgia, from which point Howell Cobb escorted her to Macon. It was here that Clay caught up with her on February 10, 1865.[48]

For the next three months, Clement and Virginia Clay led an almost nomadic life. A large segment of the Confederacy's population was in motion, as each day the area that was safe from the enemy diminished in size. Communications were on the verge of collapse as the enemy cut rail lines, while the wet spring weather turned wagon roads into quagmires. During his week's sojourn in Macon, Clay was invited to address the Georgia legislature, but declined because he must hasten on to Richmond. At the same time, Lawson, writing from Richmond, warned him, "If you think it necessary to come on, do so at once; don't delay. Leave sister; don't undertake to bring her in the present uncertain condition of the Railroad connection between here & the Georgia line."

Clement and Virginia boarded "the cars" in Macon on February 18, 1865, and bumped over the hundred miles of line in operation to Washington, Georgia, where they stopped with the Toombs family. Beyond stretched 140 miles where rail transportation had ceased to exist. Clay went on alone in Robert Toombs' carriage the fifty-five miles to Abbeville, South Carolina, where at the house of Armistead Burt he was taken ill and decided to return to Washington, Georgia. Here, at Robert Toombs', Virginia nursed Clement through a monthlong illness.[49]

On March 25, 1865, Clay set out once more, this time on Toombs' "gray mare, attended by his servant Wallace." Two days of steady riding brought him to Newberry Court House. Here he

48 Virginia Clay, Diary, 1859-1866, entries for April 30—Nov. 3, 1864, John Withers to Virginia Clay, Sept. 27, 1864, S. R. Mallory to Virginia Clay, Sept. 27, 1864, Robert W. Brown to Virginia Clay, Oct. 1, 1864, H. L. Clay to Virginia Clay, Nov. 11, 1864, Clay MSS; Clay-Clopton, *Belle of the Fifties*, 207, 212, 231, 240f; Louise (Wigfall) Wright, *A Southern Girl in '61* (New York, 1905), 179.

49 J. W. Clay to Susanna Clay and Clay, Sr., March 28, 1865, H. L. Clay to Clay, Jr., Feb. 15, 1865, Clay, Jr., Diary, Jan. 31—March 29, 1865, Clay, Jr., holo. memoranda [ca. May 12, 1865], Clay MSS; Toombs to Stephens, March 16, 23, 1865, Toombs-Stephens-Cobb, *Correspondence*, II, 660f; Chesnut, *Diary from Dixie*, 473.

managed to hire an open wagon, which in three days slogged through the forty-two miles of mud to Chester, South Carolina, where he rested briefly and called on Mrs. Chesnut of *Diary from Dixie* fame. From here "the cars" still ran through to Richmond, 335 miles distant, with scarcely more than the customary wartime delays and changes. Clay left Chester on Friday, March 31, and reached Richmond at 2:30 P.M. on Sunday, April 2, a few hours after Davis had been called from church by the news that Lee could no longer hold the lines at Petersburg.

Clay delivered his dispatches and reports to Benjamin, and then hastened to Davis. He found that distracted man in the midst of packing clothes and archives. In the confusion, Clay did not record his activities for the remainder of that day, but he was one of the many passengers on the last evacuation train which left Richmond about eleven o'clock that night, carrying the heads of government, the archives, subordinate officials, and as many frightened citizens as could push their way into the overcrowded cars. It was not until five o'clock on Monday afternoon, April 3, that the train had covered the 140 miles to Danville, Virginia, where the government established itself for, as it turned out, only a week.[50]

His official obligations discharged, Clay felt no compelling reason to remain with the retreating government, and so after resting for four days with his cousin, Dr. Robert Enoch Withers, he pushed on to Charlotte, North Carolina, and after a few days to Chester, South Carolina, where on April 19 the news of Lee's surrender turned him "pale as a sheet." While with his friends Paul F. Hammond and James Ryder Randall in Augusta, Georgia, Clay first heard of Lincoln's assassination "& expressed my regret on ground that it would complicate our affairs, exacerbate the feelings of the North & render an adjustment of our differences more difficult." On May 1, 1865, the three Clay men, Lawson, Withers, and Clement, together with Virginia and Celeste, were

50 Clay, Jr., to Virginia Clay, March 26, 30, 1865, Clay, Jr., holo. memoranda [ca. May 12, 1865], Clay MSS; Chesnut, *Diary from Dixie*, 512; Clay-Clopton, *Belle of the Fifties*, 244f; Jones, *RWCD*, II, 465-67; Stephen Russell Mallory, "Unpublished Chapters of History: Last Days of the Confederate Government, from Papers Left by Stephen R. Mallory, Secretary of the Navy in the Confederate Cabinet," *McClure's Magazine*, XVI (Dec., 1900), 102-105; J. H. Averill, "Richmond, Virginia: The Evacuation of the City and the Days Preceding It," *SHSP*, XXV (1897), 267-69; Dallas D. Irvine, "The Fate of Confederate Archives," *AHR*, XLIV (July, 1939), 823-41; Alfred Jackson Hanna, *Flight into Oblivion* ([Richmond, Va.], 1938), 11, 15.

all gathered at Forsyth, Georgia. Here Clement, "contemplating a trip to a foreign country," gave Virginia a power of attorney to act for him in all business transactions and made out a hasty memorandum for her guidance. "My Deeds, Patents, Bonds, Notes & accounts," he noted were left at Macon. "Collect what is due if you can. . . . My clothes should be sold. . . . Sell everything you can for gold or silver. . . . You should sell every thing left—lands, houses, carriage, books &c, if you can."[51]

The next scene of the story took place at Lagrange, Georgia, where at Benjamin H. Hill's spacious home were gathered Clement and Virginia Clay, Louis and Charlotte Wigfall, Stephen and Angela Mallory, Thomas J. and Myra (Knox) Semmes, and some fifteen children and young people. Here Clay and Wigfall were perfecting their plans for a rapid journey to Texas, while all pored over maps and speculated on Davis' whereabouts and his prospects for escape. Preparing to return to Huntsville, Virginia Clay on May 10, 1865, drove to the Lagrange railroad station to inquire what kind of currency would purchase her ticket and to get the latest news from passengers on the incoming Atlanta train. A friend in the crowd thrust into her hand a newspaper with the flaming headline: "$360,000 REWARD! THE PRESIDENT OF THE UNITED STATES HAS ISSUED HIS PROCLAMATION announcing that the Bureau of Military Justice have reported upon indubitable evidence, that JEFFERSON DAVIS, CLEMENT CLAY, JACOB THOMPSON, GEORGE N. SAUNDERS: BEVERLEY TUCKER AND W. C. CLEARY, incited and concerted the Assassination of Mr. Lincoln and the attempt on Mr. Seward. He therefore offers for the arrest of Davis, Clay and Thompson, One Hundred Thousand Dollars each; for that of Saunders and Tucker, Twenty-five Thousand Dollars each, and for that of Cleary, Ten Thousand Dollars."[52]

A trembling and hysterical Virginia Clay rushed back to the Hill household, where Clay sat quietly reading Burton's *Anatomy*

[51] Clay, Jr., holo. memoranda [ca. May 12, 1865], "Memoranda for My Dear Wife," power of attorney, May 1, 2, 1865, Clay MSS; Robert Enoch Withers, *Autobiography of an Octogenarian* (Roanoke, Va., 1907), 214-17.

[52] Clay-Clopton, *Belle of the Fifties*, 246-50; Beverley Tucker, *Address of Beverley Tucker, Esq., to The People of the United States, 1865*, ed. by James Harvey Young (Atlanta, 1948). The frontispiece of this publication is a reproduction of the broadside here quoted. The original and only known copy is in the library of Emory University. It was printed and distributed from Athens, Ga., and dated May 9, 1865. Other broadsides of similar context were issued from other headquarters. That here quoted contains an error in the amount of reward offered; the correct amounts were $100,000 for Davis, and $25,000 each for Thompson and Clay.

of Melancholy. The appalling news sent all present into frightened protests and wild urgings of immediate flight. At this moment, Clay's old friend Philip Phillips arrived and shocked everyone into silence by asking, "Mr. Clay I wish that you would first tell me what you think you ought to do." Clay replied, "As I know myself to be entirely innocent of the foul charge my judgment is that I should at once surrender myself to Genl. Wilson." And to that officer, in command at Macon, Clay telegraphed, "Seeing the Proclamation of the President of the United States, I go today with Hon. P. Phillips, to deliver myself to your custody." Among the notes he made for his own defense was this: "I never saw or heard of Booth before he killed Lincoln, unless he had an assumed name, & never suggested or heard any one suggest the killing of L. Not a shadow of truthful evidence can be offered to implicate me with his murder."[53]

[53] Clay, Jr., to James H. Wilson, May 11, 1865, Clay, Jr., holo. memoranda [May 12, 1865], Clay MSS; Benjamin Harvey Hill to Andrew Johnson, Nov. 26, 1865, Andrew Johnson MSS; Philip Phillips to Virginia Clay, May 16, 1882, Philip Phillips MSS.

12 ~

The Prisoner of State

VIRGINIA CLAY was "heart stricken" and "confused with sorrow and dread" as she set out with Clement and Philip Phillips for Macon. The news that Jefferson Davis had been captured increased their gloom and apprehension, and caused Clay to exclaim that his own surrender had been a mistake. But it was too late to turn back, and after one day with friends in Macon, Clement and Virginia Clay were instructed by General James H. Wilson to be ready for departure on the evening of May 13, 1865. Through streets full of Union soldiers and sad-faced citizens, they drove to the railroad station, where they encountered two dilapidated vehicles, the first bearing Jefferson Davis, still erect and dignified in a new Confederate uniform, the second containing the four Davis children together with Mrs. Davis and her young sister. Alongside rode her brother and members of Davis' staff, Burton N. Harrison, William Preston Johnston, Francis R. Lubbock, and Postmaster General Reagan.

Aboard the train leaving Macon, the prisoners found themselves accompanied by a guard of three officers and twenty men. Sleep was only for the children during that weary all-night ride to Atlanta, where a special train with breakfast aboard was waiting to take them on to Augusta. Here a brief visit with friends was so fraught with hysteria that Clement and Virginia were glad of the necessity to hasten on. During the night, Alexander H. Stephens, General Joseph Wheeler, and four officers of his staff had been added to the party. As the prisoners drove to the Augusta wharves, one of the spectators was eight-year-old Woodrow Wilson.[1]

The prisoners found the small river steamer they now boarded devoid of all arrangements for their comfort. In the absence of even a chair, Jefferson Davis, now ill, sat on the floor, propped against luggage. The "rest of us," wrote Stephens, "were all crowded together in a small space on the deck. The night was cool, the air on the water damp. . . . Clay and I combined our cloaks, coats, shawls, etc.; General Wheeler sent us a blanket; Mrs. Davis sent us a mattress, and we made a joint bed in the open air on deck. I put the carpet-bags under our heads." The physical strain and mental anguish of recent weeks was beginning to tell on all. Clay and Stephens were in a semi-invalid state. Wheeler and his men had been captured when exhaustion forced them to stop for sleep in the Georgia woods. At Savannah all were transferred to a more commodious boat, and at Hilton Head to the *William P. Clyde,* under escort of the sloop-of-war *Tuscarora.* It was now the afternoon of May 16, 1865.

Three days later the *Clyde* anchored off Fortress Monroe, Virginia, in lower Chesapeake Bay. The journey had been rough, and nearly everyone except Clay had been seasick. Prisoners and guards all thought they were going to Washington for immediate trial, but now it turned out otherwise, as the War Department made a hasty policy. One by one the prisoners were transferred to other vessels and sent on their way to the various forts, until only Clay and Davis remained. Fortress Monroe was their destination. This bastion, on the tip of Old Point Comfort, had stone walls over 30 feet in height, 95 feet thick at the foundation, and 50 feet thick at a higher level where 94 casemates (chambers in the walls) provided space for troops and gun emplacements. Surrounding the walls was a moat 8 feet deep and up to 150 feet wide.[2]

[1] Myra Knox Semmes to Sister Bernard, May [12], 1865, Marie D — — to Virginia Clay, May 17, 1865, Clay MSS; Philip Phillips to Virginia Clay, May 16, 1882, Philip Phillips MSS; Benjamin D. Pritchard to Stanton, May 25, 1865, *O.R.,* I, xlix, pt. 1, p. 537; *Jefferson Davis, Constitutionalist,* VII, 1-19; Ray Stannard Baker, *Woodrow Wilson: Life and Letters* (Garden City, N. Y., 1925-1927, 6 vols.), I, 52; Clay-Clopton, *Belle of the Fifties,* 246-379 (these pages cover the entire story of this chapter; hence this work will not be cited again).

[2] Alexander H. Stephens, *Recollections of Alexander H. Stephens: His Diary Kept when a Prisoner at Fort Warren, Boston Harbour, 1865,* ed. by Myrta Lockett Avary (New York, 1910), 111-24 (cited hereinafter as Stephens, *Diary*); Pritchard to Stanton, May 25, 1865, *O.R.,* I, xlix, pt. 1, p. 537; Joseph Wheeler, "An Effort to Rescue Jefferson Davis," *Century Magazine,* LVI (May, 1898), 88; Chester D. Bradley, "Dr. Craven and the Prison Life of Jefferson Davis," *Virginia Magazine of History and Biography,* LXII (Jan., 1954), 51.

At one o'clock on Monday, May 22, 1865, General Nelson A. Miles came aboard to take the two "arch-conspirators and traitors" into that fort. Clement and Virginia had their leavetaking in private, and Virginia did not appear on deck. The Davis family had a more public parting, during which "he exhibited no great emotion, though he was violently affected." Assistant Secretary of War Charles A. Dana, on hand to witness the event, reported the arrival of the prisoners: a guard detachment "was followed by General Miles, holding Davis by the right arm. Next came half a dozen soldiers, and then Colonel Pritchard with Clay, and last the guard. . . . The arrangements were excellent . . . and not a single curious spectator was anywhere in sight. Davis bore himself with a haughty attitude. His face was somewhat flushed, but his features were composed and his step firm. In Clay's manner there was less expression of bravado and dramatic determination. Both were dressed in gray, with drab slouched hats."

At this point the desolation among the women, still aboard the *Clyde,* was complete. Varina Davis gave way to uncontrolled weeping. Virginia Clay however refused to shed tears before a Yankee and put up a much braver front than Varina could manage at this time. Orders respecting them had already been issued. They read, "The women and children, constituting the family of Davis, and Mrs. Clay are not prisoners . . . and . . . will be sent . . . in the steamer Clyde . . . to Savannah, Ga. . . . The baggage, rooms, beds, and persons of the passengers . . . will be thoroughly searched and all papers retained. After the Clyde leaves here the ladies and children will be under no restraint, and on reaching Savannah will be left at perfect liberty."

On the morning of May 23, two gaudily dressed women came aboard to conduct the search of "baggage, rooms, . . . and persons." Even this trying situation did not daunt Virginia Clay, who calmly twirled a pistol while the investigator tumbled the contents from trunks and satchels, with many a comment on the variety and quality of "rebel" clothing, particularly some borrowed French lingerie that had come through the blockade. Then came the personal search, as the inquisitor removed Virginia's clothing piece by piece, examining each minutely. With her corsets the next garment to be removed, Virginia's mischievous spirit took over. The day was sultry; and already perspiration had streaked the investigator's lavishly applied cosmetics. By taking a deep breath and holding it, Virginia made removal of the corsets impossible. Her inquisitor struggled, pried, took time out to fan, and tried again. Finally both women were worn out with the game, the search was finished, and then Virginia forced the investigator to dress her. When Virginia went to see how the others had fared, she found Varina Davis weeping, humiliated, and unclad.[3]

The journey back to Savannah was full of alarms, discomforts, and seasickness, in addition to the mental anguish that beset both women. Besides the care of her four children, Varina Davis now had to nurse her sister, who was seriously ill. Virginia helped as best she could with these responsibilities. The *Clyde* was now filled with released prisoners of war and Negroes, an alarming assortment to women who had never before traveled without proper masculine escort. They soon learned to be thankful for the Union soldiers stationed as guards near their cabins. The "perfect liberty" promised them on reaching Savannah turned out to be liberty to scramble up the steep riverbank as best they could, bag, baggage, and children. No advance notice of their arrival had been permitted, and they were not allowed to send for carriages to meet them. News of their coming circulated through the city quickly, however, and friends and sympathizers soon flocked to them. Mrs. Davis spent most of the summer in Savannah, under some surveillance, and cooped up in one or two hotel rooms, with her children subjected to the taunts of thoughtless or vengeful Union soldiers.[4]

Virginia remained for two weeks with friends in Savannah, then went on to Augusta and Macon, where she sought advice as to her future course of action. In the meantime, she sent off to the North many letters to old friends asking their help in Clement's defense, and waited, often in vain because of disrupted mail service, for replies. Finally, on August 21, 1865, Virginia came once more to Huntsville, after an absence of nearly three years. She returned to chaos and destruction and to more responsibility than she had ever

[3] Dana to Stanton, May 22, 1865, Stanton to Halleck, May 21, 1865, Halleck to Miles, May 22, 1865, *O.R.*, II, viii, 562, 564, 566; Eron Rowland, *Varina Howell, Wife of Jefferson Davis* (New York, 1931, 2 vols.), II, 446-53.

[4] Martha Levy to Virginia Clay, June 27, July 12, 1865, Virginia Clay to Ben Wood, Aug. 4, 1865, Clay MSS; Arthur Marvin Shaw (ed.), "My Dearest Friend: A Letter from Mrs. Jefferson Davis" [to William Preston Johnston, Oct. 3, 1865], *Southwest Review*, XXXIII (Spring, 1948), 137-40; *Jefferson Davis, Constitutionalist,* VII, 44-48; John Joseph Craven, *Prison Life of Jefferson Davis* (New York, 1866), 331-48.

before known. She found "Our poor old parents . . . very feeble
& helpless. . . . Father . . . at times confined to his bed . . . I
devote myself to him, . . . making his toddy, or mixing his medicine, keeping off flies, or refreshing him with cologne." "I will,"
she assured Clement, "try to evoke order out of chaos & will leave
nothing undone to promote the comfort of our poor old parents."

As for other members of the family, Virginia wrote that "Bro
W.[ithers] is doing nothing. . . . Sister Mary looks thin, but is
well. Works like a trojan . . . teaching." Lawson, who had just
visited his father, had returned to Georgia. "His house," Virginia
reported, "was completely destroyed. He sold his furniture & every
thing he could. Neither of yr. bros: have any tho't of attempting
to work freedmen and women. The place is for rent." After
detailing news of their former slaves, Virginia summed up the
situation thus: "There is no crop on the place, but a good many
of the negroes have asked & obtained permission to live in the
houses, being homeless. . . . It amuses and distresses me to see
your photograph stuck up in all the negro houses I enter. It is
a singular commentary on the times."

Regarding their own property, Virginia added, "The Freed-
man's Bureau is in your office, *all* your property is confiscated . . .
& I am really afraid to say my soul is my own for fear some vile
negro will report it . . . for confiscation. Our house & my baggage
has been so repeatedly searched, that I asked, & have obtained,
from Gen. G[rierson] an exemption from such further indignity."

The search for Clay's papers, begun at the time of his surrender,
had been unsuccessful until August, 1865, when President Johnson
sent the notorious Lafayette C. Baker, head of the secret service, to
"seize . . . and bring to Washington, all correspondence, papers,
and documents belonging to Clement C. Clay." Arrived at Huntsville, the callous Baker found the infirmities of the elder Clays so
pathetic that even he had "never so reluctantly obeyed an order
as the one to search this house." But his search was unrewarding,
and so he hastened on to Macon, where he found Virginia Clay's
trunks and examined them in her absence, taking all the papers
he found. The one item he missed was the small black notebook
containing copies of Clay's dispatches from Canada.[5]

[5] Virginia Clay to Clay, Jr., Sept. 3, Nov. 3, 1865, Clay MSS; Lafayette C. Baker,
History of the United States Secret Service (Philadelphia, 1867), 565.

For the next few months Virginia Clay struggled with a situation bordering on destitution. The plantation yielded neither cotton nor food; the family's major investment, Memphis and Charleston Railroad stock, was worth no more than half its face value and not readily convertible into cash; and it was impossible to collect anything on debts long since due. Actually, the most likely source of income was to rent rooms to officials of the occupation. Amid all these difficulties, even more trouble lay ahead for the Clays. On January 1, 1866, Susanna Clay was stricken with apoplexy and died the next morning. "Her life," wrote Mary Clay, "had become a weary burden to her; mortified pride, disappointed ambition, loss of fortune & the crowning sorrow that broke her heart Bro. C's imprisonment were too much for her feeble frame."

Since Virginia Clay had gone to Washington to work for Clement's release, Mary and Withers saw "no way now but for us to live with Father." Lawson (in Huntsville for his mother's funeral) took a gloomy view of this arrangement. "I think the children annoy father," he wrote, "they are very boisterous rude & undisciplined—& he is too feeble . . . to be harassed by the tumult of children running hither & thither, slamming doors or leaving them open . . . always talking, laughing or crying." Mary Clay's description of her household was somewhat different: "Withers & myself sleep in Father's room & W. takes care of him. . . . We place his chair before the fire & have every thing convenient for him. W. makes a bright fire for him & either he or I make his toddy. We have nice mackerel & cheese for him & vary the fare with good steak & hash."

A week later, on January 26, 1866, Father Clay "was stricken with paralysis of the limbs & arms & for 10 or 12 days Withers was obliged to nurse him like a babe. It is providential," continued Mary Clay, "that Withers is not in business for every moment of his time was demanded by Father." And, she added, the "chess board" over which Withers had sat while his wife supported the family "has not been seen for two months, grief for his mother the one best beloved on earth by him & care of an invalid Father have been sure preventives to any kind of pleasure." Not only was there little pleasure in the Clay household; for a time the diet was so poor that "several of the children & I," wrote Withers, "have had . . . a touch of scurvy, from deficiency of vegetable food, pickle & fruits, the Drs. say . . . the complaint is very prevalent."[6]

Over this sea of trouble hung the all-pervading and ever-present pall of "fearful forebodings" about the prisoners. The wave of vindictiveness that gripped the North, the summary trial and execution of Lincoln's assassins, and the popular clamor that Davis be hanged were circumstances not calculated to be reassuring to Virginia Clay and Varina Davis. Along with many other Confederate women, they were left prey to their wildest fears and apprehensions while their husbands were held incommunicado in distant Union forts.

But what of the prisoners themselves? Clay and Davis each occupied "the inner room of a casemate," its window being "heavily barred." Three doors, each guarded by two or more sentries, separated them from liberty, while the rooms on either side were filled with guards, and outside three lines of sentries provided further security. The officer of the guard was under orders "to see his prisoners every fifteen minutes" and to aid him a "lamp is constantly kept burning in each of the rooms." Each prisoner had a hospital bed, a chair, a table, a Bible, and "soldiers' rations, cooked by the guard." Further orders were: "No person will be permitted to communicate with the prisoners verbally or in writing. No sentinel will be permitted to speak to them or to answer any questions." Under these regulations Clay and Davis had entered Fortress Monroe as prisoners of state. On the following morning, May 23, 1865, General Miles had iron fetters placed on Davis' ankles, ostensibly for adequate security while the wooden doors leading to the casemate were replaced with others of grated iron. So great was the public outcry at this indignity that Stanton himself ordered the fetters removed, which was done on May 28.[7]

"Owing to the delicate health . . . of the prisoner Clay," Surgeon John Joseph Craven at the end of June requested modification of the most stringent regulations. He put both Clay and Davis on a hospital diet, having their meals prepared in his own kitchen. Each prisoner was now allowed a spoon, but no knife or fork, "lest he should commit suicide." The presence of

[6] H. L. Clay to Virginia Clay, Sept. 20, 1865, Jan. 14, 1866, Mary Clay to Virginia Clay, Jan. 1, 2, 21, Feb. 12, 1865, J. W. Clay to Virginia Clay, Nov. 25, 1865, Clay MSS.

[7] Special Orders No. 3, May 24, 1865, Clay MSS; Dana to Stanton, May 22, 1865, Stanton to Miles, May 28, 1865, Miles to Stanton, May 28, 1865, *O.R.*, II, viii, 564f, 577; Craven, *Prison Life of Jefferson Davis,* 33-66.

two guards constantly in the cell with him was the greatest annoyance Clay had to endure. The changing of these guards every two hours, with the resultant noise of clanging doors, voices, boots, and arms clattering on stone floors, so disturbed Clay's sleep that he was soon in a state of "nervous prostration." To alleviate this condition, the guards were withdrawn to stations just outside the cell door, and Clay was allowed to walk for an hour a day in the open air (under guard of course). But, as he wrote to Stanton, "I experience little relief, if any. The opening of the outer door & entry of six men & exit of six men every two hours arouse me, if asleep, & I am often awakened at other times by unavoidable noises in the front room. . . . I rarely get half the sleep I need, & then only by the use of medicine." In September he again became so feeble that the guard was further removed to the corridor. The beneficial result Clay noted in his prayer book: "Sept. 15, 65. Slept last night about 6 hours. without waking. More than I have any night during my 116 nights in this prison." Not until the end of July did Clay and Davis see each other, when they were permitted to shake hands. By early August, Clay's privileges were further enlarged. He could now have any book of a "religious character," and he received the first newspapers he had seen since May—carefully selected, as he thought, for their paucity of news. As autumn approached, warmer and drier quarters for the prisoners became necessary. First- and second-floor rooms in the officers' quarters of Carroll Hall were prepared, and in October, Clay and Davis moved into that building. The new arrangement meant, however, that guards were again stationed just outside the doors.[8]

Aboard the *Clyde* on May 22, 1865, Virginia had the promise of General Miles to keep her informed of Clement's health and condition. On June 8 she sent him a note begging him to keep that promise. His reply of June 20, assuring her that Clay was well, did not reach Virginia until late July. Meantime, she had appealed to General Wilson at Macon for information and for any mail that might have been addressed to his care. He could only assure her that Clay was still at Fortress Monroe. Virginia then

[8] Clay, Jr., to Stanton, Aug. 19, 1865, E. M. Stanton MSS, vol. 28, no. 55561; Clay, Jr., to Virginia Clay, Aug. 11, 21, 1865, Clay MSS; Clay, Jr., notations in Jay's *Family Prayers*, Ada Sterling MSS; *O.R.*, II, viii, 744, 767; Craven, *Prison Life of Jefferson Davis*, 223; Dorris, *Pardon and Amnesty under Lincoln and Johnson*, 263-71.

wrote again to General Miles, who on July 29 replied that her husband was well, and added, "You may be reassured he will not be allowed to suffer while within the limits of my command." Thus more than two months passed before Virginia had any news of Clement's welfare other than such scraps of unreliable information as she could glean from the newspapers.

In mid-August, Miles transmitted to the War Department "two letters from Mrs. C. C. Clay, one addressed to myself and one to Clay. I desire to know if Mr. Clay can be permitted to read the one addressed to him." Two days later Stanton granted such permission, and so it was that thirteen weeks after he had entered Fortress Monroe, Clement received Virginia's letter of July 27. Regulations issued on August 18 stipulated that Clay's and Davis' letters to their wives "must relate only to family matters and be first submitted to the Attorney-General's inspection." Under these restrictions Clement wrote five letters to Virginia during the remainder of 1865. In these inspected letters he soft-pedaled all complaints and spoke kindly of his jailors. Even so, his second letter was returned for deletion of some objectionable passages.

Like many another prisoner, Clay soon found other means of communication. In the course of a few months he had made friends with some of the officers of his guard and ultimately felt he could trust them. Surgeon Craven, too, was distinctly sympathetic, and during a short visit to Richmond in September, he called on Clay's cousin, Thomas Withers, who was thereafter in a position to send the prisoner occasional parcels of food and clothing, and to give Virginia recent and accurate news of Clement's health. Indeed, Craven was relieved as post surgeon because he presumed to order an overcoat for Jefferson Davis without authorization from superior officers. The regiment on guard at the fort went out of service early in November, 1865. At that time a friendly officer took out a letter from Clement to Virginia, other officers wrote to her shortly thereafter giving her news of Clement, and several of them promised "to try to get him parolled." In this smuggled letter Clay described General Miles as "a low born & low bred Yankee, from Mass., without learning, sensibility, or sentiment."[9]

9 N. A. Miles to Virginia Clay, July 29, 1865, Virginia Clay to Clay, Jr., July 27, 1865, Clay, Jr., to Virginia Clay, Aug. 21, Sept. 18, Oct. 25, 1865, Clay MSS; E. D. Townsend to N. A. Miles, Aug. 18, 1865, *O.R.*, II, viii, 719; Bradley, "Dr. Craven and the Prison Life of Jefferson Davis," 54.

Early in August, Clay received permission to write Virginia a letter to be delivered only in case of his death. In it he set down his most solemn thoughts on his own situation and the troubles of the times. "God bears me witness," he wrote, "that I am unconscious of having committed any crime against the U. S. . . . & that I feel . . . I have done my duty as a servant of the State of Ala.—to whom alone I owed allegiance—both before & since she seceded from the Federal Union. I have not changed my opinion as to the sovereignty of the States & the right of a state to secede; . . . I think the utter subversion of our political & social systems & sudden enfranchisement of 4.000.000 slaves a great crime & one of the most terrible calamities that ever befel any people; that generations yet unborn will feel it in sorrow & suffering. . . . Had I forseen this, I should, doubtless, have been in favor of enduring lesser evils & wrongs from the North & postponing this calamity, for it would have come, . . . but perhaps not in our day. I never doubted, as we had no children, that our interest would be best served by preserving the old Union, under which I might have enjoyed wealth & honor all my life. I felt that I was acting against my own interest in favoring secession, but tho't it my duty to my State & the South. Hence I have nothing to reproach myself for as to my course in that respect." He advised Virginia that "you had best make yr. home in some city or large town, where the white population prevails." He ended the first installment of his letter on a religious note: "I have studied the Bible, searched my own heart & reviewed my life more earnestly, prayerfully & anxiously than in all my days before coming in here." Later sections of the letter, dated September 10 and October 16, of a less exalted tone, reviewed the conditions of his imprisonment and the feebleness of his health, but, he continued, the "great improvement in my health since I was allowed to sleep encourages the belief that I can bear a great deal more.— Thank God, I think, with His help, I can even live thro' 5 months more of such torture as I have endured. I think," he speculated, "they would let me out, if I would beg pardon; but, as I am conscious of no crime, I cannot do it. . . . I fear it is a devilish spirit, but I have been reluctant to humble myself to men whom I regarded as criminals far more than myself touching all the woes & wrongs, the destruction & desolation of the South." In a hasty conclusion, he wrote on October 16, "I avail myself of a chance to send you these sheets, lest they should never reach you, if I die in prison. I must impress on you the propriety of *concealing this communication . . . & never alluding to it.*"[10]

Virginia Clay lost no time in beginning her appeals to friends and officials in behalf of Clay. Aboard the *Clyde* returning to Savannah, Virginia wrote at least six letters. Her first, to Joseph Holt pleading for a *"fair & impartial trial,"* closed with an appeal to the "heavenly spirit" of his "angelic wife" and to the "memory of that happy & hallowed time when you esteemed my husband all that was noble, true & brave." She did not then know that war hatred had changed this onetime friend into a vicious, vengeful Radical. She appealed to Ben Wood to "influence . . . public opinion favorably towards all the prisoners now held by Federal power." As legal counsel for Clay, she sought the aid of several prominent men: Thomas W. Pierce of Boston, Charles O'Conor of New York, James Mandeville Carlisle of Washington, Jeremiah Sullivan Black of Pennsylvania, and George Shea of New York, junior counsel and protege of Horace Greeley. Virginia had written her letters, but how could she get them mailed? As she sat in her cabin pondering this problem, a passing Union soldier tossed in a bit of paper on which was written, "I will mail your letters. Trust me." When the *Clyde* stopped at Hilton Head, Virginia slipped him the letters with a gold coin to pay for postage. Some hours later the coin was tossed back, landing squarely on her berth, and her campaign to free Clement was under way.[11]

Some of Virginia's letters sped north in no more than a week; others required nearly a month. The prompt and sympathetic replies did not reach her at Macon until late July and early August. Meantime, Black and O'Conor had offered their services as counsel for Davis and Clay. Their applications to see their clients were refused by the War Department and the attorney general. This reduced their efforts "to mere professional preparation for the possible but by no means certain event" of a trial.

10 Clay, Jr., to Virginia Clay, Aug. 11, 1865, Clay MSS.
11 Virginia Clay to Joseph Holt, May 23, 1865, Joseph Holt MSS; Virginia Clay to Benjamin Wood, May 27, 1865, Douglas Southall Freeman (ed.), *Calendar of Confederate Papers* (Richmond, 1908), 440; Virginia Clay to George Shea, May 27, 1865, Virginia Clay to Thomas W. Pierce, May 29, 1865, Virginia Clay to J. S. Black, May 29, 1865, Clay MSS; Joseph Cyrillus Walsh, "Charles O'Conor," American-Irish Historical Society *Journal*, XXVII (1928), 285-313; Brigance, *Black*, 158f.

Indeed, all five of the legal counsel agreed that no "attempt will be made to try Mr. Clay or any other of the Southern leaders on the charge of complicity in the Assassination of Lincoln." O'Conor accurately predicted that the Confederate leaders "may be obliged to suffer imprisonment until it shall be determined, as a matter of policy, whether they ought to be tried for treason and, as a matter of fact, whether they can be convicted of that offence. . . . Even if convicted of treason I do not believe that any of them will ever suffer the penalty prescribed." "If there be any good sense" in the government, he added, "the project of trying these gentlemen for any offence on account of their participation in the late War, will ere long be abandoned." These reassurances were no more than cold comfort to an emotional and impatient woman like Virginia Clay, who believed that if she were just in Washington she could accomplish Clement's release immediately.[12]

Meantime, other friends were speaking out in behalf of Clay and Davis. From their Canadian sanctuary, Beverley Tucker and George N. Sanders immediately denounced Johnson's proclamation of May 2, 1865, as "a living, burning lie." James Murray Mason from London and later Jacob Thompson from Halifax wrote offering to meet all expenses incurred in Davis' defense. Clay's friends, S. N. Salomon and Richard Jacobs Haldeman, appealed to Robert J. Walker and Thaddeus Stevens, both of whom later used their influence to hasten Clay's release. Virginia Clay subsequently enlisted the aid of other prominent northern men. Her first goal, however, was to get to Washington. Since "arch-rebels" were not yet free to travel everywhere, Virginia asked her old friend Duff Green and his son Ben. E. Green to seek a permit for her to visit Washington. Ben Green had to cool his heels repeatedly in White House corridors before being told that "an application for permission to visit Washington made by Mrs. C. C. Clay over her own name will be considered."

Virginia received this information on September 16, 1865, and that same day sent off her most heart-rending appeal to Andrew

12 Dates of the replies were: Carlisle, June 11, Wood, June 15, Pierce, June 16, 21, O'Conor, June 29, Shea, July 3, Black, July 3, 1865, Clay MSS; O'Conor to Black, June 7, July 1, 1865, Black to Andrew Johnson, July 3, 1865, J. S. Black MSS; O'Conor to Jefferson Davis, July 2, 1865, E. D. Townsend to Black, July 26, 1865, *O.R.*, II, viii, 634, 712; James Speed to O'Conor, July 6, 1865, O'Conor to J. M. Mason, July 9, 1865, J. M. Mason MSS; Charles M. Blackford, "The Trials and Trial of Jefferson Davis," *SHSP*, XXIX (1901), 54; Roy Franklin Nichols, "United States vs. Jefferson Davis, 1865-1869," *AHR*, XXXI (Jan., 1926), 266-84.

Johnson. "Months ago," she wrote, "*I* wd have presented myself to you, to beg to be allowed to visit my husband, & to sue for his release. But wiser heads & riper judgments than mine, assured me that *no appeal* in behalf of Mr. Clay, wd be considered by you, until *after some disposition* of Mr. Davis's case. I have waited, for nearly four long months . . . in vain! . . . I wd hurry to Washington instantly to prefer this request in *person,* but for lack of means to expend in what might prove a fruitless journey. . . . Say that I can see my husband . . . or give me one hope of his release & I will fly to you, with words & tears of grateful thanks for yr justice magnanimity & clemency."

At the end of three weeks, impatient Virginia asked Ben Green to ascertain whether the President had received her letter. He had, but with his customary indecision and procrastination, Johnson had not yet acted on it. And so, Ben Green continued, "My advice is to come on at once & see the President in person. . . . 'Tis said that the President likes the opportunity of granting personal favors direct to the parties on their own application—That he don't like intermediaries—and that the ladies never fail with him."

By November 1, 1865, Virginia had decided to follow this advice, despite warnings of probable failure from family and friends. A Huntsville merchant advanced her one hundred dollars in gold and silk for a new dress. Thus prepared, Virginia set out about November 13, 1865, in the company of William Echols and two other Huntsville neighbors. They traveled by way of Nashville, where Virginia's thoughts went back to her schooldays there twenty-five years before. Thence to Louisville she rode for the first time in a sleeping car, an event the more memorable because she found that a raccoon had already gone to sleep in her berth. Major Echols had to be called to remove the intruder. Because her escorts knew "*all* the R. R. men," Virginia reported, "I have paid literally nothing thus far." From Louisville the party proceeded by boat. A stopover in Cincinnati enabled Virginia to see her old friends, the George H. Pendletons.[13]

13 Beverley Tucker, *Address of Beverley Tucker, Esq., to the People of the United States, 1865,* p. 26; Mason to O'Conor, June 19, 1865, J. M. Mason MSS; Thompson to Black, Sept. 2, 1865, J. S. Black MSS; Salomon to Virginia Clay, June 30, 1865, R. J. Haldeman to Virginia Clay, June 28, 1865, B. E. Green to Virginia Clay, Sept. 5, Oct. 21, 1865, Duff Green to Andrew Johnson, Sept. 5, 1865, Virginia Clay to Susanna Clay, Nov. 15, 1865, Clay MSS; Virginia Clay to B. E. Green, Sept. 16, Oct. 7, 1865, Duff Green MSS; Virginia Clay to Andrew Johnson, Sept. 16, 1865, Johnson MSS, vol. 77.

It was November 17, 1865, when Virginia Clay once again set foot in Washington. She went immediately to Willard's Hotel, where many old friends flocked to see her, for the capital was full of Southerners seeking pardons and other favors. Virginia lost no time in requesting an interview with President Johnson. During her first week in Washington, she conferred with J. S. Black, Judge James Hughes, Frederick Aiken (counsel for Mrs. Surratt), and no less a personage than General Grant himself. He greeted her sympathetically, assured her of his belief in Clay's innocence, and proved his good will on the spot by writing to the President:

"As it has been my habit heretofore to intercede for the release of all prisoners who I thought could be safely left at large, either on parole or by amnesty, I now respectfully recommend the release of Mr. C. C. Clay.

"The manner of Mr. Clay's surrender I think is a full guarantee that if released on parole to appear when called for, either for trial or otherwise, that he will be forthcoming . . . so . . . I respectfully recommend that C. C. Clay, now a state prisoner, be released on parole."

Virginia's first interview with the President, on November 22, 1865, was enlivened by the unexpected assistance of beauteous Adele Douglas, widow of Stephen A. Douglas. Virginia opened the assault with a stream of arguments for Clement's immediate release or speedy trial, together with pleas that she be allowed to see him. Johnson managed to remain noncommittal, whereupon Adele Douglas burst into tears and threw herself at his feet, urging Virginia to do likewise. Not even to free Clement could Virginia bring herself to kneel before Andrew Johnson, whom she contemned for his lowly background, his unionist beliefs, and now for his lack of resolution. The uneasy President managed to edge these emotional females out of his office and pass them on to Stanton.

At the War Department, Virginia waited in haughty silence until Stanton sought her out. She repeated her arguments in Clement's behalf, to which Stanton replied, "I am not your husband's judge. . . . Neither am I his accuser!" Attaching much importance to these disclaimers, Virginia promised to repeat them to the President, and ended her only interview with the secretary of war. A few days later, armed with Grant's letter, Virginia went again to the President, high with hope that this precious document would open prison doors. But Johnson's defenses held firm, as she learned from his secretary who informed her that "the Pres't has the letter of Gen'l Grant. No action has yet been had—I will bring the matter before the Pres't during the day and will advise you."[14]

With affairs at this stalemate, Virginia went off to New York to enlist aid from sympathizers there. "I met hosts of friends in N. Y.," she reported, "as the N. Y. Hotel is the rendezvous for rebels. . . . Hospitalities without number were proferred. And, will you believe it, thousands of dollars!" She conferred with O'Conor and Shea, and had from Horace Greeley a personal promise of sympathetic publicity in the *Tribune*. The *Herald's* James Gordon Bennett grudgingly agreed to "take the subject in hand." When Virginia returned to Washington on December 10, she could only write to Clement that "fortitude & patience must be yet further taxed. But I am *very hopeful* still my darling, & will you know, leave no avenue of assistance untried."

The first tangible result of her efforts came at Christmas, when Johnson gave Virginia an order permitting her to visit Clement. Enroute to Fortress Monroe, Virginia found another sympathetic friend in the Yankee steamboat captain who ordered his line to "pass free Mrs. C. C. Clay, rooms and meals included, to all points as she wishes." Arriving at the fortress in the chill blackness of a winter morning, Virginia waited at the wharf office for daylight, when two officers in an "ambulance" drove her to headquarters. General Miles was courteous, examined her order from the President, and asked her to wait. She declined a proffered breakfast, remarking that she would have that meal with her husband. As the morning wore on, Virginia waited with outward patience, but mounting inward dismay. In her state of nervous distress she was unable to eat the lunch brought her at noon. At every opportunity she pleaded with Miles to allow her to go to Clement. As her hysteria and weeping increased, Miles was apologetic but adamant, refusing even to let her send a telegram to the President.

Meanwhile, the ever-timorous Miles was keeping the wires busy while he asked Stanton whether the President's order should be

[14] U. S. Grant to Andrew Johnson, Nov. 26, 1865, Johnson MSS; Robert Johnson to Virginia Clay, Nov. 30, 1865, Virginia Clay to Clay, Jr., Dec. 10, 1865, Clay MSS; Sister Marie Perpetua Hayes, "Adele Cutts, Second Wife of Stephen A. Douglas," *Catholic Historical Review*, XXXI (July, 1945), 180-91.

honored. Finally authorization came through, and late in the afternoon Miles sent Virginia to Carroll Hall for her long-awaited reunion with Clement. The few hours they had together were all too short for the torrent of news Virginia had to pour out. She had brought with her various documents and notes which she left for Clement's later perusal. Back in Washington, Virginia indignantly told the President how his order had been ignored. He now assured her that such an incident would not occur again and that she was free to visit Clement whenever she wished. During her second visit in the last week of January, 1866, Virginia had time to discuss in detail with Clement her future efforts for his release. She now also enjoyed the hospitality of Mrs. George Cooper, southern wife of the new "Black Republican" post surgeon.[15]

During these seven months of imprisonment, Clay and Davis had been kept in complete ignorance of the evidence against them. Even as they disappeared within the confines of Fortress Monroe, the military commission was hearing testimony designed to prove that Lincoln's assassins had been "incited and encouraged thereunto by Jefferson Davis, George N. Sanders, Beverly Tucker, Jacob Thompson, William C. Cleary, Clement C. Clay, George Harper, George Young, and others unknown."[16] The panic and hysteria that gripped the country upon Lincoln's assassination is something impossible now to comprehend. In the crisis, control of the government fell, actually, into the hands of Edwin M. Stanton, described by one prominent Confederate as a "spy under Buchanan, a tyrant under Lincoln, and a traitor to Johnson." Cer-

15 Virginia Clay to Susanna Clay and Clay, Sr., Dec. 10, 1865, Horace Greeley to Virginia Clay, Dec. 8, 1865, R. B. Rhett, Jr., to Virginia Clay, Dec. 19, 1865, Virginia Clay to Clay, Jr., Dec. 10, 1865, Clay MSS.
16 The military commission to try Lincoln's assassins was established by Presidential proclamation on May 1, 1865; the trial opened on May 10 and concluded on June 29. Part of the testimony, especially that relating to Clay and the other Confederates, was taken in secret, but it leaked to the press and was published in New York newspapers, June 5-7, 1865. By the end of 1865, several versions of the proceedings appeared in book form. Most important are these three: *The Assassination of President Lincoln and the Trial of the Conspirators*, comp. by Benn Pitman, recorder to the commission (Cincinnati, 1865) (cited hereinafter as Pitman, *Conspiracy Trial*); *The Trial of the Assassins and Conspirators at Washington City, D. C., May and June, 1865*, by correspondents and reporters of the Philadelphia *Daily Inquirer* (Philadelphia, [1865]) (often referred to as the Associated Press or Peterson edition); *Conspiracy Trial for the Murder of the President*, ed. by Ben: Perley Poore (Boston, 1865, 3 vols.) (referred to as the Poore edition). Secondary accounts are those by David Miller DeWitt: *The Judicial Murder of Mary E. Surratt* (Baltimore, 1895); *The Impeachment and Trial of Andrew Johnson, Seventeenth President of the United States: A History* (New York, 1903); *The Assassination of Abraham Lincoln and Its Expiation* (New York, 1909).

tainly Stanton's violent and excitable temperament ill fitted him
to cope with an emergency demanding steadfastness and caution.
That the assassination was a vast conspiracy, the last desperate
blow of a dying Confederate government, was a natural suspicion.
In Stanton's inflamed mind however, suspicion hardened into
absolute conviction, and on that basis he operated with ruthless
energy.[17] He sent out Lafayette C. Baker, armed with all the
resources of the War Department, to round up suspects. Joseph
Holt's Bureau of Military Justice swung into action, offering
rewards for evidence to prove existence of the conspiracy he and
Stanton already believed in. To Holt's office flocked hundreds
of witnesses who swore to mountains of testimony.

Testimony concerning Clay and the other Confederates fell into
three categories: that taken between April 20 and May 3, 1865, on
which Johnson's proclamation of May 2 was based; that given
between May 12 and June 27, 1865, during the trial of Lincoln's
assassins; evidence gathered during the remainder of 1865. First
to testify were Richard Montgomery and James B. Merritt, who
rushed to Washington before the end of April. They were soon
joined by Sanford Conover, who later brought in many other
witnesses. They all told a story of Confederate conspiracy to
assassinate and to carry out other desperate exploits. From their
voluminous testimony, Holt compiled his own report, designed
to prove that Clay, resident in Canada during 1864, in "intimate
association with Jacob Thompson, Cleary, Sanders, and others
. . . engaged in maturing treasonable enterprises in violation of
the laws . . . of . . . war." Thompson was equally guilty, for
he had declared that he could "have the tyrant Lincoln . . . put
out of the way [and] would not consider it a crime when done for
the cause of the Confederacy." And Clay declared, "That is so;
we are all . . . ready to go any lengths . . . to serve our cause."
A witness had later observed Clay in "confidential conversation"
with Lewis Payne, "the conspirator [who] attempted the life of
Secretary Seward." In February, 1865, Clay "was present at a
meeting of prominent rebels at Montreal" when "a letter from

---

[17] Richard Taylor, *Destruction and Reconstruction: Personal Experiences of the
Late War*, ed. by Richard B. Harwell (New York, 1955), 295; William H. Crook,
*Through Five Administrations: Reminiscences of Colonel William H. Crook, Body-
Guard to President Lincoln* (New York, 1910), 35f; Frank Burt Friedell, *Francis
Lieber, Nineteenth Century Liberal* (Baton Rouge, 1947), 370-75.

Jefferson Davis was read by Sanders [expressing] approbation of
. . . the making away with President Lincoln." "The end would
justify the means," Clay reportedly said, while of a later corroboration, Thompson presumably said, "this makes the thing all right."
Another witness saw at Clay's house in St. Catherines "a secret
cipher used among the rebels in Canada" exactly the same as the
"cipher found among the effects of Booth." A third witness testified that he had been enlisted in the plot with other Confederates
and assigned the task of killing Stanton, but that was later turned
over to others, and he was invited to participate in the expedition
to burn New York City. This, declared Holt, was Clay's "most
flagrant" crime. "For this gigantic scheme . . . Clay is morally
as well as legally responsible."

The St. Albans raid, which the North always viewed as "brigand-
age," was, continued Holt, "not only authorized, but fully approved by Clay." And worst of all, the alleged plot to introduce
yellow fever into northern cities by means of infected clothing had
"Clay's cognizance and approval." Holt's statement was based on
the testimony of Godfrey J. Hyams, who had betrayed the Confederates in August, 1864. In conclusion, Holt recommended that
as soon as the evidence was complete, Clay should be "brought
before a military commission upon charges, not only of complicity
in the plot of assassination, but also of violation of the laws of
war." "Can it be supposed," he asked, "that a man who had done
all this in the interest of the rebellion would hesitate to take any
single life . . . even though it should be the life of the President
of the United States?" A few weeks later, three new witnesses
testified that Clay's "enterprise" in Canada "was the taking of the
lives of Abraham Lincoln . . . and his Cabinet." At least eight
witnesses swore that they had seen Clay in Canada in February or
March, 1865. Two others told of interviews with Jefferson Davis
in the summer of 1863 concerning a plot to kidnap Lincoln and
bring him to Richmond.[18]

Who were these witnesses who had testified to Confederate
guilt? By July, 1866, the truth had come to light, chiefly through
the work of Levi C. Turner, a judge advocate in Holt's office, and
Andrew Jackson Rogers of New Jersey, the fearless minority

18 Pitman, *Conspiracy Trial*, 54-56; *O.R.*, II, viii, 847-61, 878-85; Robinson, *The
Infamous Perjuries of the "Bureau of Military Justice" Exposed*, 1-10.

member of the House Judiciary Committee, whose report exposed what had been going on. Said Rogers, "one by one I find each and all of the witnesses brought forward . . . to implicate Jefferson Davis, Clement C. Clay, Jacob Thompson, and others, to be either convicted perjurers or men of infamous life. . . . All the testimony taken to establish said complicity . . . is wholly unworthy of credit . . . an act highly reprehensible, discreditable to the officers of the court, a disgrace to the nation."[19]

Richard Montgomery, the doublecrosser who had worked both sides, was the first witness. Actually, he had held a commission in a New York regiment, but was discharged for fraud and later faced civil charges for seduction and robbery. But he had gained the confidence of some of the Confederates in Canada and doubtless had some real knowledge of their activities. The second witness, Dr. James B. Merritt, a native of western New York, late in 1864 settled in the village of Ayr, near Windsor, Ontario. Here he represented himself as a large landowner from Tennessee, where, he said, he had been the personal physician of Andrew Johnson and "Parson" Brownlow. His story was that after the Emancipation Proclamation he had turned Confederate, had been a surgeon in the Confederate army, had been taken prisoner, and after escaping had made his way into Canada. His neighbors in Ayr and Windsor soon discovered him in dubious business transactions, and concluded that he was no more than a "disreputable swindler" whom they "would not believe on his oath." After his testimony before the military commission they denounced him "as a spy or a traitor, or both."

But the most notorious witness was Sanford Conover, whose real name was Charles A. Dunham. A native of Croton, New York, he was educated as a lawyer. From western New York he entered Canada late in 1864, where, under the name of James Watson Wallace, he became intimate with many Confederates and no doubt learned something of what they were doing. At the trial of the St. Albans raiders he swore that he was a native of Virginia and had visited Richmond on Confederate business in September, 1864. When he testified before the military commission in Washington on May 20, 1865, he amended this story by saying that he had been conscripted into the Confederate service,

19 USC, 39:1, HR Jud. Com. *Rep.* no. 104, p. 37.

but had been detailed as a clerk in the Confederate war department, had later gone through the lines to Canada, and had become
a correspondent for the New York *Tribune*. His lengthy testimony as to a Confederate conspiracy, taken in secret, leaked to
the press and was published in the New York papers, June 5-7,
1865. By that time Conover had rejoined his Confederate friends
in Canada, who immediately confronted him with the record of
his testimony. To get out of this spot, he made an affidavit
declaring that the person who testified before the military commission was not himself, and offered $500 reward for arrest of the
"infamous and perjured scoundrel who recently personated me
under the name of Sanford Conover, and deposed to a tissue of
falsehoods before the Military Commission at Washington." Holt
rescued Conover and brought him back to Washington for further
testimony. To make his story even better, Conover now swore
that the Confederates had ganged up on him in Canada and that
this affidavit had been made at the point of a pistol. This was
as much a lie as all his other testimony.[20]

Holt believed implicitly every shred of testimony given by
Conover and all the other witnesses. For a man of Conover's
stripe, Holt's gullibility opened up unlimited opportunities. He
had little difficulty in persuading Holt to employ him in a search
for witnesses who would swear to Confederate guilt. Conover
traveled all over the country, and from various points in the
North, South, and Canada he wrote to Holt, telling that he had
found witnesses, was hot on the trail of others, and, always, needed
additional funds, which Holt never failed to send. Between
September, 1865, and February, 1866, Conover brought in at
least eight witnesses who swore to elaborate details of a Confederate assassination conspiracy.

Conover's schemes were succeeding beautifully until the spring
of 1866, when two of his witnesses, William Campbell and Joseph
Snevel, were brought back to Washington to testify before the
House Judiciary Committee. In reply to questions about his
testimony, Campbell, now suffering pangs of conscience, declared,
"This is all false; I must make a clean breast of it; I can't stand
it any longer." "Why did you make it?" the Judiciary Committee

20 Pitman, *Conspiracy Trial*, 28-34; Cleary, *The Protest of W. W. Cleary*, 3-53;
DeWitt, *Judicial Murder of Mary E. Surratt*, 62-64.

asked. Said Campbell, "I was informed by Conover that Judge Holt had offered a reward of one hundred thousand dollars for the capture of Jefferson Davis . . . now . . . they had not enough against him to justify them in what they had done; that Judge Holt wanted to get witnesses to prove that Davis was interested in the assassination of Mr. Lincoln, so as to justify him in paying the $100,000. I went to Canada," he continued, "to hunt up a witness to swear false. . . . Conover wrote out the evidence and I learned it by heart. I made it to make money. . . . I received $625 . . . $100 from Conover and $500 from Judge Holt." Snevel had received $475, and Dr. Merritt had collected a total of $6,000 from the War Department for his testimony. Conover steadfastly refused to tell how much he had been paid.[21]

Judge Advocate Levi Turner's investigations brought these additional facts to light about the witnesses. William Campbell, whose real name was Joseph A. Hoare, was "a gas-fixer by trade; born in the State of New York and never south of Washington." Joseph Snevel, the alias of William H. Roberts, was "formerly ticket agent on Harlem Railroad, then kept tavern at Yonkers, &c.; was never South." Other witnesses, all with assumed names, turned out to be a brickyard worker on Long Island, a justice of the peace at Nyack, and "a licensed peddler in New York [who] sometimes drives a one-horse cart." Conover's wife and sister also had given testimony under false names. Turner later proved that Conover had forged all the letters ostensibly written by his suborned witnesses. In spite of these disclosures, Holt sent Conover back to New York to find more of his witnesses. There Conover disappeared and was not heard of again until the following November, when he was arrested and later tried and convicted of perjury. During the impeachment trial, James M. Ashley and other Radicals intent on removing the President from office connived with Conover for more of his evidence to use against Johnson. In spite of all his evil designs, Conover, in February, 1869, received a pardon from President Johnson.[22]

In the face of such conclusive evidence, Joseph Holt was forced to abandon his Confederate-conspiracy theory. Reluctantly he admitted that it was his "duty . . . formally to withdraw these

21 USC, 39:1, HR Jud. Com. *Rep.* no. 104, pp. 36-40; *O.R.,* II, viii, 921-23.
22 *O.R.,* II, viii, 921-23, 962-64, 978-80; DeWitt, *Impeachment and Trial of Andrew Johnson,* 154-56, 278-81.

depositions for the present from the consideration of the Government." "The testimony . . . as to the utter falsity of the depositions," he confessed, "has left a strong impression on my mind that Conover has been guilty of a most atrocious crime, committed under what promptings I am wholly unable to determine." The whole affair "left a strong impression" on others that Holt had been in guilty collusion with Conover to organize the plot of the perjurers. Actually Holt was not guilty; he simply believed what he wanted to believe. Yet the fact that "the plotters did . . . operate through the Bureau of Military Justice . . . looked . . . like a shield extended . . . to save certain officers of the government from the charge of having been betrayed into . . . the blunders of an excitement, which it was their province to allay or control, not to increase or share; but still extended over acknowledged, self-convicted, most wicked perjury; and the fact that Mr. Holt did himself pay moneys . . . to those who acknowledge they swore for money, may awaken suspicion that there was bribery as well as perjury—perhaps not conscious bribery, but the payment for false testimony was committed; though it may have been done innocently, it produced the usual effect of subornation of perjury."[23]

Thus in little more than a year did the truth come to light. Clay, Davis, and the other Confederates stood vindicated. But spreading that truth to the general public took much longer; and indeed, twenty-five years later one member of the military commission still believed all the perjured evidence. But in January, 1866, the truth soon to be revealed was not much help to Clement and Virginia Clay. After reading Holt's report on his case, Clay wrote in considerable alarm, "Before a Military Court where everything touching myself in C.[anada] would be admitted, I should have a slight chance of escaping a judicial murder." Of the witnesses he said, "all must be base men of bad characters; but this must be proven by competent witnesses. They have united in a plot against my life, & may take it, if I am taken from prison to trial & not allowed time & means of exposing their falsehood and infamy." As his legal mind pondered the situation, he continued, "You do not know how hard it is to prove a negative.

23 Joseph Holt to Stanton, July 3, 1866, *O.R.*, II, viii, 843f; USC, 39:1, HR Jud. Com. *Rep.* no. 104, pp. 36-38.

How am I to disprove positive assertions that I said this or that at such a time? unless by showing I was not there (or an *alibi*) or by discrediting the witness." Judge Holt, Clement concluded, "is determined to sacrifice me. . . . He may do so if I am not allowed the libty to seek witnesses & prepare my defence, or if I am subjected to the mockery of a military Court,—where all the charges he can make may be brought against me in a great drag net."[24]

Clay did not then know that two of his friends still in Canada had for months been hard at work to prove alibis for him, themselves, Jacob Thompson, and other Confederates, and to discredit all the witnesses who had testified before Holt and the military commission. The Reverend Stuart Robinson, exiled from Kentucky for his Confederate sympathies, had, as early as the summer of 1865, published a pamphlet denouncing Hyams, Montgomery, and Merritt as perjurers. Late in 1865 W. W. Cleary brought out a much more elaborate exposure containing affidavits of many Canadians designed to prove that he, Clay, Thompson, Sanders, Tucker, and other Confederates were not present at the places and times when Conover's witnesses said they were, and consequently that it was impossible that the Confederates had any part in or knowledge of the assassination. Two affidavits particularly dealt with the time of Clay's departure from Canada, proving that Conover's witnesses could not possibly have seen or talked with him in Canada in January or February, 1865.[25]

Meantime, Clay did what little he could in his own defense by addressing letters to Stanton and Johnson. Protesting to Stanton the conditions of his imprisonment, Clay continued, "But no relaxation of physical discipline [can] ever compensate for the crucifixion of soul to wh. I am subject. While I am isolated here . . . the world is busy with my name & character . . . the public mind is being impressed with my guilt, & may be immoveably convinced of it, before I am permitted to offer a word in my defense. And when, at last I am allowed to reply to my accusers, the evidence of my innocence may have been lost, or destroyed, or removed beyond my reach. I am even denied means of per-

24 Clay, Jr., to Virginia Clay, memorandum [ca. Jan. 1, 1866], Clay MSS; Thomas Mealley Harris, *Assassination of Lincoln: A History of the Great Conspiracy, Trial of the Conspirators by a Military Commission, and a Review of the Trial of John H. Surratt* (Boston, 1892), *passim*.
25 Robinson, *Infamous Perjuries of the "Bureau of Military Justice" Exposed*, 1-3; Cleary, *Protest of W. W. Cleary*, 49-52.

peturating & preserving whatever my own mind may suggest as essential to my defense, while all my mental faculties, like my physical, are being impaired. . . . I cannot now recall names, dates & events, which once occurred to me as aids to prove my innocence, but wh. I had no means of recording." To Andrew Johnson he wrote, "Conscious of my innocence of either concerting, consenting to, conceiving or being privy to this crime, or anything base, cowardly or dishonorable, or unwarranted by the laws of war & the example of the U. S.; confident that no act or word of mine could be tortured into complicity in any such crime; & trusting & expecting that I would ere long be allowed means & opportunity of removing from my name a stain more painful than any wound you could have inflicted on my body; I parted from those who have escaped arrest. . . . I felt & feel that neither liberty nor life is valuable with a dishonored name. . . . I, therefore, surrendered myself with the expectation that I would long since have been relieved from a disgraceful charge, that has weighed like an incubus upon my spirits."

After her visit to Clement, Virginia Clay redoubled her efforts. During the next three months she addressed lengthy written appeals to the President; she haunted the White House day and night, seeing Johnson at every opportunity, volubly pouring out her story, and sometimes chiding the President for his vacillation and procrastination. Her first letter of January 11, 1866, which Johnson promised to read at a cabinet meeting, made an emotional appeal based on Susanna Clay's recent death. "Oh! Mr. Johnson," Virginia wrote, "what a fearful blow to my noble husband, your unhappy prisoner! He was her idolized son, her first-born; . . . upon whose precious lineaments she had not rested her longing eyes for three weary, desolate years." In another vein she continued, "Mr. Clay, always delicate, is dying daily. His thin pale face daggered my heart to look upon! He told me he was dying, but resigned to God's will and perfectly willing to perish in those four walls if his country would be thereby benefitted. Mr. President, I am not such a Christian or patriot, . . . my husband is . . . my all. . . . Give him to me for a little while at least. . . . Do not force him to feel himself the victim of misplaced confidence in the magnanimity of the Govt. but give him the parole I ask."

Two months later Virginia wrote, "My last communication to

you was from a sorrowing heart;—this, is from an indignant one!
My patience is fled, & I am outraged that Mr. Clay should be still,
denied the right of trial, & yet refused a parole. If the Gov.
thinks him guilty, why does it not try him & *prove* his guilt? If he
be innocent . . . is it so lost to every sense of Honor & Justice
as to desire to murder by inches an innocent man. . . . Shall a
brave but fallen foe be trampled & crushed without a hearing?—
a foe who staked his life & liberty in *your* hands Mr President,
that he might be given the opportunity to vindicate his honor
& his innocence? . . . And Sir, he will yet do it. . . . He is
neither afraid or ashamed to tell you for what purposes he went
to Canada, nor what he accomplished while there. . . . Only
allow him the aid of counsel. . . . Or if this be too great a
liberty . . . give *me* the privilege of free correspondence with my
husband & free conference with Mr. Davis, not subject to the
surveillance of the Govt; & its officials—thro' whom hired witnesses
may learn to fit their testimony to an altered state of case . . . &
even I, a feeble woman (no, thank God not a feeble, but strong
woman . . .) will lay bare as diabolical a plot as was ever conceived to compass the judicial murder of an innocent man."[26]

In addition to General Grant's letter, Virginia now had recommendations from three influential men, two of them prominent
Radicals. Vitriolic Thaddeus Stevens himself wrote, "In answer
to your question about Mr. Clay, I say that having acknowledged
him a belligerent I should treat him as such and in no other light
unless he were in conspiracy to assassinate Mr Lincoln of which I
have seen no evidence and do not believe. But I would confiscate
his property and that of most of the others and let them go." No
less surprising was the action of abolitionist Henry Wilson, who
came unannounced to George Parker's house, where Virginia was
now a guest, to express his sympathy and declare his belief in
Clay's innocence. He followed this visit with a letter to Johnson
recommending that Clay be allowed "to go to his home on parole."
"I have no hesitation," he continued, "in recommending its favorable consideration, if only from motives of humanity, as I have no
doubt Mr. Clay will be forthcoming when his presence is again
required by the government." From Robert J. Walker came a

---

[26] Clay, Jr., to Stanton, June 30, 1865, Clay Letterbook, Clay, Jr., to Andrew
Johnson, Nov. 23, 1865, Clay MSS; Virginia Clay to Andrew Johnson, Jan. 11,
March 12, 1866, Johnson MSS, vol. 93.

stronger statement. "I have known Mr. Clay many years," he declared, "and unhesitatingly pronounce him incapable of such a crime. There has arisen great public sympathy for him, and a general desire that, if not pardoned, he may be paroled. . . . Under the circumstances of his voluntary surrender for a trial, can there be any apprehension that he would break his parole to avoid a trial? Permit me to say that among the hundreds of loyal men, who have conversed with me on this subject, I have *never met one,* who believed Mr. Clay guilty of any complicity in the murder of Mr. Lincoln."[27]

Fortified with these endorsements, Virginia pressed her efforts with renewed vigor. During the many hours she spent in White House anterooms, frequent brief notes, penciled on calling cards, passed between her and the President. On one Virginia wrote, "Can I see you this Evening? I await an answer in the Audience room"; to which Johnson replied, "There is Committee here in consultation—I cannot tell what time they will leave—I fear too late for you." On another occasion Virginia asked, "Shall I go, or can you see me? I can wait 20 minutes only." "My dear friend," replied the President, "it will be impossible to see you until it is too late—I am pressed to death." And so the tantalizing business went on day after day, until on the evening of April 17 Virginia and her constant companion, Mary E. (Parker) Bouligny, came again to the White House.[28] Johnson's evasive promises of early action had hardened Virginia's determination not to leave that night until she held in her own hands Clement's parole. The evening wore on while the two women waited and Johnson busied himself with work which took him many times from his desk to an adjoining committee room. It was near eleven when the President had occasion to pause at his desk. Seizing the moment, Virginia repeated her demand for the order and her determination to remain until she had it. As she stood angry and imperious

27 Virginia Clay to Andrew Johnson, March 12, 1866, Thaddeus Stevens to R. J. Haldeman, Jan. 8, 1866, Henry Wilson to Andrew Johnson, March 3, 1866, R. J. Walker to Andrew Johnson, Feb. 2, 1866, Johnson MSS, vol. 93; Virginia Clay to Henry Wilson, March 1, 1866, Clay MSS.

28 Undated holo. notes, Clay MSS; Douglass Zevely, "Old Houses on C. Street and Those Who Lived There," Columbia Historical Society *Records,* V (1902), 151-75. Mary E. P. Bouligny was the daughter of George Parker, wealthy merchant of Washington, in whose home Virginia Clay was a guest for most of her sojourn in Washington at this time. Mary Bouligny was the widow of John Edward Bouligny, Louisiana congressman who died in 1864. She later married George Collins Levy and lived in England.

beside the President, the moment came toward which she had striven for five months: Johnson sat down and wrote the order releasing her husband.

And so on the morning of April 18, 1866, Clement Clay was a free man again. To Virginia's query of whether he would come to Washington, he replied, "I am too enfeebled by my long & painful confinement to bear the excitement of a visit to W., & I am too anxious to see my dear old parents. . . . Let us hurry to them. . . . I need rest & air & exercise & *liberty*—wh. I will get with my dear kin & friends in Petersburg. . . . I shall await you there expecting to go thence thro' Tenn. to home. I am grateful," he continued, "for the Presdts' favors, because I believe they have been cheerfully rendered & only so long delayed because of his difficulties & embarrassments. May God help him to save what is left the unhappy south. I shall gladly give him the feeble aid in my power. . . . Get yr. & my letters & the *restoration of our property if possible*—& also, some enlargement of Mr. D's. imprisonment."[29]

After a few days filled with a flurry of congratulations and farewells, Virginia joined Clement in Petersburg. Together they reached Huntsville on Sunday, April 29, where a spontaneous reception greeted them. The local press described it: "Mr. Clay reached home on Sunday morning . . . and as soon as it became known, a large number of friends hastened to greet him at the residence of his venerable father; and on yesterday the parlors of the mansion were thronged with gentlemen from the city and country who came to greet their respected fellow-citizen, and welcome him home again. He met his visitors with that hearty cordiality which evidences how rejoiced he was to see old faces after so long and so eventful a separation. We hardly expected to see him looking so well as he does. The trouble, harassment and deprivations of prison life, have, however, left visible marks upon his frame, and his head is sprinkled with premature gray. His conversation partook largely of recitals of his prison experiences, but it was free from any bitterness of censure or acrimony of feeling. Indeed he seemed disposed to speak more of the acts of kindness shown him than to recall the petty, mean indignities that he was sometimes treated with by some who could not appre-

29 *O.R.*, II, vii, 899; Clay, Jr., to Virginia Clay, April 19, 1866, Clay MSS. Clement had not yet been told of his mother's death.

ciate the courtesy due to a gentleman in misfortune so far superior to them in all the elements of true manhood. Mr. Clay did not go to Washington, as was so positively affirmed in the Northern press, but proceeded immediately to Petersburg, Va., from which place he came directly home. Mrs. Clay is with her husband, and is an equal sharer in the esteem and admiration that is so justly due her, not only for her unrivaled virtues and graces, but for that exalted womanly devotion which in the true heart is only the more developed and fixed when the trials of adversity encompass us about. We wish them a long and joyous life after the eventful and discordant scenes through which they have passed."[30]

30 Huntsville *Daily Independent,* May 1, 1866.

13 ⁓

Reconstructing Life

THE JOY AND RELIEF that Clement first experienced in his freedom and reunion with family and friends soon gave way to despair as he surveyed the loss and destruction that had befallen his neighbors and his state. Property and capital amounting to $500,000,000 were wiped out. Devastation in North Alabama exceeded even that made on Sherman's march through Georgia. The town of Athens was a shambles after its pillaging at the hands of the notorious Turchin, whose "brigade has stolen a hundred thousand dollars' worth of watches, plate, and jewelry in northern Alabama." "Decatur is a ruin," wrote another observer. "Its streets are dug up in trenches, and made impassable by earthworks. Shanties abound." "Our beautiful town is dessolated [sic]," mourned one resident of Huntsville. "Our Churches are injured. . . . The Methodist Church was burned." Huntsville's railroad yards and shops had been destroyed in 1862, many residences had been burned, and others had been taken over by the army of occupation. Every building yet standing was in need of repairs and paint. In the country, plantation houses and buildings, gin-houses, and fences had been burned or otherwise destroyed, and farm animals had long since vanished. The planters were the heaviest losers; with their capital in slaves and plantation improvements gone, they were almost as destitute as the poorest Negro. The planter stood amid his thousands of acres now reverted to wilderness and puzzled over where to start.[1]

Lawson Clay voiced the universal feeling of despair when he wrote to Clement, "I fear your return to Huntsville will be everything except pleasant. The changes that have occurred in our own family, not to mention the altered condition & circumstances of friends, will bring sorrow. Death & misfortune have pursued us & those we esteemed from the very commencement of our ill-fated revolution. You & I homeless & almost penniless, John in little better condition & father very much injured in estate & in bad health present contrasts to what we were in 1860 . . . painful, to regard at any time or anywhere, especially in Huntsville. . . . It is no place for a poor man to reside in, especially one who has heretofore lived there as a man of fortune & been so regarded by the community. Comparative contentment may be secured among a people who never knew us in our better days; but, to be conscious that we live among those who were our inferiors, socially, mentally, & pecuniarily, & that they now take the lead in society and in public affairs, is enough to make each day of life less supportable than the preceding one."[2]

Although Lawson alone had inherited his mother's overweening pride, Clement could take little comfort from the position in which the Clay family now found itself. Like many another Confederate, he faced a blank wall. How could he salvage something from the chaos? What should he try to do? The naked question was, how was he going to make a living?

During the preceding decade, Clay's chief sources of income had been these: his salary as a senator; the hire of his and Virginia's slaves; dividends on railroad and other stocks; rents, legal fees, and interest. In 1858, a typical year, he had as income $3,000 salary as United States senator, $1,250 from the hire of twelve slaves, $100 in dividends on bank stock, and about $600 in legal fees. This gave him an income of $4,950, without counting his senatorial mileage, repayment of personal loans made to neighbors in Huntsville, and dividends on Memphis and Charleston Railroad stock.

1 Susanna Clay to Clay, Jr., March 14, 1865, Clay MSS; *O.R.*, I, xvi, pt. 1, pp. 479-81, pt. 2, p. 80; John Beatty, *Memoirs of a Volunteer, 1861-1863*, ed. by Harvey S. Ford (New York, 1946), 117; *De Bow's Review*, n.s. I (Feb., March, 1866), 218, 332; Fleming, *Civil War and Reconstruction in Alabama*, 254-59.

John Basil Turchin, born in Russia, commanding the Nineteenth Illinois Volunteer Infantry, was found guilty of unwarranted depredations, but before he could be dismissed from the service, he was promoted to the rank of brigadier general.

2 H. L. Clay to Clay, Jr., April 23, June 14, 1866, Clay MSS.

The war had wiped out all this income. Clay's salary as a senator had of course ceased on February 17, 1864. Income from Negro hire ended for practical purposes at the close of 1864, and terminated legally with the adoption of the Thirteenth Amendment on December 18, 1865. However, money still due on hire contracts made during the war was generally viewed as a collectable debt any Southerner was in honor bound to pay. No southern railroad was in a position to pay dividends at this time. Finally, the Freedmen's Bureau had taken over Clay's office building as abandoned property and was occupying it rent free. As for his peripheral sources of income, his other buildings had been burned; as a paroled prisoner he could not resume law practice, even if there had been any prospect of profit in it; his other stocks and investments were worthless; and it was impossible to collect loans from debtors who had no money. Clement spent the summer and autumn pondering these catastrophic changes and trying to find a way out.

To a northern friend he summarized his situation thus: "Many sad & strange changes have occurred here & throughout the South. Hopes have been blighted, hearts crushed, fortunes destroyed, & society disorganized ever since our banner went down. . . . I need scarcely assure you, that none have fared worse than myself & my kindred. . . . Nothing has been left me, worth naming, that could be destroyed or carried off. My lands, a three-storied brick building in this city (that could not be burned without destroying a large part of this city) some good debts, my Bank stocks & my wifes rail road stock remain. The lands were stripped of all improvements & are unoccupied, the M. & C. R. R. Stock is, as yet, yielding no dividend, owing to expense of repairs &c. & my brick office is held by the Govt. without paying me rent. I have no income & am living on my credit. The rail R. Stock was worth all it called for in 1860-61—about $15,000. . . . The lands, about 2.500 acres, mostly wild & unimproved, were worth at least $10.000, in 1860, without the improvements on 60 acres, in 3½ miles of Huntsville, where I lived & my dwelling, other houses, fences, &c. were all burned. . . . The brick building in the city was then worth $6000. The Bank stock is probably, valueless. Of the debts due me I think I will realize $6000. I think I may safely say that the property left my wife & self would command $30.000—if peace, tranquillity & confidence were restored." Clay did not at this time mention the doubtful asset of his other lands purchased during his United States senatorship. On his 1,800 acres of land in Pine and Chisago counties, Minnesota, he now owed back taxes, and his large tract nine miles from Superior, Wisconsin, was almost worthless until railroad lines should reach that area. There was little prospect for the sale of any of these holdings.[3]

As Clement and Lawson worried with the problem of their invalid father's estate, they agreed that the town property should be sold. But, Lawson warned, "I do not believe the lot will bring in its dilapidated condition what you believe it will command. . . . Remember, [the] house is by no means modern in its architecture—it is not convenient in its construction, nor is its location esteemed desirable by most persons. If $10.000.*00* could be had, *it would be well sold.* . . . The next question is, how to dispose of the plantation *in the family.* . . . Father could give [it] to his sons, or sell to one or two of them at a fair price." But before anything could be settled upon, Clement Comer Clay died on September 6, 1866.

His three sons were of course the sole heirs, though in the preceding spring, Lawson, in a codicil to his father's will, had taken the precaution of transferring Clement's share to Virginia Clay, in order to avoid possible confiscation proceedings. Now, however, Clement became executor, and in that capacity he described his father's estate as "consisting of a plantation near the M. & C. R. R. of about 2300 acres of wh. 1,000 are open & in cultivation by a renter; an improved city lot of 5 acres, on wh. he lived & died, & something over $13.000 of Memphis & Chas. R. R. Stock—has been appraised at $80.000. It owes about $23.000." As 1866 drew to a close, Clement was busy with initial moves in settling the estate. The first item was the family residence in Huntsville. Even though it was now freshly painted and repaired (at a cost of $508.61), there was little prospect of its sale. The next best solution was to rent it, but even that was not easy, as Clement revealed when he wrote, "On New Year's day there were so few people in town, & it was so cold & cloudy, that I did not offer the

[3] Clay, Jr., to T. W. Pierce, Dec. 8, 1866, Hiram Hayes to Clay, Jr., July 20, 1866, George Culver to Clay, Jr., Aug. 3, 1866, G. G. Beardsley to George Culver, June 17, 1876, [Clay, Jr., to Virginia Clay], fragment, n.d., but perhaps Oct. 5, 1868, Clay MSS.

house for rent at auction, as advertised. . . . If it do not go up to $800.00 I shall bid it in & we will occupy it." Ten days later he reported to Virginia, who was in Washington, "I bid in the house, at Auction, on Monday last, at $500,—there being no other bidder but Mr. Alfred Clay, who went up to $475!! He is an aspiring gentleman of color." Clement continued, "I have sold nearly $300 worth of furniture & am still selling." "I shall only retain enough furniture to keep up two chambers, dining & sitting room. . . . I have fished up many old things in attic, cellar, & elsewhere, not inventoried, wh. are useful. And have recovered some treasured relics—such as *most of my notes in rhyme to you,* in the halcyon days of courtship! I expect poor mother scattered them in trying to hide from the enemy our manuscripts."[4]

Sometimes the whole prospect almost overwhelmed him, as when he wrote, "If I did not keep busy . . . I should die of melancholy in this dreary domicil . . . amid the memorials of so many blasted hopes & bitter disappointments." "Imagine me in the room where both of my parents died, sitting where they sat so long, near where both fell, to rise no more, & resting at night where one of them slept his last sleep—poring over manuscripts from their fingers, or ours . . . gathering up what may be useful or is interesting & destroying what is unvalued—& you may know that I am never gay & seldom cheerful."

These sad reveries were often interrupted by more immediate problems, one of which was Withers Clay's family. "Do not," Clement admonished Virginia, "buy any useless things for Bro. W.'s children." So Virginia sent flannel, which, Clement assured her, "was a godsend to that poor family. They are in a truly pitiable condition, & bro. W. very unhappy. He confessed to me that he feared he could not feed & clothe his family & supply them necessary fuel thro' this winter. . . . They seem to be doomed to hard trials & bitter tribulation. Sister M.," Clement continued, "looks for her 11th in 10 days, I'm told, & is preparing for that accustomed event." Pursuing the subject a week later, Clement wrote, "Don't covet children, but thank God that he has not

4 H. L. Clay to Clay, Jr., June 14, Aug. 2, 1866, Clay, Jr., to T. W. Pierce, Dec. 8, 1866, Mary Clay to Virginia Clay, Oct. 17, 1866, Clay, Jr., to Virginia Clay, Jan. 4, 13, 1867, Clay MSS.
Alfred had been one of the Clays' most intelligent and trusted slaves. Alfred later apologized for bidding, saying he had done it for the family's sake.

given you the care of them. Bro. W.'s case is enough to satisfy me that they are too heavy a responsibility for me. And without help he could not bear it. I do not think he or sister M. look upon the new comer with any pleasure, but rather with grief & regret. I am truly sorry for them."[5]

Of the three Clay men, Withers was most demoralized by the debacle. For months he had neither occupation nor income and admitted, wrote Clement, that "he cannot pay his debts, with all the property he holds—is utterly insolvent. His house shows it—it presents a beggarly appearance, that is very distressing to me." By February, 1866, Withers was "busy arranging his accounts . . . & will try & collect his debts . . . being persuaded by hundreds of persons to recommence his paper." Because of possible adverse effects, Withers deferred its revival while Clement was still in prison, and so the first postwar issue of the Huntsville *Democrat* did not appear until October 19, 1866. Amid the general poverty, however, he did not "get the patronage he expected," and though he managed to keep the paper going, the income from it furnished at best a precarious support for his family. On one occasion his employees struck when he was unable to pay them.[6]

Pride and wartime destruction of his home combined to dissuade Lawson Clay from returning to Huntsville. He and Celeste remained among her relatives in Georgia, while Lawson busied himself with trying to "collect money that may be necessary yet to feed me." But such picayunish business as this and the selling of his furniture in Huntsville did not satisfy Lawson's ambitious nature. The prospect of quick money from high-priced cotton lured him, and so as he explained, "I & John Comer have hired negroes & work Maj. Comer's plantation on joint account. . . . We have near 450 acres in cotton & have as good prospects as our neighbors for a good crop. The life is not only very laborious . . . but it is irksome. . . . The shirking from work, the misunderstanding of plain contracts, the thefts, lies, complaints are almost as unendurable as innumerable." Lawson had never had a taste for planting with slave labor; his troubles now with freedmen were almost more than dire necessity could force him to.

5 Clay, Jr., to Virginia Clay, Dec. 9, 1866, Jan. 13, 16, 27, Feb. 5, 1867, Clay MSS. Virginia Clay had often expressed great unhappiness because she had no children.
6 Mary Clay to Virginia Clay, Feb. 12, 1866, H. L. Clay to Clay, Jr., Aug. 2, 1866, March 23, 1872, Clay, Jr., to Virginia Clay, Jan. 13, 17, 1867, J. W. Clay to Clay, Jr., Nov. 3, 1866, Clay MSS.

A month later he reported that "Our prospects for making money in planting cotton seem daily diminishing. . . . A severe storm . . . blew down fences . . . & tore off the tops of the tender plant. . . . Now, we are all alarmed at the proposed tax of 5c per lb. & are almost ready to abandon the plantation in despair to the free-negro & the exciseman."

By midsummer he feared "the golden anticipation with which I commenced the year will be far from realization at its close; yet, there is consolation in knowing that I have not spared myself in the attempt to succeed. . . . I hope to have enough the next winter to pay the $1200.00 I owe in Huntsville." But at the end of the year he had no money, and indeed "tried to borrow" but "has failed," as Clement related, "& must sell his R. R. stock to meet his obligations," while at the same time he was *"reluctantly compelled"* to ask Clement to help out by repaying a personal loan made in Confederate currency and by lending him "$1000 for 12 months, of the money arising from rent of the plantation!" This Clement could not do. In spite of these reverses, Lawson tried planting in Georgia for another year. But Major John Comer's death on August 27, 1867, and the subsequent breakup of his estate, changed the situation, and so at the end of that year Lawson and Celeste returned to Huntsville. They soon built a house just outside the town, and Lawson again took up the practice of law and worked his share of his father's plantation.[7]

The year of 1867 thus opened gloomily for all the Clays. As for Clement, this was how his affairs stood: confiscation proceedings were pending against his property; he himself was indicted for treason and liable to arrest; he owed at least $5,000 to creditors in Huntsville; he was responsible for $23,000 in debts against his father's estate, and three months hence creditors would begin suing; he could not even rent, much less sell, his father's town residence; if he sold any of the estate's property at auction, it might be liable for confiscation; and even if he could sell property at auction, it would not bring more than one-fourth of its appraised value. The picture had only two bright spots: the plantation was rented for $3,000, and it was possible that Clem-

7 H. L. Clay to Clay, Sr., Oct. 21, 1865, H. L. Clay to Virginia Clay, Jan. 14, 1866, Aug. 29, 1867, H. L. Clay to Clay, Jr., April 23, May 26, June 14, 1866, Clay, Jr., to Virginia Clay, Dec. 12, 1866, Clay, Jr., to H. L. Clay, Dec. 15, 1866, Virginia Clay to Clay, Jr., May 27, 1868, Clement Clay III to Virginia Clay, Jan. 7, 1869, Clay MSS.

ent's property held by the Freedmen's Bureau might soon be returned to him.[8]

In the preceding October, Clement and Virginia had journeyed to Washington and New York, chiefly for the purpose of obtaining an order to drop the confiscation proceedings against their property. Clement consulted Jeremiah S. Black on this problem, as well as on the prospects of bringing suit against Sanford Conover and Joseph Holt. Since such litigation would be expensive, they sought aid from Jacob Thompson, who expressed interest, but did not follow through financially. Clement and Virginia also planned to write a book exposing Holt, and to that end gathered a quantity of material, but they were denied access to the archives which would furnish the most pertinent and damaging information. Though Clement thought they might "make $10,000 by that book," the volume never took shape. On his homeward journey, Clement stopped at Fortress Monroe to visit Jefferson Davis, while Virginia remained in New York and Washington, not returning to Huntsville until March, 1867.[9]

On November 25, 1866, President Johnson gave Virginia an order for the release of Clay's property. But Clement saw many legal flaws in the document and predicted that it would not be honored. Nevertheless, he forwarded the order to Major General Wager Swayne, assistant commissioner for the Freedmen's Bureau in Alabama, who immediately directed his deputy in Huntsville to turn over the office building to Clay. But when Clement attempted to get possession, he found that scalawag officials of the district court refused. They intended to force a court action whereby they would collect $200 in costs, a profitable practice that had been filling their pockets for some time. The only way to circumvent this would be an order from Attorney General Henry Stanbery to dismiss the suit without costs. Virginia got just such an order from Stanbery on January 16, 1867. This the court was bound to honor, and so at the next term, not only were the suits

<hr />

[8] Clay, Jr., to Virginia Clay, Dec. 3, 4, 7, 9, 12, 18, 1866, Clay, Jr., to H. L. Clay, Dec. 15, 1866, Clay, Jr., to T. W. Pierce, Dec. 8, 1866, Clay MSS.
[9] N. A. Miles to Virginia Clay, Sept. 29, 1866, William H. Carroll to Clay, Jr., Oct. 26, 1866, J. S. Black to Clay, Jr., Oct. 27, 1866, J. S. Black to Jacob Thompson, Nov. 6, 1866, Jacob Thompson to J. S. Black, July 7, 1867, Clay, Jr., to Virginia Clay, Dec. 12, 1866, Jan. 2, 13, 16, 20, Feb. 5, 1867, and undated fragment, ca. Jan., 1867, Mary E. P. Bouligny to Virginia Clay, March 3, 1867, Clay MSS. Jefferson Davis was released from Fortress Monroe on May 13, 1867. He lived in Memphis for several years.

against Clay's property dismissed, but the indictment for treason was suspended as well. In the meantime, as Clement reported to Virginia, the marshal "yield[ed] me my office, & the tenants have agreed to pay me reasonable rent." On April 11, 1867, he received from the Freedmen's Bureau $415.16 as rent from November 25, 1866.[10] Clement was now assured of an income of one hundred dollars a month.

One hundred dollars a month in inflated greenbacks might sustain life, but it would not pay debts, make repairs, or buy equipment. The Clays had always been used to large-scale operations and the credit system. To continue in the old way was perfectly natural; to do otherwise did not occur to them. This was evidenced by Lawson's plunge into large-scale planting. It was equally obvious in Clement's outlook when he explained to Thomas W. Pierce, "I wish to borrow 15, or $20,000 on 3 yrs credit paying the interest annually . . . with the privilege of paying part or all of the principal whenever I chose, for wh. I will give the joint & several bond of my brothers, my wife & myself. If I can effect such a loan, I feel confident I can save what is left of my own & my father's estate. . . . With ready money I could discharge the debts at a discount of from 10 to 15 pr ct." "One creditor offered to deduct 40 pr ct. for cash!" But Pierce, like all others in the North, feared to risk large capital with no other security than declining southern land values and honorable intentions, and so he replied that it was "utterly out of his power to make the loan." "So end my hopes of relief," sighed Clement. "I must sacrifice property to meet the demands of Crs. who are growing importunate."[11]

The business of settling his father's estate occupied most of Clement's time for almost three years. Claims presented against the estate amounted to nearly $23,000. These claims consisted mostly of notes due (some going back to 1859), and unpaid accounts with numerous business establishments in Huntsville.

10 Andrew Johnson, Order dated Nov. 25, 1866, Clay, Jr., to Virginia Clay, Dec. 4, 19, 23, 1866, Jan. 13, 1867, Wager Swayne to Clay, Jr., Dec. 15, 1866, Clay, Jr., to Wager Swayne, Dec. 23, 1866, John Benton Callis to Clay, Jr., April 11, 1867, Clay MSS; USC, 40:1, HR Jud. Com. *Rep.* no. 7 (Ser. 1314), *Impeachment Investigation: Testimony Taken before the Judiciary Committee of the House of Representatives in the Investigation of the Charges against Andrew Johnson* (Washington, 1867), 446, 448, 550-53, 811.

11 Clay, Jr., to T. W. Pierce, Dec. 8, 1866, Clay, Jr., to Virginia Clay, Jan. 13, Feb. 5, 1867, Clay MSS.

From 1867 to 1869 Clement paid out nearly $1,200 in taxes on
the estate, and a slightly smaller sum for repairs. He sold furniture
to the amount of $500, received in rents $3,500, sold 533 shares of
railroad stock for something over $9,000, and the family home
for $10,000. The purchaser of this last was Reuben Chapman,
whose own house had been burned during the war. By the middle
of 1872 the vexed business of the estate was finally concluded,
Clement having "fully paid and discharged all debts." In the
settlement, Withers sold his share to his brothers, so that the lands
were now entirely in the hands of Clement and Lawson Clay
and their wives.[12]

Physical ills beset Clement along with financial worries during
these bleak years. He suffered almost constantly from asthma,
sometimes severely. One such attack led him to try the cure he
had used in 1851, namely an extended horseback journey. Setting
out on May 7, 1868, with young Charles Shelby as his companion,
Clay traveled through middle Tennessee and Kentucky, as far as
Mammoth Cave. Two months of daily riding in the open air
brought a marked improvement. And in his wanderings he visited
many old friends and acquaintances, including Bennett Young.
Clement expended little money, as his overnight sojourns, though
often in the private homes of strangers, seldom involved payment
for food and lodging, since he was welcomed as a martyr of the
Lost Cause. He returned to the plantation on July 1, 1868, and
that same day Virginia set off for New York to attend the Democratic convention. In 1870 a severe attack of asthma sent Clay to
Minnesota for several months, where he further suffered several
broken ribs when he was thrown from a buggy. In another riding
accident two years later, a severely fractured left arm incapacitated
Clement for several months.[13]

About this time, Clay embarked on the only business venture of
his career. In these years the insurance business was experiencing
a great boom all over the country. The scores of fire- and life-
insurance companies organized throughout the South were often

12 Virginia Clay to Clay, Jr., Nov. 3, 1865, Aug. 20, 1871, Clay, Jr., Executor's
Book, 1866-1869, Clay, Jr., Account Book, Aug. 24, 1868, Clay MSS; Madison County
Archives, Probate Record, July 13, 1872, vol. 32, p. 564.
13 Clay, Jr., to Virginia Clay, May 16, 19, 22, June 3, 7, 14, 21, July 12, 1868,
Virginia Clay to Clay, Jr., July 12, 1868, Jefferson Davis to Virginia Clay, Aug. 8,
1870, J. J. B. Hilliard to Virginia Clay, Sept. 23, 1870, T. A. Faries to Virginia
Clay, Dec. 29, 1870, T. O. Chestney to Clay, Jr., Feb. 21, 1871, Clay MSS; Virginia
Clay to Jefferson Davis, Nov. 21, 1873, *Jefferson Davis, Constitutionalist,* VII, 378.

headed by generals or other equally prominent ex-Confederates. Late in 1869 Jefferson Davis became president of the Carolina Life Insurance Company, recently formed in Memphis. Davis quickly proposed that Clay be made a regional agent, but negotiations to that end were interrupted by Clay's attack of asthma in 1870. The next year, however, Clay became state agent (apparently on a trial basis) for the Anchor Life Insurance Company of New Jersey, and on June 1, 1871, he arrived in Mobile to begin work. The procedure was to organize in every city a board of directors, each of whom would subscribe for a life-insurance policy of $5,000. It was uphill work, but after two weeks Clay could report, "I did well in Mobile—getting a Board of 10 first rate men, at policies of $5,000 each."[14]

Indeed, for the moment, opportunities seemed to multiply as the possibilities of the life-insurance boom revealed themselves to Clay. He wrote that the newly organized Mobile Life Insurance Company "propose . . . to employ me as Genl. Agt." "Genl. Butler wants me to take Admiral Buchanan's place, as State Manager, of the Life Association of America, with a guarantee of $3.000 a year & my travelling expenses. So I hope something good will turn up from my visit to Mobile." "I will make the best bargain I can."[15]

Late in July, 1871, Clay went to St. Louis to complete his arrangements with the Life Association of America. The company office he described as "a grand affair, 3 stories, elegantly furnished, with 20 clerks." With his appointment in this company as agent for Alabama, Clement, riding a wave of optimism, wrote, "I think they will advance me $10,000, to settle my debts. . . . I'm in high hope that they will lift me out of the mire. At all events I think I see the way to something more profitable than cotton planting." Clay soon returned to Mobile, but his insurance work was interrupted at various times by the need to look after his plantation, and by his own illness. As early as the spring of 1872 he wrote,

14 Virginia Clay to Clay, Jr., June 2, 1871, Clay, Jr., to Virginia Clay, June 14, July 5, 1871, Clay MSS; Jefferson Davis to R. S. Guernsey, April 9, 1870, *Jefferson Davis, Constitutionalist*, VII, 268; *Western Insurance Review* (St. Louis), I-VIII (1867-1875), *passim;* Roscoe Carlyle Buley, *The American Life Convention, 1906-1952: A Study in the History of Life Insurance* (New York, 1953, 2 vols.), I, 77, 91; J. Owen Stalson, *Marketing Life Insurance: Its History in America* (Cambridge, Mass., 1942), 433-35.
15 Clay, Jr., to Virginia Clay, June 16, 18, 26, July 3, 5, 25, 1871, Clay MSS; *Western Insurance Review*, IV (July, 1871), 618; Charles Lee Lewis, *Admiral Franklin Buchanan, Fearless Man of Action* (Baltimore, 1929), 253-58.

"I am getting uneasy . . . about our Ins. Co. The long delay of the report of the Actuaries . . . makes me fear all is not well; while some N. Y. papers say it will be pronounced insolvent. . . . And if it prove of doubtful solvency I must quit it for my own sake." Indeed, the insurance boom had gone into a nosedive. The Anchor Company had already fallen "from an assumed condition of high prosperity to a state of shameless bankruptcy." In 1875 Jefferson Davis' Carolina Life Company failed because of "excessive mortality and policy loans." By the spring of 1872 Clay was "heartily sick" of the insurance business, though he stayed at it for another year. The Life Association of America was in difficulties long before it finally failed in 1879, when all six of the life-insurance companies of St. Louis were "in the hands of receivers, and in different stages of decomposition."[16]

While Clay was pursuing the chimera of insurance, another and more substantial opportunity passed him by. In the struggle to wrest the state university from scalawag and Radical control, the alumni in the summer of 1871 took things into their own hands. Clay was widely spoken of for the presidency, but when the alumni balloted, they chose Matthew Fontaine Maury. Such a position would have been more suited to Clay's talents than insurance, certainly, but the difficult problems of finance and administration in reorganizing the university might have required more patient perseverance and business acumen than Clay possessed. As it turned out, Maury never actually filled the office, and the university opened in October, 1871, under the presidency of Nathaniel Thomas Lupton.[17]

Upon abandoning the insurance business, Clay returned to his plantation and there strove, during the remaining years of his life, to make a living. The sale in 1868 of the family home in Huntsville had necessitated a considerable change in living arrangements. By the autumn of that year, Clement was settled in the small cabin on the plantation and was struggling with the manifold problems of an uncertain labor force. "Have had nothing done in the field for want of hands & no hauling of lumber, boards

16 Clay, Jr., to Virginia Clay, July 5, 25, 1871, May 19, 1872, Clay MSS; Western Insurance Review, XIII (Nov., 1879), 66; Insurance Blue Book, 1876-1877 (New York, 1877), 233.

17 Clay, Jr., to Virginia Clay, June 14, 18, 22, 1871, Clay MSS; M. F. Maury to Rutson Maury, Sept. 16, 1871, M. F. Maury MSS; Sellers, Hist. of the Univ. of Ala., I, 308-17.

or anything," he wrote. "If I cannot get another horse & 2 more hands I do not see how I can get the houses here repaired this year." "I am oppressed with many things but most with want of hands to do what is needed. Monroe, Dudley, Byron & Salina—all sick . . . almost every body sick." At other times he was busy supervising his "hirelings . . . in cutting rails to fence in the plantation, wh. would not be worth cultivating with only the present fence to protect the crops [except for the bordering] broad hedge of briars that defy the cows & hogs & mock our lazy agriculture." At the same time, Clement was in quest of a "well digger." The one he found did not do altogether satisfactory work, for he later reported that "the new well has caved in so as to prevent getting water . . . & the old . . . well is nearly dry & too muddy to use." He was still struggling with the problem of a well in 1875, when he had "engaged the well borers . . . & they are to be here tomorrow with their engine & drills to begin work. I have to feed them (3 men)." To Virginia, who was then in Huntsville, he continued, "I will send down your basket tomorrow morning— Try to return it with Bakers' bread & some cooked meat by the 2½ p.m. passenger train tomorrow or next day. If you could get a good ham . . . boil it, & send a roast (some beef or mutton) for them. They will sleep in a tent. . . . I dislike the increased expense of boring an Artesian well, but I must have water."

While Clement was thus occupied, Virginia was spending the autumn of 1868 in New York and Washington. "I am trying to prepare our log cabin for yr reception," Clement wrote her, and "am doing my best, with my small means, to make it comfortable. If it were possible," mused Clement, "for you to love me & enjoy my company as I love you & enjoy yrs, we might be happy in our seclusion." But, knowing Virginia, he continued, "I am trying hard to rent the whole place that we may live elsewhere. If you should find it too lonely & are not content to stay here, we will try to get elsewhere."[18]

Actually, Virginia stayed at the plantation as little as possible. She boarded in Huntsville part of the time until the spring of 1872, when Clement turned over to her the office building on the square. With the installation of gas and plumbing, she made

[18] Clay, Jr., to Virginia Clay, July 12, Oct. 11, 14, Nov. 16, 22, 1868, July 13, 1869, June 2, 1875, Clay MSS.

these rooms into living quarters for herself, and for Clement when leisure or business brought him to town. He commuted the eighteen miles between town and plantation by Memphis and Charleston trains which stopped at the "Tank," a water tank around which grew the hamlet of Gurleysville.

During Clement's venture into insurance, however, it was necessary for Virginia to supervise the plantation, where the vexations of dilatory servants and tenants led her to this outburst, "But for stern duty I wd. not remain here one hour I am sure! There is nothing to delight & much to Endure. While I write, Wood's wife (self-invited) sits by sewing & nursing her baby by turns, happier than I ever was in my life! . . . I staid in town from the 27th ult to 7th inst. . . . In my absence all things went wrong. The house-well is nearly dry, & the *field* [well], full of dead rats, impossible to use the water. Grace had neglected my cows till they were nearly dry, & no butter, no eggs, no chickens. . . . I had the yard well cleaned yes: . . . To-day I made Levi W. clean the other also. . . . Two or three milkings saltings & feedings have doubled the milk & general vigilance is beginning to tell. I certainly seem by my presence to inspirit the field hands & hope to increase fodder saving, & maybe get some hay. Already between 7 & 8000 bundles are pulled, & to-day they are hauling."

These vexations Virginia abandoned as often as possible for the delights of a livelier society to be found with her friends, the Goodmans, in Memphis. On one of her visits to that city she wrote, "I find scores of friends . . . found big Lushe Lamar here. . . . Senator Henry called & kissed me! . . . We dine at the Peabody with Dr. Arrington. . . . The dinner was superb & wine abundant . . . the Hollenbergs . . . have entertained me elegantly . . . the Opera is charming. . . . We went to see Jo Jefferson last night . . . & Thursday . . . an complimentary party . . . a select few, will meet us, & Clara Fitzgerald will play the harp—&c." "I am more than ever disenchanted of H[untsville]," she wrote on another occasion. "Memphis was never so gay outdoors as this past week. Two great theatrical attractions—four grand festivals for churches, the Elmwood cemetery celebration—& cars running with flags flying make it very gay." It all illustrated another friend's comment to Virginia, "that *your* proper sphere is in the midst of elegance comfort refinement wealth & luxury, & God knows NO ONE more deserves it." Delightful as she found the social whirl, bitter reality always hovered in the background, as Virginia wrote in response to a gloomy letter from Clement, "I feel lonely & sad & poor & miserable enough be sure, tho' I try to smile thro' it all. When I see the luxurious homes of the Parkers & Bartletts & trousseaux from Paris, & think of my lot, my home & my one black silk dress,—I do not need in addition one word from you or any other one to realize my situation."[19]

Clay's financial situation was certainly not improving. His repeated efforts to obtain a large loan from northern friends never succeeded. With such a loan, he felt he could make a fresh start by paying off all accumulated debts, often at a large discount for cash. But the intangibles of crop failures, falling prices, and the panic of 1873, followed by years of depression, were formidable handicaps to success. As it was, Clement struggled along with the aid of a few small loans: $1,000 from W. W. Corcoran in 1868, and $1,400 from J. J. B. Hilliard, Virginia's cousin, who was slowly climbing the financial ladder in a Louisville banking house. Regarding repayment of Corcoran's loan, Clement instructed Virginia in 1871, "You must raise by sale of a Bl. of cotton, or otherwise, $60 & remit in a check to W. W. Corcoran . . . to pay interest . . . & beg another year's indulgence on score of our short crop, &c, &c." Early in 1872 Clement and Virginia sold their Memphis and Charleston Railroad stock at 38 percent of its face value, realizing from it $5,700. At the same time, Virginia wrote, "Outerbridge, I hear wants 3 or 400 acres of land, & do lets sell *quick* if he'll give 15$ per. acre. 400 wd. bring 6.000, 4.000 *ours*, & this sum, with the proceeds of R. R. stock, 5.700 & yr. cotton now on hand wd. nearly make you free! Then we wd. own more than a 1.000 acres of the plantation. . . . Lets sell till out of debt." But that happy circumstance did not come to pass, for three years later, Clement, commenting on the "hard bondage of debt," wrote, "Altho' I have extinguished more than 50,000 of debts since 1866, I am still owing about 7,000."[20]

[19] Clay, Jr., to Virginia Clay, Dec. 1, 1871, Jan. 1, 1872, Virginia Clay to Clay, Jr., Nov. 11, 1868, Jan. 10, 11, Sept. 8, 1870, May 19, 1871, April 20, 1872, Leo Wheat to Virginia Clay, Nov. 23, 1867, Clay MSS.
[20] Clay, Jr., to Virginia Clay, Nov. 5, 1868, Gerrit Smith to Clay, Jr., Sept. 16, 1869, Clay, Jr., to J. J. B. Hilliard, Feb. 23, April 11, 1870, Clay, Jr., to Virginia Clay, Dec. 9, 1871, Jefferson Davis to Clay, Jr., Jan. 12, 1872, Davis to Virginia Clay, Jan. 25, 1872, Virginia Clay to Clay, Jr., Jan. 16, 1872, Clay MSS; Clay, Jr., to Jefferson Davis, Oct. 30, 1875, *Jefferson Davis, Constitutionalist*, VII, 461.

Clay operated his plantation by a combination of all the labor and tenant systems then in use. The first two or three postwar crops were produced under the supervision of a managerial tenant, who rented the plantation for a stipulated amount and took all responsibility for management and the supplying of labor and equipment. This was the arrangement when, late in 1866, Clay "rented the plantation to Parker for $3,000 payable 1st Novr. next." After Clement moved to the plantation in 1868, he became his own manager, and the next year he entered into a partnership with a man named May. The results were unfortunate, for May's thievery, Clement wrote, "cost me all my profits from our planting. I am trying to get off from him peaceably, & to save as much as I can. He has been shipping & selling more cotton!!" In his labor force Clay had some tenants with equipment, sharecroppers with no equipment, and hands to whom he paid a cash wage. This was so unsatisfactory that in 1871 he was determined to get "hands with their *own stock* to cultivate the plantation next year. . . . I am determined . . . not to furnish stock or food to laborers next year. . . . I have tried it for 3 years to my cost & harassment beyond endurance another year."

Building up equipment had been Clay's greatest problem and expense. The loans from J. J. B. Hilliard were used to purchase horses, plows, and cotton seed. But the case of the harness illustrates some of his difficulties. Having ordered the needed harness, Clement reported, "Moore refused to trust me for one week . . . 'how are the mighty fallen!!' Think of my being refused credit for one week for $40.00!—& denied an article ordered . . . for want of cash. Well, I have borrowed . . . the harness I need . . . & have ordered from Nashville [where] . . . I hope I shall get a cheaper & better set of Harness . . . which will soothe my mortified pride or vanity. . . . A good name . . . is not equal to pure gold, or impure green backs."[21]

As cotton prices declined, Clay attempted to improve his prospects by more diversified farming. But his wheat crops were not successful. After he spent a week in finding "a man & machine" to thresh his wheat, the threshing itself took another week, during

21 Clay, Jr., to Virginia Clay, Dec. 18, 1866, Nov. 5, 1868, Jan. 6, 1870, Aug. 18, 1871, Clay, Jr., to J. J. B. Hilliard, Feb. 23, April 11, 1870, Clay MSS; Clay, Jr., to Jefferson Davis, Nov. 28, 1869, Jefferson Davis MSS; John Spencer Bassett, "The Industrial Decay of the Southern Planter," *SAQ*, II (April, 1903), 107-13.

which Clay "had to provide not only food & lodging" for the four men operating the threshing machine, "but from 6 to 8 hands & a wagon & team, each day, wh. was not easily commanded. The wheat," Clement continued, "turned out miserably—not averaging more than 4 bushels to the acre, when I expected not less than 10: it will hardly pay expenses." The next year the trouble was the low price. As Clement explained, "I cannot sacrifice my little wheat by selling it at $1. per bushel. . . . Flour will pay much better. . . . It should make me . . . $250, besides bran for cows & mules." His project for quarrying and selling lithographer's stone did not get under way because the stone on his land proved to be of too poor quality. A few years later he tried lumbering, having "put up a saw mill, with a 30 horse power steam engine. . . . I wish," Clement elaborated, "to run gist [*sic*] mills and shingle and lath machines by the same power, so as to utilize all my timber." But he found that in 1875 the demand for lumber was not brisk, and the freight charges were too high for shipping to urban centers.[22]

In the troubles that beset him, Clay was not alone or unique. Thousands of other Southerners were no more successful than he in regaining their prewar financial standing. A. H. Colquitt expressed it succinctly when he wrote to Virginia, "I have a good deal of property, *plantations,* and a great deal owing to me, but I have many & large debts to pay. I cant collect any money, I cant sell the plantations. I dun, and suffer duns—pay a little and extend much—dread the future and have no hope in the present—struggle hard to out live the storm, but the clouds thicken and the night grows darker." Under similar circumstances, Clay wrote on one occasion, "If I can find a vocation that suits me, tolerably, & will pay me $100 a month, I had best part with the plantation for $2,000 & give away all else I hold on it." Indeed, most people were making a bare living. Only the shrewdest, the most energetic, and the most untiring attained financial success in these trying years. Clay had neither the business acumen nor the physical energy for success in competitive enterprise; his talents lay in other channels.

In spite of the vexations of plantation management, Clement

22 Clay, Jr., to Virginia Clay, July 12, 1868, July 10, 1869, Aug. 23, 1876, Jefferson Davis to Clay, Jr., Dec. 5, 1875, Clay MSS; Clay, Jr., to Davis, Oct. 30, 1875, *Jefferson Davis, Constitutionalist,* VII, 461f.

was content to live in the quiet and isolation of his rural home, even though it lacked the romantic aura with which Jefferson Davis invested it on his occasional visits to the Clays. "That lovely cove is in my memory like a dream land," wrote Davis after one visit, and again, "It would be to me rest indeed if I could . . . be with you . . . in your mountain retreat . . . that abode of hospitality and rural beauty." "How often have I recalled the happy hours we . . . spent together . . . around your broad chimney place, with its grandly hospitable fire."[23]

Ordinarily that household was limited, however, to Clement, Matt, a favorite dog, a pet cat, and one or two servants. Apropos of his pets Clement wrote on one occasion, "Matt met me at the door with the sad news that he found Lina dead . . . lying before her box & kittens. . . . You can imagine my grief over my poor dead cat—that showed more love for me than any cat ever did, & wh. I loved more than I ever did another—& how I miss her meek & gentle & reverential expressions of regard & respect. We gave her xtian burial, with her feet to the east." Of a cow that had just died, Clement added, "That I do not regret her loss half so much as Lina's shows that I am not a philosopher or wise economist, but a childlike sentimentalist."

"Matt and I," wrote Clement on another occasion, "have taken to hard study, early bed time & rising, abstemious living & other virtuous things." "Abstemious living" was sometimes an elusive goal for both Clement and Lawson. "Bro. L. has not *tasted* one drop of spirits, beer, wine or anything since Xmas. Says he is resolved to live sober," reported Virginia in the spring of 1872. Clement's frequent attacks of asthma often necessitated the use of various drugs which tended to be habit forming. "I have had no excuse for taking laudanum or whiskey, & have not touched either, or chloroform," he wrote in 1869. At another time, after a long, cold ride "thro mud, rain & water . . . I was," confessed Clement, "sorely tempted to take some stimulant at Woodville & Camden . . . & felt that I needed it & that it would warm my frozen feet; but I did not & have not touched anything stronger than coffee since we parted. Trust me, I am a 'sadder but wiser man' than formerly." "I did not know that you felt so apprehensive of my *falling*," Clement wrote to Virginia while he was

23 A. H. Colquitt to Virginia Clay, Jan. 15, 1874, Jefferson Davis to Virginia Clay, Oct. 22, 1871, Sept. 14 [1872], Sept. 8, 1874, Jan. 3, 1875, June 15, 1882, Clay MSS.

in Mobile on insurance business. "I am . . . ," he assured her, "living very abstemiously & not taking any stimulant save tea & coffee. . . . I have dined & supped, when all but myself took wine or something stronger . . . & have been subjected to various temptations which I have had grace given me to resist. . . . Trust me—I will keep my word, with God's help; for I do not trust myself, but in his mercy & earnest prayer."

Such expression of religious faith came from Clement more frequently in these later years of his life. During his imprisonment he had turned to religion for solace, and in 1867 he became a member of Huntsville's Church of the Nativity (Episcopal). The women of the family had long been members, and Withers Clay had for many years been a vestryman. While always considering himself a Christian gentleman, Clement, like his father, had not made religion a major factor in his life.[24]

As the tribulations of Reconstruction settled down upon Alabama, Clay could feel no interest in politics. Commenting on some of its aspects in 1871, he wrote to Virginia, "I am at the Madison House,—where we last sojourned in my reelection to U. S. Sen. Nov. 1857. What an age ago . . . I have been looking in upon the two Houses of the Legislature with painful emotions. How changed since I stood in the lobby's last in 1863! In the House there are 15 negroes, of all colors, but most of them very black & kinky heads. They sit promiscuously, & seem, with a few exceptions, to be uncomfortable & unhappy. There is but one ebony face in the Senate who seems 'wrapt in the solitude of his own originality.' "

With the revival of the Democratic party, however, and the approaching presidential contest of 1872, Clay developed considerable enthusiasm for the election of Greeley. When the Talladega Greeley Club asked him to address one of its meetings, Clay declined, but agreed to attend and make the necessary excuses on behalf of himself and General John B. Hood, who had also declined to speak. The result was somewhat astonishing, as Clement wrote to Virginia, "Would you believe that I got up to excuse him & myself from speaking, and spoke nearly 2 hours! I quite forgot the excuse and only made it for him at close of my

[24] Clay, Jr., to Virginia Clay, March 25, 1874, July 13, 1869, Jan. 6, 1870, Aug. 23, 1871, May 10, 1872, Virginia Clay to Clay, Jr., April 24, 1872, Celeste Clay to Virginia Clay, April 23 [1867], Clay MSS.

talk. I was assured by old & new friends that I never spoke better or more effectively & that my voice was as clear as a bell. On my word I did not mean to talk 5 minutes when I arose, but the tremen*dious* [*sic*] applause stirred me like the trumpet does an old war horse, making him tho' spavined & stiff prick his ears & snort & cavort with all his might. They wish me to canvass the state, & if out of debt I think I'd try."

The Democratic victory in Alabama in 1874 was an occasion of great rejoicing, but it had unpleasant repercussions, as Clement noted. "The negroes . . . look sullen, but subdued, distressed & distrustful. I have been assuring them that the Demo. Party had no purpose to enslave or oppress them, but would preserve & protect all their rights. . . . But while they protest they are not for social equality, they are for stealing & as bent on it as ever. . . . Yesterday Ragsdale & I caught Pete Diel & Frank Jumper carrying off to sell about 10 to 12$ worth of cotton in the seed. . . . The negroes, too, are resolved . . . not to get out their crops before Xmas. They lost all the last week—monday, tuesday & wednesday, in preparing to vote, voting, & counting the votes; thursday, friday & saturday in cursing & lamentation."[25]

Eight years later, Clay passed by another opportunity to reenter politics. The circumstance was a senatorial vacancy caused by the death of George Smith Houston. Clay's friends thought he could be elected, and so urged him to apply for the removal of his political disabilities. Virginia heartily endorsed the idea and entrusted to Senator John Tyler Morgan "the delicate duty" of persuading Clay that to make the necessary application would not be construed as an admission of guilt. And so Clay finally wrote, "I respectfully ask that the disabilities imposed upon me under sections 3 of the fourteenth amendment of the Constitution of the United States in consequence of my participation in the war waged by Alabama and other States against the United States, or my having given aid or comfort to the enemies of the United States, may be removed." Senator Morgan put the necessary bill through Congress, and on June 16, 1880, Clement Clay was once more in possession of all the rights and privileges of a citizen of the United States.

But in spite of Morgan's urgings, Clay concluded that his friends

25 Clay, Jr., to Virginia Clay, Dec. 1, 4, 1871, Oct. 2, 1872, Nov. 8, 1874, Clay MSS.

had overrated his popularity, and so declined to seek the senatorship. "I am entirely content," he wrote another friend, "with the
honors wh. Ala. has conferred upon me, & covet nothing but independence & repose. . . . I am, indeed, too poor to seek office save
for its emoluments,—& no man worthy of it would aspire to the
U. S. S. for its salary. . . . I shall never seek office of Ala. again,
for I have already recd. more than I merited." Clay's decision was
probably wise, for it is doubtful that he could have been elected
after a withdrawal from Alabama politics of almost twenty years.[26]

In the New South that was taking shape around him, Clay had
no part. Like Davis, he clung to the old. For them both, life
had ended with the defeat of the Confederacy. Though Clay was
barely fifty years of age when he was released from prison, he felt
himself too old to make a new start. "I have lived ½ a 100 yrs.
in vain," he wrote on his fiftieth birthday. Indeed, as he struggled
with his problems, he often looked forward to death "with
pleasure. For life," as he wrote Davis, "has lost its chiefest joys
with me, & I do not even hope to recover them. If I could only
settle my a/cs in this world, & leave the property I hold, without
incumbrance, to my wife, I should be content to go away from it
at once. Debt is my heaviest cross & I long to lay it down."

Clay's life came to an end on January 3, 1882, following an
attack of pneumonia. In a quickly written but moving elegy,
Virginia Clay epitomized her husband's life:[27]

> 'Th' applause of List'ning Senate to command'
> Was thine in happy days forever past;
> Belov'd and honor'd were thou in the land,
> E'en under dire Misfortune's bitter blast.
>
> But, not for lov'd ones, friends or country dear,
> Can sorrow visit thy sad heart again,
> Which broke: when, folded o'er a Nation's bier,
> Her banner lay, embalmed in tears of pain.

Clay's chief desire, to leave his estate to Virginia "without
incumbrance," was unfulfilled. The administrator found that

<hr />

[26] J. T. Morgan to Virginia Clay, March 11, 1880, Clay, Jr., to J. H. Clanton,
Sept. 27, 1880, Clay MSS; USC, *Cong. Record*, 64:2, X, pt. 4, p. 3896, pt. 5, pp.
4267, 4314, 4402, 4620, May 28, June 7, 9, 11, 16, 1880; Dorris, *Pardon and Amnesty
under Lincoln and Johnson*, 387f.

[27] Clay, Jr., to Virginia Clay, Dec. 13, 1866, Clay MSS; Clay, Jr., to Jefferson
Davis, May 26, 1873, Davis MSS; Huntsville *Democrat*, Jan. 5, 1882.

Clay's indebtedness at the time of his death amounted to about $12,000, whereas the real property had a valuation of $6,750. Consequently the estate was declared insolvent. Under petition for assignment of dower, Virginia was entitled to personal property to the value of $1,000. The office building on the square, which had been mortgaged in 1876, was now sold for $2,650. When the lands came up for sale, they were bid in by Virginia, Lawson, William Lewis Clay (Withers' son), and (in Jackson County) by "Thomas Gurley, colored." Thus was Clement's estate kept in the family. It was perhaps some consolation for the Clays to learn that the estate of another prominent Huntsville family, the Walkers, was also insolvent.[28]

Virginia must now perforce live on the plantation and derive from it the best income she could. To this end Lawson tried to impress her with "the *necessity* there is for you to look well into your business affairs now." But Virginia had small interest in the details of business and no talent whatsoever for financial management and thrift. Her rustic home, which she now named "Wildwood," was located on a hillside spot overlooking the Memphis and Charleston Railroad tracks and the road that would in later years become U. S. 72. The household too had increased, for about 1875 two young orphaned cousins came to live with the Clays. They were Fannie Weatherford and Bettie Lumsden, daughters of sisters of Tom Tait Tunstall. Though the girls both married in the 1880's, they remained in the vicinity and in later years returned to live at "Wildwood," where they devoted themselves to caring for Virginia in her advanced age[29] and where their descendants still reside.

In the summer of 1884, Virginia achieved her lifelong ambition of European travel. She chaperoned two young cousins, Nannie Whitmell Tunstall and Mary Lou Dearing, on an extensive tour which included Ireland, England, and Scotland, a journey up the Rhine, and the chief tourist attractions of Switzerland and France. Virginia enjoyed another social triumph when she returned as a visitor in the winter of 1885-1886 to official Washington society, once more under the Democratic aegis. Her undiminished popu-

28 Madison County Archives, Office of Probate Court, Case no. 3609, Record Book 36, pp. 52, 276, Minute Book 21, p. 511.
29 Whitmore Morris, *The First Tunstalls in Virginia and Some of Their Descendants* (San Antonio, Texas, 1950), 86f.

larity after an absence of twenty-five years is undeniable proof of her social grace and leadership.[30]

On November 29, 1887, Virginia Clay was married to Judge David Clopton of the Alabama supreme court. The wedding took place at Lawson Clay's home and was attended by many prominent Southerners. Clopton had made the law his career, first in his youthful days in Georgia, then in Tuskegee, Alabama, where he lived from 1844 until he moved to Montgomery in 1866. In politics a Democrat and secessionist, he had been Clay's colleague in Congress for one term (1859-1861) and served in the Confederate house of representatives 1861-1865. He campaigned for the Democratic party in various postwar elections, but retained his judicial office until his death on February 5, 1892. As Mrs. Clopton, Virginia was again in official capital society and lived most of the time at Montgomery, but plantation matters and family responsibilities involving Fannie and Bettie took her often to "Wildwood." David Clopton also had many family and financial responsibilities involving the children of his two previous marriages.

In the years following Clopton's death, Virginia hoped to realize something from his estate, in which she was one of seven heirs. But the administrator, Clifford A. Lanier (brother of Sidney Lanier and Clopton's son-in-law), had to inform her that debts and losses from bad investments had cut her estimated $10,000 inheritance down to a few hundred dollars. Virginia ultimately received some land in the Birmingham area.[31]

As the years passed, other family changes occurred. Late in 1884 Withers Clay suffered a cerebral hemorrhage so severe that he was an invalid until his death on March 29, 1896. His wife Mary survived him by only two years. When he was incapacitated in 1884, his two daughters, Susanna and Virginia Clementine Clay, took over editorship of the Huntsville *Democrat* and conducted it until its demise in 1919. Lawson Clay was also stricken with paralysis on January 30, 1887, and again on March 10, 1889, and died

30 Clay MSS, June—Oct., 1884, *passim*. Virginia also wrote a series of letters which Withers Clay published in the Huntsville *Democrat* during the same period; Clay Scrapbooks, II, 1, IV, 64.

31 Mary Clay to Virginia Clay, Jan. 30, 1887, Virginia Clopton to David Clopton, Dec. 27, 28, 30, 1890, Clifford A. Lanier to Virginia Clay-Clopton, March 19, 1896, March 8, 1898, Virginia Clementine Clay to Virginia Clay-Clopton, Feb. 17, 1898, Virginia Clay-Clopton to C. A. Lanier, March 11, 1898, Clay MSS; and Clay MSS, 1887-1914, *passim;* Octavia Zollicoffer Bond, "South of the Line: A Belle of the Fifties," *Southern Woman's Magazine*, V (Sept., 1915), 16f, 33.

December 28, 1890. Celeste Clay continued to live in Huntsville until her death on March 18, 1902. With her was her widowed sister, Loula (Comer) Hammond, who died December 3, 1914.

Following the five years spent mainly in Montgomery, Virginia returned again to "Wildwood," there to pursue a variety of activities that diminished little with advancing years. She now adopted the hyphenated name of Clay-Clopton. Being an independent, active woman herself, she naturally espoused the cause of women's rights and became a local leader in the movement for woman suffrage. She frequently attended Confederate veterans' reunions, where she always enjoyed a social triumph, led the grand march around the ballroom, and sometimes addressed the assembled veterans. She was of course an active member, and honorary life president, of the Alabama Daughters of the Confederacy. Her occasional writings, published in newspapers or southern magazines, were concerned always with some incident of Clay's career. At seventy-five years of age, Virginia finally began the book of memoirs that she had projected ever since 1866. Under the urgings of her faithful friend Ellelee Humes (daughter of Reuben Chapman), and with the editorial guidance of Ada Sterling, a New York journalist who came to "Wildwood" and spent several months with Virginia, the book took shape. Virginia's richly stored memory supplied an endless stream of anecdotes of her earlier life, which Ada Sterling reduced to an organized, readable, interesting, and reasonably accurate narrative. The volume, *A Belle of the Fifties,* was published in 1904—one of a great number of memoirs appearing about that time by participants in the war for southern independence.

January 16, 1915, was a great occasion in Huntsville. On that day Virginia celebrated her ninetieth birthday with a great reception given by her friend, Mrs. Milton Humes. "Gowned in black velvet and duchess lace, with a great pink corsage rose gleaming in the soft light of ninety candles on her birthday cake," Virginia enjoyed to the full her last great social triumph. Six months later, on June 23, 1915, a short illness terminated the life of a woman whose career had embraced drama as exciting as any fiction she could have invented.[32]

[32] Bond, "South of the Line," 15-17, 33.

14 ~

A Historical Estimate

ONE HUNDRED YEARS had passed between the day when Clement Comer Clay married Susanna Withers in 1815 and the day their daughter-in-law died in 1915. What had been the family's place in Alabama history and in national history during a century that had taken Alabama from frontier through revolution and debacle into industrialization, and the nation from a weak, isolated, young country to a world power?

The Clays' services to their state have been exceeded by few if any others among Alabama's political leaders. Clement Comer Clay, growing with his frontier state, wisely assayed its needs and worked tirelessly for its development. As a Democrat of the strictest school, he vigorously advocated the Jacksonian program as the only proper solution for the nation's problems. And in so doing, he developed that undeviating party loyalty which characterized his own and his son's political careers. Despite his stern and unbending character, the elder Clay was a sufficiently skillful politician to remain on top in the fierce and unending scramble for place and power in Huntsville and North Alabama, where annual elections and campaigning kept politics constantly seething. That was no mean accomplishment. He did it, in large degree, by his control of the party organ, the Huntsville *Democrat,* whose editorial policy he guided from the sidelines for almost thirty years. The extent of that control cannot be fully charted, but it assuredly existed.

While the elder Clay carried into mature life something of the eighteenth-century exhilaration and the breath of the Revolution, young Clement was emphatically a product of the Romantic Age. The influence of romanticism only intensified his natural bent to emotionalism, sentimentality, exaggerated feeling, flowery language, and an overacute sense of "honor" which could too easily be "insulted." Admittedly, he built his career on the foundation laid by his father. Endowed with superior intellectual powers, young Clement was a precocious youth, an avid reader, a man cut out for scholarship in such fields as history, philosophy, or political science. Training and environment turned him to law and politics, where his talents had a wide and congenial range of usefulness. While his services to the state of Alabama were not so diversified as his father's had been, yet C. C. Clay, Jr., must be counted a leader second only to Yancey in Alabama's secession movement. His contemporaries held in highest esteem his services, his abilities, and his character.

This picture of the Old South as it is revealed in the story of the Clay family contains all the elements attributed to southern society. It is not a complete picture, for it represents but one class —the planting, slaveholding, ruling class. But of their class, the Clay family, individually or collectively, exhibit every facet of that life: pride of lineage, social position, ambition, arrogance, graciousness, hospitality, generosity, sophistication, and provincialism.

This strong localism, evident in all sections of the country, was deeply entrenched in the South. Living as they did in an interior town and amid an agricultural economy remote from the centers of trade and industry, the Clays had little comprehension of the rapidly changing needs of an increasingly complex society. Their occasional visits to the North and East gave them only a superficial knowledge of the problems of other sections. Neither Clement, Sr., nor his son can be credited with outstanding contributions to national policy, for both were concerned first with the welfare of their state and section. In this they did not differ from most of their colleagues, whether from North, South, or West. Indeed, as state-rights Democrats, they did not look upon the United States as a nation, but rather as a confederation of sovereign states. Both believed that the goals they sought could best be attained through a firm adherence to state rights, strict economy, and the least possible concentration of power in the federal government.

Increasing this parochialism was the vast gulf created by the slavery controversy. The younger Clay's career in the United States Senate was set in abnormal times when every subject, no matter what its nature, somehow became entangled in the slavery issue. C. C. Clay, Jr., did nothing in his public life to ease sectional tension, and much to exacerbate it. In doing so, he did only what every other state-rights leader was doing. In the slow retreat of the South from a position of equality and power in the national councils, Clay and his southern colleagues were fighting a negative, defensive, obstructive battle. They could not have a positive program.

Clay himself had a strong sense of duty, integrity, and morality, and an earnest conviction that he acted always from principle. Because he could see no other way out for the South, he fell back on "rights" and clamored ultimately for "protection" of slavery in the territories, even though he knew it had no practical meaning. As he denounced the "Black Republicans" year after year, he ultimately came to believe all the things he said about them. Like the majority of his section, he would not surrender the balance of power and control of the government by southern Democrats and their allies without a fight. So he became more fiercely state-rights as the problems became more insoluble. Clay always wished to strive for southern rights within the framework of the Democratic party, and so he opposed the formation of a southern sectional party until he could see no other way out. He then joined Yancey and the other ultra-southern-rights men in breaking up the Democratic party and leading the South out of the Union. Why? Essentially because Clay could not endure the idea of being in the minority. Though an oversimplification, this idea is basic in explaining the action of the secessionists. The loss of power in 1860 to a northern sectional party avowedly hostile to the social and economic complex of a slaveholding society foreboded so many dangers, real or imagined, that southern-rights leaders plunged into action on the basis of the theories they had long proclaimed.

So they set up a "purified" American republic, cleansed (so they hoped) of all the ambiguities which had beset the old Constitution. The more naive and unthinking even believed that the new government would operate in an atmosphere of perfect unity and harmony.

Clement Clay was too good a politician to entertain any such utopian notion, but he and the other leaders of the Confederacy were not prepared for all the bickering and problems that beset them. Why did the Confederate government make such a poor showing? Two factors seem to be fundamental. The generation of 1861 was ignorant of the nature and consequences of war. True, many men of the South had fought in the Mexican War. But that was a small war, waged mainly on foreign soil, by a limited number of troops. The people as a whole had no comprehension of war. In the dual situation of having to fight a major war and at the same time operate and stabilize a new government, the novel and overwhelming problems were more than Confederate leadership could handle. With all eyes, thoughts, and energies concentrated on fighting the invader, Confederates let their civil government die of neglect. Clay, as a member of the Confederate senate, worked as best he could to keep the legislative wheels turning, but neither he nor his colleagues envisioned the real nature of their problems or understood the desperate urgency for speedy, decisive, and unified action on emergency legislation in a time of crisis. When the times cried for unity with every leader supporting his government in order to win a war, too much brain-power was dissipated in unproductive ways. Through his long discipline in loyalty, Clay faithfully supported Davis and the government. He at least stayed at the job he knew best, and did not join those political leaders who wasted their talents in destructive opposition, or as bumbling political generals. Who can say what the result would have been if such men as Robert Toombs, Alexander H. Stephens, Joseph E. Brown, Louis T. Wigfall, and others had cast their strength for the government, rather than against it?[1]

It was Clay's strong sense of honor that led him to surrender voluntarily in 1865. This high-minded act he could only vainly regret while he suffered the misfortunes it brought in its train and discovered that the hatreds of war had warped in others the sense of justice and honor which he thought all gentlemen possessed.

Clay's personal life was beyond reproach and singularly happy. For Virginia Clay he had a deep and chivalric love, mingled with admiration and wonder at her accomplishments. Virginia, though she might be given to flirtations, adored him and looked upon him

[1] Allan Nevins, *The Statesmanship of the Civil War* (New York, 1953), 1-56.

as the South's greatest statesman. Her efforts for his release from prison, heroic and harrowing though they were, also satisfied her craving for the dramatic and for ceaseless activity.

Thus in 1866, Clement, without the discipline of youthful hardships, and Virginia, who best graced the drawing room, were not equipped to cope with adversity. A society queen could not be content as a housewife. A former senator could not take some niggling work beneath his station. For fifty years Clement had lived the "good life" as a member of the privileged class of southern society. In the day of its destruction he had not the energy or the kind of talent that could build anew in a situation full of difficulties. But he never regretted his course or wished that he had done otherwise. He had striven for what he thought best and wisest for the South, but in so doing, he had helped to destroy what he was trying to save.

BIBLIOGRAPHICAL NOTE

THIS BIOGRAPHY is based mainly on the Clement Claiborne Clay Manuscripts (1811-1925) acquired in 1930 by Duke University Library (Durham, N. C.) from Mrs. Bettie V. Adams, legatee of Virginia Clay. This large collection of family papers (8,545 items) contains the following categories of material: Personal, political, and business letters, legal documents, literary and political holographs, letterbooks, diaries, accounts, memoranda, and other records. Printed materials acquired with the collection include scrapbooks (8 vols.), clippings, broadsides, photographs, calling cards, and pamphlets. The pamphlets, all of them speeches of C. C. Clay, Sr., and C. C. Clay, Jr., contain a few rare imprints, but are generally also available in the *Congressional Globe*.

More than fifty other manuscript collections were consulted. Of them, the following proved especially valuable: (at Duke University Library), David Campbell MSS, Sterling Gee MSS, George Smith Houston MSS, Placebo Houston MSS, Ada Sterling MSS, Henry Watson MSS; (at the Alabama Department of Archives and History, Montgomery), William Phineas Browne MSS, John Coffee MSS, Thomas Butler Cooper MSS, J. L. M. Curry MSS, Bolling Hall MSS, Robert McKee MSS, William Flewellen Samford MSS, John Williams Walker MSS, William Lowndes Yancey MSS; (at the Library of Congress, Washington, D. C.), Jeremiah Sullivan Black MSS, J. L. M. Curry MSS, James Knox Polk MSS, L. T. Wigfall MSS; (at the University of Kentucky, Lexington), Thomas Henry Hines MSS (used in microfilm copy).

The other sources now to be listed fall naturally, and with little overlapping into several large chronological periods which follow the Clays from Alabama politics, to national politics, and through the Confederate period. The sources and secondary works included are limited to those which provided significant information, guidance, or background for this study, and by no means cover everything consulted or even everything cited in the footnotes.

THE CLAYS IN ALABAMA'S EARLY DEVELOPMENT AND POLITICS

Governor Clay's conduct of the Creek War (1836) is detailed in the Governors' Letterbooks (1822-1836), Official Correspondence, and Military Archives, at the Alabama Department of Archives and History (Montgomery).

The following documentary publications relate to Alabama's early history: *Journal of the Convention of the Alabama Territory, Begun July 5, 1819* (Huntsville, 1819 [Washington, D. C., 1909, photofacsimile reprint]); Alabama Legislature, House *Journal* (1819-date) and Senate *Journal* (1819-date) (Cahaba, Tuscaloosa, Montgomery, 1819-date).

Three contemporaries of the Clays recorded their impressions and knowledge of nineteenth-century Alabama in these volumes: William Garrett, *Reminiscences of Public Men in Alabama for Thirty Years* (Atlanta, 1872); Anne (Newport) Royall, *Letters from Alabama on Various Subjects: To Which Is Added an Appendix, Containing Remarks on Sundry Members of the 20th & 21st Congress, and Other High Characters &c. &c. at the Seat of Government* (Washington, 1830); and James Edmonds Saunders, *Early Settlers of Alabama . . . with Notes and Genealogies,* by his Granddaughter, Elizabeth Saunders Blair Stubbs (New Orleans, 1899). Alabama's great pioneer archivist, Thomas McAdory Owen, expanded these early efforts in his *History of Alabama and Dictionary of Alabama Biography* (Chicago, 1921, 4 vols.).

Chroniclers of Huntsville and Madison County were: Edward Chambers Betts, *Early History of Huntsville, Alabama, 1804 to 1870* (Montgomery, Ala., 1916, rev. ed.); and Thomas Jones Taylor, "Early History of Madison County," *Alabama Historical Quarterly,* I (1930), 101-11, 149-68, 308-17, 489-505, II (1940), 86-91, and continued with the title, "Later History of Madison County," in II, 239-47, 342-64, 493-536. Taylor's account, first published in the Huntsville *Independent* in 1883-1884, is more detailed and better organized than is Betts'. Both were written from the reminiscent, antiquarian point of view, but contain a wealth of information about the locality where the Clays spent their lives.

Genealogical information on the Clay, Comer, Tunstall, Withers, and related families is available in these volumes: Reginald Fitz Hugh Bigg-Wither, *Materials for a History of the Wither Family* (Winchester, Eng., 1907); Whitmore Morris, *The First Tunstalls in Virginia, and Some of Their Descendants* (San Antonio, 1950); Frederick Zachariah Smith and Mary Rogers Clay, *The Clay Family; Part First: The Mother of Henry Clay . . . Part Second: The Genealogy of the Clays . . .* (Louisville, 1899); Anne Kendrick Walker, *Braxton Bragg Comer. His Family Tree from Virginia's Colonial Days* (Richmond, 1947); and Robert Edwin Withers, *Withers Family of the County Lancaster, England, and of Stafford County, Virginia, Establishing the Ancestry of Robert Edwin Withers, III . . .* (Richmond, 1947).

The most important source for ante bellum Huntsville, however, is its newspapers. The *Alabama Republican* (1816-1825) provides coverage for the early period. In the latter year this paper was united with the *Alabamian* to form the *Southern Advocate* (1825-1865). Under the later editorship of William Bibb Figures it became the Whig organ of North Alabama, though it was nominally Democratic after 1856. The Huntsville *Democrat* (1823-1919), after its controversial beginnings under William B. Long and Andrew Wills, soon passed into the hands of Philip Woodson, whose daughter married into the Withers family. This family connection enabled Clement Comer Clay to guide

Woodson in making that paper the Democratic organ of North Alabama. In 1856 Woodson retired and sold out to John Withers Clay, under whose editorship the paper became even more strongly state-rights. Its last editors were Susanna Withers and Virginia Clementine Clay, daughters of John Withers Clay. Extensive files of all these papers are in the Alabama Department of Archives and History and in the Library of Congress.

Four scholarly monographs parallel the period of the Clays' political careers: Thomas Perkins Abernethy, *The Formative Period in Alabama, 1815-1828* (Montgomery, 1922); Clarence Phillips Denman, *The Secession Movement in Alabama* (Montgomery, 1933); Lewy Dorman, *Party Politics in Alabama from 1850 through 1860* (Wetumpka, Ala., 1935); and Theodore Henley Jack, *Sectionalism and Party Politics in Alabama, 1819-1842* (Menasha, Wis., 1919). Abernethy's "pioneer" work makes good use of the materials to which he had access, but leaves many questions for later research to answer; Denman's well-written summary of events, 1848-1861, is somewhat lacking in depth of interpretation; Dorman's insight into the workings of Alabama politics is on the whole good, although his style is pedestrian; Jack achieves that concise and reasoned appraisal which William E. Dodd required of all his students.

The following periodical articles, some of them reminiscent and others representative of recent scholarship, add substantially to the rather limited body of materials on Alabama's history to 1861: Gordon T. Chappell, "Some Patterns of Land Speculation in the Old Southwest," *Journal of Southern History*, XV (1949), 462-77; Malcolm Cook McMillan, "The Alabama Constitution of 1819: A Study in Constitution-Making on the Frontier," *Alabama Review*, III (1950), 263-85; Ruth Ketring Nuermberger, "The 'Royal Party' in Early Alabama Politics," *Alabama Review*, VI (1953), 81-98, 198-212; Frank Lawrence Owsley, "John Williams Walker," *Alabama Review*, IX (1956), 100-19; George Petrie, "William F. Samford: Statesman and Man of Letters," Alabama Historical Society *Transactions*, IV (1899-1903), 465-85; Henderson Middleton Somerville, "Trial of the Alabama Supreme Court Judges in 1829; and Its Lessons to Posterity. An Address Delivered before the Alabama State Bar Association, June 16, 1899, at Montgomery, Ala.," Alabama State Bar Association *Proceedings*, 1899 (Montgomery, 1899), 59-96.

THE CLAYS IN NATIONAL POLITICS

For any career in the United States Congress, the records of that body are the obvious chief source. U. S. Congress, House *Journal* (Washington, 1826-date) and Senate *Journal* (Washington, 1820-date), together with *Register of Debates* (Washington, 1825-1837) and *Congressional Globe* (Washington, 1834-1873), record both Clays' activities in House and Senate. The social scene is recorded in Virginia Clay-Clopton, *A Belle of the Fifties; Memoirs of Mrs. Clay, of Alabama, Covering Social and Political Life in Washington and the South, 1853-66. Put into Narrative Form by Ada Sterling* (New York, 1905), Written by journalist Ada Sterling both from oral recollections of Virginia Clay and from the Clay MSS, this account is both interesting and valuable, but cannot be relied on for complete accuracy. It supplements the unfiltered material in the Clay MSS, and is chiefly useful in reflecting Virginia Clay's character.

Newspapers are the next most valuable source for following a political career. For ease of reference, all the newspapers used are listed here, even though they might not fall strictly within the bounds of this portion of the Clays' lives.

ALABAMA

Cahaba *Dallas Gazette*
Eufaula *Spirit of the South*
Greensboro *Alabama Beacon*
Huntsville *Alabama Republican*
Huntsville *Confederate* and *Daily Confederate*
Huntsville *Daily Independent*
Huntsville *Democrat*
Huntsville *Southern Advocate*
Jacksonville *Republican*
Mobile *Commercial Register and Patriot*
Mobile *Register and Journal*
Montgomery *Advertiser and State Gazette*
Montgomery *Weekly Advertiser*
Montgomery *Alabama Journal* and *Weekly Alabama Journal*
Montgomery *Daily Confederation* and *Weekly Confederation*
Montgomery *Weekly Mail*
Tuscaloosa *Independent Monitor*
Tuscaloosa *State Rights Expositor and Spirit of the Age*

OTHERS

Baltimore (Maryland) *Weekly Sun*
Burlington (Vermont) *Daily Free Press*
Buffalo (New York) *Commercial Advertiser*
Buffalo *Daily Courier*
Buffalo *Morning Express*
Charleston (South Carolina) *Mercury*
Nashville (Tennessee) *Union*
New York *Daily News*
New York *Herald*
New York *Times*
New York *Tribune*
Richmond (Virginia) *Enquirer* and *Daily Enquirer*
Richmond *Daily Examiner*
Richmond *Whig and Public Advertiser*
Washington (D.C.) *Globe*
Washington *National Intelligencer* and *Daily National Intelligencer*
Washington *New Era*
Washington *Sentinel*
Washington *United States Telegraph*
Washington *Union*

General works for the period 1830-1860 are: Charles Sackett Sydnor, *The Development of Southern Sectionalism, 1819-1848* (Baton Rouge, 1948); Avery Odell Craven, *The Growth of Southern Nationalism, 1848-1861* (Baton Rouge, 1953); George Fort Milton, *The Eve of Conflict. Stephen A. Douglas and the Needless War* (Boston, 1934); Allan Nevins, *Ordeal of the Union* (New York, 1948, 2 vols.), and *The Emergence of Lincoln* (New York, 1950, 2 vols.); Roy Franklin Nichols, *The Disruption of American Democracy* (New York, 1948). While Nevins writes from the northern—even New England—point of view, and seems ill at ease in his dealing with the South, the other four exhibit a nice balance between the sections, or avowedly make the South the focal area of consideration.

Of the many biographies consulted, a few have been especially useful. Eugene Irving McCormac, *James K. Polk: A Political Biography* (Berkeley, Calif., 1922) is a work of much insight but lacks any personal touch. This omission is rectified in Charles Grier Sellers, Jr., *James K. Polk, Jacksonian, 1795-1843* (Princeton, N. J., 1957), a work of admirable scholarship. Roy Franklin Nichols, *Franklin Pierce, Young Hickory of the Granite Hills* (Philadelphia, 1931), delineates the fourteenth President in a realistic and personal style. Two monographs cover the public-land question: Roy Marvin Robbins, *Our Landed Heritage: The Public Domain, 1776-1936* (Princeton, 1942); and Payson Jackson Treat, *The National Land System, 1785-1820* (New York, 1910).

Among periodical articles, the following titles are self-explanatory of their relevance: Walter Lynwood Fleming, "The Buford Expedition to Kansas," *American Historical Review,* VI (1900-1901), 38-48; James Leonidas Murphy, "Alabama and the Charleston Convention," *Alabama Historical Society Transactions,* V (1904), 239-66; Albert Ray Newsome (ed.), "Letters of Lawrence O'Bryan Branch, 1856-1860," *North Carolina Historical Review,* X (1933), 44-79; James Garfield Randall, "Senator Bagby of Alabama," *South Atlantic Quarterly,* X (1911), 169-79; Roy Marvin Robbins, "Preemption—A Frontier Triumph," *Mississippi Valley Historical Review,* XVIII (1931-1932), 331-49; Shepherd H. Roberts, "Benjamin Fitzpatrick and the Vice-Presidency," Alabama Historical Society *Transactions,* IV (1899-1903), 357-64; John B. Sanborn, "Some Political Aspects of Homestead Legislation," *American Historical Review,* VI (1900-1901), 19-38; Sutton Selwyn Scott, "Recollections of the Alabama Democratic State Convention of 1860," Alabama Historical Society *Transactions,* IV (1899-1903), 313-21; Austin L. Venable, "The Conflict between the Douglas and Yancey Forces in the Charleston Convention," *Journal of Southern History,* VIII (1942), 226-41; James Eyers Davis Yonge, "Conservative Party in Alabama, 1848-1860," Alabama Historical Society *Transactions,* IV (1899-1903), 501-26.

THE CLAYS IN THE CONFEDERATE PERIOD

The dominant story of the years 1861-1863 is C. C. Clay, Jr.'s service in the Confederate senate. For this there are three sources. First in importance is the War Department Collection of Confederate Records (RG 109) at the National Archives (Washington, D. C.). This large file of Confederate Congressional Bills and Resolutions (1861-1865), and the folio volume (XI) titled Confederate Senate Register (1862-1864) provide the basic material for following Clay in the Confederate senate. The parallel and equally important printed source is *Journal of the Congress of the Confederate States of America, 1861-1865* (Washington, 1904-1905, 7 vols. [U. S. Congress, 58th Cong., 2d Sess., Senate Document no. 234]). There is no official publication of the debates in the Confederate congress. To supply this want, the Southern Historical Society, under the impetus of Douglas Southall Freeman, undertook to publish transcripts of the debates as reported in the Richmond newspapers (chiefly the *Examiner*). These are to be found in Southern Historical Society *Papers* (Richmond, 1876-date). Volumes 44-50 carry the record from February 18, 1862, through February 18, 1864. With the death of Dr. Freeman in 1953, the single remaining member of the Society transferred its assets to the Virginia Historical Society, which issued volume 50. Two volumes remain to be published. Useful as this publication is, reports are sometimes fragmentary and do not include debate in secret session.

Confederate congressmen left few personal records of their service. Two of considerable value deserve mention: Herschel Vespasian Johnson, "From the Autobiography of Herschel V. Johnson," *American Historical Review*, XXX (1924-1925), 311-36, and Franklin Barlow Sexton, "Diary of a Confederate Congressman, 1862-1863," ed. by Mary S. Estill, *Southwestern Historical Quarterly*, XXXVIII (1934-1935), 270-301, XXXIX (1935-1936), 33-65. Another, written long after and containing little more than a superficial summary, is in John Goode, *Recollections of a Life-Time* (New York, 1906). Biographical sketches, and even full-length biographies of men who served in the Confederate congress, for the most part ignore, or skip over with only passing comment, their services in that body. Two general articles on the Confederate congress may be noted. Edward A. Pollard, "The Confederate Congress. A Chapter in the History of the Late War," *Galaxy*, VI (1868), 749-58, is an account by a contemporary in a position to know, but Pollard's violent hostility to Davis and to the whole Confederate government so strongly biased his account that it has only incidental value. Daniel M. Robison, "The Whigs in the Politics of the Confederacy," East Tennessee Historical Society *Publications*, no. 11 (1939), is a most useful and provocative analysis, but admittedly it is tentative and based on research undertaken primarily for study of a later period.

General and special works on the Confederacy, all of them of a high caliber of scholarship, are: Ellis Merton Coulter, *The Confederate States of America, 1861-1865* (Baton Rouge, 1950); Clement Eaton, *A History of the Southern Confederacy* (New York, 1954); John Knox Bettersworth, *Confederate Mississippi, The People and Policies of a Cotton State in Wartime* (Baton Rouge, 1943); Jefferson Davis Bragg, *Louisiana in the Confederacy* (Baton Rouge, 1941); Walter Lynwood Fleming, *Civil War and Reconstruction in Alabama* (New York, 1905); Burton Jesse Hendrick, *Statesmen of the Lost Cause: Jefferson Davis and His Cabinet* (Boston, 1939); Ella Lonn, *Foreigners in the Confederacy* (Chapel Hill, 1940); Albert Burton Moore, *Conscription and Conflict in the Confederacy* (New York, 1924); Allan Nevins, *The Statesmanship of the Civil War* (New York, 1953); Frank

Lawrence Owsley, *State Rights in the Confederacy* (Chicago, 1925); Rembert Wallace Patrick, *Jefferson Davis and His Cabinet* (Baton Rouge, 1944); William Morrison Robinson, *Justice in Grey: A History of the Judicial System of the Confederate States of America* (Cambridge, Mass., 1941).

Of the several biographies for the period, these three have special pertinence: John Witherspoon DuBose, *The Life and Times of William Lowndes Yancey . . .* (Birmingham, Ala., 1892); Joseph Thomas Durkin, *Stephen R. Mallory: Confederate Navy Chief* (Chapel Hill, 1954); and Robert Douthat Meade, *Judah P. Benjamin, Confederate Statesman* (New York, 1943). Finally, there are those two standbys of all Confederate researchers: Mary Boykin (Miller) Chesnut, *A Diary from Dixie,* ed. by Ben Ames Williams (Boston, 1949), and John Beauchamp Jones, *A Rebel War Clerk's Diary at the Confederate States Capital . . . ,* ed. by Howard Swiggett (New York, 1935, 2 vols.).

These periodical articles proved to be valuable: Walter Lynwood Fleming, "The Peace Movement in Alabama during the Civil War," *South Atlantic Quarterly,* II (1903), 114-24, 246-60; William Lowndes Yancey, "Letters," *Alabama Historical Quarterly,* II (1940), 256-61, 334-41; and Richard E. Yates, "Zebulon B. Vance as War Governor of North Carolina, 1862-1865," *Journal of Southern History,* III (1937), 43-75.

THE CONFEDERATES IN CANADA

Dispatches by and about the Confederate commissioners in Canada are found in these archives: Confederate States of America, State Department, Record Letterbook XIV (Library of Congress); Clay MS Letterbook (Duke University Library); and Canadian Archives (Ottawa), Governor General's Office, Letters to the Secretary of State (1864), G12, vol. 69, and Governor General's Numbered Files, no. 57, vol. 1, 1864-1870. Next in importance are those two great printed repositories of material: U. S. Navy Department, *Official Records of the Union and Confederate Navies in the War of the Rebellion . . .* (Washington, 1894-1922, 30 vols.), and U. S. War Department, *War of the Rebellion: A Compilation of the Official Records of the Union and Confederate Armies . . .* (Washington, 1880-1901, 70 vols. in 128).

Of monographs the best by far is Wood Gray, *The Hidden Civil War: The Story of the Copperheads* (New York, 1942), which provides both background and detailed information on the complicated story. It is written from the northern point of view. James David Horan, *Confederate Agent, A Discovery in History* (New York, 1954), is a popular work with Thomas Henry Hines the central figure, and so slanted as to make him the Confederate hero in all operations from Canada. Though it tells a good story, this work contains several errors of fact.

The following accounts by Confederate participants are all of value, but vary considerably in their skill of presentation: John Breckin-ridge Castleman, *Active Service* (Louisville, Ky., 1917); John William Headley, *Confederate Operations in Canada and New York* (New York, 1906); Thomas Henry Hines, "The Northwestern Conspiracy," *Southern Bivouac,* V (1886-1887), 437-45, 500-10, 567-74, 699-704; Daniel Bedinger Lucas, *Memoir of John Yates Beall: His Life; Trial; Correspondence; Diary; and Private Manuscript Found among His Papers, Including His Own Account of the Raid on Lake Erie* (Mont-real, 1865); Percy L. Rainwater (ed.), "Letters to and from Jacob Thompson," *Journal of Southern History,* VI (1940), 95-111; and Bennett Henderson Young, "Secret History of the St. Albans Raid," *Vermonter,* VII (1902), 22-27.

Contemporary and reminiscent accounts of the "Northwestern Con-spiracy" by Northerners include: I. Winslow Ayer, *The Great North-western Conspiracy in All Its Startling Details* . . . (Chicago, 1865); Felix Grundy Stidger (ed.), *Treason History of the Order of Sons of Liberty* . . . (Chicago, 1903); [James Roberts Gilmore], "The Chi-cago Conspiracy," *Atlantic Monthly,* XVI (1865), 108-20; Thomas H. Keefe, "How the Northwest Was Saved. A Chapter from the Secret Service Records of the Civil War," *Everybody's Magazine,* II (1900), 82-91; Frederick Boyd Stevenson, "The Johnson Island Conspiracy. An Episode of the Civil War," *Frank Leslie's Popular Monthly,* XLVI (1898), 257-66.

For the St. Albans raid, the fullest account was published in the Burlington (Vermont) *Daily Free Press* (complete file in the Fletcher Free Public Library, Burlington). Two documentary compilations also provide detailed information: L. N. Benjamin (comp.), *The St. Albans Raid: Or Investigation into the Charges against Lieut. Bennett H. Young and Command, for Their Acts at St. Albans, Vt., on the 19th October, 1864* . . . (Montreal, 1865); *The St. Albans Raid. Investigation by the Police Committee, of the City Council of Mont-real, into the Charges Preferred by Councillor B. Devlin against Guillaume Lamothe, Esq., Chief of Police; and the Proceedings of the Council in Reference Thereto* (Montreal, 1864). Other pertinent items are: Henri Têtu, *David Têtu et les raiders de Saint-Alban. Épisode de la guerre américaine, 1864-1865* (Quebec, 1891, 2d ed.); Mrs. Gregory J. Smith, "An Incident of the Civil War," *Vermonter,* IV (1899), 101-104.

Sources for the "Niagara Falls Peace Conference" are to be found in many of the items previously listed. Most of the dispatches are available in many places. Fullest newspaper coverage was given in the three Buffalo (New York) newspapers, *Commercial Advertiser, Daily Courier,* and *Morning Express.* Supplementing these accounts are: John Hay, *Letters of John Hay and Extracts from Diary* . . . *Selected by Henry Adams,* ed. by Mrs. Hay (Washington, 1908, 3 vols.); Abraham Lincoln, *Collected Works* . . . , ed. by Roy P. Basler

(New Brunswick, N. J., 1953-1955, 9 vols.). General accounts are in: Elbert J. Benton, *The Movement for Peace without Victory during the Civil War* (Cleveland, 1918); Edward Chase Kirkland, *The Peacemakers of 1864* (New York, 1927); and Frank Hayward Severance, "The Peace Conference at Niagara," in *Peace Episodes on the Niagara: Other Studies and Reports* (Buffalo, N. Y., 1914). Greeley's part in the "Peace Conference" is dealt with in some detail in these biographies: Ralph Ray Fahrney, *Horace Greeley and the Tribune in the Civil War* . . . (Cedar Rapids, Iowa, 1936); and William Harlan Hale, *Horace Greeley, Voice of the People* (New York, 1950).

THE AFTERMATH OF WAR

Clay's personal story during the collapse of the Confederacy, his subsequent imprisonment, and his problems during the Reconstruction years can be told from the Clay MSS, but it stands against the vast and complex background of national hysteria, the trial and execution of Lincoln's assassins, and the imprisonment of hundreds of Confederate leaders. Many of the sources listed in the preceding two sections carry over into this postwar period. In addition, the most important printed documents are these: U. S. Congress, 39th Cong., 1st Sess., House Committee on Judiciary, *Report* no. 104, "Assassination of Lincoln" (Washington, 1866); U. S. Congress, 40th Cong., 1st Sess., House Committee on Judiciary, *Report* no. 7, *Impeachment Investigation. Testimony Taken before the Judiciary Committee of the House of Representatives in the Investigation of the Charges against Andrew Johnson* (Washington, 1867, ser. 1314).

The three records of the trial of Lincoln's assassins, all listed under "David E. Herold, defendant," are *The Assassination of President Lincoln and the Trial of the Conspirators* . . . , comp. by Benn Pitman (Cincinnati, 1865); *The Conspiracy Trial for the Murder of the President, and the Attempt to Overthrow the Government by the Assassination of Its Principal Officers,* ed. by Ben: Perley Poore (Boston, 1865, 3 vols.); *The Trial of the Assassins and Conspirators at Washington City, D. C., May and June, 1865. For the Murder of President Abraham Lincoln* . . . , by the Special Correspondents and Reporters of the Philadelphia *Daily Inquirer* (Philadelphia, 1865). David Miller DeWitt used these records and assessed them critically in his three volumes entitled, *The Judicial Murder of Mary E. Surratt* (Baltimore, 1895); *The Impeachment and Trial of Andrew Johnson, Seventeenth President of the United States, A History* (New York, 1903); and *The Assassination of Abraham Lincoln and Its Expiation* (New York, 1909).

Three contemporary pamphlets were issued to prove that the Confederates in Canada were not implicated in the plot to assassinate Lincoln. They are: William W. Cleary, *The Protest of W. W. Cleary, against the Proclamation of President Johnson, of May 2nd, with a Complete Exposure of the Perjuries before the Bureau of Military Justice upon Which That Proclamation Issued* (Toronto, 1865); Stuart Robinson, *The Infamous Perjuries of the "Bureau of Military Justice" Exposed. Letter of Rev. Stuart Robinson to Hon. Mr. Emmons* (n.p., n.d.); Beverley Tucker, *Address of Beverley Tucker, Esq., to The People of the United States, 1865,* ed. by James Harvey Young (Atlanta, 1948).

Other contemporary or reminiscent works include: John Joseph Craven, *Prison Life of Jefferson Davis. Embracing Details and Incidents in His Captivity, Particulars Concerning His Health and Habits, Together with Many Conversations on Topics of Great Public Interest* (New York, 1866); Charles Anderson Dana, *Recollections of the Civil War: With the Leaders at Washington and in the Field in the Sixties* (New York, 1902); Alexander Hamilton Stephens, *Recollections of Alexander H. Stephens, His Diary Kept when a Prisoner at Fort Warren, Boston Harbour, 1865; Giving Incidents and Reflections of His Prison Life and Some Letters and Reminiscences,* ed. by Myrta Lockett Avary (New York, 1910).

Two works of recent scholarship deal with particular aspects of the period: Jonathan Truman Dorris, *Pardon and Amnesty under Lincoln and Johnson: The Restoration of the Confederates to Their Rights and Privileges, 1861-1898* . . . (Chapel Hill, 1953); and Alfred Jackson Hanna, *Flight into Oblivion* (Richmond, 1938).

Periodical articles for the postwar years include: [John Spencer Bassett], "The Industrial Decay of the Southern Planter," *South Atlantic Quarterly,* II (1903), 107-13; J. F. Bivins, "The Life and Character of Jacob Thompson," *Trinity College Historical Society Papers,* ser. II (Durham, N. C., 1898), 83-91; Octavia Zollicoffer Bond, "South of the Line: A Belle of the Fifties," *Southern Woman's Magazine,* V (Sept., 1915), 16-17, 33; Chester D. Bradley, "Dr. Craven and the Prison Life of Jefferson Davis," *Virginia Magazine of History and Biography,* LXII (1954), 50-94; Dallas D. Irvine, "The Fate of Confederate Archives," *American Historical Review,* XLIV (1938-1939), 823-41; Stephen Russell Mallory, "Unpublished Chapters of History. Last Days of the Confederate Government. From Papers Left by Stephen R. Mallory, Secretary of the Navy in the Confederate Cabinet," *McClure's Magazine,* XVI (1900-1901), 100-107, 239-48; Roy Franklin Nichols, "United States *vs.* Jefferson Davis, 1865-1869," *American Historical Review,* XXXI (1925-1926), 266-84; Arthur Marvin Shaw (ed.), "My Dearest Friend. A Letter from Mrs. Jefferson Davis," *Southwest Review,* XXXIII (1948), 137-40; Joseph Wheeler, "An Effort to Rescue Jefferson Davis," *Century Magazine,* LVI (May, 1898), 84-91.

INDEX